OSWALD SPENGLER

THE DECLINE

OF THE WEST

AN ABRIDGED EDITION BY

HELMUT WERNER

ENGLISH ABRIDGED EDITION PREPARED BY

ARTHUR HELPS

FROM THE TRANSLATION BY

CHARLES FRANCIS ATKINSON

THE MODERN LIBRARY
New York

THE DECLINE OF THE WEST

VOLUME I: FORM AND ACTUALITY
Copyright 1926 by Alfred A. Knopf, Inc.
Published April 23, 1926
Originally published as *Der Untergang des Abendlandes, Gestalt und Wirklichkeit,* copyright 1918 by C. H. Beck'sche Verlagsbuchhandlung, Munich

VOLUME II: PERSPECTIVES OF WORLD-HISTORY
Copyright 1928 by Alfred A. Knopf, Inc.
Published November 9, 1928
Originally published as *Der Untergang des Abendlandes, Welthistorische Perspektiven,* copyright 1922 by C. H. Beck'sche Verlagsbuchhandlung, Munich

ONE-VOLUME EDITION
Published November 15, 1932

Wenn im Unendlichen dasselbe
Sich wiederholend ewig fliesst,
Das tausendfältige Gewölbe
Sich kräftig ineinander schliesst;
Strömt Lebenslust aus allen Dingen,
Dem kleinsten wie dem grössten Stern,
Und alles Drängen, alles Ringen
Ist ewige Ruh in Gott dem Herrn.

GOETHE

OSWALD SPENGLER

by ARTHUR HELPS

A CASSANDRA is not out of place in Germany, so the revival of interest in Spengler in his native country should not be regarded as a bad sign, though young Germans may wonder how it was that a profound philosopher of history, professing to follow in the footsteps of Goethe, should look forward to Nihilism after the style of Nietzsche. They will, nevertheless, come to the conclusion that there is much good sense in Spengler to balance an occasional excess of Romantic paradox.

It would be a pity if his reputation as a pessimist were to deter English readers from *The Decline of the West*. They would miss a wealth of poetry and eloquence, of encyclopaedic knowledge, and of challenging views, illuminated by a mordant wit and much cheerful vituperation. If Spengler was a pessimist, so was the prophet Isaiah, whom he admires and emulates. His recurrent theme that "cultures," embodying forms of government, religions, arts and crafts, sciences, peculiar to one culture and that culture alone, rise and fall, and leave nothing behind, would be depressing if one accepted it literally. His cultures are "organic" (the word having a more mystical than biological connotation); they go through the prescribed stages, which he calls spring, summer, autumn and winter, and then fade away. World-history is the sum of such cultures.

Spengler rejected linear progress. For him, as for Goethe, evolution is the fulfilment of a form. A culture blossoms from the soil of an exactly definable landscape and dies when it has exhausted all its possibilities. Thus did species such as the fugue and the Greek statue pass away, and never recur. These cultures, sublimated like essences, grow with the same superb aimlessness as the flowers of the field. *Alles Vergängliche ist nur ein*

Gleichnis, a symbol of the inner, invisible life, which is eternal and supersensual, over which presides Destiny (Providence).

We live, says Spengler, in an intellectual age, which understands by destiny a relation between cause and effect which the brain can detect; not so Shakespeare, who took his stories as he found them and filled them with the force of an inward necessity. Anyone who looks for an inner form of history, based on cause and effect, must always, if he is honest, find a burlesque comedy. Do not the deaths of Gustavus Adolphus and Alexander seem like expedients of a nonplussed playwright? Day is not the cause of night, nor youth of age, nor blossom of fruit.

The keynote of Spengler's condemnation of his own time is in the word "Civilization," which, as used by him, connotes the death of a culture and a consequent transformation of values. Rousseau, Socrates and Buddha, who were contemporaries in the Spenglerian sense, signalized the end of a culture. Each buried a millennium of spiritual depth. Life is presented by them as the intellect sees it; it is judged by utilitarian or "rational" criteria. The brain rules because the soul has abdicated.

Spengler could not forgive St. Paul for travelling to the "urban" West, thus intellectualizing what he calls "Magian" Christianity even in the lifetime of Christ's disciples. In the ambience of the apocalyptic there is no intellect. Religion is not the metaphysic of knowledge, argument, proof, which is mere philosophy and learning, but a lived and experienced metaphysic; the unthinkable as a certainty, the supernatural as a fact.

In the springtime of a culture men could say *credo quia absurdum* because they felt certain that the understandable and the non-understandable were necessary ingredients of the world, of that Nature which Giotto painted, and into which reason can penetrate only so far as the Deity permits. From a sort of jealousy arises the idea that what cannot be understood is valueless, that only what is proven is of value. The new religion without any secrets is philosophy. The old religion, said Aristotle, is necessary only for the uneducated; Confucius, Buddha, Voltaire and Lessing were of the same opinion.

Spengler, unfortunately, was obsessed by politics, and his political views were progressively darkened by the frustration of his hopes. He gave up his post as a high-school teacher of mathematics and history at the time of the Agadir incident in 1911, when he was thirty-one. He foresaw war and hoped for an imperial future for a victorious Germany, which he feared might deteriorate like Rome after the Punic Wars. His book was intended as a guide to its rulers. He was disqualified for military service by a bad heart, so he continued to write steadily throughout the First World War. He had very small means, and later, looking back on his life, he felt that the *Decline* had cost him dearly in depriving him of marriage and of a more normal existence. The first volume was finished in 1917, and after some difficulty found a publisher in 1918. The military collapse of that year and the triumph of radical ideas plunged him into despair, and confirmed him in Machiavellianism.

This attitude is most clearly expressed in the description contained in the second volume of the *Decline,* published in 1922, of what he calls a scene appallingly distinct and overwhelming in its symbolism, such as the world had never before, and never since, seen—the trial of Jesus before Pilate. Pilate's question— What is Truth?—implies that practical politics and ethics are poles apart. This is borne out by Jesus' unspoken reply—What is Reality? Spengler insists elsewhere that the words "My kingdom is not of this world" do not admit any glossing over. It is not Truth nor Righteousness nor Justice, but the Roman, the Cromwellian, the Prussian that is a fact. It is personality that counts. It was not the Christian Gospel but the Christian martyr that conquered the world, and the martyr derived his strength not from doctrines, but from the example of the Man on the Cross. The genuine statesman does not believe in high-sounding phrases. Pilate's question is always on his lips. He does not confuse the logic of events with the logic of systems. He has convictions, but as a private individual he is not hampered by didactic principles. The man of action, says Goethe, is always conscienceless. The great Popes and English party leaders acted on the same principles as the conquerors of all ages. Take Innocent III, who very nearly succeeded in making a world dominion of the Church, and deduce therefrom the catechism of success. It will be found to be in utter contradiction to Religion and Morality. Yet, without it there would have been no bearable existence for any church, not to mention English Colonies. It is life, not the individual that is conscienceless. (In spite of his unwarranted assertion that England acquired her Colonies by immoral methods Spengler implies that the world was the gainer thereby.)

With Spengler's suspicion of intellectuals—other than mathematicians—goes his emphasis on breeding (*Zucht*) as against mere book-learning. By breeding he meant the instilling of traditions, without which a nation loses "form." He cites the training of a mediaeval page, cloister education, the training of the Prussian Officers Corps, English public-school and university training for the Indian Civil Service, the training for the Roman Catholic priesthood, and Bismarck's failure to train a political elite competent to deal with foreign affairs.

When ball-game players are "in form," rash strokes "come off." An Art Period is in form when its tradition is second nature, as counterpoint was to Bach. Napoleon's army was in form at Austerlitz, Moltke's at Sedan. The English over a period of 200 years had only one Pitt, but their tradition enabled them to survive Ramsay MacDonald and Lloyd George. It does not matter if the leaders come up from the People; the mighty tide of tradition takes hold of them, all unwilling, and rules their conduct. He prophesies that the British democratic system will be introduced into Africa, but that without the tradition it cannot succeed. So far from benefiting, like port from a journey round the Cape, it loses its flavour in crossing the British Channel. It is a purely local growth like the Rococo.

It goes without saying that Spengler hated materialistic Humanists, Utopians, "World Betterers" and Pacifists. World Peace is always a one-sided resolve. "Man is a beast of prey, I shall say it again and again." The coloured races are not pacifists; they do not cling to a life whose length is its sole value. He protested accordingly against the Japanese alliance, thereby angering the Nazis, with whom he failed to see eye to eye. He called them everlasting youths, raving like mendicant monks. "Aryan" and "Semite" were silly catchwords borrowed from philology; the idea of a 1,000-year Reich was ridiculous. After publishing a pamphlet entitled *The Hour of Destiny*, he thought he would be obliged to leave Germany, but an interview with Hitler on the introduction of Frau Wagner prevented this. Spengler died in 1936 before Nazism reached its zenith.

Spengler reverts frequently to the subject of "Megapolis," which he considers the worst feature of "Civilization." He foresees cities laid out for twenty million inhabitants, covering vast areas of countryside. Almost hopefully he dwells on the subject of the vanished cities of the past. Regular rectangular blocks astounded Herodotus in Babylon and Cortez in Tenochtitlán.

Pataliputra, Asoka's capital, was an immense and completely un-inhabited waste when Hsüan Tsang visited it about A.D. 635. Antioch had five miles of colonnades, while Nisibis, now 200 wretched hovels, had a revenue in A.D. 969 of 5,000,000 dirhems. The towns of Saba, with buildings twenty stories high, were attributed to supernatural builders. Eventually the huge cities stand empty except for a few fellaheen camping in the ruins like Stone Age men in caves. This then is the conclusion of the city's history, from primitive barter centre to culture city, and at last to world city, and so, doomed, it moves on to certain destruction.

On the other hand his prophecies for the future of Russia are surprisingly optimistic. He sees in her the saviour of the world. On three occasions Russia has been victimized by having Western influences thrust upon her—by Peter the Great, by the Czar Alexander at the time of the Holy Alliance and by Lenin. Marxism, based on a typically British poor man's hatred of the rich, coupled with Jewish memories of the Old Testament curse on manual labour, was adopted by Russia under an ardent misunderstanding. The Russian does not fight Capital; he does not understand it. By "Petrinism" and Bolshevism, which is not the contrary but the final issue of Petrinism, a people which should have lived for many generations more without history was forced into a false and artificial history of which the soul of Old Russia was incapable.

The Russian instinct has very truly and fundamentally divided Europe from Mother Russia with the hostility that we can see embodied in Tolstoi, Aksakov or Dostoievski. Inwardly, though, Tolstoi is tied to the West. He is the spokesman of Petrinism even when he is denying it. A soul, such as Dostoievski, can look beyond the things we call social, for the things of this world seem to be so unimportant as not to be worth improving. What has Communism to do with the agony of a soul? Dostoievski is a saint but Tolstoi only a revolutionary. He spoke of Christ but he meant Marx. To Dostoievski will the next 1,000 years belong.

Living temporarily under the crust of urban-thinking Bolshevism, the Russian has freed himself from Western Economy. To him, thinking in terms of money is a sin (Gorki's *Night Asylum*). Russia will produce a third [1] issue of Christianity, priestless and

---

[1] Following the "Magian" and the "Faustian."

founded on the gospel of St. John. They will even develop a new architectural style and abandon the onion cupolas forced on them by the Holy Synod in place of the steep eight-sided tent roof which was universal from Norway to Manchuria.

Spengler did not quite live up to his scorn of nineteenth-century painting and of music since Beethoven. He played Verdi and Wagner as well as old Italian music. His walls were hung with German pictures of the Romantic period, such as one sees in the Schack gallery at Munich. Out of the profits of the *Decline* he could afford to convert two rooms of a top-floor apartment on Widermayer Strasse, facing the Isar, into a sort of gallery, where he paced up and down and looked out on the mountains. When he left Munich it was usually to visit Italy, where his favourite spot was Lake Iseo. He was quiet and amiable in his conversation except when roused. "Then one heard a harsh contemptuous laugh and saw his eyes shining behind thick spectacles like those of a troll." He appreciated claret and cigars, and this may partly account for the liverishness of his political pamphlets, which, in fact, detracted from his reputation. He was intended to be a poet, not a pamphleteer.

There is a certain "wheel wobble" in the last chapters of the *Decline*, evidence of the stress between optimism and pessimism, faith and spleen, always present in Spengler, and also perhaps of haste to get his task finished.

"The machine forces the entrepreneur not less than the workman to obedience. They are its slaves, not its masters. But the machine depends upon its priest, the engineer; in future generations, suppose," asks Spengler, "that the very elite of intellect that is now concerned with the machine becomes overpowered with a growing sense of its Satanism (the step from Roger Bacon to Bernard of Clairvaux), then nothing can hinder the end of the great drama that has been a play of intellects with hands as mere auxiliaries. So long as the Machine dominates the earth, every non-European will try to fathom the secret of this terrible weapon. Nevertheless, inwardly he abhors it, be he Indian or Japanese, Russian or Arab." The attitude of Gandhi supported Spengler, but can India in the long run hold out against industrialism, the idea of wealth? Spengler replies that the dictatorship of money is an idea, and, as such, must fade out as soon as it has thought its economic world through to finality. Unfortunately the conqueror of the dictatorship of money and its political weapon, democracy, is "Caesarism." A power can be overcome only by another power, not by a principle, such as Socialism. The Sword is victorious over Money, the Master Will defeats the Plunderer Will.

Spengler's end-product, Caesarism, the analogy from the Roman Empire, is quite arbitrary. It is remarkable how his genius is outweighed by bile when describing the present or prophesying the future. He falls victim to a schematic dogmatism. Events must follow prescribed phases of cultures seen from the Spenglerian standpoint. His claim to observe from a neutral standpoint shows a neglect of the relativity which is his favourite weapon. If the whole of reality is being constantly transformed in a continuum of aspects from perpetually changing viewpoints, it must be impossible to obtain a precise picture.

The schoolmaster persists in Spengler. Having dazed the class with splendid rhetoric, he rubs in his points, if not by paradoxes, by striking antitheses; intuition and analysis; history and nature; experience and perception; and so on. To keep the boys attentive he feels entitled to exaggerate, as he certainly does in insulating his cultures absolutely from one another. This may be a partial explanation of the brutality of his political prophecies, in entire contrast with his metaphysical mind. Kant also saw the inner and the outer world as quite separate, if that is the meaning of the words "I feel the moral law within me and I see the starry heavens above me." Spengler regards "the personal," destiny, time, as interchangeable words. We are Time. He quotes Augustine: *"In te, anime meus, tempora metior";* Destiny and with it the Ego stand outside time in the ordinary sense of the word. For political purposes, however, Spengler reverts to the good old German gods. His friend and contemporary and posthumous critic, Professor Schröter, is reminded of the grim Hagen in the Nibelungenlied, the daemonic form of purposeless and sinister power, destroying others and finally himself. Spengler, disowned by the Nazis, cannot be acquitted of egging them on to their doom. In 1927 he wrote a character sketch of his fellow countrymen: "Our unlimited need to serve, to follow, to honour someone, true as a dog, blind in belief in spite of all obstacles. . . . No cause, no leader, or even the caricature of one, is elsewhere so certain of an unquestioning following, a treasure of immense value to him who knows how to use it."

In his pamphlet *The Duties of German Youth* he wrote: "Who cannot hate is no Man, and history is made by Men. That we Germans can at last hate is one of the few results of this period which hold out promise for the future." In his last publication he said: "The ancient barbarism which has been held down for centuries . . . is waking again with a warlike delight in its own strength. This barbarism is what I call strong Race (Race which one has, not a race to which one belongs; one is Ethos, the other Zoology), the eternal warlike in the type of the beast of prey—Man. The only form-giving power is the warlike 'Prussian' spirit; not only in Germany the legions of Caesar march again." The romantic, the admirer of Hölderlin, Novalis and Brentano, has turned very sour. Professor Schröter remarks: "Never since the days of Amos and Isaiah has ripening actuality and its recognition been so closely connected."

Spengler's prophecy that Western Europe would lose its world hegemony has been fulfilled. Must Western culture also go under? Is a global culture, to take its place, even remotely conceivable? Would Ancient Greece, the leader of the Western world, have survived if the small individual states had joined together? Western Europe has made several attempts to combine in the course of the last 400 years—Charles V, Philip II (an Anglo-Spanish Empire over South America?), Louis XIV, Napoleon and finally the criminal Hitler. Continental historians point out that England was invariably the stumbling-block, but in every case she had good cause. Has she still? As to the other countries, would France, for example, share the Sahara—seeing that, in 1898, when it seemed of little value, she was prepared to fight England for it? Must Germany again go berserk? Heine said that, whereas deed follows thought as thunder follows lightning, German thunder is slow like the German, but when the German revolution comes, the French will be an idyll in comparison. The Germans have had their revolution, and though *Kadavergehorsam* is in their blood, the berserk mood, Spengler thinks, may not reappear for several centuries.

On one point Spengler is very definite. The polarity between the pull of the visible and the invisible worlds is more important than other tensions—for example, that between East and West. When the Roman Empire fell it bequeathed Christianity to the world. Western Europe offers science and its child, technology. Nevertheless, Spengler perceives that the balance will swing and the invisible will regain the hold over the Western world that it has lost since the Middle Ages.

It is noticeable that he expects the initiative in ideas, particularly political and economic, to come from England.

PREFACE

TO THE FIRST EDITION

THE complete manuscript of this book—the outcome of three years' work—was ready when the Great War broke out. By the spring of 1917 it had been worked over again and—in certain details—supplemented and cleared up, but its appearance in print was still delayed by the conditions then prevailing.

Although a philosophy of history is its scope and subject, it possesses also a certain deeper significance as a commentary on the great epochal moment of which the portents were visible when the leading ideas were being formed.

The title, which had been decided upon in 1912, expresses quite literally the intention of the book, which was to describe, in the light of the decline of the Classical age, one world-historical phase of several centuries upon which we ourselves are now entering.

Events have justified much and refuted nothing. It became clear that these ideas must necessarily be brought forward at just this moment and in Germany, and, more, that the war itself was an element in the premises from which the new world-picture could be made precise.

For I am convinced that it is not merely a question of writing one out of several possible and merely logically justifiable philosophies, but of writing *the* philosophy of our time, one that is to some extent a natural philosophy and is dimly presaged by all. This may be said without presumption; for an idea that is historically essential—that does not occur within an epoch but itself makes that epoch—is only in a limited sense the property of him to whose lot it falls to parent it. It belongs to our time as a whole and influences all thinkers, without their knowing it; it is but the accidental, private attitude towards it (without which no philosophy can exist) that—with its faults and its merits—is the destiny and the happiness of the individual.

Oswald Spengler

MUNICH
December 1917

PREFACE

TO THE REVISED EDITION

AT the close of an undertaking which, from the first brief sketch to the final shaping of a complete work of quite unforeseen dimensions, has spread itself over ten years, it will not be out of place to glance back at what I intended and what I have achieved, my standpoint then and my standpoint today.

In the Introduction to the 1918 edition—inwardly and outwardly a fragment—I stated my conviction that an idea had now been irrefutably formulated which no one would oppose, once the idea had been put into words. I ought to have said: once that idea had been understood. And for that we must look—as I more and more realize—not only in this instance but in the whole history of thought—to the new generation that is *born* with the ability to do it.

I added that this must be considered a first attempt, loaded with all the customary faults, incomplete and not without inward opposition. The remark was not taken anything like as seriously as it was intended. Those who have looked searchingly into the hypotheses of living thought will know that it is not given to us to gain insight into the fundamental principles of existence without conflicting emotions. A thinker is a person whose part it is to symbolize time according to his vision and understanding. He has no choice; he thinks as he has to think. Truth in the long run is to him the picture of the world which was born at his birth. It is that which he does not invent but rather discovers within himself. It is himself over again: his being expressed in words; the meaning of his personality formed into a doctrine which so far as concerns his life is unalterable, because truth and his life are identical. This symbolism is the one essential, the vessel and the expression of human history. The learned philosophical works that arise out of it are superfluous and serve only to swell the bulk of a professional literature.

I can then call the essence of what I have discovered "true"— that is, *true for me,* and as I believe, true for the leading minds of the coming time; not true in itself as dissociated from the conditions imposed by blood and by history, for that is impossible. But what I wrote in the storm and stress of those years was, it must be admitted, a very imperfect statement of what stood clearly before me, and it remained to devote the years that followed to the task of correlating facts and finding means of expression which should enable me to present my idea in the most forcible form.

To perfect that form would be impossible—life itself is only fulfilled in death. But I have once more made the attempt to bring up even the earliest portions of the work to the level of definiteness with which I now feel able to speak; and with that I take leave of this book with its hopes and disappointments, its merits and its faults.

The result has in the meantime justified itself as far as I myself am concerned and—judging by the effect that it is slowly beginning to exercise upon extensive fields of learning—as far as others are concerned also. Let no one expect to find everything set forth here. It is *but one side* of what I see before me, a new outlook on *history and the philosophy of destiny*—the first indeed of its kind. It is intuitive and depictive through and through, written in a language which seeks to present objects and relations illustratively instead of offering an army of ranked concepts. It addresses itself solely to readers who are capable of living themselves into the word-sounds and pictures as they read. Difficult this undoubtedly is, particularly as our awe in face of mystery—the respect that Goethe felt—denies us the satisfaction of thinking that dissections are the same as penetrations.

Of course, the cry of "pessimism" was raised at once by those who always live in the yesterday and therefore oppose every idea that is intended for the pathfinder of tomorrow only. But I have not written for people who imagine that delving for the springs of action is the same as action itself; those who make definitions do not know destiny.

By understanding the world I mean being equal to the world. It is the hard reality of living that is the essential, not the concept of life, which the ostrich-philosophy of idealism propounds.

Those who refuse to be bluffed by enunciations will not regard this as pessimism; and the rest do not matter. For the benefit of serious readers who are seeking a glimpse at life and not a definition, I have—in view of the far too great concentration of the text—mentioned in my notes a number of works which will carry that glance into more distant realms of knowledge. [These references are not included in the present abridged edition.]

And now, finally, I feel urged to name once more those to whom I owe practically everything: Goethe and Nietzsche. Goethe gave me method, Nietzsche the questioning faculty—and if I were asked to find a formula for my relation to the latter I should say that I had made of his "outlook" (*Ausblick*) an "overlook" (*Überblick*). But Goethe was, without knowing it, a disciple of Leibniz in his whole mode of thought. And, therefore, that which has at last (and to my own astonishment) taken shape in my hands I am able to regard and, despite the misery and disgust of these years, proud to call *a German philosophy.*

Oswald Spengler

BLANKENBURG AM HARZ
December 1922

EDITOR'S PREFACE

TO THE GERMAN-LANGUAGE
ABRIDGED EDITION

THE present abridged edition has been prepared for the sake of the intellectually alert reader who, today, is prevented by the pressing claims of his professional and civic responsibilities from reading the more monumental works outside his increasingly narrowing special field. To fill a genuine need by opening the way to a significant contemporary work, it became necessary and possible to set aside such scruples as might, in principle, assert themselves against the abridgment of an original creation.

This is a condensation of the two volumes of the original [German-language] edition of *The Decline of the West*, faithfully reprinted page for page since 1924, 140,000 copies of which have by now (1959) come off press. *Of the fundamental first volume, extensive portions have been retained almost in their entirety.* A more selective treatment has been given particularly to the chapters in the second volume entitled "Origin and Landscape," "Cities and Peoples," "The State," and "The Form-World of Economic Life." Here the chief stress has been laid on the interpretations of the late phases, especially of our own Western culture. Here and there, simplifying transitional passages, in italic type, serve to pull the whole together. These are intended to help the reader find his way in an often far-ranging ramification of thought. It was not always possible to prevent such synoptic passages, though couched largely in Spengler's own terms, from seeming at first rather abstract and difficult—especially where important new terms had to be introduced—the more so in that Spengler's terms were often chosen for the symbolic values of their sound, and for what they suggest of personal experience. However, the copiously treated great themes themselves (architecture, religion, natural science, etc.), occasionally used as images of a great thought, are elucidation enough. They express sufficiently the fundamental fatalism that moved many theologians to concern themselves with Spengler. The survey tables of the various cultures had to be sacrificed. Though the present text may have passed over many a subtle distinction, it does contain everything necessary for a comprehension of the whole; nothing essential has been left out. Beyond this, such passages as are especially characteristic of Spengler's power of poetic vision and language have also been included.

The publication of this condensed version offers an opportunity to correct certain misconceptions. Many expressions coined by Spengler are in circulation today. The reader will find that their meaning in the original is quite different from that often attributed to them, even, sometimes, in scholarly works. "Napoleonism," "Caesarism," "second religiousness," and the terms "culture" and "civilization," which are a specifically Spenglerian pair of concepts, are often falsely applied, even when the originator is cited. The concept of "pseudomorphosis" too, though invoked in Spengler's name, is often distorted and falsified. That there are fruitful relationships between the various cultures, such as particularly the exchanging and passing along of cultural goods which may stimulate new creations of a more or less autonomous character, has been often enough stressed by Spengler. Pseudomorphosis, however, is his own term for two special cases of cultural history in which the totality of an awakening culture succumbs to the influence of a matured culture and takes on a veneer of the latter's alien formal structures. The cases under consideration are, specifically, the awakening Russian consciousness and, most of all, the "Magian Culture," whose autonomous existence beneath the surface of a variety of historical forms Spengler was the first to grasp. Extensively reprinted here, the chapter on the Magian Culture—the discovery of which by Spengler has been appreciated by such scholars as the great historian of antiquity Eduard Meyer and the distinguished Islamist C. H. Becker—is one of the best illustrations of Spengler's incomparably objective historical perception and, at the same time, his genius for historical empathy.

The much abridged disquisitions on race and spirit, blood and soil—which Spengler sees as opposites, in contrast to the National Socialists' use of them—nation and language, define Spengler's metaphysically grounded position as compared with the materialistic views of man, whether nationalistic or Marxist. It is wrong to connect Spengler with any doctrines or theories of race such as are still current even today. The constantly reiterated assertion of Spengler's "biologistic concept of history" stems from a superficial reading of his text. That this touches on a merely external aspect of Spengler's thought will now be realized by a larger circle of readers able to see for themselves. Lastly, let me point out that the title of the work was not inspired by the German defeat of 1918, as has often been believed, but was chosen before the First World War, which, when it came, Spengler expected to end in a German victory. He chose the title *The Decline of the West* in 1912, on the model of Otto Seeck's *History of the Decline of Antiquity.*

Like every daring conception, *The Decline of the West* calls for readers with a wide intellectual horizon and a certain equanimity of spirit. Even a condensed version will not lessen the demands upon the reader in this respect. If a large readership may be expected to possess these qualifications, this edition might contribute something to the strengthening and deepening of modern man's insight into himself. The debate over Spengler has slackened not because his work has been superseded, but because everywhere an irresistible conviction has been making itself felt that Spengler "might have been right, after all." But the importance of Spengler does not rest on the fact that, within the space of fifty years since the conception of his work, many events have confirmed his predictions. Of greater moment is the fact that, on the one hand, Spengler has decisively influenced our view of the world and of history as a whole and in detail, and continues to do so. Even many of the special fields of scholarship so long antagonistic to him have made his suggestions bear fruit. On the other hand, it has become apparent today more than ever how much Spengler's world view represents the living spirit, and his epistemology, the philosophical style of our epoch. His work having been suppressed after 1933, and at first unwelcome after 1945, it is hoped that this edition may now assist even younger readers to order the wealth, or perhaps the burden, of their recent experience and of the present world confusion into a convincing design profoundly realistic and close to life.

Finally, I hope that despite the condensation of the text, the true stature of this work, not only as a phenomenal achievement of thought but also as a great work of art, has not been obscured.

And now I ask the reader's indulgence for a personal remark. As this book went into print, death came, in Munich, after a grave illness, at the age of forty-nine, to Dr. Hildegard Kornhardt. She was the niece and last surviving relative of Oswald Spengler. In addition to her own professional scholarly labors as a philologist, she served as executor of Spengler's literary remains. Several new editions of his works appeared, after the Second World War, with informative introductions from her pen. She was, most regrettably, prevented from completing the difficult tasks imposed by Spengler's literary legacy, which consisted essentially of a mass of brief notes toward his work on "Primary Problems" which he had projected since the twenties. I am indebted to her for much valuable advice, especially regarding the work of this condensed version. Therefore, I should like to dedicate this book to her memory.

Helmut Werner
TRANSLATED BY SOPHIE WILKINS

Reutlingen, May 4, 1959

CONTENTS

THE

DECLINE

OF THE

WEST

EXPLANATORY NOTE

The italic passages within brackets are the work of Helmut
Werner, translated or modified by Arthur Helps. They
serve to summarize certain lengthy passages that have
been omitted where a link would nevertheless appear to be
necessary. Otherwise no indication is given of where the
countless cuts have been made in order to reduce the work
to considerably less than half its original extent.

The abbreviation *At.* at the end of a footnote indicates
that the note is the work of the original translator, Charles
Francis Atkinson.

I

INTRODUCTION

IN this book is attempted for the first time the venture of prede-
termining history, of following the still untravelled stages in the
destiny of a Culture, and specifically of the only Culture of our
time and on our planet which is actually in the phase of fulfilment—the West European–American.

Is there a logic of history? Is there, beyond all the casual and
incalculable elements of the separate events, something that we
may call a metaphysical structure of historic humanity, something that is essentially independent of the outward forms—social, spiritual and political—which we see so clearly? Are not
these actualities indeed secondary or derived from that something? Does world-history present to the seeing eye certain grand
traits, again and again, with sufficient constancy to justify certain conclusions? And if so, what are the limits to which reasoning from such premises may be pushed?

Is it possible to find in life itself—for human history is the
sum of mighty life-courses which already have had to be endowed with ego and personality, in customary thought and expression, by predicating entities of a higher order like "the Classical" or "the Chinese Culture," "Modern Civilization"—a series of
stages which must be traversed, and traversed moreover in an
ordered and obligatory sequence? For everything organic the notions of birth, death, youth, age, lifetime, are fundamentals—
may not these notions, in this sphere also, possess a rigorous
meaning which no one has as yet extracted? In short, is all history founded upon general biographic archetypes?

The decline of the West, which at first sight may appear, like
the corresponding decline of the Classical Culture, a phenomenon limited in time and space, we now perceive to be a philosophical problem that, when comprehended in all its gravity, includes within itself every great question of Being.

If therefore we are to discover in what form the destiny of

the Western Culture will be accomplished, we must first be clear as to what culture *is,* what its relations are to visible history, to life, to soul, to nature, to intellect, what the forms of its manifestation are and how far these forms—peoples, tongues and epochs, battles and ideas, states and gods, arts and craftworks, sciences, laws, economic types and world-ideas, great men and great events—may be accepted and pointed to .as symbols.

The means whereby to identify dead forms is Mathematical Law. The means whereby to understand living forms is Analogy. By these means we are enabled to distinguish polarity and periodicity in the world.

It is, and has always been, a matter of knowledge that the expression-forms of world-history are limited in number, and that eras, epochs, situations, persons, are ever repeating themselves true to type. Napoleon has hardly ever been discussed without a side-glance at Caesar and Alexander—analogies of which, as we shall see, the first is morphologically quite inacceptable and the second is correct. Frederick the Great, in his political· writings— such as his *Considérations,* 1738—moves among analogies with perfect assurance. Thus he compares the French to the Macedonians under Philip and the Germans to the Greeks. "Even now," he says, "the Thermopylae of Germany, Alsace and Lorraine, are in the hands of Philip," therein exactly characterizing the policy of Cardinal Fleury. We find him drawing parallels also between the policies of the Houses of Habsburg and Bourbon and the proscriptions of Antony and of Octavius.

Still, all this was only fragmentary and arbitrary, and usually implied rather a momentary inclination to poetical or ingenious expressions than a really deep sense of historical forms. In this region no one hitherto has set himself to work out a *method,* nor has had the slightest inkling that there is here a root, in fact the only root, from which can come a broad solution of the problems of History. Analogies, insofar as they laid bare the organic structure of history, might be a blessing to historical thought. Their technique, developing under the influence of a comprehensive idea, would surely eventuate in inevitable conclusions and logical mastery. But as hitherto understood and practised, they have been a curse, for they have enabled the historians to follow their own tastes, instead of soberly realizing that their first and

4

hardest task was concerned with the symbolism of history and its analogies.

Thus our theme, which originally comprised only the limited problem of present-day civilization, broadens itself into a new philosophy—*the* philosophy of the future, so far as the metaphysically exhausted soil of the West can bear such, and in any case the only philosophy which is within the *possibilities* of the West European mind in its next stages. It expands into the conception of a *morphology of world-history,* of the world-as-history in contrast to the morphology of the world-as-nature that hitherto has been almost the only theme of philosophy. And it reviews once again the forms and movements of the world in their depths and final significance, but this time according to an entirely different ordering, which groups them, not in an ensemble picture inclusive of everything known, but in a picture of *life,* and presents them not as things-become, but as things-becoming.

The *world-as-history,* conceived, viewed and given form from out of its opposite, the *world-as-nature*—here is a new aspect of human existence on this earth. As yet, in spite of its immense significance, both practical and theoretical, this aspect has not been realized, still less presented. Some obscure inkling of it there may have been, a distant momentary glimpse there has often been, but no one has deliberately faced it and taken it in with all its implications. We have before us two possible ways in which man may inwardly possess and experience the world around him. With all rigour I distinguish (as to form, not substance) the organic from the mechanical world-impression, the content of images from that of laws, the picture and symbol from the formula and the system, the instantly actual from the constantly possible, the intents and purposes of imagination ordering according to plan from the intents and purposes of experience dissecting according to scheme; and—to mention even thus early an opposition that has never yet been noted, in spite of its significance—the domain of *chronological* from that of *mathematical number.*

Consequently, in a research such as that lying before us, there can be no question of taking spiritual-political events, as they become visible day by day on the surface, at their face value, and arranging them on a scheme of "causes" or "effects" and following them up in the obvious and intellectually easy directions. Such a "pragmatic" handling of history would be nothing but a piece of "natural science" in disguise, and for their part, the supporters of the materialistic idea of history make no secret about it—it is their adversaries who largely fail to see the similarity of the two methods. What concerns us is not what the historical facts which appear at this or that time *are,* per se, but what they signify, what they point to, *by appearing.* I have not hitherto found one who has carefully considered the *morphological relationship* that inwardly binds together the expression-forms of *all* branches of a Culture. Yet, viewed from this morphological standpoint, even the humdrum facts of politics assume a symbolic and even a metaphysical character, and—what has perhaps been impossible hitherto—things such as the Egyptian administrative system, the Classical coinage, analytical geometry, the cheque, the Suez Canal, the book-printing of the Chinese, the Prussian Army, and the Roman road-engineering can, as symbols, be made *uniformly* understandable and appreciable.

But at once the fact presents itself that as yet there exists no theory-enlightened art of historical treatment. What passes as such draws its methods almost exclusively from the domain of that science which alone has completely disciplined the methods of cognition, viz., physics, and thus we imagine ourselves to be carrying on historical research when we are really following out objective connexions of cause and effect. Judged by the standards of the physicist and the mathematician, the historian becomes *careless* as soon as he has assembled and ordered his material and passes on to interpretation. That there is, besides a necessity of cause and effect—which I may call the *logic of space*—another necessity, an organic necessity in life, that of Destiny—the *logic of time*—is a fact of the deepest inward certainty, a fact which suffuses the whole of mythological religions and artistic thought and constitutes the essence and kernel of all history (in contradistinction to nature) but is unapproachable through the cognition-forms which the *Critique of Pure Reason* investigates. This fact still awaits its theoretical formulation.

Mathematics and the principle of Causality lead to a naturalistic, Chronology and the idea of Destiny to a historical ordering of the phenomenal world. Both orderings, each on its own account, cover the *whole* world. The difference is only in the eyes by which and through which this world is realized.

6

THE MEANING OF HISTORY FOR THE INDIVIDUAL

Nature is the shape in which the man of higher Cultures synthesizes and interprets the immediate impressions of his senses. History is that from which his imagination seeks comprehension of the living existence of the world in relation to his own life, which he thereby invests with a deeper reality. Whether he is capable of creating these shapes, which of them it is that dominates his waking consciousness, is a primordial problem of all human existence.

Man, thus, has before him two possible ways of regarding the world. But it must be noted, at the very outset, that these possibilities are not necessarily *actualities,* and if we are to enquire into the sense of all history we must begin by solving a question which has never yet been put, viz., *for whom* is there History? The question is seemingly paradoxical, for history is obviously for everyone to this extent, that every man, with his whole existence and consciousness, is a part of history. But it makes a great difference whether anyone lives under the constant impression that his life is an element in a far wider life-course that goes on for hundreds and thousands of years, or conceives of himself as something rounded off and self-contained. For the latter type of consciousness there is certainly no world-history, no *world-as-history*. But how if the self-consciousness of a whole nation, how if a whole Culture rests on this ahistoric spirit? How must actuality appear to it? The world? Life?

ANTIQUITY AND INDIA: UNHISTORICAL

What diaries and autobiographies yield in respect of an individual, that historical research in the widest and most inclusive sense—that is, every kind of psychological comparison and analysis of alien peoples, times and customs—yields as to the soul of a Culture as a whole. But the Classical Culture possessed no *memory*, no organ of history in this special sense. The memory of the Classical man—so to call it, though it is somewhat arbitrary to apply to alien souls a notion derived from our own—is something different, since past and future, as arraying perspectives in the working consciousness, are absent and the "pure

Present," which so often roused Goethe's admiration in every product of the Classical life and in sculpture particularly, fills that life with an intensity that to us is perfectly unknown. This pure Present, whose greatest symbol is the Doric column, in itself predicates the *negation of time* (of direction). For Herodotus and Sophocles, as for Themistocles or a Roman consul, the past is subtilized instantly into an impression that is timeless and changeless, *polar and not periodic* in structure—in the last analysis, of such stuff as myths are made of—whereas for our world-sense and our inner eye the past is a definitely periodic and purposeful organism of centuries or millennia. For this reason, although Classical man was well acquainted with the strict chronology and almanac-reckoning of the Babylonians and especially the Egyptians, and therefore with that eternity-sense and disregard of the present-as-such which revealed itself in their broadly conceived operations of astronomy and their exact measurements of big time-intervals, none of this ever became *intimately* a part of him.

As regards Classical history-writing, take Thucydides. The mastery of this man lies in his truly Classical power of making alive and self-explanatory the events of the *present,* and also in his possession of the magnificently *practical outlook* of the born statesman who has himself been both general and administrator. In virtue of this quality of *experience* (which we unfortunately confuse with the historical sense proper), his work confronts the merely learned and professional historian as an inimitable model, and quite rightly so. But what is absolutely hidden from Thucydides is perspective, the power of surveying the history of centuries, that which for us is implicit in the very conception of a historian. The fine pieces of Classical history-writing are invariably those which set forth matters within the political present of the writer, whereas for us it is the direct opposite, our historical masterpieces without exception being those which deal with a distant past. Thucydides would have broken down in handling even the Persian Wars, let alone the general history of Greece, while that of Egypt would have been utterly out of his reach. He, as well as Polybius and Tacitus (who, like him, were practical politicians), loses his sureness of eye from the moment when, in looking backwards, he encounters motive forces in any form that is unknown in his practical experience. For Polybius even the First Punic War, for Tacitus even the reign of Augustus, is inexplicable. As for Thucydides, his lack of historical feeling—in our sense of the phrase—is conclusively demonstrated on the very first page of his book by the astounding statement that before his time (about 400 B.C.) no events of importance had occurred (οὐ μεγάλα γενέσθαι) in the world! [1]

EGYPTIAN AND WESTERN MAN: HISTORICAL

The Egyptian soul, conspicuously historical in its texture and impelled with primitive passion towards the infinite, perceived past and future as its *whole* world, and the present (which is identical with waking consciousness) appeared to him simply as the narrow common frontier of two immeasurable stretches. The Egyptian Culture is an embodiment of *care*—which is the spiritual counterpoise of distance—care for the future expressed in the choice of granite or basalt as the craftsman's materials,[2] in the chiselled archives, in the elaborate administrative system, in the net of irrigation works,[3] and, necessarily *bound up therewith,* care for the past. The Egyptian mummy is a symbol of the first importance. The body of the dead man was *made everlasting,* just as his personality, his "Ka," was immortalized through

[1] The attempts of the Greeks to frame something like a calendar or a chronology after the Egyptian fashion, besides being very belated indeed, were of extreme naïveté. The Olympiad reckoning is not an era in the sense of, say, the Christian chronology, and is, moreover, a late and purely literary expedient, without popular currency. The people, in fact, had no general need of a numeration wherewith to date the experiences of their grandfathers and great-grandfathers, though a few learned persons might be interested in the calendar question. We are not here concerned with the soundness or unsoundness of a calendar, but with its currency, with the question of whether men regulated their lives by it or not.

[2] Contrast with this the fact, symbolically of the highest importance and unparalleled in art-history, that the Hellenes, though they had before their eyes the works of the Mycenaean Age and their land was only too rich in stone, *deliberately reverted to wood;* hence the absence of architectural remains of the period 1200–600. The Egyptian plant-column was from the outset of stone, whereas the Doric column was wooden, a clear indication of the intense antipathy of the Classical soul towards duration.

[3] Is there any Hellenic city that ever carried out one single comprehensive work that tells of care for future generations? The road and water systems which research has assigned to the Mycenaean—i.e., the preClassical—Age fell into disrepair and oblivion from the birth of the Classical peoples—i.e., from the Homeric period.

9

the portrait-statuettes, which were often made in many copies and to which it was conceived to be attached by a transcendental likeness.

There is a deep relation between the attitude that is taken towards the historic past and the conception that is formed of death, and this relation is expressed in the *disposal of the dead.* The Egyptian denied mortality, the Classical man affirmed it in the whole symbolism of his Culture. The Egyptians embalmed even their history in chronological dates and figures. From pre-Solonian Greece nothing has been handed down, not a year-date, not a true name, not a tangible event—with the consequence that the later history (which alone we know) assumes undue importance—but for Egypt we possess, from the third millennium, and even earlier, the names and even the exact reign-dates of many of the kings, and the New Empire must have had a complete knowledge of them. Today, pathetic symbols of the will to endure, the bodies of the great Pharaohs lie in our museums, their faces still recognizable.

No great Greek ever wrote down any recollections that would serve to fix a phase of experience for his inner eye. Not even Socrates has told, regarding his inward life, anything important in our sense of the word. It is questionable indeed whether for a Classical mind it was even possible to react to the motive forces that are presupposed in the production of a Parzival, a Hamlet, or a Werther. In Plato we fail to observe any conscious evolution of doctrine; his separate works are merely treatises written from very different standpoints which he took up from time to time, and it gave him no concern whether and how they hung together. On the contrary, a work of deep self-examination, the *Vita Nuova* of Dante, is found at the very outset of the spiritual history of the West. How little therefore of the Classical pure Present there really was in Goethe, the man who forgot nothing, the man whose works, as he avowed himself, are only fragments of a *single great confession!*

After the destruction of Athens by the Persians, all the older art-works were thrown on the dustheap (whence we are now extracting them), and we do not hear that anyone in Hellas ever troubled himself about the ruins of Mycenae or Phaistos for the purpose of ascertaining historical facts. In the West, on the contrary, the piety inherent in and peculiar to the Culture manifested itself in Petrarch—the collector of antiquities, coins and manuscripts, the very type of historically sensitive man, viewing the distant past and scanning the distant prospect (was he not the first to attempt an Alpine peak?), living in his time, yet essentially not of it. The soul of the collector is intelligible only by having regard to his conception of Time. Even more passionate perhaps, though of a different colouring, is the collecting-bent of the Chinese. In China, whoever travels assiduously pursues "old tracks" (*Ku-tsi*), and the untranslatable *Tao,* the basic principle of Chinese existence, derives all its meaning from a deep historical feeling. In the Hellenistic period, objects were indeed collected and displayed everywhere, but they were curiosities of mythological appeal (as described by Pausanias) as to which questions of date or purpose simply did not arise.

Amongst the Western peoples, it was the Germans who discovered the mechanical *clock,* the dread symbol of the flow of time, and the chimes of countless clock towers that echo day and night over West Europe are perhaps the most wonderful expression of which a historical world-feeling is capable.[4] In the timeless countrysides and cities of the Classical world, we find nothing of the sort. Till the epoch of Pericles, the time of day was estimated merely by the length of shadow, and it was only from that of Aristotle that the word ὥρα received the (Babylonian) significance of "hour"; prior to that there was no exact subdivision of the day. In Babylon and Egypt water-clocks and sun-dials were discovered in the very early stages, yet in Athens it was left to Plato to introduce a practically useful form of clepsydra, and this was merely a minor adjunct of everyday utility which could not have influenced the Classical life-feeling in the smallest degree. It is a bizarre, but nevertheless psychologically exact, fact that the Hellenic physics—being statics and not dynamics—neither knew the use nor felt the absence of the time-element, whereas we on the other hand work in thousandths of a second. The one and only evolution-idea that is timeless, ahistoric, is Aristotle's entelechy.

---

[4] It was about A.D. 1000 and therefore contemporaneously with the beginning of the Romanesque style and the Crusades—the first symptoms of a new Soul—that Abbot Gerbert (Pope Sylvester II), the friend of Emperor Otto III, invented the mechanism of the chiming wheel-clock. In Germany too, the first tower-clocks made their appearance, about 1200, and the pocket watch somewhat later. Observe the significant association of time measurement with the edifices of religion.

This, then, is our task. We men of the Western Culture are, with our historical sense, an exception and not a rule. World-history is *our* world picture and not all mankind's. Indian and Classical man formed no image of a world in progress, and perhaps when in due course the civilization of the West is extinguished, there will never again be a Culture and a human type in which "world-history" is so potent a form of the waking consciousness.

WHAT IS WORLD-HISTORY?

What, then, *is* world-history? Certainly, an ordered presentation of the past, an inner postulate, the expression of a capacity for feeling form. But a feeling for form, however definite, is not the same as form itself. No doubt we feel world-history, experience it and believe that it is to be read just as a map is read. But, even today, it is only partial shapes of it that we know and not *the* shape of it, which is the mirror-image of *our own* inner life.

Thanks to the subdivision of history into "Ancient," "Mediaeval" and "Modern"—an incredibly jejune and *meaningless* scheme, which has, however, entirely dominated our historical thinking—we have failed to perceive the true position in the general history of higher mankind of the little part-world which has developed on West European [5] soil from the time of the German-Roman Empire, to judge of its relative importance and above all to estimate its direction. The Cultures that are to come will find it difficult to believe that the validity of such a scheme with its simple rectilinear progression and its meaningless proportions, becoming more and more preposterous with each cen-

---

[5] The word "Europe" ought to be struck out of history. There is historically no "European" type, and it is sheer delusion to speak of the Hellenes as "European Antiquity" and to enlarge upon their "mission" to bring Europe and Asia closer together. It is thanks to this word "Europe" alone, and the complex of ideas resulting from it, that our historical consciousness has come to link Russia with the West in an utterly baseless unity—a mere abstraction derived from the reading of books—that has led to immense real consequences. In the shape of Peter the Great, this word has falsified the historical tendencies of a primitive human mass for two centuries, whereas the Russian *instinct* has very truly and fundamentally divided "Europe" from "Mother Russia" with the hostility that we can see embodied in Tolstoi, Aksakov or Dostoievski. "East" and "West" are notions that contain real history, whereas "Europe" is an empty sound.

tury, incapable of bringing into itself the new fields of history as they successively come into the light of our knowledge, was, in spite of all, never wholeheartedly attacked. It is not only that the scheme circumscribes the area of history. What is worse, it rigs the stage. The Western European area is regarded as a fixed pole, a unique patch chosen on the surface of the sphere for no better reason, it seems, than because we live on it—and great histories of millennial duration and mighty faraway Cultures are made to revolve around this pole in all modesty. It is a quaintly conceived system of sun and planets! We select a single bit of ground as the natural centre of the historical system, and make it the central sun. From it all the events of history receive their real light; from it their importance is judged in *perspective*.

It is self-evident that for the Cultures of the West the existence of Athens, Florence or Paris is more important than that of Loyang or Pataliputra. But is it permissible to found a scheme of world-history on estimates of such a sort? If so, then the Chinese historian is quite entitled to frame a world-history in which the Crusades, the Renaissance, Caesar and Frederick the Great are passed over in silence as insignificant. How, *from the morphological point of view,* should our eighteenth century be more important than any other of the sixty centuries that preceded it? Is it not ridiculous to oppose a "modern" history of a few centuries, and that history to all intents localized in West Europe, to an "ancient" history which covers as many millennia—incidentally dumping into that "ancient history" the whole mass of the pre-Hellenic cultures, unprobed and unordered, as mere appendix-matter? This is no exaggeration. Do we not, for the sake of keeping the hoary scheme, dispose of Egypt and Babylon—each as an individual and self-contained history quite equal in the balance to our so-called "world-history" from Charlemagne to the World War and well beyond it—as a *prelude* to Classical history? Do we not relegate the vast complexes of Indian and Chinese Culture to footnotes, with a gesture of embarrassment? As for the great American Cultures, do we not, on the ground that they do not "fit in" (with what?), entirely ignore them?

The most appropriate designation for this current West European scheme of history, in which the great Cultures are made to follow orbits round us as the presumed centre of all world-happenings, is the *Ptolemaic system* of history. The system that is put forward in this work in place of it I regard as the *Copernican discovery* in the historical sphere, in that it admits no sort of privileged position to the Classical or the Western Culture as against the Cultures of India, Babylon, China, Egypt, the Arabs, Mexico—separate worlds of dynamic being which in point of mass count for just as much in the general picture of history as the Classical, while frequently surpassing it in point of spiritual greatness and soaring power.

The scheme "ancient-mediaeval-modern" in its first form was a creation of the Magian world-sense. It first appeared in the Persian and Jewish religions after Cyrus, received an apocalyptic sense in the teaching of the Book of Daniel on the four world-eras and was developed into a world-history in the post-Christian religions of the East, notably the Gnostic systems.

This important conception, within the very narrow limits which fixed its intellectual basis, was unimpeachable. Neither Indian nor even Egyptian history was included in the scope of the proposition. For the Magian thinker the expression "world-history" meant a unique and supremely dramatic act, having as its theatre the lands between Hellas and Persia, in which the strictly dualistic world-sense of the East expressed itself not by means of polar conceptions like the "soul and spirit," "good and evil" of contemporary metaphysics, but by the figure of a catastrophe, an epochal change of phase between world-creation and world-decay. No elements beyond those which we find stabilized in the Classical literature, on the one hand, and the Bible (or other sacred book of the particular system), on the other, came into the picture, which presents (as "the Old" and "the New," respectively) the easily grasped contrasts of Gentile and Jewish, Christian and Heathen, Classical and Oriental, idol and dogma, nature and spirit *with a time connotation*—that is, as a drama in which the one prevails over the other. The historical change of period wears the characteristic dress of the religious "Redemption." This "world-history" in short was a conception narrow and provincial, but within its limits logical and complete. Necessarily, therefore, it was specific to this region and this humanity, and incapable of any *natural* extension.

But to these two there has been added a third epoch, the epoch that we call "modern," on Western soil, and it is this that for the first time gives the picture of history the look of a progression. The oriental picture was *at rest*. It presented a self-contained antithesis, with equilibrium as its outcome and a unique divine act as its turning-point. But, adopted and assumed by a wholly new type of mankind, it was quickly transformed (without any-one's noticing the oddity of the change) into a conception of a *linear progress:* from Homer or Adam—the modern can sub-stitute for these names the Indo-German, Stone Age, or the Pithecanthropus—through Jerusalem, Rome, Florence and Paris according to the taste of the individual historian, thinker or artist, who has unlimited freedom in the interpretation of the three-part scheme.

This third term, "modern times," which in form asserts that it is the last and conclusive term of the series, has in fact, ever since the Crusades, been stretched and stretched again to the elastic limit at which it will bear no more. It was at least implied, if not stated in so many words, that here, beyond the ancient and the mediaeval, something definitive was beginning, a Third Kingdom in which, somewhere, there was to be fulfilment and culmination, and which had an objective point. As to what this objective point is, each thinker, from Schoolman to present-day Socialist, backs his own peculiar discovery.

On the very threshold of the Western Culture we meet the great Joachim of Floris (c. 1145–1202), the first thinker of the Hegelian stamp, who shattered the dualistic world-form of Au-gustine, and with his essentially Gothic intellect stated the new Christianity of his time in the form of a third term to the reli-gions of the Old and the New Testaments, expressing them re-spectively as the Age of the Father, the Age of the Son and the Age of the Holy Ghost. His teaching moved the best of the Fran-ciscans and the Dominicans, Dante, Thomas Aquinas, in their inmost souls and awakened a world-outlook which slowly but surely took entire possession of the historical sense of our Cul-ture. Lessing—who often designated his own period with refer-ence to the Classical as the "after-world" (*Nachwelt*)—took his idea of the "education of the human race," with its three stages of child, youth and man, from the teaching of the fourteenth-century mystics. Ibsen treats it with thoroughness in his *Em-peror and Galilean* (1873), in which he directly presents the Gnostic world-conception through the figure of the wizard Maxi-mus, and advances not a step beyond it in his famous Stockholm address of 1887. It would appear, then, that the Western con-sciousness feels itself urged to predicate a sort of finality inher-ent in its own appearance.

But the creation of the Abbot of Floris was a *mystical* glance into the secrets of the divine world-order. It was bound to lose all meaning as soon as it was used in the way of reasoning and made a hypothesis of *scientific* thinking, as it has been—ever more and more frequently—since the seventeenth century.

It is a quite indefensible method of presenting world-history to begin by giving rein to one's own religious, political or social convictions and endowing the sacrosanct three-phase system with tendencies that will bring it exactly to one's own standpoint. This is, in effect, making of some formula—say, the "Age of Reason," Humanity, the greatest happiness of the greatest number, enlightenment, economic progress, national freedom, the conquest of nature or world-peace—a criterion whereby to judge whole millennia of history. And so we judge that they were ignorant of the "true path," or that they failed to follow it, when the fact is simply that their will and purposes were not the same as ours. Goethe's saying "What is important in life is life and not a result of life" is the answer to any and every senseless attempt to solve the riddle of historical form by means of a *programme*.

It is the same picture that we find when we turn to the historians of each special art or science (and those of national economics and philosophy as well). We find:

"Painting" from the Egyptians (or the cave-men) to the Impressionists, or

"Music" from Homer to Bayreuth and beyond, or

"Social Organization" from Lake Dwellings to Socialism, as the case may be,

presented as a linear graph which steadily rises in conformity with the values of the (selected) arguments. No one has seriously considered the possibility that arts may have an allotted span of life and may be attached as forms of self-expression to particular regions and particular types of mankind, and that therefore the total history of an art may be merely an additive compilation of separate developments, of special arts, with no bond of union save the name and some details of craft-technique.

We know it to be true of every organism that the rhythm, form and duration of its life, and all the expression-details of that life as well, are determined by the *properties of its species*. No one, looking at the oak, with its millennial life, dare say that it is at this moment, now, about to start on its true and proper course. No one as he sees a caterpillar grow day by day expects that it will go on doing so for two or three years. In these cases we feel, with an unqualified certainty, a *limit*, and this sense of the limit is identical with our sense of the inward form. In the case of higher human history, on the contrary, we take our ideas as to the course of the future from an unbridled optimism that sets at naught all historical, i.e. *organic*, experience, and everyone therefore sets himself to discover in the accidental present terms that he can expand into some striking progression-series, the existence of which rests not on scientific proof but on predilection.

"Mankind," however, has no aim, no idea, no plan, any more than the family of butterflies or orchids. "Mankind" is a zoological expression, or an empty word.[6] But conjure away the phantom, break the magic circle, and at once there emerges an astonishing wealth of *actual* forms—the Living with all its immense fullness, depth and movement—hitherto veiled by a catchword, a dry-as-dust scheme and a set of personal "ideals." I see, in place of that empty figment of *one* linear history which can be kept up only by shutting one's eyes to the overwhelming multitude of the facts, the drama of *a number* of mighty Cultures, each springing with primitive strength from the soil of a mother-region to which it remains firmly bound throughout its whole life-cycle; each stamping its material, its mankind, in *its own* image; each having *its own* idea, *its own* passions, *its own* life, will and feeling, *its own* death. Here indeed are colours, lights, movements, that no intellectual eye has yet discovered. Here the Cultures, peoples, languages, truths, gods, landscapes bloom and age as the oaks and the pines, the blossoms, twigs and leaves—but there is no aging "Mankind." Each Culture has its own new possibilities of self-expression which arise, ripen, decay and never return. There is not *one* sculpture, *one* painting, *one* mathematics, *one* physics, but many, each in its deepest essence different from the others, each limited in duration and self-contained, just as each species of plant has its peculiar blossom or fruit, its special type of growth and decline. These Cultures, sublimated life-essences, grow with the same superb aimlessness as the flowers of the field. They belong, like the plants and the animals, to the living Nature of Goethe, and not to the dead

[6] "Mankind? It is an abstraction. There are, always have been, and always will be, men and only men." (Goethe to Luden.)

Nature of Newton. I see world-history as a picture of endless formations and transformations, of the marvellous waxing and
waning of organic forms. The professional historian, on the contrary, sees it as a sort of tapeworm industriously adding onto
itself one epoch after another.

But the series "ancient-mediaeval-modern history" has at last
exhausted its usefulness. Angular, narrow, shallow though it
was as a scientific foundation, still we possessed no other form
that was not wholly unphilosophical in which our data could be
arranged, and world-history (as hitherto understood) has to
thank it for filtering our classifiable solid residues. But the number of centuries that the scheme can by any stretch be made to
cover has long since been exceeded, and with the rapid increase
in the volume of our historical material—especially of material
that cannot possibly be brought under the scheme—the picture
is beginning to dissolve into a chaotic blur.

HISTORICAL RELATIVITY

When Plato speaks of humanity, he means the Hellenes in contrast to the barbarians, which is entirely consonant with the
ahistoric mode of the Classical life and thought, and his
premisses take him to conclusions that *for Greeks* were complete and significant. When, however, Kant philosophizes, say on
ethical ideas, he maintains the validity of his theses for men of
all times and places. He does not say this in so many words, for,
for himself and his readers, it is something that goes without
saying. In his aesthetics he formulates the principles, not of
Phidias' art, or Rembrandt's art, but of Art generally. But what he
poses as necessary forms of thought are in reality only necessary forms of Western thought, though a glance at Aristotle and
his essentially different conclusions should have sufficed to show
that Aristotle's intellect, not less penetrating than his own, was of
different structure from it.

It is *this* that is lacking to the Western thinker, the very
thinker in whom we might have expected to find it—insight into
the *historically relative* character of his data, which are expressions of one *specific existence and one only;* knowledge of the
necessary limits of their validity; the conviction that his "unshakable" truths and "eternal" views are simply true for him and

eternal for his world-view; the duty of looking beyond them to find out what the men of other Cultures have with equal certainty evolved out of themselves. That and nothing else will impart completeness to the philosophy of the future, and only through an understanding of the living world shall we understand the symbolism of history. Here there is nothing constant, nothing universal. We must cease to speak of the forms of "Thought," the principles of "Tragedy," the mission of "the State." Universal validity involves always the fallacy of arguing from particular to particular.

But something much more disquieting than a logical fallacy begins to appear when the centre of gravity of philosophy shifts from the abstract-systematic to the practical-ethical and our Western thinkers from Schopenhauer onward turn from the problem of cognition to the problem of life (the will to life, to power, to action). Here it is not the ideal abstract "man" of Kant that is subjected to examination, but actual man as he has inhabited the earth during historical time, grouped, whether primitive or advanced, by peoples; and it is more than ever futile to define the structure of his highest ideas in terms of the "ancient-mediaeval-modern" scheme with its local limitations. But it is done, nevertheless.

Consider the historical horizon of Nietzsche. His conceptions of decadence, militarism, the transvaluation of all values, the will to power, lie deep in the essence of Western civilization and are for the analysis of that civilization of decisive importance. But what, do we find, was the foundation on which he built up his creation? Romans and Greeks, Renaissance and European present, with a fleeting and uncomprehending side-glance at Indian philosophy—in short "ancient, mediaeval and modern" history. Strictly speaking, he never once moved outside the scheme, nor did any other thinker of his time. And is the thought-range of Schopenhauer, Comte, Feuerbach, Hebbel or Strindberg any wider? Is not their whole psychology, for all its intention of world-wide validity, one of purely West European significance?

What the West has said and thought, hitherto, on the problems of space, time, motion, number, will, marriage, property, tragedy, science, has remained narrow and dubious, because men were always looking for *the* solution of *the* question. It was never seen that many questioners implies many answers, that any philosophical question is really a veiled desire to get an explicit affirmation of what is implicit in the question itself, that the great questions of any period are fluid beyond all conception, and that therefore it is only by obtaining a *group of historically limited solutions* and measuring it by *utterly impersonal* criteria that the final secrets can be reached. In other Cultures the phenomenon talks a different language, for other men there are different truths. The *thinker* must admit the validity of all, or of none. How greatly, then, Western world-criticism can be widened and deepened! How immensely far beyond the innocent relativism of Nietzsche and his generation one must look—how fine one's sense for form and one's psychological insight must become —how completely one must free oneself from limitations of self, of practical interests, of horizon—before one dare assert the pretension to understand world-history, the *world-as-history*.

THE HISTORICAL EYE

In opposition to all these arbitrary and narrow schemes, derived from tradition or personal choice, into which history is forced, I put forward the natural, the "Copernican," form of the historical process which lies deep in the essence of that process and reveals itself only to an eye perfectly free from prepossessions.

Such an eye was Goethe's. That which Goethe called *Living Nature* is exactly that which we are calling here world-history, *world-as-history*. Goethe, who as artist portrayed the life and development, always the life and development, of his figures, the thing-becoming and not the thing-become (*Wilhelm Meister* and *Dichtung und Wahrheit*), hated Mathematics. For him, the world-as-mechanism stood opposed to the world-as-organism, dead nature to living nature, law to form. As naturalist, every line he wrote was meant to display the image of a thing-becoming, the "impressed form" living and developing. Sympathy, observation, comparison, immediate and inward certainty, intellectual *flair*—these were the means whereby he was enabled to approach the secrets of the phenomenal world in motion. *Now these are the means of historical research*—precisely these and no others. It was this *godlike* insight that prompted him to say at the bivouac fire on the evening of the Battle of Valmy: "Here and now begins a new epoch of world history, and you, gentlemen, can say that you 'were there.'" No general, no diplomat, let alone the philosophers, ever so directly felt history "becoming." It is the deepest judgment that any man ever uttered about a great historical act in the moment of its accomplishment.

And just as he followed out the development of the plant-form from the leaf, the birth of the vertebrate type, the process of the geological strata—*the Destiny in nature and not the Causality*—so here we shall develop the form-language of human history, its periodic structure, its *organic logic*, out of the profusion of all the challenging details.

In other aspects, mankind is habitually, and rightly, reckoned as one of the organisms of the earth's surface. Its physical structure, its natural functions, the whole phenomenal conception of it, all belong to a more comprehensive unity. Only in *this* aspect is it treated otherwise, despite that deeply felt relationship of plant destiny and human destiny which is an eternal theme of all lyrical poetry, and despite that similarity of human history to that of any other of the higher life-groups which is the refrain of endless beast-legends, sagas and fables. But only bring analogy to bear on this aspect as on the rest, letting the world of human Cultures intimately and unreservedly work upon the imagination instead of forcing it into a ready-made scheme. Let the words "youth," "growth," "maturity," "decay"—hitherto, and today more than ever, used to express subjective valuations and entirely personal preferences in sociology, ethics and aesthetics—be taken at last as objective descriptions of organic states. Set forth the Classical Culture as a self-contained phenomenon embodying and expressing the Classical soul, put it beside the Egyptian, the Indian, the Babylonian, the Chinese and the Western, and determine for each of these higher individuals what is typical in their surgings and what is necessary in the riot of incident. And then at last will unfold itself the picture of world-history that is natural to us, men of the West, and to us alone.

ONE-SIDED INTERPRETATIONS OF THE PICTURE OF CLASSICAL HISTORY

Our narrower task, then, is primarily to determine, from such a world-survey, the state of West Europe and America as at the epoch of 1800–2000—to establish the chronological position of this period in the ensemble of Western culture-history, its significance as a chapter that is in one or other guise necessarily found in the biography of every Culture, and the organic and symbolic meaning of its political, artistic, intellectual and social expression-forms.

Considered in the spirit of analogy, this period appears as chronologically parallel—"contemporary" in our special sense—with the phase of Hellenism, and its present culmination, marked by the World War, corresponds with the transition from the Hellenistic to the Roman age. *Rome,* with its rigorous realism—uninspired, barbaric, disciplined, practical, Protestant, *Prussian* —will always give us, working as we must by analogies, the key to understanding our future. The *break of destiny that we express by hyphening the words "Greeks-Romans" is occurring for us also, separating that which is already fulfilled from that which is to come.* Long ago we might and should have seen in the "Classical" world a development which is the complete counterpart of our own Western development, differing indeed from it in every detail of the surface but entirely similar as regards the inward power driving the great organism towards its end.

Unfortunately, this requires an interpretation of the picture of Classical history very different from the incredibly one-sided, superficial, prejudiced, limited picture that we have in fact given to it. We have in truth been only too conscious of our near relation to the Classical Age, and only too prone in consequence to unconsidered assertion of it. Superficial similarity is a great snare, and our entire Classical study fell a victim to it as soon as it passed from the (admittedly masterly) ordering and critique of the discoveries to the interpretation of their spiritual meaning. The whole religious-philosophical, art-historical and social-critical work of the nineteenth century has been necessary to enable us, not to *understand* Aeschylus, Plato, Apollo and Dionysus, the Athenian state and Caesarism (which we are far indeed from doing), but to begin to realize, once and for all, how immeasurably alien and distant these things are from our inner selves—more alien, maybe, than Mexican gods and Indian architecture.

[*Our judgments of the Graeco-Roman Culture have always swung between two extremes. Economists, politicians, jurists, are inclined to take the "progress" of present mankind as a standard for judging everything earlier. Conversely, artists, poets, philologists and philosophers may feel*

22

themselves out of their element in the present, and choose a standpoint in this or that past epoch, that is just as absolute and dogmatic from which to condemn today. Both are superficial pragmatists. Briefly, there are two ways of regarding the Classical—the materialistic and the ideological. In the juxtaposing of cause and effect the materialist classes the purely political facts as causes and the religious, intellectual, artistic facts as effects. The ideologues lose themselves in cults, mysteries, customs, in the secrets of the strophe and the line, scarcely throwing a side-glance at commonplace daily life.]

The one type is foreshadowed from the very outset in Petrarch; it created Florence and Weimar and the Western classicism. The other type appears in the middle of the eighteenth century, along with the rise of civilized,[7] economic-megalopolitan [8] politics, and England is therefore its birthplace (Grote). At bottom, the opposition is between the conceptions of culture-man and those of civilization-man, and it is too deep, too essentially human, to allow the weaknesses of *both standpoints alike* to be seen or overcome.

In all history there is no analogous case of one Culture making a passionate cult of the memory of another. We have projected our own deepest spiritual needs and feelings onto the Classical picture. To worshippers of the Classical it seems blasphemous to talk of Roman central-heating or book-keeping in preference to the worship of the Great Mother of the Gods.

But the other school sees *nothing but* these things. They think it exhausts the essence of this Culture, alien as it is to ours, to regard the Greeks as no different from themselves and obtain their conclusions by means of simple factual substitutions, ignoring altogether the Classical *soul.* That there is not the slightest inward correlation between the things meant by "Republic," "freedom," "property" and the like then and there and the things meant by such words here and now, it has no notion whatever.

Not that religious and artistic phenomena are more primitive

---

[7] As will be seen later, the words *zivilisierte* and *Zivilisation* possess in this work a special meaning.—*At.*

[8] English not possessing the adjective-forming freedom of German, we are compelled to coin a word for the rendering of *grossstädtisch,* an adjective not only frequent but of emphatic significance in the author's argument.—*At.*

than social and economic, any more than the reverse. For the man who in these things has won his unconditional freedom of outlook, beyond *all* personal interests whatsoever, there is no dependence, no priority, no relation of cause and effect, no differentiation of value or importance. That which assigns relative ranks amongst the individual detail-facts is simply the greater or less purity and force of their form-language, their symbolism, beyond all questions of good and evil, high and low, useful and ideal.

THE PROBLEM OF "CIVILIZATION"

Looked at in this way, the "Decline of the West" comprises nothing less than the problem of *Civilization*. We have before us one of the fundamental questions of all higher history. What is Civilization, understood as the organico-logical sequel, fulfilment and finale of a culture?

For every Culture has *its own* Civilization. In this work, for the first time the two words, hitherto used to express an indefinite, more or less ethical, distinction, are used in a *periodic* sense, to express a strict and necessary *organic succession*. The Civilization is the inevitable *destiny* of the Culture, and in this principle we obtain the viewpoint from which the deepest and gravest problems of historical morphology become capable of solution. Civilizations are the most external and artificial states of which a species of developed humanity is capable. They are a conclusion, the thing-become succeeding the thing-becoming, death following life, rigidity following expansion, intellectual age and the stone-built, petrifying world-city following mother-earth and the spiritual childhood of Doric and Gothic. They are an end, irrevocable, yet by inward necessity reached again and again.

So, for the first time, we are enabled to understand the Romans as the *successors* of the Greeks, and light is projected into the deepest secrets of the late-Classical period. What, but this, can be the meaning of the fact—which can only be disputed by vain phrases—that the Romans were barbarians who did not *precede* but *closed* a great development? Unspiritual, unphilosophical, devoid of art, clannish to the point of brutality, aiming relentlessly at tangible successes, they stand between the Hellenic Culture and nothingness. An imagination directed purely to practical objects was something which is not found at all in Athens. In a word, Greek *soul*—Roman *intellect;* and this antithesis is the differentia between Culture and Civilization. Nor is it only to the Classical that it applies. Again and again there appears this type of strong-minded, completely non-metaphysical man, and in the hands of this type lies the intellectual and material destiny of each and every "late" period. *Pure* Civilization, as a historical process, consists in a progressive exhaustion of forms that have become inorganic or dead.

The transition from Culture to Civilization was accomplished for the Classical world in the fourth, for the Western in the nineteenth century. From these periods onward the great intellectual decisions take place, no longer all over the world where not a hamlet is too small to be unimportant, but in three or four world-cities that have absorbed into themselves the whole content of History, while the old wide landscape of the Culture, become merely provincial, serves only to feed the cities with what remains of its higher mankind. *World-city and province*—the two basic ideas of every civilization—bring up a wholly new form-problem of History, the very problem that we are living through today with hardly the remotest conception of its immensity. In place of a world, there is a *city, a point,* in which the whole life of broad regions is collecting while the rest dries up. In place of a type-true people, born of and grown on the soil, there is a new sort of nomad, cohering unstably in fluid masses, the parasitical city dweller, traditionless, utterly matter-of-fact, religionless, clever, unfruitful, deeply contemptuous of the countryman and especially that highest form of countryman, the country gentleman. This is a very great stride towards the inorganic, towards the end—what does it signify?

The world-city means cosmopolitanism in place of "home" [9] . . . To the world-city belongs not a folk but a mob. Its uncomprehending hostility to all the traditions representative of the Culture (nobility, church, privileges, dynasties, convention in art and limits of knowledge in science), the keen and cold intelligence that confounds the wisdom of the peasant, the new-fashioned naturalism that in relation to all matters of sex and

---

[9] A profound word which obtains its significance as soon as the barbarian becomes a culture-man and loses it again as soon as the civilization-man takes up the motto *"Ubi bene, ibi patria."*

society goes back far to quite primitive instincts and conditions, the reappearance of the *panem et circenses* in the form of wage-disputes and sports stadia—all these things betoken the definite closing down of the Culture and the opening of a quite new phase of human existence—anti-provincial, late, futureless, but quite inevitable.

This is what has to be *viewed,* and viewed not with the eyes of the partisan, the ideologue, the up-to-date moralist, not from this or that "standpoint," but in a high, time-free perspective embracing whole millennia of historical world-forms, if we are really to comprehend the great crisis of the present.

To me it is a symbol of the first importance that in the Rome of Crassus—triumvir and all-powerful building-site speculator— the Roman people with its proud inscriptions, the people before whom Gauls, Greeks, Parthians, Syrians afar trembled, lived in appalling misery in the many-storied lodging-houses of dark sub-urbs, accepting with indifference or even with a sort of sporting interest the consequences of the military expansion: that many famous old-noble families, descendants of the men who defeated the Celts and the Samnites, lost their ancestral homes through standing apart from the wild rush of speculation and were re-duced to renting wretched apartments; that in depopulated Athens, which lived on visitors and on the bounty of rich foreign-ers, the mob of parvenu tourists from Rome gaped at the works of the Periclean Age with as little understanding as the Ameri-can globe-trotter in the Sistine Chapel at those of Michelangelo, every removable art-piece having ere this been taken away or bought at fancy prices to be replaced by the Roman buildings which grew up, colossal and arrogant, by the side of the low and modest structures of the old time. In such things—which it is the historian's business not to praise or to blame but to consider morphologically—there lies, plain and immediate enough for one who has learnt to see, an *idea.*

For it will become manifest that, from this moment on, all great conflicts of world-outlook, of politics, of art, of science, of feeling, will be under the influence of the same contrary factor. What is the hallmark of a politic of Civilization today, in con-trast to a politic of Culture yesterday? It is, for the Classical rhetoric, and for the Western journalism, both serving that ab-stract which represents the power of Civilization—*money.* It is the money-spirit which penetrates unremarked the historical forms of the people's existence, often without destroying or even in the least disturbing these forms—the form of the Roman state, for instance, underwent very much less alteration between the elder Scipio and Augustus than is usually imagined. Though forms subsist, the great political parties nevertheless cease to be more than reputed centres of decision. A small number of superior heads, whose names are very likely not the best-known, settle everything, while below them are the great mass of second-rate politicians—rhetors, tribunes, deputies, journalists—selected through a provincially conceived franchise to keep alive the illusion of popular self-determination.

It is possible to understand the Greeks without mentioning their economic relations; the Romans, on the other hand, can *only* be understood through these. Chaeronea and Leipzig were the last battles fought about an idea. In the First Punic War and in 1870 economic motives are no longer to be overlooked.

THE CONCLUSION—IMPERIALISM

Considered in itself, the Roman world-dominion was a negative phenomenon, being the result not of a surplus of energy on the one side—that the Romans had never had since Zama—but of a deficiency of resistance on the other. That the Romans did *not* conquer the world is certain; they merely took possession of a booty that lay open to everyone. The *Imperium Romanum* came into existence not as the result of such an extremity of military and financial effort as had characterized the Punic Wars, but because the old East forwent all external self-determinations. We must not be deluded by the appearance of brilliant military successes. With a few ill-trained, ill-led, and sullen legions, Lucullus and Pompey conquered whole realms—a phenomenon that in the period of the battle of Ipsus would have been unthinkable. The Mithridatic danger, serious enough for a system of material force which had never been put to any real test, would have been nothing to the conquerors of Hannibal. After Zama, the Romans never again either waged or were capable of waging a war against a great military Power.[1] Their classic

---

[1] The conquest of Gaul by Caesar was frankly a colonial, i.e. a one-sided, war; and the fact that it is the highest achievement in the later military history of Rome only shows that the well of real achievement was rapidly drying up.

wars were those against the Samnites, Pyrrhus and Carthage. Their grand hour was Cannae. To maintain the heroic posture for centuries on end is beyond the power of any people. The Prussian-German people have had three great moments (1813, 1870 and 1914), and that is more than others have had.

Here, then, I lay it down that *Imperialism,* of which petrifacts such as the Egyptian empire, the Roman, the Chinese, the Indian, may continue to exist for hundreds or thousands of years—dead bodies, amorphous and dispirited masses of men, scrap-material from a great history—is to be taken as the typical symbol of the end. Imperialism is Civilization unadulterated. In this phenomenal form the destiny of the West is now irrevocably set. The energy of culture-man is directed inwards, that of civilization-man outwards. And thus I see in Cecil Rhodes the first man of a new age. It is not a matter of choice—it is not the conscious will of individuals, or even that of whole classes or peoples that decides. The expansive tendency is a doom, something daemonic and immense, which grips, forces into service, and uses up the late mankind of the world-city stage, willy-nilly, aware or unaware.[2] Life is the process of effecting possibilities, and for the brain-man there are *only extensive* possibilities.[3] Hard as the half-developed Socialism of today is fighting against expansion, one day it will become arch-expansionist with all the vehemence of destiny. Here the form-language of politics, as the direct intellectual expression of a certain type of humanity, touches on a deep metaphysical problem—on the fact, affirmed in the grant of unconditional validity to the causality-principle, that *the soul is the complement of extension.*

Rhodes is to be regarded as the first precursor of a Western type of Caesar, whose day is to come though yet distant. He stands midway between Napoleon and the force-men of the next centuries, just as Flaminius, who from 232 B.C. onward pressed the Romans to undertake the subjugation of Cisalpine

~~~~~~~

[2] The modern Germans are a conspicuous example of a people that has become expansive without knowing it or willing it. They were already in that state while they still believed themselves to be the people of Goethe. Even Bismarck, the founder of the new age, never had the slightest idea of it, and believed himself to have reached the *conclusion* of a political process.

[3] This is probably the meaning of Napoleon's significant words to Goethe: "What have we today to do with destiny? Policy is destiny."

Gaul and so initiated the policy of colonial expansion, stands be‑ tween Alexander and Caesar.

Alexander and Napoleon were romantics; though they stood on the threshold of Civilization and in its cold clear air, the one fancied himself an Achilles and the other read Werther. Caesar, on the contrary, was a pure man of fact gifted with immense understanding. But even for Rhodes political success means territorial and financial success, and only that. Of this Roman‑ ness within himself he was fully aware. But Western Civilization has not yet taken shape in such strength and purity as this. It was only before his maps that he could fall into a sort of poetic trance, this son of the parsonage who, sent out to South Africa without means, made a gigantic fortune and employed it as the engine of political aims. His idea of a trans-African railway from the Cape to Cairo, his project of a South African empire, his in‑ tellectual hold on the hard metal souls of the mining magnates whose wealth he forced into the service of his schemes, his capi‑ tal Bulawayo, royally planned as a future Residence by a states‑ man who was all-powerful yet stood in no definite relation to the State, his wars, his diplomatic deals, his road-systems, his syndi‑ cates, his armies, his conception of the "great duty to civilization" of the man of brain—all this, broad and imposing, is the prelude of a future which is still in store for us and with which the history of West European mankind will be definitely *closed.*

He who does not understand that this outcome is obligatory and insusceptible of modification, that our choice is between willing *this* and willing nothing at all, between cleaving to *this* destiny or despairing of the future and of life itself; he who can‑ not feel that there is grandeur also in the realizations of power‑ ful intelligences, in the energy and discipline of metal-hard na‑ tures, in battles fought with the coldest and most abstract means; he who is obsessed with the idealism of a provincial and would pursue the ways of life of past ages—must forgo all desire to comprehend history, to live through history or to make history.

Let it be realized, then: That the nineteenth and twentieth centuries, hitherto looked on as the highest point of an ascend‑ ing straight line of world-history, are in reality a stage of life which may be observed in every Culture that has ripened to its limit—a stage of life characterized not by Socialists, Impression‑ ists, electric railways, torpedoes and differential equations (for these are only body-constituents of the time), but by a civilized spirituality which possesses not only these but also quite other creative possibilities. That, as our own time represents a transitional phase which occurs with certainty under particular conditions, there are perfectly well-defined states (such as have occurred more than once in the history of the past) *later* than the present-day state of West Europe, and therefore that the future of the West is not a limitless tending upwards and onwards for all time towards our present ideals, but a single phenomenon of history, strictly limited and defined as to form and duration, which covers a few centuries and can be viewed and, in essentials, calculated from available precedents.

SIGNIFICANCE OF THE MAIN THEME

This high plane of contemplation once attained, the rest is easy. To this *single* idea one can refer, and by it one can solve, without straining or forcing, all those separate problems of religion, art-history, epistemology, ethics, politics, economics with which the modern intellect has so passionately—and so vainly—busied itself for decades. This idea is one of those truths that have only to be expressed with full clarity to become indisputable. It is one of the inward necessities of the Western Culture and of its world-feeling.

Up to now everyone has been at liberty to hope what he pleased about the future. Where there are no facts, sentiment rules. But henceforward it will be every man's business to inform himself of what *can* happen and therefore of what with the unalterable necessity of destiny and irrespective of personal ideals, hopes or desires, *will happen*. When we use the risky word "freedom" we shall mean freedom to do, not this or that, but the necessary or nothing. The feeling that this is "just as it should be" is the hallmark of the man of fact. To lament it and blame it is not to alter it. To birth belongs death, to youth age, to life generally its form and its allotted span. The present is a civilized, emphatically not a cultured time-period.

It will no doubt be objected that such a world-outlook, which in giving this certainty as to the outlines and tendency of the future cuts off all far-reaching hopes, would be unhealthy for all and fatal for many, once it ceased to be a mere theory and was adopted as a practical scheme of life by the group of personalities effectively moulding the future.

Such is not my opinion. We are civilized, not Gothic or Rococo, people; we have to reckon with the hard cold facts of a *late* life, to which the parallel is to be found not in Pericles' Athens but in Caesar's Rome. Of great painting or great music there can no longer be, for Western people, any question. Their architectural possibilities have been exhausted these hundred years. Only *extensive* possibilities are left to them. Yet, for a sound and vigorous generation that is filled with unlimited hopes, I fail to see that it is any disadvantage to discover betimes that some of these hopes must come to nothing. And if the hopes thus doomed should be those most dear, well, a man who is worth anything will not be dismayed.

THE RELATION OF A MORPHOLOGY OF WORLD-HISTORY TO RELIGION

All genuine historical work is philosophy, unless it is mere ant-industry. But the operations of the systematic philosopher are subject to constant and serious error through his assuming the permanence of his results. He overlooks the fact that every thought lives in a historical world and is therefore involved in the common destiny of mortality. He supposes that higher thought possesses an everlasting and unalterable objectiveness (*Gegenstand*), that the great questions of all epochs are identical and that therefore they are capable in the last analysis of final answers.

But question and answer are here one, and the great questions are made great by the very fact that unequivocal answers to them are so passionately demanded, so that it is as life-symbols only that they possess significance. There are no eternal truths. Every philosophy is the expression of its own and only its own time, and—if by philosophy we mean effective philosophy and not academic triflings about judgment-forms, sense-categories and the like—no two ages possess the same philosophic intentions. The difference is not between perishable and imperishable doctrines but between doctrines which live their day and doctrines which never live at all. The immortality of thoughts-become is an illusion—the essential is, what kind of man comes to expression in them. The greater the man, the truer the philosophy, with the inward truth that in a great work of art transcends all proof of its several elements or even of their compatibility with one another. At highest, the philosophy may absorb the entire content of an epoch, realize it within itself and then, embodying it in some grand form or personality, pass it on to be developed further and further. Only its necessity to life decides the eminence of a doctrine.

For me, therefore, the test of value to be applied to a thinker is his eye for the great facts of his own time. Only this can settle whether he is merely a clever architect of systems and principles, versed in definitions and analyses, or whether it is the very soul of his time that speaks in his works and his intuitions. A philosopher who cannot grasp and command actuality as well will never be of the first rank. The Pre-Socratics were merchants and politicians *en grand*. The desire to put his political ideas into practice in Syracuse nearly cost Plato his life, and it was the same Plato who discovered the set of geometrical theorems that enabled Euclid to build up the Classical system of mathematics. Pascal—whom Nietzsche knows only as the "broken Christian" —Descartes, Leibniz, were the first mathematicians and technicians of their time.

And herein, I think, all the philosophers of the newest age are open to a serious criticism. What they do not possess is real standing in actual life. Not one of them has intervened effectively, either in higher politics, in the development of modern technics, in matters of communication, in economics or in any other *big* actuality, with a single act or a single compelling idea. Not one of them counts in mathematics, in physics, in the science of government, even to the extent that Kant counted. Let us glance at other times. Confucius was several times a minister. Pythagoras was the organizer of an important political movement akin to the Cromwellian, the significance of which is even now far underestimated by Classical researchers. Goethe, besides being a model executive minister—though lacking, alas, the operative sphere of a great state—was interested in the Suez and Panama canals (the dates of which he foresaw with accuracy) and their effects on the economy of the world, and he busied himself again and again with the question of American economic life and its reactions on the Old World, and with that of the dawning era of machine-industry. Hobbes was one of the originators of the great plan of winning South America for England, and although in execution the plan went no further than the occupation of Jamaica, he has the glory of being one of the founders of the British Colonial Empire. Leibniz, without doubt the greatest intellect in Western philosophy, the founder of the differential calculus and the *analysis situs,* conceived or co-operated in a number of major political schemes, one of which was to relieve Germany by drawing the attention of Louis XIV to the importance of Egypt as a factor in French world-policy. The ideas of the memorandum on this subject that he drew up for the Grand Monarch were so far in advance of their time (1672) that it has been thought that Napoleon made use of them for his Eastern venture. Even thus early, Leibniz laid down the principle that Napoleon grasped more and more clearly after Wagram, viz., that acquisitions on the Rhine and in Belgium would not permanently better the position of France and that the neck of Suez would one day be the key to world-dominance. Doubtless the King was not equal to these deep political and strategic conceptions of the Philosopher.

Whenever I take up a work by a modern thinker, I find myself asking: Has he any idea whatever of the actualities of world-politics, world-city problems, capitalism, the future of the state, the relation of technics to the course of civilization, Russia, Science? Goethe would have understood all this and revelled in it, but there is not one living philosopher capable of taking it in. This sense of actualities is of course not the same thing as the content of a philosophy, but, I repeat, it is an infallible symptom of its inward necessity, its fruitfulness and its symbolic importance.

We must allow ourselves no illusions as to the gravity of this negative result. It is palpable that we have lost sight of the final significance of effective philosophy. We confuse philosophy with preaching, with agitation, with novel-writing, with lecture-room jargon. It has come to this, that the very *possibility* of a real philosophy of today and tomorrow is in question. A doctrine that does not attack and affect the life of the period in its inmost depths is no doctrine and had better not be taught. And what was possible even yesterday is, today, at least not indispensable.

THE FINAL TASK

A century of purely extensive effectiveness, excluding big artistic and metaphysical production—let us say frankly an irreligious time which coincides exactly with the idea of the world-city—is a time of decline. True. But we have not *chosen* this time. We cannot help it if we are born as men of the early winter of full Civilization, instead of on the golden summit of a ripe Culture, in a Phidias or a Mozart time. Everything depends on our seeing our own position, our *destiny,* clearly, on our realizing that though we may lie to ourselves about it we cannot evade it. Only a very few of the problems of metaphysics are, so to say, allocated for solution to any epoch of thought. Even thus soon, a whole world separates Nietzsche's time, in which a last trace of romanticism was still operative, from our own, which has shed every vestige of it.

Systematic philosophy closes with the end of the eighteenth century. Kant put its utmost possibilities in forms both grand in themselves and—as a rule—final for the Western soul. He is followed, as Plato and Aristotle were followed, by a specifically megalopolitan philosophy that was not speculative but practical, irreligious, social-ethical. This philosophy—paralleled in the Chinese civilization by the schools of the "Epicurean" Yang Chu, the "Socialist" Mo Ti, the "Pessimist" Chuang-tzu, the "positivist" Mencius, and in the Classical by the Cynics, the Cyrenaics, the Stoics and the Epicureans—begins in the West with Schopenhauer, who is the first to make the *Will to life* ("creative life-force") the centre of gravity of his thought, although the deeper tendency of his doctrine is obscured by his having, under the influence of a great tradition, maintained the obsolete distinctions of phenomena and things-in-themselves and suchlike. It is the same creative will-to-life that was Schopenhauer-wise denied in *Tristan* and Darwin-wise asserted in *Siegfried;* that was brilliantly and theatrically formulated by Nietzsche in *Zarathustra;* that led the Hegelian Marx to an economic and the Malthusian Darwin to a biological hypothesis which together have subtly transformed the world-outlook of the Western megalopolis; and that produced a homogeneous series of tragedy-conceptions extending from Hebbel's *Judith* to Ibsen's *Epilogue.* It has embraced, therefore, all the possibilities of a true philosophy—and at the same time it has exhausted them.

Systematic philosophy, then, lies immensely far behind us, and ethical has been wound up. *But a third possibility, corresponding to the Classical Scepticism, still remains to the soul-world* of the present-day West, and it can be brought to light by the hitherto unknown methods of historical morphology. That which is a possibility is a necessity. The Classical scepticism is ahistoric, it doubts by denying outright. But that of the West, if it is an inward necessity, a symbol of the autumn of our spirituality, is obliged to be historical through and through. Its solutions are got by treating everything as relative, as a historical phenomenon, and its procedure is psychological. Whereas the Sceptic philosophy arose within Hellenism as the negation of philosophy—declaring philosophy to be purposeless—we, on the contrary, regard the *history of philosophy* as, in the last resort, philosophy's gravest theme. This *is* "skepsis," in the true sense, for whereas the Greek is led to renounce absolute standpoints by contempt for the intellectual past, we are led to do so by comprehension of that past as an organism.

In this work it will be our task to sketch out this unphilosophical philosophy—the last that West Europe will know. Scepticism is the expression of a pure Civilization; and it dissipates the world-picture of the Culture that has gone before. For us, its success will lie in resolving all the older problems into one, the genetic. The conviction that what *is* also *has become,* that the natural and cognizable is rooted in the historic, that the World as the actual is founded on an Ego as the potential actualized, that the "when" and the "how long" hold as deep a secret as the "what," leads directly to the fact that everything, whatever else it may be, must at any rate be *the expression of something living.* Cognitions and judgments too are acts of living men. The thinkers of the past conceived external actuality as produced by cognition and motiving ethical judgments, but to the thought of the future they are above all *expressions and symbols. The Morphology of world-history becomes inevitably a universal symbolism.*

With that, the claim of higher thought to possess general and eternal truths falls to the ground. Truths are truths only in relation to a particular mankind. Thus, my own philosophy is able to express and reflect *only* the Western (as distinct from the Classical, Indian or other) soul, and that soul *only* in its present civilized phase by which its conception of the world, its practical range and its sphere of effect are specified.

THE ORIGIN OF THIS BOOK

In concluding this Introduction, I may be permitted to add a personal note. In 1911, I proposed to myself to put together some broad considerations on the political phenomena of the day and their possible developments. At that time the World War appeared to me both as imminent and also as the inevitable outward manifestation of the historical crisis, and my endeavour was to comprehend it from an examination of the spirit of the preceding centuries—not years. In the course of this originally small task, the conviction forced itself on me that for an effective understanding of the epoch the area to be taken into the foundation-plan must be very greatly enlarged, and that in an investigation of this sort it was impossible to restrict oneself to a single epoch and its political actualities, or to confine oneself to a pragmatical framework, or even to do without purely metaphysical and highly transcendental methods of treatment. It became evident that a political problem could not be comprehended by means of politics themselves and that, frequently, important factors at work in the depths could only be grasped through their artistic manifestations or even distantly seen in the form of scientific or purely philosophical ideas. Even the politico-social analysis of the last decades of the nineteenth century—a period of tense quiet between two immense and outstanding events: the one which, expressed in the Revolution and Napoleon, had fixed the picture of West European actuality for a century and another of at least equal significance that was visibly and ever more rapidly approaching—was found in the last resort to be impossible without bringing in *all* the great problems of Being in all their aspects. For, in the historical as in the natural world-picture, there is found nothing, however small, that does not embody in itself the entire sum of fundamental tendencies. And thus the original theme came to be immensely widened. A vast number of unexpected (and in the main entirely novel) questions and interrelations presented themselves. And finally it became perfectly clear that no single fragment of history could be thoroughly illuminated unless and until the secret of world-history itself, to wit the story of higher mankind as an organism of regular structure, had been cleared up. And hitherto this has not been done, even in the least degree.

Thereafter I saw the present—the approaching World War—in a quite other light. It was no longer a momentary constellation of casual facts due to national sentiments, personal influences or economic tendencies endowed with an appearance of unity and necessity by some historian's scheme of political or social cause-and-effect, but the type of *a historical change of phase* occurring within a great historical organism of definable compass at the point preordained for it hundreds of years ago. The mark of the great crisis is its innumerable passionate questionings and probings. In our own case there were books and ideas by the thousand; but, scattered, disconnected, limited by the horizons of specialisms as they were, they incited, depressed and confounded but could not free. Hence, though these questions are seen, their identity is missed. Consider those art-problems that (though never comprehended in their depths) were evinced in the disputes between form and content, line and space, drawing and colour, in the notion of style, in the idea of Impressionism and the music of Wagner. Consider the decline of art and the failing authority of science; the grave problems arising out of the victory of the megalopolis over the countryside, such as childlessness and land-depopulation; the place in society of a fluctuating Fourth Estate; the crisis in materialism, in Socialism, in parliamentary government; the position of the individual *vis-à-vis* the State; the problem of private property with its pendant the problem of marriage. Consider at the same time what is apparently an entirely different field, the voluminous work that was being done in the domain of folk-psychology on the origins of myths, arts, religions and thought—and done, moreover, no longer from an ideal but from a strictly morphological standpoint. It is my belief that every one of these questions was really aimed in the same direction as every other, viz., towards that *one* Riddle of History that had never yet emerged with sufficient distinctness in the human consciousness. The tasks before men were not, as supposed, infinitely numerous—they were one and the same task. Everyone had an inkling that this was so, but no one from his own narrow standpoint had seen the single and comprehensive solution. And yet it had been in the air since Nietzsche, and Nietzsche himself had gripped all the decisive problems although, being a romantic, he had not dared to look strict reality in the face.

But herein precisely lies the inward necessity of the *stock-taking* doctrine, so to call it. It had to come, and it could only come at this time. Our scepticism is not an attack upon, but rather the verification of, our stock of thoughts and works. It *confirms* all that has been sought and achieved for generations past, in that it integrates all the truly living tendencies which it finds in the special spheres, no matter what their aim may be.

Above all, there discovered itself the *opposition of History and Nature* through which alone it is possible to grasp the essence of the former. As I have already said, man as an element and representative of the World is a member not only of nature but also of history—which is a second Cosmos different in structure and complexion, entirely neglected by Metaphysics in favour of the first. I was originally brought to reflect on this *fundamental* question of our world-consciousness through noticing how present-day historians as they fumble round tangible events, things-become, believe themselves to have already grasped History, the happening, the becoming itself. This is a prejudice common to all who proceed by reason and cognition, as against intuitive perception.[4] And it had long ago been a source of perplexity to the

~~~~~~

[4] The philosophy of this book I owe to the philosophy of Goethe, which is practically unknown today, and also (but in a far less degree) to that of Nietzsche. The position of Goethe in West European metaphysics is still not understood in the least; when philosophy is being discussed he is not even named. For unfortunately he did not set down his doctrines in a rigid system, and so the systematic philosophy has overlooked him. Nevertheless, he was a philosopher. His place *vis-à-vis* Kant is the same as that of Plato—who similarly eludes the would-be systematizer—*vis-à-vis* Aristotle. Plato and Goethe stand for the philosophy of Becoming, Aristotle and Kant the philosophy of Being. Here we have intuition opposed to analysis. Something that it is practically impossible to convey by the methods of reason is found in individual sayings and poems of Goethe, e.g. in the *Orphische Urworte*, and stanzas like *Wenn im Unendlichen* and *Sagt es Niemand*, which must be regarded as the expression of a *perfectly definite* metaphysical doctrine. I would not have one single word changed in this: "The Godhead is effective in the living and not in the dead, in the becoming and the changing, not in the become and the set-fast; and therefore, similarly, the reason (*Vernunft*) is concerned only to strive towards the divine through the becoming and the living, and the understanding (*Verstand*) only to make use of the become and the set-fast" (to Eckermann). This sentence comprises my entire philosophy.

great Eleatics with their doctrine that through cognition there could be no becoming, but only a being (or having-become). In other words, History was seen as Nature (in the objective sense of the physicist) and treated accordingly, and it is to this that we must ascribe the baneful mistake of applying the principles of causality, of law, of system—that is, the structure of rigid being—to the picture of happenings. It was assumed that a human culture existed just as electricity or gravitation existed, and that it was capable of analysis in much the same way as these. The habits of the scientific researcher were eagerly taken as a model, and if, from time to time, some student asked what Gothic, or Islam, or the Polis *was,* no one inquired why such symbols of something living *inevitably* appeared just *then, and there, in that form, and for that space of time.* That every phenomenon *ipso facto* propounds a metaphysical riddle, that the time of its occurrence is *never* irrelevant; that it still remained to be discovered what kind of a *living* interdependence (apart from the inorganic, natural-law interdependence) subsists within the world-picture, which radiates from nothing less than the whole man and not merely (as Kant thought) from the cognizing part of him; that a phenomenon is not only a fact for the understanding but also an expression of the spiritual, not only an object but a symbol as well, be it one of the highest creations of religion or art or a mere trifle of everyday life—all this was, philosophically, something new.

And thus in the end I came to see the solution clearly before me in immense outlines, possessed of full inward necessity, a solution derived from one single principle that though discoverable had never been discovered, that from my youth had haunted and attracted me, tormenting me with the sense that it was there and must be attacked and yet defying me to seize it. Thus, from an almost accidental occasion of beginning, there has arisen the present work, which is put forward as the provisional expression of a new world-picture. The book is laden, as I know, with all the defects of a first attempt, incomplete, and certainly not free from inconsistencies. Nevertheless I am convinced that it contains the incontrovertible formulation of an idea which, once enunciated clearly, will (I repeat) be accepted without dispute.

If, then, the narrower theme is an analysis of the Decline of that West European Culture which is now spread over the entire globe, yet the object in view is the development of a philosophy and of the operative method peculiar to it, which is now to be tried, viz., the method of comparative morphology in world-history. The work falls naturally into two parts. The first, "Form and Actuality," starts from the form-language of the great Cultures, attempts to penetrate to the deepest roots of their origin and so provides itself with the basis for a science of Symbolic. The second part, "Perspectives of World-History," starts from the *facts of actual life,* and from the historical practice of higher mankind seeks to obtain a quintessence of historical experience that we can set to work upon the formation of our own future.

II

THE MEANING OF NUMBERS

[IT *may be better to begin by drawing attention to certain basic terms which are sometimes employed in this book in a novel sense, although in the course of the argument their meaning becomes clear.*

1. Goethe's distinction between "becoming" and the "become" [1] *can be adopted in place of the customary distinction between "being" and "becoming." Of these two elements in the results that we obtain by and in consciousness, becoming is always the basic element, not the other way round.*

*2. The words "proper" (individual) and "alien" (*das Eigne *as against* das Fremde*) represent two primal facts in consciousness. The element called "alien" is always related to "perception," i.e. the outer world, the life of sensation. The element called "proper" is involved with the basic fact known as feeling, i.e. the inner life.*

3. Human consciousness is identical with the opposition between the soul and the world. There are gradations in consciousness, varying from a dim perception, sometimes suffused by an inner light, to an extreme sharpness of pure reason that we find in the thought of Kant, for whom soul and world have become subject and object. This elementary structure of consciousness is not capable of further analysis; both factors are always present together and appear as a unity.

4. Life, perpetually fulfilling itself as an element of becoming, is what we call "the present," and it possesses that mysterious property of "direction," which men have tried to rationalize by means of the enigmatic word "time."

5. Life is the form in which the realization of the possible is fulfilled. The soul, as the repository of feelings, represents

~~~~~~~

[1] See note on page 38.

the possible, that which is to be fulfilled; the world is the actual, *the completed, and life the fulfilment.*

6. There are two ways of regarding the entirety of knowledge—becoming and the become, life and the lived, according to whether the becoming, the realization of the possible, or the become, the world fulfilled—whether direction *or* extension *dominates the effect which cannot solely be attributed to either. It is not the question of an alternative, but of a series of perpetually varying possibilities, the extremes being a purely organic and a purely mechanical view of the world.*

One is the world as history, *the other the world as* nature *(these words being used in an unusual sense). The mechanism of a pure nature-picture such as the world of Newton and Kant is cognized and reduced to a system. The organism of a pure history-picture, such as the world of Plotinus, Dante and Giordano Bruno is intuitively seen and inwardly experienced.*

7. In order to obtain such a world-picture, which can be called a higher world-consciousness, it is necessary to study the language of a Culture. We can differentiate between possible *and* actual *Culture, i.e. Culture as an idea in the (general or individual) existence, and Culture as the embodiment of that idea, as the total of its visible tangible expressions, such as arts and sciences. Higher history, intimately related to life and to becoming, is the actualizing of possible Culture.*]

NUMBER AS THE SIGN OF COMPLETED DEMARCATION

In order to exemplify the way in which a soul seeks to actualize itself in the picture of its outer world—to show, that is, in how far Culture in the "become" state can express or portray an idea of human existence—I have chosen *number*, the primary element on which all mathematics rests. I have done so because mathematics, accessible in its full depth only to the very few, holds a quite peculiar position amongst the creations of the mind. It is a science of the most rigorous kind, like logic but more comprehensive and very much fuller; it is a true art, along with sculpture and music, as needing the guidance of inspiration and as developing under great conventions of form; it is, lastly, a metaphysic of the highest rank, as Plato and above all Leibniz show us. Every philosophy has hitherto grown up in conjunction with a mathematic *belonging* to it. Number is the symbol of causal necessity. Like the conception of God, it contains the ultimate meaning of the world-as-nature. The existence of numbers may therefore be called a mystery, and the religious thought of every Culture has felt their impress.

Just as all becoming possesses the original property of *direction* (irreversibility), all things-become possess the property of *extension*. But these two words seem unsatisfactory in that only an artificial distinction can be made between them. The real secret of all things-become, which are *ipso facto* things extended (spatially and materially), is embodied in mathematical number as contrasted with chronological number. Mathematical number contains in its very essence the notion of a *mechanical demarcation,* number being in that respect akin to *word,* which, in the very fact of its comprising and denoting, fences off world-impressions. The deepest depths, it is true, are here both incomprehensible and inexpressible. But the actual number with which the mathematician works, the figure, formula, sign, diagram, in short the *number-sign which he thinks, speaks or writes exactly,* is (like the exactly used word) from the first a symbol of these depths, something imaginable, communicable, comprehensible to the inner and the outer eye, which can be accepted as representing the demarcation. The origin of numbers resembles that of the myth. It is by means of names and numbers that the human understanding obtains power over the world. Consequently, in all acts of the intellect germane to mathematical number—measuring, counting, drawing, weighing, arranging and dividing—men strive to delimit the extended in words as well, i.e. to set it forth in the form of proofs, conclusions, theorems and systems; and it is only through acts of this kind (which may be more or less unintentioned) that waking man begins to be able to use numbers, normatively, to specify objects and properties, relations and differentiae, unities and pluralities—briefly, that structure of the world-picture which he feels as necessary and unshakable, calls "Nature" and "cognizes." *Nature is the numerable,* while History, on the other hand, is the aggregate of that which has no relation to mathematics— hence the mathematical certainty of the laws of Nature, the astounding rightness of Galileo's saying that Nature is "written in mathematical language," and the fact, emphasized by Kant, that exact natural science reaches just as far as the possibilities of applied mathematics allow it to reach.

Nevertheless, mathematics—meaning thereby the capacity to think practically in figures—must not be confused with the far narrower scientific mathematics, that is, the *theory* of numbers as developed in lecture and treatise. The mathematical vision and thought that a Culture possesses within itself is as inadequately represented by its written mathematic as its philosophical vision and thought by its philosophical treatises. Number springs from a source that has also quite other outlets. Gothic cathedrals and Doric temples are *mathematics in stone*. Doubtless Pythagoras was the first in the Classical Culture to conceive number scientifically as the principle of a world-order of comprehensible things—as *standard* and as *magnitude*—but even before him it had found expression, as a noble arraying of sensuous-material units, in the strict canon of the statue and the Doric order of columns. The great arts are, one and all, modes of interpretation by means of limits based on number (consider, for example, the problem of space-representation in oil painting). A high mathematical endowment may, without any mathematical science whatsoever, come to fruition and full self-knowledge in *technical* spheres. In the presence of so powerful a number-sense as that evidenced, even in the Old Kingdom,[2] in the dimensioning of pyramid temples and in the technique of building, water-control and public administration (not to mention the calendar), no one surely would maintain that the valueless arithmetic of Ahmes belonging to the New Empire represents the level of Egyptian mathematics.

It is the style of a Soul that comes out in the world of numbers, and the world of numbers includes something more than the science thereof.

EVERY CULTURE HAS ITS OWN MATHEMATIC

From this there follows a fact of decisive importance which has hitherto been hidden from the mathematicians themselves. If

---

[2] Dynasties I–VIII, or, effectively, I–VI. The Pyramid period coincides with Dynasties IV–VI. Cheops, Chephren and Mycerinus belong to the IVth Dynasty, under which also great water-control works were carried out between Abydos and the Fayum.—*At.*

mathematics were a mere science like astronomy or mineralogy, it would be possible to define their object. *There is no mathematic but only mathematics.* What we call "the history of mathematics"—implying merely the progressive actualizing of a single invariable ideal—is in fact, below the deceptive surface of history, a complex of self-contained and independent developments, an ever-repeated process of bringing to birth new form-worlds and appropriating, transforming and sloughing alien form-worlds, a purely organic story of blossoming, ripening, wilting and dying within the set period. The student must not let himself be deceived. The mathematic of the Classical soul sprouted almost out of nothingness, the historically constituted Western soul, already possessing the Classical science (not inwardly, but outwardly as a thing learnt), had to win its own by apparently altering and perfecting, but in reality destroying the essentially alien Euclidean system. In the first case, the agent was Pythagoras, in the second Descartes. In both cases the act is, at bottom, the same.

The relationship between the form-language of a mathematic and that of the cognate major arts, is in this way put beyond doubt. The temperament of the thinker and that of the artist differ widely indeed, but the expression-methods of the waking consciousness are inwardly the same for each. The sense of form of the sculptor, the painter, the composer, is essentially mathematical in its nature. The same inspired ordering of an infinite world which manifested itself in the geometrical analysis and projective geometry of the seventeenth century, could vivify, energize and suffuse contemporary music with the harmony that it developed out of the art of thorough-bass (which is the geometry of the sound-world) and contemporary painting with the principle of perspective (the felt geometry of the space-world that only the West knows). To Goethe we owe the profound saying: "The mathematician is only complete insofar as he feels within himself the *beauty* of the true." Here we feel how nearly the secret of number is related to the secret of artistic creation.

Mathematics, then, are an art. The development of the great arts ought never to be treated without an (assuredly not unprofitable) side-glance at contemporary mathematics. In the very deep relation between changes of musical theory and the analysis of the infinite, the details have never yet been investigated, although aesthetics might have learned a great deal more from these than from all so-called "psychology." Still more revealing would be a history of musical instruments written, not (as it always is) from the technical standpoint of tone-production, but as a study of the deep spiritual bases of the tone-colours and tone-effects aimed at. For it was the wish, intensified to the point of a longing, to fill a spatial infinity with sound which produced—in contrast to the Classical lyre and reed (lyra, kithara; aulos, syrinx) and the Arabian lute—the two great families of keyboard instruments (organ, pianoforte, etc.) and bow instruments, and that as early as the Gothic time. The organ and clavichord belong certainly to England, the bow instruments reached their definite forms in upper Italy between 1480 and 1530, while it was principally in Germany that the organ was developed into the *space-commanding* giant that we know, an instrument the like of which does not exist in all musical history. The free organ-playing of Bach and his time was nothing if it was not analysis—analysis of a strange and vast tone-world.

CLASSICAL NUMBERS AS MAGNITUDE

When, about 540 B.C., the circle of the Pythagoreans arrived at the idea that *number is the essence of all things,* it was not "a step in the development of mathematics" that was made, but a wholly new mathematic that was born. Long heralded by metaphysical problem-posings and artistic form-tendencies, now it came forth from the depths of the Classical soul as a formulated theory, a mathematic born in one act at one great historical moment—just as the mathematic of the Egyptians had been, and the algebra-astronomy of the Babylonian Culture with its ecliptic co-ordinate system—and new—for these older mathematics had long been extinguished and the Egyptian was never written down.

The most valuable thing in the Classical mathematic is its proposition that number is the essence of all things *perceptible to the senses.* Defining number as a measure, it contains the whole world-feeling of a soul passionately devoted to the "here" and the "now." Measurement in this sense means the measurement of something near and corporeal. Consider the content of the Classical art-work, say the free-standing statue of a naked man; here every essential and important element of Being, its whole rhythm, is exhaustively rendered by surfaces, dimensions and the sensuous relations of the parts. The Pythagorean notion of the harmony of numbers, although it was probably deduced from music—a music, be it noted, that knew not polyphony or harmony, and formed its instruments to render single, plump, almost fleshy, tones—seems to be the very mould for a sculpture that has this ideal. The worked stone is only a something insofar as it has considered limits and measured form; what it *is* is what it *has become* under the sculptor's chisel. Apart from this it is a *chaos,* something not yet actualized, in fact for the time being a null. The same feeling transferred to the grander stage produces, as an opposite to the state of chaos, that of *cosmos,* which for the Classical soul implies a cleared-up situation of the external world, a harmonic order which includes each separate thing as a well-defined, comprehensible and present entity. The sum of such things constitutes neither more nor less than the whole world, and the interspaces between them, which for us are filled with the impressive symbol of the Universe of Space, are for them the nonent ($\tau\grave{o}$ $\mu\grave{\eta}$ $\mathring{o}\nu$). And, looking backward from this standpoint, we may perhaps see into the deepest concept of the Classical metaphysics, Anaximander's $\check{\alpha}\pi\epsilon\iota\rho o\nu$—a word that is quite untranslatable into any Western tongue. It is that which possesses no "number" in the Pythagorean sense of the word, no measurable dimensions or definable limits, and therefore no being; the measureless, the negation of form, the statue not yet carved out of the block; the $\mathring{a}\rho\chi\grave{\eta}$ optically boundless and formless, which only becomes a something (namely, the world) after being split up by the senses. It is the underlying form *a priori* of Classical cognition, bodiliness as such, which is replaced exactly in the Kantian world-picture by that Space out of which Kant maintained that all things could be "thought forth." The whole Classical mathematic is at bottom *Stereometry* (solid geometry). To Euclid, who rounded off its system in the third century, the triangle is of deep necessity the bounding surface of a body, never a system of three intersecting straight lines or a group of three points in three-dimensional space. He defines a line as "length without breadth" ($\mu\hat{\eta}\kappa o\varsigma$ $\mathring{a}\pi\lambda\alpha\tau\acute{e}\varsigma$). In our mouths such a definition would be pitiful—in the Classical mathematic it was brilliant.

Numbers belong exclusively to the domain of extension. But

there are precisely as many possibilities—and therefore necessities—of ordered presentation of the extended as there are Cultures. Classical number is a thought-process dealing not with spatial relations but with visibly limitable and tangible units, and it follows naturally and necessarily that the Classical knows only the "natural" (positive and whole) numbers, which on the contrary play in our Western mathematics a quite undistinguished part in the midst of complex, hypercomplex, non-Archimedean and other number-systems.

On this account, the idea of irrational numbers—the unending decimal fractions of our notation—was unrealizable within the Greek spirit. Euclid says—and he ought to have been better understood—that incommensurable lines are *"not related to one another like numbers."* In fact, it is the idea of irrational number that, once achieved, separates the notion of number from that of magnitude, for the magnitude of such a number (π for example) can never be defined or exactly represented by any straight line. Moreover, it follows from this that in considering the relation, say, between diagonal and side in a square the Greek would be brought up suddenly against a quite other sort of number, which was fundamentally alien to the Classical soul, and was consequently feared as a secret of its proper existence too dangerous to be unveiled.[3] There is a singular and significant late-Greek legend, according to which the man who first published the hidden mystery of the irrational perished by shipwreck, "for the unspeakable and the formless must be left hidden forever."[4]

~~~~~~~

[3] One may be permitted to add that according to legend, both Hippasus, who took to himself public credit for the discovery of a sphere of twelve pentagons, viz., the regular dodecahedron (regarded by the Pythagoreans as the quintessence—or aether—of a world of real tetrahedrons, octahedrons, icosahedrons and cubes), and Archytas, the eighth successor of the Founder, are reputed to have been drowned at sea. The pentagon from which his dodecahedron is derived, itself involves incommensurable numbers. The "pentagram" was the recognition badge of Pythagoreans and the ἄλογον (incommensurable) their special secret. It would be noted, too, that Pythagoreanism was popular till its initiates were found to be dealing in these alarming and subversive doctrines, and then they were suppressed and lynched—a persecution which suggests more than one deep analogy with certain heresy-suppressions of Western history.

[4] The idea $\sqrt{2}$ for the diagonals, the length of the sides being 1, was known to Eudoxus. In spite of this knowledge of them the Greeks did not use the irrational number.—H.W.

It is the deep metaphysical fear that the sense-comprehensible and present in which the Classical existence had entrenched itself would collapse and precipitate its cosmos (largely created and sustained by art) into unknown primitive abysses. And to understand this fear is to understand the final significance of Classical number—that is, *measure in contrast to the immeasurable*—and to grasp the high ethical significance of its limitation.

Now, the Classical soul felt the principle of the irrational, which overturned the statuesquely ordered array of whole numbers and the complete and self-sufficing world-order for which these stood, as an impiety against the Divine itself. In Plato's *Timaeus* this feeling is unmistakable. For the transformation of a series of discrete numbers into a continuum challenged not merely the Classical notion of number but the Classical world-idea itself, and so it is understandable that even *negative* numbers, which to us offer no conceptual difficulty, were impossible in the Classical mathematic, let alone *zero as a number,* that refined creation of a wonderful abstractive power which, for the Indian soul that conceived it as base for a positional numeration, was nothing more nor less than the key to the meaning of existence. Every product of the waking consciousness of the Classical world, then, is elevated to the rank of actuality by way of sculptural definition. That which cannot be drawn is not "number." Archytas and Eudoxus use the terms surface- and volume-numbers to mean what we call second and third powers, and it is easy to understand that the notion of higher integral powers did not exist for them, for a fourth power would predicate at once, for the mind based on the plastic feeling, an extension in four dimensions, and four *material* dimensions into the bargain, "which is absurd." Expressions like ϵ^{-it}, which we constantly use, or even the fractional index (e.g. $5^{\frac{1}{2}}$), which is employed in the Western mathematics as early as Oresme (fourteenth century), would have been to them utter nonsense. Euclid calls the factors of a product its sides ($\pi\lambda\epsilon\upsilon\rho\alpha\iota$) and fractions (finite of course) were treated as whole-number relationships between two lines. Clearly, out of this no conception of zero as a number could possibly come, for from the point of view of a draughtsman it is meaningless. We, having minds differently constituted, must not argue from our habits to theirs and treat their mathematic as a "first stage" in the development of "Mathematics." Within and for the purposes of the world that Classical man evolved for himself, the Classical mathematic was a complete thing—it is merely not so *for us*.

THE WORLD ACCORDING TO ARISTARCHUS. DIOPHANTUS AND THE MAGIAN MATHEMATIC

Numbers are images of the perfectly desensualized understanding, of pure thought, and contain their abstract validity within themselves. Their exact application to the actuality of conscious experience is therefore a problem in itself—a problem which is always being posed anew and never solved—and the congruence of mathematical system with empirical observation is at present anything but self-evident. Although the lay idea—as found in Schopenhauer—is that mathematics rest upon the direct evidences of the senses, Euclidean geometry, superficially identical though it is with the popular geometry of all ages, is only in agreement with the phenomenal world approximately and within very narrow limits—in fact, the limits of a drawing-board. Extend these limits, and what becomes, for instance, of Euclidean parallels? They meet at the line of the horizon—a simple fact upon which all our art-perspective is grounded. But Euclid, as a thinker of the Classical age, was entirely consistent with its spirit when he refrained from proving the phenomenal truth of his axioms by referring to, say, the triangle formed by an observer and two infinitely distant fixed stars. For these can neither be drawn nor "intuitively apprehended" and his feeling was precisely the feeling which shrank from the irrationals, which did not dare to give nothingness a value as zero (i.e. a number) and even in the contemplation of cosmic relations shut its eyes to the Infinite and held to its symbol of Proportion.

Aristarchus of Samos, who in 288–277 belonged to a circle of astronomers at Alexandria that doubtless had relations with Chaldaeo-Persian schools, projected the elements of a heliocentric world-system.[5] Rediscovered by Copernicus, it was to shake

---

[5] In the only writing of his that survives, indeed, Aristarchus maintains the geocentric view; it may be presumed therefore that it was only temporarily that he let himself be captivated by a hypothesis of the Chaldaean learning.

the metaphysical passions of the West to their foundations—witness Giordano Bruno—to become the fulfilment of mighty premonitions, and to justify that Faustian, Gothic world-feeling which had already professed its faith in infinity through the forms of its cathedrals. But the world of Aristarchus received his work with entire indifference and in a brief space of time it was forgotten—designedly, we may surmise. In fact, the Aristarchian system had no spiritual appeal to the Classical Culture and might indeed have become dangerous to it. And yet it was differentiated from the Copernican (a point always missed) by something which made it perfectly conformable to the Classical world-feeling, viz., the assumption that the cosmos is *contained* in a materially finite and optically appreciable *hollow sphere*, in the middle of which the planetary system, arranged as such on Copernican lines, moved. In the Classical astronomy, the earth and the heavenly bodies are consistently regarded as entities of two different kinds, however variously their movements in detail might be interpreted. Equally, the opposite idea that the earth is *only a star among* stars is not inconsistent in itself with either the Ptolemaic or the Copernican systems. But by this device of a celestial sphere the principle of infinity which would have endangered the sensuous-Classical notion of bounds was smothered. One would have supposed that the infinity-conception was inevitably implied by the system of Aristarchus—long before his time, the Babylonian thinkers had reached it. But no such thought emerges. On the contrary, in the famous treatise on the grains of sand Archimedes proves that the filling of this stereometric body (for that is what Aristarchus' Cosmos is, after all) with atoms of sand leads to very high, but *not* to infinite, figure-results. This proposition, quoted though it may be, time and again, as being a first step towards the Integral Calculus, amounts to a denial (implicit indeed in the very title) of everything that we mean by the word "analysis." Eudoxus, Apollonius and Archimedes, certainly the keenest and boldest of the Classical mathematicians, completely worked out, in the main with rule and compass, a *purely optical* analysis of things-become on the basis of sculptural-Classical bounds. With these methods also should be classed the exhaustion-method of Archimedes, given by him in his recently discovered letter to Eratosthenes on such subjects as the quadrature of the parabola section by means of inscribed rectangles (instead of through similar polygons).

But the very subtlety and extreme complication of his methods, which are grounded in certain of Plato's geometrical ideas, make us realize, in spite of superficial analogies, what an enormous difference separates him from Pascal. Apart altogether from the idea of Riemann's integral, what sharper contrast could there be to these ideas than the so-called quadratures of today? The name itself is now no more than an unfortunate survival, the "surface" is indicated by a bounding function, and the *drawing*, as such, has vanished. Nowhere else did the two mathematical minds approach each other more closely than in this instance, and nowhere is it more evident that the gulf between the two souls thus expressing themselves is impassable.

Numbers are symbols of the mortal. Set forms are the negation of life, formulae and laws spread rigidity over the face of nature, numbers make dead—and the "Mothers" of *Faust II* sit enthroned, majestic and withdrawn, in

> *The realms of Image unconfined.*
> *. . . Formation, transformation,*
> *Eternal play of the eternal mind*
> *With semblances of all things in creation*
> *For ever and for ever sweeping round.*[6]

Goethe draws very near to Plato in this divination of one of the final secrets. For his unapproachable Mothers are Plato's Ideas— the possibilities of a spirituality, the unborn forms to take shape as active and purposed Culture, as art, thought, polity and religion, in a world ordered and determined by that spirituality. And so the number-thought and the world-idea of a Culture are related, and by this relation, the former is elevated above mere knowledge and experience and becomes a view of the universe, there being consequently as many mathematics—as many number-worlds—as there are higher Cultures. Only so can we understand, as something *necessary*, the fact that the greatest mathematical thinkers, the creative artists of the realm of numbers, have been brought to the decisive mathematical discoveries of their several cultures by a deep religious intuition. Classical, Apollinian number we must regard as the creation of Pythagoras —*who founded a religion*. It was an instinct that guided Nico-

---

[6] Dr. Anster's translation.—*At.*

laus Cusanus, the great Bishop of Brixen (c. 1450), from the idea of the unendingness of God in nature to the elements of the Infinitesimal Calculus. Leibniz himself, who two centuries later definitely settled the methods and notation of the Calculus, was led by purely metaphysical speculations about the divine principle and its relation to infinite extent to conceive and develop the notion of an *analysis situs*—probably the most inspired of all interpretations of pure and emancipated space. And Kepler and Newton, strictly religious natures both, were and remained convinced, like Plato, that it was precisely through the medium of number that they had been able to apprehend intuitively the essence of the divine world order.

The Classical arithmetic, we are always told, was first liberated from its sense-bondage, widened and extended by Diophantus (A.D. 250), who did not indeed create algebra (the science of undefined magnitudes) but brought it to expression within the framework of the Classical mathematic that we know —and so suddenly that we have to assume that there was a pre-existent stock of ideas which he worked out. But this amounts, not to an enrichment of, but a complete victory over, the Classical world-feeling. In Diophantus, unconscious though he may be of his own essential antagonism to the Classical foundations on which he attempted to build, there emerges from under the surface of Euclidean *intention* the new limit-*feeling* which I designate the "Magian." He did not widen the idea of number as magnitude, but (unwittingly) eliminated it. No Greek could have stated anything about an *undefined* number *a* or an *undenominated* number 3—which are neither magnitudes nor lines.

In Diophantus, number has ceased to be the measure and essence of *plastic things*. Diophantus does not yet know zero and negative numbers, it is true, but he has *ceased* to know Pythagorean numbers. And this Arabian indeterminateness of number is, in its turn, something quite different from the controlled variability of the later Western mathematics, the variability of the *function*.

The Magian mathematic—we can see the outline, though we are ignorant of the details—advanced through Diophantus (who is obviously not a starting-point) boldly and logically to a culmination in the Abbassid period (ninth century) that we can appreciate in Al-Khwarizmi and Alsidzshi.

WESTERN MATHEMATIC AS FUNCTION

The decisive act of Descartes, whose geometry appeared in 1637, consisted not in the introduction of a new method or idea in the domain of traditional geometry (as we are so frequently told), but in the definitive conception of *a new number-idea*, which conception was expressed in the emancipation of geometry from servitude to optically realizable constructions and to measured and measurable lines generally. With that, the analysis of the infinite became a fact. In place of the sensuous element of concrete lines and planes—the specific character of the Classical feeling of bounds—there emerged the abstract, spatial, un-Classical element of the *point* which from then on was regarded as a group of co-ordered pure numbers. The idea of magnitude and of perceivable dimension derived from Classical texts and Arabian traditions was destroyed and replaced by that of variable relation-values between positions in space. It is not in general realized that this amounted to the *supersession of geometry,* which thenceforward enjoyed only a fictitious existence behind a façade of Classical tradition. The word "geometry" has an inextensible Apollinian meaning, and from the time of Descartes what is called the "new geometry" is made up in part of synthetic work upon the *position of points* in a space which is no longer necessarily three-dimensional (a "manifold of points"), and in part of analysis, in which numbers are defined through point-positions in space. And this replacement of lengths by positions carries with it a purely spatial, and no longer a material, conception of extension. The clearest example of this destruction of the inherited optical-finite geometry seems to me to be the conversion of angular functions—which in the Indian mathematic had been numbers (in a sense of the word that is hardly accessible to our minds)—into *periodic* functions, and their passage thence into an infinite number-realm, in which they become series and not the smallest trace remains of the Euclidean figure. In all parts of that realm the circle-number π, like the Napierian base ϵ, generates relations of all sorts which obliterate all the old distinctions of geometry, trigonometry and algebra, which are neither arithmetical nor geometrical in their nature, and in which no one any longer dreams of actually drawing circles or working out powers.

At the moment exactly corresponding to that at which (c. 540) the Classical soul in the person of Pythagoras discovered its own proper Apollinian number, the measurable magnitude, the Western soul in the persons of Descartes and his generation (Pascal, Fermat, Desargues) discovered a notion of number that was the child of a passionate *Faustian* tendency towards the infinite. Number as *pure magnitude* inherent in the material presentness of things is paralleled by numbers as *pure relation*,[7] and if we may characterize the Classical "world," the cosmos, as being based on a deep need of visible limits and composed accordingly as a sum of material things, so we may say that our world-picture is an actualizing of an infinite space in which things visible appear very nearly as realities of a lower order, limited in the presence of the illimitable. The symbol of the West is an idea of which no other Culture gives even a hint, the idea of *Function*. Function is anything rather than an expansion of, it is complete emancipation from, any pre-existent idea of number. Not only the Euclidean geometry (and with it the common human geometry of children and laymen, based on everyday experience) but also the Archimedean arithmetic, ceased to have any value for the really *significant* mathematic of Western Europe. Henceforward, this consisted solely in abstract analysis. Even the power, which in the beginning denotes numerically a set of multiplications (products of equal magnitudes), is, through the exponential idea (logarithm) and its employment in complex, negative and fractional forms, dissociated from all connexion with magnitude and transferred to a transcendent relational world which the Greeks, knowing only the two positive whole-number powers that represent areas and volumes, were unable to approach. Think, for instance, of expressions like

$$\epsilon^{-x}, \sqrt[r]{x}, a^{\frac{1}{i}}.$$

Every one of the significant creations which succeeded one another so rapidly from the Renaissance onward—imaginary and complex numbers, introduced by Cardanus as early as 1550; infinite series, established theoretically by Newton's great discovery of the binomial theorem in 1666; differential geometry,

---

[7] Similarly, coinage and double-entry book-keeping play analogous parts in the money-thinking of the Classical and Western Cultures respectively.

the definite integral of Leibniz; the aggregate as a new number-unit, hinted at even by Descartes; new processes like those of general integrals; the expansion of functions into series and even into infinite series of other functions—is a victory over the popular and sensuous number-feeling in us, a victory which the new mathematic had to win in order to make the new world-feeling actual.

In all history, so far, there is no second example of one Culture paying to another Culture long extinguished such reverence and submission in matters of science as ours has paid to the Classical. It was very long before we found courage to think our proper thought. But though the wish to emulate the Classical was constantly present, every step of the attempt took us in reality further away from the imagined ideal. The history of Western knowledge is thus one of *progressive emancipation* from Classical thought, an emancipation never willed but enforced in the depths of the unconscious. *And so the development of the new mathematic consists of a long, secret and finally victorious battle against the notion of magnitude.*

The present-day sign-language of mathematics perverts its real content. It is principally owing to that tendency that the belief in numbers as magnitudes still rules today even amongst mathematicians, for is it not the base of all our written notation? But it is not the separate signs (e.g., x, π, 5) serving to express the functions, *but function itself as unit*, as element, the variable relation no longer capable of being optically defined, that constitutes the new number; and this new number should have demanded a new notation built up with entire disregard of Classical influences.

Consider the difference between two equations (if the same word can be used of two such dissimilar things) such as $3^z + 4^z = 5^z$ and $x^n + y^n = z^n$ (the equation of Fermat's theorem). The first consists of several Classical numbers—i.e. magnitudes—but the second is *one number* of a different sort, veiled by being written down according to Euclidean-Archimedean tradition in the identical form of the first. In the first case, the sign $=$ establishes a rigid connexion between definite and tangible magnitudes, but in the second it states that within a domain of variable images there exists a relation such that from certain alterations certain other alterations necessarily follow. The first equation has as its aim the specification by measurement of a concrete magnitude, viz., a "result," while the second has, in general, no result but is simply the picture and sign of a relation which for $n > 2$ (this is the famous Fermat problem) *can probably be shown to* exclude integers. A Greek mathematician would have found it quite impossible to understand the purport of an operation like this, which was not meant to be "worked out."

In fact, directly the essentially anti-Hellenic idea of the irrationals is introduced, the foundations of the idea of number as concrete and definite collapse. Thenceforward, the series of such numbers is no longer a visible row of increasing, discrete, numbers capable of plastic embodiment but a unidimensional *continuum* in which each "cut" (in Dedekind's sense) represents a number. Such a number is already difficult to reconcile with Classical number, for the Classical mathematic knows only *one* number between 1 and 3, whereas for the Western the totality of such numbers is an infinite aggregate. But when we introduce further the imaginary ($\sqrt{-1} = i$) and finally the complex numbers (general form $a + bi$), the linear continuum is broadened into the highly transcendent form of a number-body, i.e. the content of an aggregate of homogeneous elements in which a "cut" now stands for a number-surface containing an infinite aggregate of numbers of a lower "potency" (for instance, all the real numbers), and there remains not a trace of number in the Classical and popular sense. These number-surfaces, which since Cauchy and Gauss have played an important part in the theory of functions, are *pure thought-pictures*. Even positive irrational number (e.g. $\sqrt{2}$) could be conceived in a sort of negative fashion by Classical minds; they had, in fact, enough idea of it to ban it as ἄρρητος and ἄλογος. But expressions of the form $x + yi$ lie beyond every possibility of comprehension by Classical thought, whereas it is on the extension of the mathematical laws over the whole region of the complex numbers, within which these laws remain operative, that we have built up the function theory which has at last exhibited the Western mathematic in all purity and unity. Not until that point was reached could this mathematic be unreservedly brought to bear in the parallel sphere of our *dynamic* Western physics; for the Classical mathematic was fitted precisely to its own stereometric world of individual objects and to *static* mechanics as developed from Leucippus to Archimedes.

The brilliant period of the Baroque mathematic—the counterpart of the Ionian—lies substantially in the eighteenth century and extends from the decisive discoveries of Newton and Leibniz through Euler, Lagrange, Laplace and D'Alembert to Gauss. Once this immense creation found wings, its rise was miraculous. Men hardly dared believe their senses. The age of refined scepticism witnessed the emergence of one seemingly impossible truth after another.[8] Regarding the theory of the differential coefficient, D'Alembert had to say: "Go forward, and faith will come to you." Logic itself seemed to raise objections and to prove foundations fallacious. But the goal was reached. This century was a very carnival of abstract and immaterial thinking, in which the great masters of analysis and, with them, Bach, Gluck, Haydn and Mozart—a small group of rare and deep intellects—revelled in the most refined discoveries and speculations, from which Goethe and Kant remained aloof; and in point of content it is exactly paralleled by the ripest century of the Ionic, the century of Eudoxus and Archytas (440–350) and, we may add, of Phidias, Polycletus, Alcamenes and the Acropolis buildings—in which the form-world of Classical mathematic and sculpture displayed the whole fullness of its possibilities, and so ended.

DREAD AND LONGING

We have already observed that, like a child, a primitive mankind acquires (as part of the inward experience that is the birth of the ego) an understanding of number and *ipso facto* possession of an external world referred to the ego. As soon as the primitive's astonished eye perceives the dawning world of *ordered* extension, and the *significant* emerges in great outlines from the welter of mere impressions, and the irrevocable parting of the outer world from his proper, his inner, world gives form and direction to his waking life, there arises in the soul—instantly conscious of its loneliness—the root-feeling of *longing* (*Sehnsucht*). It is this that urges "becoming" towards its goal, that motives the fulfilment and actualizing of every inward possi-

---

[8] Thus Bishop Berkeley's *Discourse Addressed to an Infidel Mathematician* (1735) shrewdly asked whether the mathematician were in a position to criticize the divine for proceeding on the basis of faith.—*At.*

bility, that unfolds the idea of individual being. It is the child's longing, which will presently come into the consciousness more and more clearly as a feeling of constant *direction* and finally stand before the mature spirit as the *enigma of Time*— queer, tempting, insoluble. Suddenly, the words "past" and "future" have acquired a fateful meaning.

But this longing which wells out of the bliss of the inner life is also, in the intimate essence of every soul, a *dread* as well. As all becoming moves towards a having-become wherein it *ends,* so the prime feeling of becoming—the longing—touches the prime feeling of having-become, the dread. In the present we feel a trickling away, the past implies a passing. Here is the root of our eternal dread of the irrevocable, the attained, the final—our dread of mortality, of the world itself as a thing-become, where death is set as a frontier like birth—our dread of the moment when the possible is actualized, the life is inwardly fulfilled and consciousness stands at its goal. It is the deep world-fear of the child—which never leaves the higher man, the believer, the poet, the artist—that makes him so infinitely lonely in the presence of the alien powers that loom, threatening in the dawn, behind the screen of sense-phenomena. The element of direction, too, which is inherent in all "becoming," is felt owing to its inexorable *irreversibility* to be something alien and hostile, and the human will-to-understanding ever seeks to bind the inscrutable by the spell of a name. It is something beyond comprehension, this transformation of future into past, and thus time, in its contrast with space, has always a queer, baffling, oppressive ambiguity from which no serious man can wholly protect himself.

This world-fear is assuredly the most *creative* of all prime feelings. Man owes to it the ripest and deepest forms and images, not only of his conscious inward life, but also of the infinitely varied external culture which reflects this life. Like a secret melody that not every ear can perceive, it runs through the form-language of every true art-work, every inward philosophy, every important deed, and, although those who can perceive it in that domain are the very few, it lies at the root of the great problems of mathematics. Only the spiritually dead man of the autumnal cities—Hammurabi's Babylon, Ptolemaic Alexandria, Islamic Baghdad, Paris and Berlin today—only the pure intellectual, the sophist, the sensualist, the Darwinian, loses it or is able to evade it by setting up a secretless "scientific world-view" between himself and the alien. As the longing attaches itself to that impalpable something whose thousand-formed elusive manifestations are comprised in, rather than denoted by, the word "time," so the other prime feeling, dread, finds its expression in the intellectual, understandable, outlinable symbols of *extension;* and thus we find that every Culture is aware (each in its own special way) of an opposition of time and space, of direction and extension, the former underlying the latter as becoming precedes having-become. It is the longing that underlies the dread, *becomes* the dread, and not vice versa. The one is not subject to the intellect, the other is its servant. The role of the one is purely to experience, that of the other purely to know (*erleben, erkennen*). In the Christian language, the opposition of the two world-feelings is expressed by: "Fear God and love Him."

In the soul of all primitive mankind, just as in that of earliest childhood, there is something which impels it to find means of dealing with the alien powers of the extension-world that assert themselves, inexorable, in and through space. The subtlest, as well as the most powerful, form of this defence is causal and systematic knowledge, delimitation by label and number.

The world-fear is stilled when an intellectual form-language hammers out brazen vessels in which the mysterious is captured and made comprehensible. The method common to all the great Cultures—the only way of actualizing itself that the soul knows —is the *symbolizing of extension,* of space or of things; and we find it alike in the conceptions of absolute space that pervade Newtonian physics, Gothic cathedral-interiors and Moorish mosques, and the atmospheric infinity of Rembrandt's paintings and again the dark tone-worlds of Beethoven's quartets; in the regular polyhedrons of Euclid, the Parthenon sculptures and the pyramids of Old Egypt, the Nirvana of Buddha, the aloofness of court-customs under Sesostris, Justinian I and Louis XIV, in the God-idea of an Aeschylus, a Plotinus, a Dante; and in the world-embracing spatial energy of modern technics.

GEOMETRY AND ARITHMETIC

In the Classical world the starting-point of every formative act was, as we have seen, the ordering of the "become," insofar as this was present, visible, measurable and numerable. The Western, Gothic, form-feeling on the contrary is that of an unrestrained, strong-willed, far-ranging soul, and its chosen badge is pure, imperceptible, unlimited space. Our universe of infinite space, whose existence, for us, goes without saying, simply does not exist for Classical man. It is not even capable of being presented to him. The fact is that the infinite space of our physics is a form of very numerous and extremely complicated elements tacitly assumed, which have come into being only as the copy and expression of *our* soul, and are actual, necessary and natural only for *our* type of waking life. The simple notions are always the most difficult. The whole of our mathematic from Descartes onward is devoted to the theoretical interpretation of this great and wholly religious symbol. In the Classical mathematics and physics the content of this word is simply *not known*.

Here, too, Classical names, inherited from the literature of Greece and retained in use, have veiled the realities. Geometry means the art of measuring, arithmetic the art of numbering. The mathematic of the West has long ceased to have anything to do with both these forms of defining, but it has not managed to find new names for its own elements—for the word "analysis" is hopelessly inadequate.

The beginning and end of the Classical mathematic is consideration of the properties of individual bodies and their boundary-surfaces; thus indirectly taking in conic sections and higher curves. *We,* on the other hand, at bottom know only the abstract space-element of the point, which can neither be seen, nor measured, nor yet named, but represents simply a centre of reference. The straight line, for the Greeks a measurable edge, is for us an infinite continuum of points. Leibniz illustrates his infinitesimal principle by presenting the straight line as one limiting case and the point as the other limiting case of a circle having infinitely great or infinitely little radius. But for the Greek the circle is a *plane* and the problem that interested him was that of bringing it into a commensurable condition. Thus the *squaring of the circle became for the Classical intellect the supreme problem of the finite.* The deepest problem of world-form seemed to it to be to alter surfaces bounded by curved lines, without change of magnitude, into rectangles and so to render them measurable. For us, on the other hand, it has become the usual, and not specially significant, practice to represent the number π by algebraic means, regardless of any geometrical image.

The Classical mathematician knows only what he sees and grasps. Where definite and defining visibility—the domain of his thought—ceases, his science comes to an end. The Western mathematician, as soon as he has quite shaken off the trammels of Classical prejudice, goes off into a wholly abstract region of infinitely numerous "manifolds" of n (no longer 3) dimensions, in which his so-called geometry always can and generally must do without every commonplace aid.

[*The figured signs used by the Pythagoreans are informatory. The number 1, conceived as ἀρχή, the prime stuff of the number-series, was also the symbol of the mother-womb. The digit 2, the first true number, which doubles the 1, was therefore correlated with the male principle. Finally, the holy 3, the combination of the first two numbers, represented the act of propagation—the erotic suggestion in adding and multiplying, the only two processes of increasing magnitude known to Classical man.*]

Thus, inevitably, the Classical became by degrees the Culture of the *small*. The Apollinian soul had tried to tie down the meaning of things-become by means of the principle of *visible limits;* its taboo was focused upon the immediately-present and proximate alien. What was far away, invisible, was *ipso facto* "not there." Just as the Greek tongue—again and again we shall note the mighty symbolism of such language-phenomena—possessed *no word for space,* so the Greek himself was destitute of our feeling of landscape, horizons, outlooks, distances, clouds, and of the idea of the far-spread fatherland embracing the great nation. The Classical temple, which can be taken in in one glance, is the smallest of all first-rate architectural forms. Classical geometry from Archytas to Euclid—like the school geometry of today, which is still dominated by it—concerned itself with small, manageable figures and bodies, and therefore remained unaware of the difficulties that arise in establishing figures of astronomical dimensions, which in many cases are not amenable to Euclidean geometry. Otherwise the subtle Attic spirit would almost surely have arrived at some notion of the problems of non-Euclidean geometry, for its criticism of the well-known "parallel" axiom, the doubtfulness of which soon aroused opposition yet could not in any way be elucidated, brought it very close indeed to the decisive discovery. The Classical mind as unquestioningly devoted and limited itself to the study of the small and the near as ours has to that of the infinite and ultra-visual. All the mathematical ideas that the West found for itself or borrowed from others were automatically subjected to the form-language of the Infinitesimal —and that long before the actual Differential Calculus was discovered. Arabian algebra, Indian trigonometry, Classical mechanics, were incorporated as a matter of course in analysis. In a certain measure, geometry may be treated algebraically and algebra geometrically, that is, the eye may be switched off or it may be allowed to govern. We take the first alternative, the Greeks the second. Archimedes, in his beautiful management of spirals, touches upon certain general facts that are also fundamentals in Leibniz's method of the definite integral; but his processes, for all their superficial appearance of modernity, are subordinated to stereometric principles; in like case, an Indian mathematician would naturally have found some trigonometrical formulation.[9]

From this fundamental opposition of Classical and Western numbers there arises an equally radical difference in the relationship of element to element in each of these number-worlds. The nexus of *magnitudes* is called *proportion,* that of *relations* is comprised in the notion of *function.* The significance of these two words is not confined to mathematics proper; they are of high importance also in the allied arts of sculpture and music. Quite apart from the role of proportion in ordering the parts of the *individual* statue, the typically Classical art-forms of the statue, the relief and the fresco, admit *enlargements and reductions of scale—words that in music have no meaning at all.* In the domain of Function, on the contrary, it is the idea of *transformation of groups* that is of decisive importance, and the musician will readily agree that similar ideas play an essential part in modern composition-theory. I need only allude to one of the most elegant orchestral forms of the eighteenth century, the *Tema con Variazioni.*

All proportion assumes the constancy, all transformation the variability of the constituents. Compare, for instance, the con-

---

[9] It is impossible to say, with certainty, how much of the Indian mathematics that we possess is old, i.e. before Buddha.

gruence theorems of Euclid, the proof of which depends in fact on the assumed ratio 1:1, with the modern deduction of the same by means of angular functions.

The alpha and omega of the Classical mathematic is *construction* (which in the broad sense includes elementary arithmetic), that is, the production of a single visually present figure.

Every *construction* affirms, and every *operation* denies appearances, in that the one works out that which is optically given and the other dissolves it. And so we meet with yet another contrast between the two kinds of mathematic; the Classical mathematic of small things deals with the concrete *individual instance* and produces a once-for-all construction, while the mathematic of the infinite handles whole *classes* of formal possibilities, *groups* of functions, operations, equations, curves, and does so with an eye, not to any result they may have, but to their course. And so for the last two centuries—though present-day mathematicians hardly realize the fact—there has been growing up *the idea of a general morphology of mathematical operations,* which we are justified in regarding as the real meaning of modern mathematics as a whole. All this, as we shall perceive more and more clearly, is one of the manifestations of a general tendency inherent in the Western intellect, proper to the Faustian spirit and Culture and found in no other. The great majority of the problems which occupy our mathematic, and are regarded as "our" problems in the same sense as the squaring of the circle was the Greeks'—e.g. the investigation of convergence in infinite series (Cauchy) and the transformation of elliptic and algebraic integrals into multiple-periodic functions (Abel, Gauss) —would probably have seemed to the Ancients, who strove for simple and definite quantitative results, to be an exhibition of rather abstruse virtuosity. And so indeed the popular mind regards them even today.

THE CLASSICAL LIMIT-PROBLEM AND THE LIBERATION FROM THE VISUAL

Thus, finally, the whole content of Western number-thought centres itself upon the historic *limit-problem* of the Faustian mathematic, the key which opens the way to the Infinite, that *Faustian infinite* which is so different from the infinity of Arabian and Indian world-ideas. Whatever the guise—infinite series, curves or functions—in which number appears in the particular case, the *essence* of it is the *theory of the limit.* This limit is the absolute opposite of the limit which (without being so called) figures in the Classical problem of the quadrature of the circle. Right into the eighteenth century, Euclidean popular prepossessions obscured the real meaning of the differential principle. The idea of infinitely small quantities lay, so to say, ready to hand, and however skilfully they were handled, there was bound to remain a trace of the Classical constancy, the *semblance of magnitude,* about them, though Euclid would never have known them or admitted them as such. Thus, zero is a constant, a whole number in the linear continuum between $+ 1$ and $- 1$; and it was a great hindrance to Euler in his analytical researches that, like many after him, he treated the differentials as zero. Only in the nineteenth century was this relic of Classical number-feeling finally removed and the Infinitesimal Calculus made logically secure by Cauchy's definitive elucidation of the *limit-idea;* only the intellectual step from the "infinitely small quantity" to the "lower limit of *every possible* finite magnitude" brought out the conception of a variable number which oscillates beneath any assignable number that is not zero. A number of this sort has ceased to possess any character of magnitude whatever: the limit, as thus finally presented by theory, is no longer that which is approximated to, but *the approximation, the process, the operation itself. It is not a state, but a relation.*

The liberation of geometry from the visual, and of algebra from the notion of magnitude, and the union of both, beyond all elementary limitations of drawing and counting, in the great structure of function-theory—this was the grand course of Western number-thought. The constant number of the Classical mathematic was dissolved into the variable. Geometry *became* analytical and dissolved all concrete forms, replacing the mathematical bodies from which the rigid geometrical values had been obtained, by abstract spatial relations which in the end ceased to have any application at all to sense-present phenomena. It began by substituting for Euclid's optical figures geometrical loci referred to a co-ordinate system of arbitrarily chosen "origin," and reducing the postulated objectiveness of existence of the geometrical object to the one condition that during the operation (which itself was one of equating and not of measurement) the selected co-ordinate system should not be changed. But these co-ordinates immediately came to be regarded as values pure and simple, serving not so much to determine as to represent and replace the position of points as space-elements. Number, the boundary of things-become, was represented, not as before pictorially by a figure, but symbolically by an equation. "Geometry" altered its meaning; the co-ordinate system as a picturing disappeared and the point became an entirely abstract number-group.

This mathematics of ours was bound in due course to reach the point at which not merely the limits of artificial geometrical form but the limits of the visual itself were felt by theory and by the soul alike as limits indeed, as obstacles to the unreserved expression of inward possibilities—in other words, the point at which the ideal of transcendent extension came into fundamental conflict with the limitations of immediate perception. Mathematical, "absolute" space, we see then, is utterly un-Classical, and from the first, although mathematicians with their reverence for the Hellenic tradition did not dare to observe the fact, it was something different from the indefinite spaciousness of daily experience and customary painting, the *a priori* space of Kant which seemed so unambiguous and sure a concept. It is a pure abstract, an ideal and unfulfillable postulate of a soul which is ever less and less satisfied with sensuous means of expression and in the end passionately brushes them aside. *The inner eye has awakened.*

And then, for the first time, those who thought deeply were obliged to see that the Euclidean geometry, which is the *true and only* geometry of the simple of all ages, is when regarded from the higher standpoint nothing but a *hypothesis*, the general validity of which, since Gauss, we know it to be quite impossible to prove in the face of other and perfectly non-perceptual geometries. The critical proposition of this geometry, Euclid's axiom of parallels, is an *assertion*, for which we are quite at liberty to substitute another assertion. We may assert, in fact, that through a given point, no parallels, or two, or many parallels may be drawn to a given straight line, and all these assumptions lead to completely irreproachable geometries of three dimensions, which can be employed in physics and even in astronomy, and are in some cases preferable to the Euclidean.[1]

Even the simple axiom that extension is boundless (bound-

---

[1] Compare note 4 on page 95.

lessness, since Riemann and the theory of curved space, is to be distinguished from endlessness) at once contradicts the essential character of all immediate perception, in that the latter depends upon the existence of light-resistances and *ipso facto* has material bounds. But abstract principles of boundary can be imagined which transcend, in an entirely new sense, the possibilities of optical definition. For the deep thinker, there exists even in the Cartesian geometry the tendency to get beyond the three dimensions of *experiential* space, regarded as an unnecessary restriction on the symbolism of number. And although it was not till about 1800 that the notion of *multi-dimensional space* (it is a pity that no better word was found) provided analysis with broader foundations, the real first step was taken at the moment when powers—that is, really, logarithms—were released from their original relation with sensually realizable surfaces and solids and, through the employment of irrational and complex exponents, brought within the realm of function as perfectly general relation-values. It will be admitted by everyone who understands anything of mathematical reasoning that directly we passed from the notion of a^3 as a natural maximum of that of a^n, the unconditional necessity of three-dimensional space was done away with.

Once the space-element or point had lost its last persistent relic of visualness and, instead of being represented to the eye as a cut in co-ordinate lines, was defined as a group of three independent numbers, there was no longer any inherent objection to replacing the number 3 by the general number n. The notion of dimension was radically changed. It was no longer a matter of treating the properties of a point metrically with reference to its position in a visible system, but of representing the entirely abstract properties of a number-group by means of any dimensions that we please. The number-group—consisting of n independent ordered elements—is an image of the point and it is *called* a point. Similarly, an equation logically arrived therefrom is called a plane and is the image of a plane. And the aggregate of all points of n dimensions is *called* an n-dimensional space.[2] In these transcendent space-worlds, which are remote from every sort of

[2] From the standpoint of the theory of "aggregates" (or "sets of points"), a well-ordered set of points, irrespective of the dimension figure, is called a corpus; and thus an aggregate of $n - 1$ dimensions is considered, *relatively* to one of n dimensions, as a surface. Thus the limit (wall, edge) of an "aggregate" represents an aggregate of lower "potentiality."

sensualism, lie the relations which it is the business of analysis to investigate and which are found to be consistently in agreement with the data of experimental physics. This space of higher degree is a symbol which is through-and-through the peculiar property of the Western mind. That mind alone has attempted, and successfully too, to capture the "become" and the extended in *these* forms, to conjure and bind—to "know"—the alien by *this* kind of appropriation or taboo. Not until such spheres of number-thought are reached, and not for any men but the few who have reached them, do such imaginings as systems of hypercomplex numbers (e.g. the quaternions of the calculus of vectors) and apparently quite meaningless symbols like ∞^n acquire the character of something actual. And here if anywhere it must be understood that actuality is not only sensual actuality. The spiritual is in no wise limited to perception-forms for the actualizing of its idea.

From this grand intuition of symbolic space-worlds came the last and conclusive creation of Western mathematic—the expansion and subtilizing of the function theory in that of *groups*. Groups are aggregates or sets of homogeneous mathematical images—e.g. the totality of all differential equations of a certain type—which in structure and ordering are analogous to the Dedekind number-bodies. Here are worlds, we feel, of perfectly new numbers, which are nevertheless not utterly sense-transcendent for the *inner* eye of the adept; and the problem now is to discover in those vast abstract form-systems certain elements which, relatively to a particular group of operations (viz., of transformations of the system), remain unaffected thereby, that is, possess invariance. In mathematical language, the problem, as stated generally by Klein, is—given an n-dimensional manifold ("space") and a group of transformations, it is required to examine the forms belonging to the manifold in respect of such properties as are not altered by transformation of the group.

And with this culmination our Western mathematic, having exhausted every inward possibility and fulfilled its destiny as the *copy and purest expression of the idea of the Faustian soul*, closes its development in the same way as the mathematic of the Classical Culture concluded in the third century. Both those sciences (the only ones of which the organic structure can even today be examined historically) arose out of a wholly new idea of number, in the one case Pythagoras', in the other Descartes's.

Both, expanding in all beauty, reached their maturity one hundred years later; and both, after flourishing for three centuries, completed the structure of their ideas at the same moment as the Cultures to which they respectively belonged passed over into the phase of megalopolitan Civilization. The deep significance of this interdependence will be made clear in due course. It is enough for the moment that for us the time of the *great* mathematicians is past. Our tasks today are those of preserving, rounding off, refining, selection—in place of big dynamic creation, the same clever detail-work which characterized the Alexandrian mathematic of late Hellenism.

III

THE PROBLEM OF
WORLD-HISTORY

PHYSIOGNOMIC AND SYSTEMATIC

[TO *review the whole fact of Man from an extreme distance is to imitate Copernicus in the field of history. This the Western intellect achieved in the field of Nature, when it passed from the Ptolemaic world-system to one valid today.* Nature *and* History *are the opposite extreme terms in man's range of possibilities of picturing the world. The cognized and Nature are one and the same thing. Nature is the sum of necessities imposed by law. Everything cognized is* timeless, *neither past nor future but simply "there" and so permanently valid. Law and the domain of law are antihistoric.*

Pure Becoming, *pure life, on the other hand, is irreversible. Every happening is unique and incapable of being repeated. Becoming lies beyond the domain of cause and effect, law and measurement. But history, as positively treated, is not pure becoming; it is an image radiated from the waking-consciousness of the historian, in which the becoming dominates the become.*

The possibility of extracting scientific results from history depends upon the proportion of things-become presented in the subject treated, but when this proportion dwindles to very little, as is hypothetically the case, history is almost pure becoming and belongs to the realm of Art. Ranke said that Quentin Durward *is history at its best. Science reaches as far as the notions of truth and falsity have validity, viz., the collection, ordering and sifting of material. For real historical vision the crucial words are not "correct" and "erroneous," but "deep" and "shallow." There are no exact boundaries between "becoming" and "become." They are jointly present in every sort of understanding. If one looks at the becoming and fulfilling, one experiences History; if one dissects the become and fulfilled one cognizes Nature. The principle of Form and the principle of Law are the basic elements in picturing the world. The historical impression-process is intuitive, instinctive. It is only the quantitative that is capable of being causally defined, grasped through figures, of being captured in a law or formula. When it has achieved this, science has shot its bolt. Nevertheless, or rather, therefore, the modern mind finds nature study easy, and historical study hard. Direction and extension are the chief distinguishing marks separating the historical and the scientific impression of the world. There is knowledge of nature and knowledge of men. Scientific experience and experience of life.*]

That which Dante saw before his spiritual eyes as the destiny of the world, he *could not possibly* have arrived at by scientific methods, nor could Plotinus and Giordano Bruno have distilled their visions from researches.

All modes of comprehending the world may, in the last analysis, be described as Morphology. *The Morphology of the mechanical and the extended, a science which discovers and orders nature-laws and causal relations, is called Systematic. The Morphology of the organic, of history and life and all that bears the sign of direction and destiny, is called Physiognomic.*

In the West, the Systematic mode of treating the world reached and passed its culminating-point during the last century, while the great days of Physiognomic have still to come. In a hundred years all sciences that are still possible on this soil will be parts of a single vast Physiognomic of all things human. This is what the "Morphology of World-History" means.

CULTURES AS ORGANISMS

[*The visible foreground of history is, as it were, the pursuit of Becoming as it becomes. Becoming is visible to the historical eye insofar as state-forms, battles, arts, sciences, etc., are symbols, and the expression of a soul.* Everything transitory is only a parable. *The transitory is the symbol of a becoming which follows a form, an organism. Cultures are organisms. If we disentangle their shapes we may find the primitive Culture-form that underlies all individual Cultures and is reflected in their various manifestations. The phenomenon of the Great Cultures gives meaning and substance to the 6,000 years or so of history of higher mankind. The Culture is the prime phenomenon of all past and future world-history.*]

The deep, and scarcely appreciated, idea of Goethe, which he discovered in his "living nature" and always made the basis of his morphological researches, we shall here apply—in its most precise sense—to all the formations of man's history, whether fully matured, cut off in the prime, half opened or stifled in the seed. It is the method of living into (*erfühlen*) the object, as opposed to dissecting it. "The highest to which man can attain, is wonder; and if the prime phenomenon makes him wonder, let him be content; nothing higher can it give him, and nothing further should he seek for behind it; here is the limit." The prime phenomenon is that in which the idea of becoming is presented net. To the spiritual eye of Goethe the idea of the prime plant was clearly visible in the form of every individual plant that happened to come up, or even that could possibly come up. In his investigation of the "os intermaxillare" his starting-point was the *prime phenomenon of the vertebrate type;* and in other fields it was geological stratification, of the leaf as the prime form of the plant-organism, or the metamorphosis of the plants as the prime form of all organic becoming. "The same law will apply to everything else that lives," he wrote, in announcing his discovery to Herder. It was a look into the heart of things that Leibniz would have understood, but the century of Darwin is as remote from such a vision as it is possible to be.

At present, however, we look in vain for any treatment of history that is entirely free from the methods of Darwinism—that is, of systematic natural science based on causality. A physiognomic that is precise, clear and sure of itself and its limits has never yet arisen, and it can only arise through the discoveries of method that we have yet to make. Herein lies the great problem set for the twentieth century to solve—to explore carefully the inner structure of the organic units through and in which world-history fulfils itself, to separate the morphologically necessary from the accidental, and, by seizing the *purport* of events, to ascertain the languages in which they speak.

A boundless mass of human Being, flowing in a stream without banks; upstream, a dark past wherein our time-sense loses all powers of definition and restless or uneasy fancy conjures up geological periods to hide away an eternally unsolvable riddle; downstream, a future even so dark and timeless—such is the groundwork of the Faustian picture of human history.

Over the expanse of the water pass the endless uniform ripples of the generations. Here and there bright shafts of light broaden out, everywhere dancing flashes confuse and disturb the clear mirror, changing, sparkling, vanishing. These are what we call the clans, tribes, peoples, races which unify a series of generations within this or that limited area of the historical surface. As widely as these differ in creative power, so widely do the images that they create vary in duration and plasticity, and when the creative power dies out, the physiognomic, linguistic and spiritual identification-marks vanish also and the phenomenon subsides again into the ruck of the generations. Aryans, Mongols, Germans, Celts, Parthians, Franks, Carthaginians, Berbers, Bantus, are names by which we specify some very heterogeneous images of this order.

But over this surface, too, the great Cultures accomplish their majestic wave-cycles. They appear suddenly, swell in splendid lines, flatten again and vanish, and the face of the waters is once more a sleeping waste.

A Culture is born in the moment when a great soul awakens out of the proto-spirituality of ever-childish humanity, and detaches itself, a form from the formless, a bounded and mortal thing from the boundless and enduring. It blooms on the soil of an exactly definable landscape, to which plant-wise it remains bound. It dies when this soul has actualized the full sum of its possibilities in the shape of peoples, languages, dogmas, arts, states, sciences, and reverts into the proto-soul. But its living existence, that sequence of great epochs which define and display the stages of fulfilment, is an inner passionate struggle to maintain the Idea against the powers of Chaos without and the unconscious muttering deep down within. It is not only the artist who struggles against the resistance of the material and the stifling of the idea within him. Every Culture stands in a deeply

73

symbolical, almost in a mystical, relation to the Extended, the space, in which and through which it strives to actualize itself. The aim once attained—the idea, the entire content of inner possibilities, fulfilled and made externally actual—the Culture suddenly hardens, it mortifies, its blood congeals, its force breaks down, and it becomes *Civilization,* the thing which we feel and understand in the words Egypticism, Byzantinism, Mandarinism. As such it may, like a worn-out giant of the primeval forest, thrust decaying branches towards the sky for hundreds or thousands of years, as we see in China, in India, in the Islamic world. It was thus that the Classical Civilization rose gigantic, in the Imperial age, with a false semblance of youth and strength and fullness, and robbed the young Arabian Culture of the East of light and air.

This—the inward and outward fulfilment, the finality, that awaits every living Culture—is the purport of all the historic "declines," amongst them that decline of the Classical which we know so well and fully, and another decline, entirely comparable to it in course and duration, which will occupy the first centuries of the coming millennium but is heralded already and sensible in and around us today—the decline of the West. Every Culture passes through the age-phases of the individual man. Each has its childhood, youth, manhood and old age. It is a young and trembling soul, heavy with misgivings, that reveals itself in the morning of Romanesque and Gothic. It fills the Faustian landscape from the Provence of the troubadours to the Hildesheim cathedral of Bishop Bernward.[1] The spring wind blows over it. Childhood speaks to us also—and in the same tones—out of early-Homeric Doric, out of early-Christian (which is really early-Arabian) art and out of the works of the Old Kingdom in Egypt that began with the Fourth Dynasty. A mythic world-consciousness is fighting like a harassed debtor against all the dark and daemonic in itself and in Nature, while slowly ripening itself for the pure, day-bright expression of the existence that it will at last achieve and know. The more nearly a Culture approaches the noon culmination of its being, the more virile, austere, con-

---

[1] St. Bernward was Bishop of Hildesheim from 993 to 1022, and himself architect and metal-worker. Three other churches besides the cathedral survive in the city from his time or that of his immediate successors, and Hildesheim of all North German cities is richest in monuments of the Romanesque.—*At.*

trolled, intense the form-language it has secured for itself, the more assured its sense of its own power, the clearer its lineaments. We find every individual trait of expression deliberate, strict, measured, marvellous in its ease and self-confidence, and everywhere, at moments, the coming fulfilment suggested. Still later, tender to the point of fragility, fragrant with the sweetness of late October days, come the Cnidian Aphrodite and the Hall of the Maidens in the Erechtheum, the arabesques on Saracen horseshoe-arches, the Zwinger of Dresden, Watteau, Mozart. At last, in the grey dawn of Civilization, the fire in the soul dies down. The dwindling powers rise to one more, half-successful, effort of creation, and produce the Classicism that is common to all dying Cultures. The soul thinks once again, and in Romanticism looks back piteously to its childhood; then finally, weary, reluctant, cold, it loses its desire to be, and, as in Imperial Rome, wishes itself out of the overlong daylight and back in the darkness of proto-mysticism, in the womb of the mother, in the grave.

STYLE, TEMPO, DURATION, SYNCHRONISM

[*The style and the spiritual nature of the great historical organisms vary according to their "habitus." The habitus in the case of Cultures embraces the totality of life-expressions of the higher order, such as the choice of particular branches of art and the out-and-out rejection of others. In the "habit" we can see the style of a definite soul. To the habit of a group belong its life-duration and its tempo; it is fair to speak of the* andante *of Greece and Rome and of the* allegro con brio *of the Faustian spirit.*

The notion of the life-duration of a man, a butterfly, or an oak comprises a specific time-value independently of accidents in the individual case. Thus every Culture, every springtime, every rise and fall, has its determined phases, which invariably recur with the emphasis of a symbol. In this sense every being of any import, from intrinsic necessity, recapitulates the phases of the Culture to which it belongs.

By the homology of organs biology means their morphological equivalence—for example the lungs of land animals and the swim-bladders of fish—while lungs and gills are analogous, that is, similar in point of use. These pure phenomena are far removed from causality and cannot be explained by expediency. In homologous comparison of Cultures their forms are displayed in striking profile, though with different meanings. As they go through the same phases we can call them contemporaneous. Thus, for example, the Pyramids are contemporary with Gothic cathedrals. Analogous forms in the Cultures are dependent on the habitus of the contemporary Culture, but at times they show a precise congruence; thus antique plastic and Baroque organ music are analogous phenomena. It can almost be said that homologous and analogous phenomena are one and the same—for example Alexander the Great and Napoleon.

Given the physiognomic rhythm, it is possible, following the method of Goethe, to reconstruct the organic characteristics of whole periods of history, and even to pre-determine the features of the still unaccomplished features of our Western history.]

THE IDEA OF DESTINY AND THE PRINCIPLE
OF CAUSALITY

[The soul as the idea of an existence entails the certainty that the actualization of the possible, that life itself, must be regarded as irrevocable, fateful in every line. Such organic logic is opposed to the logic of the inorganic, and is beyond the scope of systematists like Aristotle and Kant.

The word "destiny" expresses an indescribable inward certainty: causality carries the notion of law. The physiognomic flair, by which it is possible to read a lifetime, a fate, from a face, operates without deliberate effort or any system. It is far removed from cause and effect. Still the inward feeling of certain destiny is the foundation of the recognition of cause and effect, as becoming is to the become. Causality could be described as destiny made inorganic and modelled in reason-forms. The idea of destiny governs the world-picture of history, for destiny is the true existence-mode of the prime phenomenon.

Causality, which is the existence-mode of objects, rules

and pervades the world-picture of nature. *Destiny and Causality stand in regard to each other as Time and Space. Causality has nothing to do with Time as Kantians thought. The causal connexion, strictly regarded, confines itself to the statement that something happens, not* when *it happens. Insofar as Time is concerned in this connexion, it is as an abstract product of measurement.*

Kant's Time has no relation with the past or the future. Teleology is a misdirected attempt to deal mechanically with the living *content of scientific knowledge (for knowledge implies someone to know, and though the substance of thought may be "Nature," the act of thought is History) and with life itself as an inverted causality.*

Teleology is a characteristic tendency of Darwinism. It is a caricature of the idea of destiny.]

THE PROBLEM OF TIME

[*The word "time" is a sort of charm with which we summon up that intensely personal element which with an inner certitude we oppose to an "alien" element that forces its way in among the crowding impressions of the sense-life. "Personal," "Destiny," "Time," are interchangeable words. Time cannot be thought of categorically; space can; it is a conception, but time is a* word *to indicate something inconceivable, a sound symbol, and to use it as a concept, scientifically, is utterly to misconceive its nature.*

For primitive man time can have no meaning. All of us are conscious as being "aware" of space only, and not of time. Time is a discovery which is only made by thinking. We create it as an idea and do not begin till much later to suspect that we ourselves are Time, inasmuch as we live. What one actually feels at the sound of this word "time," which is clearer in music than in language, has an organic essence as it is bound up with the living and the irreversible. Only the higher Cultures, whose ideas have reached the stage of a mechanical Nature, are capable of deriving from the idea of a measurable and comprehensible spatial, a projected image of time, the phantom time, which satisfies their need of measuring and explaining all things. What is

*merely thought, not felt and experienced, necessarily takes
a spatial form and this explains why no systematic philosopher has been able to make anything of the mystery-
clouded, far-echoing, sound symbols "Past" and "Future."
The invention of a time that is knowable and spatially rep-
resentable within causality is really wizard's gear whereby
our personal soul attempts to conjure alien powers. Goethe
speaks of "the principle of reasonable order that we bear
within ourselves, and would impress as the seal of our
powers upon everything that we touch."*

*The most profound presentation of "Time" in the elder
philosophy is in Augustine: "If no one questions me, I know;
if I would explain to a questioner, I know not."*

*While present-day philosophers "hedge" by saying that
things are in "time" as in "space," and that "outside" them
nothing is "conceivable," they are merely setting another
interpretation of space beside the ordinary one, just as one
might, if one chose, call hope and electricity the two forces
of the universe.*

*It is easy enough to come to a scientific understanding
about space, not to explain it in the ordinary sense of the
word—for that is beyond human powers; treatment of
time on the same lines breaks down utterly.]*

Every Culture possesses a wholly individual way of looking at
and comprehending the world-as-Nature; or (what comes to the
same thing) it *has* its own peculiar "Nature" which no other
sort of man can possess in exactly the same form. But in a far
greater degree still, every Culture—including the individuals
comprising it (who are separated only by minor distinctions)—
possesses a specific and peculiar sort of history.

But it is difficult enough to form an exact idea even of the
"Nature" proper to another kind of man, although in this domain
things specifically cognizable are causally ordered and unified in
a communicable system. And it is quite impossible for us to penetrate completely a historical world-aspect of "becoming" formed
by a soul that is quite differently constituted from our own. Here
there must always be an intractable residue, greater or smaller
in proportion to our historical instinct, physiognomic tact and
knowledge of men. All the same, the solution of this very prob-

lem is the condition-precedent of all really deep understanding of the world.

DESTINY AND INCIDENT

[*Destiny and Incident form an opposition in which the soul is ceaselessly trying to clothe something which consists only of feeling and living and intuition, and can only be made plain in highly subjective religious and artistic creations.*

He who is blind to the world as Divina Commedia *can only find a meaningless turmoil of incidents. The dance scene of the drunken Triumvirs in* Antony and Cleopatra *may well show Shakespeare's contempt for the pragmatic aspect of history.*

In the "late" phase of a Culture it is customary to ascribe everything to causality. Kant had carefully established causality as a necessary form of knowledge, but this was meant to refer exclusively to the understanding of man's environment by way of reason.

The supreme ethical expression of Incident and Destiny is found in the Western Christian idea of Grace—the grace of being made free to will. "Free will" is an inward certainty, but whatever one may will or do, that which actually ensues subserves *a deeper necessity, and for the eye that sweeps over the distant past visibly conforms to a major order.*

Pascal, intensely spiritual and a born mathematician, tried to bring the idea of Destiny within the schematic form of the Causality Principle. Predestination turns Grace into a nature-force bound by irrevocable law.

Yet was it not a Destiny for the world as well as for themselves that the English Puritans, who were filled with this conviction, were ruined not through any passive self-surrender but through their certainty that their will was the will of God?]

It is this insight that constitutes the singularity and the power of Shakespeare. Hitherto, neither our research nor our speculation has hit upon this in him—that he is *the Dramatist of the Incidental.* And yet this Incidental is the very heart of Western tragedy, which is a true copy of the Western history idea and with it gives the clue to that which we understand in the world—so misconstrued by Kant—"Time." It is incidental that the political situation of *Hamlet*, the murder of the King and the succession question impinge upon just that character that Hamlet is. Or, take Othello—it is incidental that the man at whom Iago, the commonplace rogue that one could pick up in any street, aims his blow is one whose person possesses just this wholly special physiognomy. And Lear! Could anything be more incidental (and therefore more "natural") than the conjunction of this commanding dignity with these fateful passions and the inheritance of them by the daughters? No one has even today realized all the significance of the fact that Shakespeare took his stories as he found them and *in the very finding of them* filled them with the force of inward necessity, and never more sublimely so than in the case of the Roman dramas. Now, Hebbel is the exact opposite, he destroys the depth of the anecdote by a system of cause and effect. The arbitrary and abstract character of his plots, which everyone feels instinctively, comes from the fact that the causal scheme of his spiritual conflicts is in contradiction with the historically motivated world-feeling and the quite other logic proper to that feeling. These people do not live, they *prove* something by coming on. One feels the presence of a great understanding, not that of a deep life. Instead of the Incident we get a Problem.

This *Western* species of the Incidental is entirely alien to the Classical world-feeling and therefore to its drama. Antigone has no incidental character to affect her fortunes in any way. What happened to Oedipus—unlike the fate of Lear—might just as well have happened to anyone else. This is the Classical "Destiny," the *Fatum* which is common to all mankind, which affects the "body" and in no wise depends upon incidents of personality.

Napoleon had in his graver moments a strong feeling for the deep logic of world-becoming, and in such moments could divine to what extent he *was*, and to what extent he *had*, a destiny. "I feel myself driven towards an end that I do not know. As soon as I shall have reached it, as soon as I shall become unnecessary, an atom will suffice to shatter me. Till then, not all the forces of mankind can do anything against me," he said at the beginning of the Russian campaign. Here, certainly, is not the thought of a pragmatist. In this moment he divined how little the logic of

Destiny needs particular instances, whether men or situations. Supposing that he himself, as "empirical person," had fallen at Marengo—then that which he *signified* would have been actualized in some other form. A melody, in the hands of a great musician, is capable of a wealth of variations; it can be entirely transformed so far as the simple listener is concerned without altering itself—which is quite another matter—fundamentally.

For if it is incidental that the history of higher mankind fulfils itself in the form of great Cultures, and that one of these Cultures awoke in West Europe about the year 1000; yet from the moment of awakening it is bound by its charter. Within every epoch there is unlimited abundance of surprising and unforeseeable possibilities of self-actualizing in detail-facts, but the epoch itself is necessary, for the life-unity is in it. That its inner form is precisely what it is, constitutes its specific determination (*Bestimmung*). Fresh incidentals can affect the shape of its development, can make this grandiose or puny, prosperous or sorrowful, but alter it they cannot.

The tragic in Napoleon's life—which still awaits discovery by a poet great enough to comprehend it and shape it—was that he, who rose into effective being by fighting British policy and the British spirit which that policy so eminently represented, completed by that very fighting the continental victory of this spirit, which thereupon became strong enough, in the guise of "liberated nations," to overpower him and to send him to St. Helena to die. It was not Napoleon who originated the expansion principle. That had arisen out of the Puritanism of Cromwell's milieu which called into life the British Colonial Empire.[2] Transmitted through the English-schooled intellects of Rousseau and Mirabeau to the Revolutionary armies, of which English philosophical ideas were essentially the driving force, it became their tendency even from that day of Valmy which Goethe alone read aright. It was not Napoleon who formed the idea, but the idea that formed Napoleon, and when he came to the throne he was obliged to pursue it further against the only power, namely England, whose purpose was *the same* as his own. His Empire was a creation of French blood but of English style. It was in London, again, that

---

[2] The words of Canning at the beginning of the nineteenth century may be recalled. "South America free! And if possible English!" The expansion idea has never been expressed in greater purity than this.

Locke, Shaftesbury, Samuel Clarke and, above all, Bentham built up the theory of "European Civilization"—the Western Hellenism—which Bayle, Voltaire and Rousseau carried to Paris. Thus it was in the name of *this* England of Parliamentarianism, business morality and journalism that Valmy, Marengo, Jena, Smolensk and Leipzig were fought, and in *all* these battles it was the English spirit that defeated the French Culture of the West.[3] The First Consul had no intention of incorporating West Europe in France; his primary object was—note the Alexander-idea on the threshold of every Civilization!—to replace the British Colonial Empire by a French one. Thereby, French preponderance in the Western culture-region would have been placed on a practically unassailable foundation; it would have been the Empire of Charles V on which the sun never set, but managed from Paris after all, in spite of Columbus and Philip, and organized as an economic-military instead of as an ecclesiastical-chivalric unit. So far-reaching, probably, was the destiny that was in Napoleon. But the Peace of Paris in 1763 had already decided the question *against* France, and Napoleon's great plans time and again came to grief in petty incidents. At Acre a few guns were landed in the nick of time from the British warships: there was a moment, again, just before the signature of the Peace of Amiens, when the whole Mississippi basin was still amongst his assets and he was in close touch with the Maratha powers that were resisting British progress in India; but again a minor naval incident [4] obliged him to abandon the whole of a carefully prepared enterprise: and, lastly, when by the occupation of Dalmatia, Corfu and all Italy he had made the Adriatic a French lake, with a view to another expedition to the East, and was negotiating with the Shah of Persia for action against India, he was defeated by the whims of the Tsar Alexander, who at times was undoubtedly willing to support a march on India and whose aid would infallibly have secured its success. It was only after the failure of all

---

[3] The Western Culture of maturity was through and through a French outgrowth of the Spanish, beginning with Louis XIV. But even by Louis XVI's time the English park had defeated the French, sensibility had ousted wit, London costume and manners had overcome Versailles, and Hogarth, Chippendale and Wedgwood had prevailed over Watteau, Boulle and Sèvres.

[4] The allusion is to the voyage of Linois's small squadron to Pondichéry in 1803, its confrontation by another small British squadron there, and the counter-order which led Linois to retire to Mauritius.—*At.*

extra-European combinations that he chose, as his *ultima ratio* in the battle against England, the incorporation of Germany and Spain, and so, raising against himself *his own* English-Revolutionary ideas, the very ideas of which he had been the vehicle, he took the step that made him "no longer necessary."

A "United States of Europe," actualized through Napoleon as founder of a romantic and popular military monarchy, is the analogue of the Realm of the Diadochi; when actualized as a twenty-first-century economic organism by a matter-of-fact Caesar, it will be the counterpart of the *imperium Romanum*. These are incidentals, but they are in the picture of history. But Napoleon's victories and defeats (which always hide a victory of England and Civilization over Culture), his Imperial dignity, his fall, the *Grande Nation*, the episodic liberation of Italy (in 1796, as in 1859, essentially no more than a change of political costume for a people long since become insignificant), the destruction of the Gothic ruin of the Roman-German Empire, are mere surface phenomena, behind which is marching the great logic of genuine and invisible History, and it was in the sense of this logic that the West, having fulfilled its French-formed Culture in the *ancien régime*, closed it off with the English Civilization. As symbols of "contemporary" epochal moments, the storming of the Bastille, Valmy, Austerlitz, Waterloo and the rise of Prussia thus correspond to the Classical-history facts of Chaeronea, Gaugamela (Arbela), Alexander's Indian expedition and the Roman victory of Sentinum.[5] And we begin to understand that in wars and political catastrophes—the chief material of our historical writings—victory is not the essence of the fight.

IS THERE A SCIENCE OF HISTORY?

[There is no science of history, but a quality of divining what actually took place. To the historical vision the actual data are always symbols.]

Is it permissible to fix upon one, any one, group of social, religious, physiological or ethical facts as the "cause" of another? "Certainly," the rationalistic school of history, and still more the

---

[5] 295 B.C., when the Romans decisively defeated the Samnites.—*At.*

up-to-date sociology, would reply. That, they would say, is what is meant by our comprehending history and deepening our knowledge of it. But in reality, with "civilized" man there is always the implicit postulate of an underlying *rational* purpose—without which indeed his world would be meaningless. Goethe's warning: "Do not, I beg you, look for anything behind phenomena. *They are themselves their own lesson (sie selbst sind die Lehre)*" had become incomprehensible to the century of Marx and Darwin. The idea of trying to read a destiny in the physiognomy of the past and that of trying to represent unadulterated Destiny as a tragedy were equally remote from them. In both domains, the cult of the useful had set before itself an entirely different aim. Shapes were called into being, not to be, but to prove something. "Questions" of the day were "treated," social problems suitably "solved," and the stage, like the history-book, became a means to that end. What historical investigation *really* is, namely pure Physiognomic, cannot be better illustrated than by the course of Goethe's nature-studies. He works upon mineralogy, and at once his views fit themselves together into a conspectus of an earth-history in which his beloved granite signifies nearly the same as that which I call the proto-human signifies in man's history. He investigates well-known plants, and the prime phenomenon of metamorphosis, the original form of the history of all plant existence, reveals itself; proceeding further, he reaches those extraordinarily deep ideas of vertical and spiral tendencies in vegetation which have not been fully grasped even yet. His studies of ossature, based entirely on the contemplation of life, lead him to the discovery of the "os intermaxillare" in man and to the view that the skull-structure of the vertebrates developed out of six vertebrae. Never is there a word of causality. He feels the necessity of Destiny just as he himself expressed it in his *Orphische Urworte:*

> So must thou be. Thou canst not Self escape.
> So erst the Sibyls, so the Prophets told.
> Nor Time nor any Power can mar the shape
> Impressed, that living must itself unfold.

History has the characteristic of the *singular-factual,* Nature that of the *continuously possible.* So long as I scrutinize the image of the world-around in order to see by what laws it *must* actualize itself, irrespective of whether it does happen or merely might happen—irrespective, that is, of time—then I am working in a genuine science. For the necessity of a nature-law (and there are no other laws) it is utterly immaterial whether it becomes phenomenal infinitely often or never. *That is, it is independent of Destiny.* There are thousands of chemical combinations that never are and never will be produced, but they are demonstrably possible and therefore they *exist*—for the fixed System of Nature though not for the Physiognomy of the whirling universe. A system consists of truths, a history rests on facts. Nature stands beyond all time, its mark is extension, and it is without directional quality. Hence, for the one, the necessity of the mathematical, and for the other, the necessity of the tragic.

In the actuality of waking existence, both worlds, that of scrutiny and that of acceptance (*Hingebung*), are interwoven, just as in a Brabant tapestry warp and woof together effect the picture. Every law must, to be *available* to the understanding at all, once have been discovered through some destiny-disposition in the history of an intellect—that is, it must have once been in experiential life; and every destiny appears in some sensible garb —as persons, acts, scenes and gestures—in which Nature-laws are operative. History and nature *within ourselves* stand opposed to one another as *life* is to *death*, as *ever-becoming time* to *ever-become space*. In the waking consciousness, becoming and become struggle for control of the world-picture, and the highest and maturest forms of both sorts are seen, in the case of the Classical soul, in the opposition of Plato and Aristotle, and, in the case of our Western, in that of Goethe and Kant—the pure physiognomy of the world contemplated by the soul of an eternal child, and its pure system comprehended by the reason of an eternal greybeard.

Before my eyes there seems to emerge, as a vision, a hitherto unimagined mode of superlative historical research that is truly Western, necessarily alien to the Classical and to every other soul but ours—a comprehensive Physiognomic of all existence, a morphology of becoming for *all* humanity that drives onward to the highest and last ideas; a duty of penetrating the world-feeling not only of our proper soul but of all souls whatsoever that have contained grand possibilities and have expressed them in the field of actuality as grand Cultures. This philosophic view—to which we and we alone are entitled in virtue of our analytical mathematic, our contrapuntal music and our perspective painting—in that its scope far transcends the scheme of the systematist, presupposes the eye of an artist, and of an artist who can feel the whole sensible and apprehensible environment dissolve into a deep infinity of mysterious relationships. So Dante felt, and so Goethe felt. Every epoch, every great figure, every deity, the cities, the tongues, the nations, the arts, in a word everything that ever existed and will become existent, are physiognomic traits of high symbolic significance that it will be the business of quite a new kind of "judge of men" (*Menschenkenner*) to interpret. There is a wondrous music of the spheres which *wills to be heard* and which a few of our deepest spirits will hear. The physiognomic of world-happening will become the *last Faustian philosophy*.

IV

MAKROKOSMOS:
THE SYMBOLISM OF THE WORLD-PICTURE AND THE SPACE-PROBLEM

---

*MACROCOSM—THE SUM TOTAL OF ALL SYMBOLS
IN RELATION TO ONE SOUL*

SYMBOLS are sensible signs, final, indivisible and, above all, unsought impressions of definite meaning. A symbol is a trait of actuality that for the sensuously alert man has an immediate and inwardly sure significance, and that is incommunicable by process of reason. The detail of a Doric or early-Arabic or early-Romanesque ornament; the forms of the cottage and the family, of intercourse, of costume and rite; the aspect, gait and mien of a man and of whole classes of peoples and men; the communication- and community-forms of man and beast; and beyond all this the whole voiceless language of Nature with her woods and pastures, flocks, clouds, stars, moonlight and thunderstorm, bloom and decay, nearness and distance—all this is the emblematical impression of the Cosmos upon us, who are both aware and in our reflective hours quite capable of listening to this language. When we wake up at once something interposes between a "here" and a "there." We live the "here" as something proper to ourselves, we experience the "there" as something alien. There is a dualizing of soul and world as poles of actuality; and in the latter there are both resistances which we grasp causally as things and properties, and impulses in which we feel beings, *numina* ("just like ourselves") to be operative. But there is in it, further, something which, as it were, eliminates the duality. Actuality—the world *in relation to* a soul—is for every individual the projection of the Directed upon the domain of the Extended—the Proper mirroring itself on the Alien; one's *actuality then signifies oneself.* By an act that is both creative and unconscious—

for it is not "I" who actualize the possible, but "it" actualizes itself through me—the bridge of symbol is thrown between the living "here" and "there." Suddenly, necessarily and completely "the" world comes into being out of the totality of received and remembered elements: and as it is an individual who apprehends the world, there is for each individual a singular world.

There are therefore as many worlds as there are waking beings and like-living, like-feeling groups of beings. The supposedly single, independent and external world that each believes to be common to all is really an ever-new, uniquely-occurring and non-recurring experience in the existence of each.

This is the *idea of the Macrocosm, actuality as the sum total of all symbols in relation to one soul.* From this property of being significant nothing is exempt. All that is, symbolizes. From the corporeal phenomena like visage, shape, mien (of individuals and classes and peoples alike), which have always been known to possess meaning, to the supposedly eternal and universally valid forms of knowledge, mathematics and physics, everything speaks out of the essence of one and only one soul.

At the same time these individuals' worlds as lived and experienced by men of *one* Culture or spiritual community are interrelated, and on the greater or less degree of this interrelation depends the greater or less communicability of intuitions, sensations and thoughts from one to another—that is, the possibility of making intelligible what one has created in the style of one's own being, through expression-media such as language or art or religion, by means of word-sounds or formulae or signs that are themselves also symbols. The degree of interrelation between one's world and another's fixes the limit at which understanding becomes self-deception. Certainly it is only very imperfectly that we can understand the Indian or the Egyptian soul, as manifested in the men, customs, deities, root-words, ideas, buildings and acts of it.

SPACE AND DEATH

Symbols, as being things actualized, belong to the domain of the extended. They are become and not becoming (although they may stand for a becoming) and they are therefore rigidly limited and subject to the laws of space. There are *only* sensible-spatial symbols. The very word "form" designates something extended in the extended. But extension is the hallmark of the fact "waking-consciousness," and this constitutes only one side of the individual existence and is intimately bound up with that existence's destinies. Consequently, every trait of the actual waking-consciousness, whether it be feeling or understanding, is in the moment of our becoming aware of it, already *past*. We can only *reflect* upon impressions, but that which for the sensuous life of the animals is *past*, is for the grammatical (*wortgebundene*) understanding of man *passing, transitory*. Follow out the destiny of the Column, from the Egyptian tomb-temple in which columns are ranked to mark the path for the traveller, through the Doric peripteros in which they are held together by the body of the building, and the early-Arabian basilica where they support the interior, to the façades of the Renaissance in which they provide the upward-striving element. As we see, an old significance never returns; that which has entered the domain of extension has begun and ended at once. A deep relation, and one which is early felt, exists *between space and death*. Man is the only being that knows death; all others become old, but with a consciousness wholly limited to the moment which must seem to them eternal. We *are* Time, but we *possess* also an image of history and in this image death, and with death birth, appear as the two riddles. It is because there is this deep and significant identity that we so often find the awakening of the inner life in a child associated with the death of some relation. The child *suddenly* grasps the lifeless corpse for what it is, something that has become wholly matter, wholly space, and at the same moment it feels itself as an individual *being* in an alien extended world. "From the child of five to myself is but a step. But from the new-born baby to the child of five is an appalling distance," said Tolstoi once. Here, in the decisive moments of existence, when man first becomes man and realizes his immense loneliness in the universal, the world-fear reveals itself for the first time as the essentially human fear in the presence of death, the limit of the light-world, rigid space. Here, too, the higher thought originates as meditation upon death. Every religion, every scientific investigation, every philosophy, proceeds from it. Every great symbolism attaches its form-language to the cult of the dead, the forms of disposal of the dead, the adornment of the graves of the dead. And thus every new Culture comes into existence with a new view of the world, that is, a sudden glimpse of death as the secret of the perceivable world. It was when the idea of the impending end of the world spread over Western Europe (about the year 1000) that the Faustian soul of this region was born. Ego-feeling and world-feeling begin to work in primitive man, and all culture, inner or outer, bearing or performance, is as a whole only the intensification of this being-human. Henceforward all that comes up against our sensations is not mere "resistance" or thing or *impression,* as it is for animals and for children also, but an *expression* as well. And thus the essence of every genuine— *unconscious and inwardly necessary*—symbolism proceeds from the knowledge of death in which the secret of space reveals itself. All symbolism implies a defensive; it is the expression of a deep *Scheu* in the old double sense of the word, and its form-language tells at once of hostility and of reverence.

Every thing-become is mortal. Every thought, faith and science dies as soon as the spirits in whose worlds their "eternal truths" were true and necessary are extinguished. Dead, even, are the star-worlds which "appeared" to the astronomers of the Nile and the Euphrates, for our eye is different from theirs; and our eye in its turn is mortal. World-experience is bound up with the essence of *depth* (i.e. *far-ness* or *distance*). In the abstract system of mathematics, "depth" is taken along with "length" and "breadth" as a "third" dimension; but this trinity of elements of like order is misleading from the outset, for in our impression of the spatial world these elements are unquestionably *not* equivalents, let alone homogeneous.

SPATIAL DEPTH AS "TIME BECOME RIGID"
THE PRIME SYMBOL

Length and breadth represent the purely sensuous impression. But depth is a representation of *expression,* of *Nature,* and with it begins the "world."

This discrimination between the "third" and the other two dimensions, so called, which needless to say is wholly alien to mathematics, is inherent also in the opposition of the notions of sensation and contemplation. Extension into depth converts the former into the latter; in fact, depth is the first and genuine dimension in the literal sense of the word. In it the waking-consciousness is active, whereas in the others it is strictly passive. It is the *symbolic content of a particular order* as understood by one particular Culture that is expressed by this original and un-analyzable element. The experiencing of depth (this is a premiss upon which all that follows is dependent) is an act, as entirely involuntary and necessary as it is creative, whereby the ego keeps its world, so to say, in subordination (*zudiktiert erhält*). Out of the rain of impressions the ego fashions a formal unit, a cinematic *picture*. Every artist has rendered "Nature" by line and by tone, every physicist—Greek, Arabian or German—has dissected "Nature" into ultimate elements, and how is it that they have not all discovered the same? Because every one of them has had his own Nature, though—with a naïveté that was really the salvation of his world-idea and of his own self—every one believed that he had it in common with all the rest. Nature is a possession which is saturated through and through with the most personal connotations. *Nature is a function of the particular Culture.*

Kant believed that he had decided the great question of whether this *a priori* element was pre-existent or obtained by experience, by his celebrated formula that Space is the form of perception which underlies all world impressions. But the "world" of the careless child and the dreamer undeniably possess this form in an insecure and hesitant way, and it is only the tense, practical, *technical* treatment of the world-around—imposed on the free-moving being which, unlike the lilies of the fields, must care for its life—that lets sensuous self-extension stiffen into rational tridimensionality.

Just as Kant confused the Time-problem by bringing it into relation with an essentially misunderstood arithmetic and—on that basis—dealing with a phantom sort of time that lacks the life-quality of direction and is therefore a mere spatial scheme, so also he confused the Space-problem by relating it to a commonplace geometry.

The outcome, then, of Gauss's discovery, which *completely* altered the course of modern mathematics,[1] was the statement that there are severally equally valid structures of three-dimensional extension. That it should even be asked which of them cor-

---

[1] So much so that Gauss said nothing about his discovery until almost the end of his life for fear of "the clamour of the Boeotians."

responds to actual perception shows that the problem was not in the least comprehended. Mathematics, whether or not it employs visible images and representations as working conveniences, concerns itself with systems that are entirely emancipated from life, time and distance, with form-worlds of pure numbers whose validity—not *fact-foundation*—is timeless and like everything else that is "known" is known by causal logic and not experienced.

With this, the difference between the intuitive method and mathematical form-language became manifest and the secret of *spatial becoming* was revealed.

As becoming is the foundation of the become, continuous living history that of fulfilled dead nature, the organic that of the mechanical, destiny that of causal law and the causally settled, so too *direction is the origin of extension. The secret of Life accomplishing itself which is touched upon by the word "time" forms the foundation of that which, as accomplished, is understood by* (or rather *indicated to an inner feeling in us by*) *the word "space."* Every extension that is actual has first been accomplished in and with an experience of depth, and what is primarily indicated by the word "time" is just this process of extending, first sensuously (in the main, visually) and only later intellectually, into depth and distance, i.e. the *step* from the planar semi-impression to the macrocosmically ordered world-picture with its mysterious-manifest kinesis.

If we can describe the basic form of the understood, viz., causality, as *destiny become rigid,* we may similarly speak of spatial depth as *a time become rigid*. While we gaze into the distance with our senses, it floats around us, but when we are startled, the alert eye sees a tense and rigid space. This space *is;* the principle of its existing at all is that it is, outside time and detached from it and from life. In it duration, a piece of perished time, resides as a known property of things. And, as we know ourselves too as *being* in this space, we know that we also have a duration and a limit, of which the moving finger of our clock ceaselessly warns us. But the rigid Space itself is transient too— at the first relaxation of our intellectual tension it vanishes from the many-coloured texture of our environment—and so it is a sign and expression of *the most elemental and powerful symbol,* of life itself.

For the involuntary and unqualified realization of depth,

which dominates the consciousness with the force of an elemental event (*simultaneously with the awakening of the inner life*), marks the frontier between child and . . . Man. The symbolic experience of depth is what is lacking in the child; distance is felt, but it does not yet speak to the soul. And with the soul's awakening, direction, too, first finds a living expression. Thus the Destiny-idea manifests itself in every line of a life. With it alone do we become members of a particular Culture, whose members are connected by a common world-feeling and a common world-form derived from it. A deep identity unites the awakening of the *soul*, its birth into clear existence in the name of a Culture, with the sudden realization of distance and time, the *birth of its outer world* through the symbol of extension; and thenceforth this symbol is and remains the *prime symbol* of that life, imparting to it its specific style and the historical form in which it progressively actualizes its inward possibilities. From the specific directedness is derived the specific prime symbol of extension, namely, for the Classical world-view the near, strictly limited, self-contained Body, for the Western infinitely wide and infinitely profound three-dimensional Space, for the Arabian the world as a Cavern. And therewith an old philosophical problem dissolves into nothing: this prime form of the world is *innate* insofar as it is an original possession of the soul of that Culture which is expressed by our life as a whole, and *acquired* insofar that every individual soul re-enacts for itself that creative act and unfolds in early childhood the symbol of depth to which its existence is predestined, as the emerging butterfly unfolds its wings. The first comprehension of depth is *an act of birth*—the spiritual complement of the bodily.[2] In it the Culture is born out of its mother-landscape, and the act is repeated by every one of its individual souls throughout its life-course. This is what Plato—connecting it with an early Hellenic belief—called anamnesis.

But the prime symbol does not actualize itself; it is operative through the form-sense of every man, every community, age and epoch and dictates the style of every life-expression. It is inherent in the form of the state, the religious myths and cults, the ethical ideals, the forms of painting and music and poetry, the

---

[2] It may not be out of place here to refer to the enormous **importance** attached in savage society to initiation-rites at adolescence.—*At.*

fundamental notions of each science—but it is not presented by these. Consequently, it is not presentable by words, for language and words are themselves *derived* symbols. Every individual symbol tells of it, but only to the inner feelings, not to the understanding. And when we say, as henceforth we shall say, that the prime symbol of the Classical soul is the material and individual body, that of the Western pure infinite space, it must always be with the reservation that concepts cannot represent the inconceivable, and thus at the most a *significative feeling* may be evoked by the sound of words.

THE CLASSICAL AND THE WESTERN
PRIME SYMBOL

What then was it that Classical man, whose insight into his own world-around was certainly not less piercing than ours, regarded as the prime problem of all being? It was the problem of ἀρχή, the *material origin and foundation* of all sensuously perceptible things. If we grasp this we shall get close to the significance of the fact—not the fact of space,[3] but the fact that made it a necessity of destiny for the space-problem to become the problem of the Western, and only the Western, soul. This very spatiality (*Räumlichkeit*) that is the truest and sublimest element in the aspect of *our* universe, that absorbs into itself and begets out of itself the substantiality of all things, Classical humanity (which knows no word for, and therefore has no idea of, space) with one accord cuts out as the nonent, τὸ μὴ ὄν, that which *is not*. The emphasis of this denial can scarcely be exaggerated. The material, the optically definite, the comprehensible, the immediately present—this list exhausts the characteristics of this kind of ex-

~~~~~~~~~

[3] Either in Greek or in Latin. Τόπος (= *locus*) means spot, locality and also social position; χώρα (= *spatium*) means space-between, distance, rank and also ground and soil (e.g., τὰ ἐκ τῆς χώρας, produce); τὸ κένον (*vacuum*) means quite unequivocally a hollow body, and the stress is emphatically on the envelope. The literature of the Roman Imperial Age, which attempted to render the *Magian* world-feeling through Classical words, was reduced to such clumsy versions as ὁρατὸς τόπος (sensible world) or *spatium inane* ("endless space," but also "wide surface"—the root of the word "spatium" means to swell or grow fat). In the true Classical literature, the idea not being there, there was no necessity for a word to describe it.

tension.[4] The Classical universe, the *Cosmos* or well-ordered aggregate of all near and completely viewable things, is concluded by the corporeal vault of heaven. More there is not. The need that is in us to think of "space" as being behind as well as before this shell was wholly absent from the Classical world-feeling. The Stoics went so far as to treat even properties and relations of things as "bodies." For Chrysippus the Divine Pneuma is a "body," for Democritus seeing consists in our being penetrated by material particles of the things seen. And the feeling finds its last and most sublime expression in the stone body of the Classical temple. The windowless interior is carefully concealed by the array of columns; but outside there is not one truly straight line to be found. Every flight of steps has a slight sweep outward, every step relatively to the next. The pediment, the roof-ridge, the sides, are all curved. Every column has a slight swell and none stand truly vertical or truly equidistant from one another. But swell and inclination and distance vary from the corners to the centres of the sides in a carefully toned-off ratio, and so the whole corpus is given a something that swings mysterious about a centre. The curvatures are so fine that to a certain extent they are invisible to the eye and only to be "sensed." But it is just by these means that direction in depth is eliminated. While the Gothic style *soars,* the Ionic *hovers.* To the principles of position, material and form we have opposed those of straining movement, force and mass, and we have defined the last-named as a constant ratio between force and acceleration, nay, finally volatilized both in the purely spatial elements of *capacity* and *intensity.* It was

~~~~~~~~

[4] It has not hitherto been seen that this fact is implicit in Euclid's famous parallel axiom ("through a point only one parallel to a straight line is possible").

This was the only one of the Classical theorems which remained unproved, and as we know now, it is incapable of proof. But it was just that which made it into a dogma (as opposed to any experience) *and therefore the metaphysical centre* and main girder of that geometrical system. Everything else, axiom or postulate, is merely introductory or corollary to this. This one proposition is necessary and universally valid for the Classical intellect, *and yet not deducible.* What does this signify?

It signifies that the statement is a *symbol* of the first rank. It contains the structure of Classical corporeality. It is just this proposition, theoretically the weakest link in the Classical geometry (objections began to be raised to it as early as Hellenistic times), that reveals its soul, and it was just this proposition, self-evident within the limits of routine experience, that the Faustian number-thinking, derived from incorporeal spatial distances, fastened upon as the centre of doubt.

an obligatory consequence also of this way of conceiving actuality that the instrumental music of the great eighteenth-century masters should emerge as a master-art—for it is the only one of the arts whose form-world is inwardly related to the contemplative vision of pure space. This prime feeling of a loosing, *Erlösung*, solution, of the Soul in the Infinite, of a liberation from all material weight which the highest moments of our music give, sets free also the energy of depth that is in the Faustian soul: whereas Classical art limits its effect to the body and brings back the eye from distance to a Near and Still that is saturated with beauty.

And now I draw the conclusions. There is a plurality of prime symbols. It is the depth-experience through which the world becomes, through which perception *extends itself* to world. Its signification is for the soul to which it belongs and only for that soul. It actualizes for every high Culture the possibility of form upon which that Culture's existence rests and it does so of deep necessity. All the primary words like our mass, substance, material, thing, body, extension (and multitudes of words of the like order in other culture-tongues) are emblems, obligatory and determined by destiny, that out of the infinite abundance of world-possibilities evoke in the name of the individual Culture those possibilities that alone are significant and therefore necessary for it. None of them is exactly transferable just as it is into the experiential living and knowing of another Culture. And none of these prime words ever recurs. The *choice of prime symbol* in the moment of the Culture-soul's awakening into self-consciousness on its own soil—a moment, that for one who can read world-history, thus contains something catastrophic—decides all.

V

MAKROKOSMOS:
APOLLINIAN, FAUSTIAN AND
MAGIAN SOUL

ARCHITECTURE AND DIVINITIES

HENCEFORTH we shall designate the soul of the Classical Culture, which chose the sensuously-present individual body as the ideal type of the extended, by the name (familiarized by Nietzsche) of the *Apollinian*. In opposition to it we have the *Faustian* soul, whose prime symbol is pure and limitless space, and whose "body" is the Western Culture that blossomed forth with the birth of the Romanesque style in the tenth century on the Northern plain between the Elbe and the Tagus.

"Space"—speaking now in the Faustian idiom—is a spiritual something, rigidly distinct from the momentary sense-present, which *could* not be represented in an Apollinian language, whether Greek or Latin. But the created *expression-space* of the Apollinian arts is equally alien to ours. In no other Culture is the firm footing, the socket, so emphasized. The Doric column bores into the ground, the vessels are always thought of from below upward, whereas those of the Renaissance float above their footing. Hence in archaic works the legs are disproportionately emphasized, the foot is planted on the full sole, and if the drapery falls straight down, a part of the hem is removed to show that the foot is standing. The Classical relief is strictly stereometrically set on a plane, and there is an interspace between the figures but no depth. A landscape of Claude Lorrain, on the contrary, is *nothing but* space, every detail being made to subserve its illustration. All bodies in it possess an atmospheric and perspective meaning purely as carriers of light and shade. The extreme of this disembodiment of the world in the service of space is Impressionism.

97

The Classical Culture begins, then, with a great *renunciation*. A rich, pictorial, almost over-ripe art lay ready to its hand. But this *could* not become the expression of the young soul, and so from about 1100 B.C. the harsh, narrow, and to our eyes scanty and barbaric, early-Doric geometrical style appears in opposition to the Minoan.

Faustian architecture, on the contrary, begins on the grand scale simultaneously with the first stirrings of a new piety (the Cluniac reform, c. 1000) and a new thought (the Eucharistic controversy between Berengar of Tours and Lanfranc, 1050), and proceeds at once to plans of gigantic intention; often enough, as in the case of Speyer, the whole community did not suffice to fill the cathedral,[1] and often again it proved impossible to complete the projected scheme. The passionate language of this architecture is that of the poems too. Far apart as may seem the Christian hymnology of the South and the Eddas of the still heathen North, they are alike in the implicit space-endlessness of prosody, rhythmic syntax and imagery. Read the *Dies Irae* together with the *Völuspá*,[2] which is little earlier; there is the same adamantine will to overcome and break all resistances of the visible. No rhythm ever imagined radiates immensities of space and distance as the old Northern does:

> *Zum Unheil werden—noch allzulange*
> *Männer und Weiber—zur Welt geboren*
> *Aber wir beide   —bleiben zusammen*
> *Ich und Sigurd.*

The accents of the Homeric hexameter are the soft rustle of a leaf in the midday sun, the rhythm of *matter;* but the *Stabreim*, like "potential energy" in the world-pictures of modern physics, creates a tense restraint in the void without limits, distant night-storms above the highest peaks. In its swaying indefiniteness all words and things dissolve themselves—it is the dynamics, not the statics, of language. The same applies to the grave rhythm of *Media vita in morte sumus*. Here is heralded the colour of Rembrandt and the instrumentation of Beethoven—*here infinite soli-*

---

[1] English readers may remember that Cobbett (*Rural Rides, passim*) was so impressed with the spaciousness of English country churches as to formulate a theory that mediaeval England must have been more populous than modern England is.—*At.*

[2] The oldest and most mystical of the poems of the *Elder Edda*.—*At.*

tude is felt as the home of the Faustian soul. Siegfried, Parzival, Tristan, Hamlet, Faust, are the loneliest heroes in all the Cultures. Read the wondrous awakening of the inner life in Wolfram's Parzival. The love of wild nature, the mysterious compassion, the ineffable sense of forsakenness—it is all Faustian and only Faustian. Every one of us knows it. The motive returns with all its profundity in the Easter scene of *Faust I.*

> *A longing pure and not to be described*
> *drove me to wander over woods and fields,*
> *and in a mist of hot abundant tears*
> *I felt a world arise and live for me.*

Of this world-experience neither Apollinian nor Magian man, neither Homer nor the Gospels, knows anything whatever. The climax of the poem of Wolfram, that wondrous Good Friday morning scene when the hero, at odds with God and with himself, meets the noble Gawan and resolves to go on pilgrimage to Tevrezent, takes us to the heart of the *Faustian* religion. Here one can feel the mystery of the Eucharist which binds the communicant to a mystic company, to a Church that alone can give bliss. In the myth of the Holy Grail and its Knights one can feel the inward necessity of the German-Northern Catholicism. In opposition to the Classical sacrifices offered to individual gods in separate temples, there is here the *one never-ending* sacrifice repeated everywhere and every day. This is the Faustian idea of the ninth–eleventh centuries, the Edda time, foreshadowed by Anglo-Saxon missionaries like Winfried but only then ripened. The Cathedral, with its High Altar enclosing the accomplished miracle, is its expression in stone.

The plurality of separate bodies which represents Cosmos for the Classical soul, requires a similar pantheon—hence the antique polytheism. The *single* world-volume, be it conceived as cavern or as space, demands the *single* god of Magian or Western Christianity. Athene or Apollo might be represented by a statue, but it is and has long been evident to our feeling that the Deity of the Reformation and the Counter Reformation can only be "manifested" in the storm of an organ fugue or the solemn progress of cantata and Mass. About the end of the seventeenth century this religiousness could no longer be limited to pictorial expression, and instrumental music came as its last and only form-language: we may say that the Catholic faith is to the Protestant as an altar-piece is to an oratorio. But even the Germanic gods and heroes are surrounded by this rebuffing immensity and enigmatic gloom. They are steeped in music and in night, for daylight gives visual bounds and therefore shapes bodily things. Night eliminates body; day, soul. Apollo and Athene have no souls. On Olympus rests the eternal light of the transparent southern day, and Apollo's hour is high noon, when great Pan sleeps. But Valhalla is lightless, and even in the Eddas we can trace that deep midnight of Faust's study-broodings, the midnight that is caught by Rembrandt's etchings and absorbs Beethoven's tone-colours. No Wotan or Baldur or Freya has "Euclidean" form. Of them, as of the Vedic gods of India, it can be said that they suffer not "any graven image or any likeness whatsoever"; and this impossibility carries an implicit recognition that eternal space, and not the corporeal copy—which levels them down, desecrates them, denies them—is the supreme symbol. This is the deep-felt motive that underlies the iconoclastic storms in Islam and Byzantium (*both,* be it noted, of the seventh century), and the closely similar movement in our Protestant North. Was not Descartes's creation of the *anti-Euclidean* analysis of space an iconoclasm?

THE EGYPTIAN AND THE CHINESE PRIME SYMBOL

That which is expressed by the soul of the West in its extraordinary wealth of media—words, tones, colours, pictorial perspectives, philosophical systems, legends, the spaciousness of Gothic cathedrals and the formulae of functions—namely, its world-feeling, is expressed by the soul of Old Egypt almost exclusively by the immediate language of *Stone*—stone, the emblem of the timeless become space. The Egyptian soul saw itself as moving down a narrow and inexorably prescribed life-path to come at the end before the judges of the dead (*Book of the Dead,* cap. 125). That was its *Destiny-idea.* The Egyptian's existence is that of the traveller who follows one unchanging direction, and the whole form-language of his Culture can be regarded as illustrating this one theme. And as we have taken *endless space* as the prime symbol of the North and *body* as that of the Classical, so we may take the word *way* as most intelligibly expressing that of the Egyptians. Strangely, and for Western thought almost incomprehensibly, the one element in extension that they emphasize is that of direction in depth. The tomb-temples of the Old Kingdom and especially the mighty pyramid-temples of the Fourth Dynasty represent, not a purposed organization of space such as we find in the mosque and the cathedral, but a rhythmically ordered *sequence* of spaces. The sacred way leads from the gate-building on the Nile through passages, halls, arcaded courts and pillared rooms that grow even narrower and narrower, to the chamber of the dead, and similarly the Sun-temples of the Fifth Dynasty are not "buildings" but a path enclosed by mighty masonry. The reliefs and the paintings appear always as rows which with an impressive compulsion lead the beholder in a definite direction. The ram and sphinx avenues of the New Empire have the same object. For the Egyptian, the depth-experience which governed his world-form was so emphatically directional that he comprehended space more or less as a continuous process of actualization. There is nothing rigid about distance as expressed here. Man must move, and so become himself a symbol of life, in order to enter into relation with the stone part of the symbolism. "Way" signifies both Destiny and third dimension. The mighty wall-surfaces, reliefs, colonnades past which he moves are "length and breadth"; that is, mere perceptions of the senses, and it is the forward-driving life that *extends* them into "world." And consequently the art of these Egyptians must aim at *plane* effects and nothing else, even when it is making use of solid means. For the Egyptian, the pyramid over the king's tomb is a *triangle*, a huge powerfully expressive *plane* that, whatever be the direction from which one approaches, closes off the "way" and commands the landscape. For him, the columns of the inner passages and courts, with their dark backgrounds, their dense array and their profusion of adornments, appear entirely as vertical strips which rhythmically accompany the march of the priests. Relief-work is—in utter contrast to the Classical—carefully restricted in one plane; in the course of development dated by the Third to the Fifth dynasties it diminishes from the thickness of a finger to that of a sheet of paper, and finally it is sunk in the plane. The dominance of the horizontal, the vertical and the right angle, and the avoidance of all foreshortening, support the two-dimensional principle and serve to insulate this directional depth-experience which coincides with the way and the grave at its end. It is an art that admits of no deviation for the relief of the tense soul.

There is, however, another Culture that, different as it most fundamentally is from the Egyptian, yet found a closely related prime symbol. This is the Chinese, with its intensely directional principle of the Tao.[3] But whereas the Egyptian treads to the end a way that is prescribed for him with an inexorable necessity, the Chinese *wanders* through his world; consequently, he is conducted to his god or his ancestral tomb not by ravines of stone, between faultless smooth walls, but by friendly Nature herself. Nowhere else has the *landscape* become so genuinely the material of the architecture. The temple is not a self-contained building but a layout, in which hills, water, trees, flowers and stones in definite forms and dispositions are just as important as gates, walls, bridges and houses. This Culture is the only one in which the art of gardening is a grand religious art. It is the architecture of the landscape, and only that, which explains the architecture of the buildings, with their flat extension and the emphasis laid on the roof as the really expressive element. And just as the devious ways through doors, over bridges, round hills and walls lead at last to the end, so the paintings take the beholder from detail to detail, whereas Egyptian relief masterfully points him in the one set direction. "The whole picture is *not* to be taken at once. Sequence in time presupposes a sequence of space-elements through which the eye is to wander from one to the next." As the Egyptian architecture dominates the landscape, the Chinese espouses it. But in both it is direction in depth that maintains the *becoming* of space as a continuously present experience.

IMITATION AND ORNAMENT

All art is *expression-language*. This expression is either *ornament or imitation*. Both are *higher* possibilities and their polarity to one another is hardly perceptible in the beginnings. Of the two, imitation is definitely the earlier and the more characteristic of race. Imitation is born of the secret rhythm of all things cosmic. Every live religion is an effort of the waking soul to reach the

---

[3] What makes Chinese—as also Indian—art so difficult a study for us is the fact that all works of the early periods (namely, those of the Hwang Ho region from 1300 to 800 B.C. and of pre-Buddhist India) have vanished without a trace.

powers of the world-around. And so too is Imitation, which in its most devoted moments is wholly religious, for it consists in an identity of inner activity between the soul and body "here" and the world-around "there" which, vibrating as one, become one. As a bird poises itself in the storm or a float gives to the swaying waves, so our limbs take up an irresistible beat at the sound of march-music. Not less contagious is the imitation of another's bearing and movements, wherein children in particular excel. It reaches the superlative when we "let ourselves go" in the common song or parade-march or dance that creates out of many units one unit of feeling and expression, a "we." A "successful" picture of a man or a landscape requires the executant to be an adept who can reveal the idea, the *soul,* of life in the play of its surface. In certain unreserved moments we are all adepts of this sort, and in such moments, as we follow in an imperceptible rhythm the music and the play of facial expression, we suddenly look over the precipice and see great secrets. All imitation is in the broadest sense dramatic; drama is presented in the movement of the brush-stroke or the chisel, the melodic curve of the song, the tone of the recitation, the line of poetry, the description, the dance.

Ornament detaches itself now from Imitation as something which does not follow the stream of life but rigidly *faces it.* Instead of physiognomic traits overheard in the alien being, we have established motives, *symbols,* which are impressed upon it. The intention is no longer to pretend but to conjure. The "I" overwhelms the "Thou." Imitation is only a *speaking* with means that are born of the moment and unreproducible—but Ornament *employs a language* emancipated from the speaking, a stock of forms that possesses duration and is not at the mercy of the individual.

Only the *living* can be imitated, and it can be imitated only in movements, for it is through these that it reveals itself to the senses of artists and spectators. To that extent, imitation belongs to Time and Direction. Ornament, on the contrary, is something removed from Time: it is pure extension, settled and stable. Whereas an imitation expresses something by *accomplishing itself,* ornament can only do so by presenting itself to the senses as a finished thing. It is Being as such, wholly independent of origin. Every imitation possesses beginning and end, while an ornament possesses only duration. In every springtime there are *two* definitely ornamental and non-imitative arts, that of building and that of decoration. In the longing and pregnant centuries before it, elemental expression belongs exclusively to Ornamentation in the narrow sense. The Carolingian period is represented only by its ornament, as its architecture, for want of the *Idea*, stands between the styles. But with the dawn of the great Culture, *architecture as ornament* comes into being suddenly and with such a force of expression that for a century mere decoration-as-such shrinks away from it in awe. The spaces, surfaces and edges of stone speak *for themselves*. The tomb of Chephren is the culmination of mathematical simplicity—everywhere right angles, squares and rectangular pillars, nowhere adornment, inscription or desinence—and it is only after some generations have passed that Relief ventures to infringe the solemn magic of those spaces and the strain begins to be eased. In the same way the noble Romanesque of Westphalia-Saxony (Hildesheim, Gernrode, Paulinzella, Paderborn), of Southern France and of the Normans (Norwich and Peterborough) managed to render the whole sense of the world with indescribable power and dignity in *one* line, *one* capital, *one* arch.

When the form-world of the springtime is at its highest, and not before, the ordained relation is that architecture is lord and ornament is vassal. The warrior figures of Dipylon vases are conceived in the spirit of ornament, and so, in a far higher degree still, are the statuary *groups* of Gothic cathedrals. And besides draperies, gestures and figure-types, even the structure of the hymn-strophe and the parallel motion of the parts in church music are ornament in the service of the all-ruling architectural idea. The spell of the great Ornamentation remains unbroken till in the beginning of a "late" period architecture falls into a *group* of civic and worldly special arts that unceasingly devote themselves to pleasing and clever imitation and become *ipso facto* personal.

Then comes the gleaming autumn of the style. Once more the soul depicts its happiness, this time conscious of self-completion. The "return to Nature" which already thinkers and poets—Rousseau, Gorgias and their "contemporaries" in the other Cultures—begin to feel and to proclaim, reveals itself in the form-world of the arts as a sensitive longing and *presentiment of the end*. A perfectly clear intellect, joyous urbanity, the pain of a farewell —such are the features of the last decades of a Culture of which

Talleyrand was to remark later: *"Qui n'a pas vécu avant 1789 ne connaît pas la douceur de vivre."* So it was, too, with the free, sunny and superfine art of Egypt under Sesostris III (c. 1850 B.C.) and the brief moments of satiated happiness that produced the varied splendour of Pericles' Acropolis and the works of Zeuxis and Phidias. A thousand years later again, in the age of the Ommaiyads, we meet it in the glad fairyland of Moorish architecture with its fragile columns and horseshoe-arches that seem to melt into air in an iridescence of arabesques and stalactites. A thousand years more, and we see it in the music of Haydn and Mozart, in Dresden shepherdesses, in the pictures of Watteau and Guardi and the works of German master-builders at Dresden, Potsdam, Würzburg and Vienna.

At the last, when Civilization sets in, true ornament and, with it, great art as a whole are extinguished. The transition consists —in every Culture—in Classicism and Romanticism of one sort or another, the former being a sentimental regard for an Ornamentation (rules, laws, types) that has long been archaic and soulless, and the latter a sentimental Imitation, not of life, but of an older Imitation. In the place of architectural style we find architectural taste. Methods of painting and mannerisms of writing, old forms and new, home and foreign, come and go with the fashion. In the end we have a pictorial and literary stock-in-trade which is destitute of any deeper significance and is employed according to taste. This final or industrial form of Ornament— no longer historical, no longer in the condition of "becoming"— we have before us not only in the patterns of oriental carpets, Persian and Indian metal-work, Chinese porcelain, but also in Egyptian (and Babylonian) art as the Greeks and Romans found it.

THE ARCHITECTURE OF THE WINDOW

The Doric soul actualized the symbol of the corporally-present individual thing. The expression to which this soul finally attained was the Doric temple with its purely outward effectiveness, set upon the landscape as a massive image but denying and artistically disregarding the space within as the $\mu\acute{\eta}$ $\ddot{o}\nu$, that which was held to be incapable of existence.

The Magian and the Faustian souls, on the contrary, built high.

Their dream-images became concrete as vaultings above significant inner-spaces, structural anticipations respectively of the mathematic of algebra and that of analysis. In the style that radiated from Burgundy and Flanders, rib-vaulting with its lunettes and flying buttresses emancipated the contained space from the sense-appreciable surface bounding it. In the Magian interior "the window is merely a negative component, a utility-form in no wise yet developed into an art-form—to put it crudely, nothing but a hole in the wall." When windows were in practice indispensable, they were for the sake of artistic impression concealed by galleries as in the Eastern basilica. The *window as architecture*, on the other hand, is peculiar to the Faustian soul and the most significant symbol of its depth-experience. In it can be felt the will to emerge from the interior into the boundless. The same will that is immanent in contrapuntal music was native to these vaultings. The incorporeal world of this music was and remained that of the first Gothic. To get rid of every trace of Classical corporeality, there was brought to bear the full force of a deeply significant Ornamentation, which defies the delimiting power of stone with its weirdly impressive transformations of vegetal, animal and human bodies (St. Pierre in Moissac), which dissolves all its lines into melodies and variations on a theme, all its façades into many-voiced fugues, and all the bodiliness of its statuary into a music of drapery-folds. It is this spirituality that gave their deep meaning to the gigantic glass-expanses of our cathedral-windows with their polychrome, *translucent and therefore wholly bodiless,* painting—an art that has never and nowhere repeated itself and forms the completest contrast that can be imagined to the Classical fresco. It is perhaps in the Sainte-Chapelle at Paris that this emancipation from bodiliness is most evident. Here the stone practically vanishes in the gleam of the glass. Whereas the fresco-painting is co-material with the wall on and with which it has grown and its colour is effective as material, here we have colours dependent on no carrying surface but as free in space as organ notes, and shapes poised in the infinite. Compare with the Faustian spirit of these churches —almost wall-less, loftily vaulted, irradiated with many-coloured light, aspiring from nave to choir—the Arabian (that is, the early-Christian Byzantine) cupola-church. The pendentive cupola, which seems to float on high above the basilica or the octagon, was indeed also a victory over the principle of natural gravity which the Classical expressed in architrave and column; it, too, was a defiance of architectural body, of "exterior." But the very absence of an exterior emphasizes the more the unbroken coherence of the wall that shuts in the Cavern and allows no look and no hope to emerge from it. An ingeniously confusing interpenetration of spherical and polygonal forms; a load so placed upon a stone drum that it seems to hover weightless on high, yet closing the interior without outlet; all structural lines concealed; vague light admitted, through a small opening in the heart of the dome but only the more inexorably to emphasize the walling in—such are the characters that we see in the masterpieces of this art, S. Vitale in Ravenna, Hagia Sophia in Constantinople, and the Dome of the Rock [4] in Jerusalem.

THE GREAT STYLE. THE HISTORY OF STYLE AS AN ORGANISM

The phenomenon of the *great style,* then, is an emanation from the essence of the Macrocosm, from the prime symbol of a *great* Culture.

The organic history of a style comprises a "pre —," a "non —" and a "post —." The bull tablet of the First Dynasty of Egypt is not yet "Egyptian." Not till the Third Dynasty do the works acquire a style—but then they do so suddenly and very definitely. Similarly the Carolingian period stands "between-styles." We see different forms touched on and explored, but nothing of inwardly necessary expression. The creator of the Aachen Minster "thinks surely and builds surely, but does not feel surely." For the whole of West Europe the period 850–950 is almost a blank. And just so today Russian art stands between two styles. The primitive wooden architecture with its steep eight-sided tent-roof (which extends from Norway to Manchuria) is impressed with Byzantine motives from over the Danube and Armenian-Persian from over the Caucasus. The church roof emerges, hillockwise, but little from the landscape, and on it sit the tent-roofs whose points are coifed with the "kokoshniks" that suppress and would abolish

<hr>

[4] "Mosque of Omar."—*At.*

the upward tendency.[5] They neither tower up like the Gothic Belfry nor enclose like the mosque-cupola, but *sit*, thereby emphasizing the horizontality of the building, which is meant to be regarded merely from the outside. When about 1760 the Synod forbade the tent-roofs and prescribed the orthodox onion-cupolas, the heavy cupolas were set upon slender cylinders, of which there may be any number and which sit on the roof-plane. It is not yet a style, only the promise of a style that will awaken when the real Russian religion awakens.

In the Faustian West, this awakening happened shortly before A.D. 1000. In one moment, the Romanesque style was there. Instead of the fluid organization of space on an insecure ground plan, there was, suddenly, a strict *dynamic of space*. From the very beginning, inner and outer construction were placed in a fixed relation, the wall was penetrated by the form-language and the form worked into the wall in a way that no other Culture has ever imagined. From the very beginning the window and the belfry were invested with their meanings. The form was irrevocably assigned. Only its development remained to be worked out.

The Egyptian style began with another such creative act, just as unconscious, just as full of symbolic force. The prime symbol of the Way came into being suddenly with the beginning of the Fourth Dynasty (2550 B.C.). The Egyptian flat-relief, which is designed to be seen at close quarters and arranged serially so as to compel the beholder to pass along the wall-planes in the prescribed direction, appears with similar suddenness about the beginning of the Fifth Dynasty.

The Egyptian style was purely architectural, and remained so till the Egyptian soul was extinguished. It is the only one in which Ornamentation as a decorative supplement to architecture is entirely absent. It allowed of no divergence into arts of entertainment, no display-painting, no busts, no secular music. In the Ionic phase, the centre of gravity of the Classical style shifted

~~~~~~~

[5] The lack of any vertical tendency in the Russian life-feeling is perceptible also in the saga-figure of Ilya Murometz. The Russian has not the smallest relation with a *Father*-God. His ethos is not a filial but purely a *fraternal* love, radiating in all directions along the human plane. Christ, even, is conceived as a Brother. The Faustian, wholly vertical, tendency to strive up to fulfilment is to the real Russian an incomprehensible pretension. The same absence of all vertical tendency is observable in Russian ideas of the state and property.

from architecture to an independent plastic art; in that of the Baroque the style of the West passed into music, whose form-language in its turn ruled the entire building art of the eighteenth century; in the Arabian world, after Justinian and Chosroes-Nushirvan, Arabesque dissolved all the forms of architecture, painting and sculpture into style-impressions that nowadays we should consider craft-art. But in Egypt the sovereignty of architecture remained unchallenged; it merely softened its language a little.

In China, in lieu of the awe-inspiring pylon with its massy wall and narrow entrance, we have the "Spirit-wall" (*yin-pi*) that conceals the way in. The Chinese slips into life and thereafter follows the Tao of life's path; as the Nile Valley is to the up-and-down landscape of the Hwang Ho, so is the stone-enclosed temple-way to the mazy paths of Chinese garden-architecture. And just so, in some mysterious fashion, the Euclidean existence is linked with the multitude of little islands and promontories of the Aegean, and the passionate Western, roving in the infinite, with the broad plains of Franconia and Burgundy and Saxony.

The Egyptian architect loved immense stone buildings, the Greek avoided it; his architecture first set itself small tasks, then ceased altogether. If we survey it as a whole, and then compare it with the totality of Egyptian or Mexican or even, for that matter, Western architecture, we are astounded at the feeble development of the style. A few variations of the Doric temple and it was exhausted. It was already closed off about 400 when the Corinthian capital was invented, and everything subsequent to this was merely modification of what existed.

The result of this was an almost bodily standardization of form-types and style-species. One might choose between them, but never overstep their strict limits—that would have been in some sort an admission of an infinity of possibilities. Similarly with the style-species of prose and the types of lyric poetry, narrative and tragedy. Universally, the expenditure of powers on the basic form is restricted to the minimum and the creative energy of the artist directed to detail-fineness. It is a statical treatment of static genera, and it stands in the sharpest possible contrast to the dynamic fertility of the Faustian with its ceaseless creation of new types and domains of form.

We are now able to see a great style sequence as an organism. Here, as in so many other matters, Goethe was the first to whom vision came. In his *Winckelmann* he says of Velleius Paterculus: "With his standpoint, it was not given to him to see all art as a living thing ($\zeta\hat{\omega}ον$) that must have an inconspicuous beginning, a slow growth, a brilliant moment of fulfilment and a gradual decline like every other organic being, though it is presented in a set of individuals." This sentence contains the entire morphology of art-history. Styles do not follow one another like waves or pulse-beats. It is not the personality or will or brain of the artist that makes the style, but the style that makes the *type* of the artist. The style, like the Culture, is a prime phenomenon in the strictest Goethian sense, be it the style of art or religion or thought, or the style of life itself. It is, as "Nature" is, an ever-new experience of waking man, his alter ego and mirror-image in the world-around. And therefore in the general historical picture of a Culture there can be but one style, *the style of the Culture*. The error has lain in treating mere style-phases—Romanesque, Gothic, Baroque, Rococo, Empire—as if they were styles on the same level as units of quite another order such as the Egyptian, the Chinese (or even a "prehistoric") style. Gothic and Baroque are simply the youth and age of one and the same vessel of forms, the style of the West as ripening and ripened. Hence Ionic columns can be as completely combined with Doric building forms as late Gothic is with early Baroque in St. Lorenz at Nürnberg, or late Romanesque with late Baroque in the beautiful upper part of the West choir at Mainz.

The task before art-history is to write the *comparative biographies of the great styles,* all of which as organisms of the same genus possess structurally cognate life-histories.

HISTORY OF THE ARABIAN STYLE

No one has yet perceived that Arabian art is a single phenomenon. It is an idea that can only take shape when we have ceased to be deceived by the crust which overlaid the young East with post-Classical art-exercises that, whether they were imitation-antique or chose their elements from proper or alien sources at will, were in any case long past all inward life. This Arabian style embraces the entire first millennium of our era.

In this as in every other Culture, Spring seeks to express its spirituality in a new ornamentation and, above all, in religious architecture as the sublime form of that ornamentation. There is in reality no such thing as a late-Classical or an early-Christian or yet an Islamic art in the sense of an art proper to each of those faiths and evolved by the community of believers as such. On the contrary, the totality of these religions—from Armenia to Southern Arabia and Axum, and from Persia to Byzantium and Alexandria—possesses a broad uniformity of artistic expression that overrides the contradictions of detail. There is something in the basilicas of Christianity, Hellenistic, Hebrew and Baal cults, and in the Mithraeum, the Mazdaist fire-temple and the Mosque, that tells of a like spirituality: it is the *Cavern*-feeling.

The artistic centre of this Culture was very definitely in the triangle of cities Edessa, Nisibis, Amida. To the westward of it is the domain of the late-Classical "Pseudomorphosis," the Pauline Christianity that conquered in the councils of Ephesus and Chalcedon, Western Judaism and the cults of Syncretism. The *architectural type of the Pseudomorphosis,* both for Jew and Gentile, is the Basilica.[6] It employs the means of the Classical to express the opposite thereof, and is unable to free itself from these means —that is the essence and the tragedy of "Pseudomorphosis." The space-feeling is different, but not—at first—the means of expressing it. In the pagan religious architecture of the Imperial Age there is a perceptible—though never yet perceived—movement from the wholly corporeal Augustan temple, in which the cella is the architectural expression of *nothingness,* to one in which the interior *only* possesses meaning. Finally the external picture of the Peripteros of the Doric is transferred to the four inside walls. Columns ranked in front of a windowless wall are a denial of space beyond—that is, for the Classical beholder, of space within, and for the Magian, of space without. It is therefore a question of minor importance whether the entire space is covered in as in the Basilica proper, or only the sanctuary as in the Sun-temple of Baalbek with the great forecourt, which later becomes a standing element of the mosque and is probably of South Arabian origin. That the Nave originates in a court surrounded by halls is suggested not only by the special development of the basilica-type in the East Syrian steppe (particularly Hau-

---

[6] The Baal-shrines in Palmyra, Baalbek and many other localities are basilicas: some of them are older than Christianity and many of them were later taken over into Christian use.

ran) but also by the basic disposition of porch, nave and choir as stages leading to the altar—for the aisles (originally the side-halls of the court) end blind, and only the nave proper corresponds with the apse. This basic meaning is very evident in St. Paul's at Rome, albeit the Pseudomorphosis (inversion of the Classical temple) dictated the technical means, viz., column and architrave. How symbolic is the Christian reconstruction of the Temple of Aphrodisias in Caria, in which the cella within the columns is abolished and replaced by a new wall outside them.

Outside the domain of the "Pseudomorphosis," on the contrary, the cavern-feeling was free to develop its own form-language, and here therefore it is *the definite roof that is emphasized* (whereas in the other domain the protest against the Classical feeling led merely to the development of an *interior*). When and where the various possibilities of dome, cupola, barrel-vaulting, rib-vaulting, came into existence as technical methods is, as we have already said, a matter of no significance. In Rome itself, Apollodorus of Damascus was employed under Trajan for the vaulting of the temple of "Venus and Rome," and the domed chambers of the Baths of Caracalla and the so-called "Minerva Medica" of Gallienus' time were built by Syrians. But the masterpiece, *the earliest of all Mosques,* is the Pantheon as rebuilt by Hadrian. Here, without a doubt, the emperor was imitating, for the satisfaction of his own taste, cult-buildings that he had seen in the East.[7]

The architecture of the central-dome, in which the Magian world-feeling achieved its purest expression, extended beyond the limits of the Roman Empire. When the Pseudomorphosis began to crumble and the last cults of Syncretism to die out, it also impressed itself victoriously upon the Basilica of the West. In Southern France—where there were Manichaean sects even as late as the Crusades—the form of the East was domesticated. Under Justinian, the interpenetration of the two produced the domical basilica of Byzantium and Ravenna. The pure basilica was pushed into the Germanic West, there to be transformed by the energy of the Faustian depth-impulse into the cathedral.

---

[7] Neither technically nor in point of space-feeling has this piece of purely *interior* architecture any connexion whatever with Etruscan round-buildings. With the cupolas of Hadrian's Villa at Tibur (Tivoli), on the contrary, its affinity is evident.

The domed basilica, again, spread from Byzantium and Armenia into Russia, where it came by slow degrees to be felt as an element of exterior architecture belonging to a symbolism concentrated in the roof. But in the Arabian world, Islam, the heir of Monophysite and Nestorian Christianity and of the Jews and the Persians, carried the development through to the end. When it turned Hagia Sophia into a mosque it only resumed possession of an old property. Islamic domical building followed Mazdaist and Nestorian along the same tracks to Shantung and to India. Mosques grew up in the Far West in Spain and Sicily, where, moreover, the style appears rather in its East Aramaean–Persian than in its West Aramaean–Syrian mode.

What is true as regards architecture is even more so as regards ornamentation, which in the Arabian world very early overcame all figure-representation and swallowed it up in itself. Then, as "Arabesque," it advanced to meet, to charm and to mislead the young art-intention of the West.

Nevertheless, the Arabian soul was cheated of its maturity— like a young tree that is hindered and stunted in its growth by a fallen old giant of the forest. Here there was no brilliant instant *felt and experienced as such,* like that of ours in which, simultaneously with the Crusades, the wooden beams of the Cathedral roof locked themselves into rib-vaulting and an interior was made to actualize and fulfil the idea of infinite space. The political creation of Diocletian was shattered in its glory upon the fact that, standing as he did on Classical ground, he had to accept the whole mass of the administrative tradition of Urbs Roma; this sufficed to reduce his work to a mere reform of obsolete conditions. And yet he was the first of the Caliphs. But so it was in all things. To this very day we admire as last creations of the Classical—because we cannot or will not regard them otherwise —the thought of Plotinus and Marcus Aurelius, the cults of Isis, Mithras and the Sun-God, the Diophantine mathematics and, lastly, the whole of the art which streamed towards us from the Eastern marches of the Roman Empire and for which Antioch and Alexandria were merely *points d'appui.*

This alone is sufficient to explain the intense vehemence with which the Arabian Culture, when released at length from artistic as from other fetters, flung itself upon all the lands that had inwardly belonged to it for centuries past. It is the sign of a soul that feels itself in a hurry, that notes in fear the first symptoms of old age before it has had youth. This emancipation of Magian mankind is without a parallel. Syria is conquered, or rather *delivered*, in 634. Damascus falls in 637, Ctesiphon in 637. In 641 Egypt and India are reached, in 647 Carthage, in 676 Samarkand, in 710 Spain. And in 732 the Arabs stood before Paris. Into these few years was compressed the whole sum of saved-up passions, postponed hopes, reserved deeds, that in the slow maturing of other Cultures suffice to fill the history of centuries.

True, all Cultures (the Egyptian, the Mexican and the Chinese excepted) have grown up under the tutelage of some older Culture. Each of the form-worlds shows certain alien traits. Thus, the Faustian soul of the Gothic, already predisposed to reverence by the Arabian origin of Christianity, grasped at the treasures of late-Arabian art. An unmistakably Southern, one might even say an Arabian, Gothic wove itself over the façades of the Burgundian and Provençal cathedrals, dominated with a magic of stone the outward language of Strassburg Minster, and fought a silent battle in statues and porches, fabric-patterns, carvings and metal-work—and not less in the intricate figures of scholastic philosophy and in that intensely Western symbol, the legend of the Grail.[8]

But the Magian soul of the Pseudomorphosis had not the courage to appropriate alien means *without yielding to them*. And this is why the physiognomic of the Magian soul has still so much to disclose to the quester.

---

[8] The Grail legend contains, besides old Celtic, well-marked Arabian elements.

VI

MUSIC AND PLASTIC:
THE ARTS OF FORM

THE clearest type of symbolic expression that the world-feeling of higher mankind has found for itself is (if we except the mathematical-scientific domain of presentation and the symbolism of its basic ideas) that of the arts of form, of which the number is legion. *And with these arts we count music,* for the formative impulse that is at work in the *wordless* arts can never be understood until we come to regard the distinction between optical and acoustic means as only a superficial one.

In reality, tones are something extended, limited and numerable just as lines and colours are; harmony, melody, rhyme and rhythm no less so than perspective, proportion, chiaroscuro and outline. The distance separating two kinds of painting can be infinitely greater than that separating the painting and the music of a period. Arts are living units, and the living is incapable of being dissected. The first act of the learned pedant has always been to partition the infinitely wide domain into provinces determined by perfectly superficial criteria of medium and technique and to endow these provinces with eternal validity and immutable (!) form-principles. But in fact the technical form-language is no more than the *mask* of the real work. Style is something inaccessible to art-reason, a revelation of the metaphysical order, a mysterious "must," a Destiny. With the material boundaries of the different arts it has no concern whatever.

If an art has boundaries at all—boundaries of its soul-become-form—they are historical and not technical or physiological boundaries.

With this, the notion of Form opens out immensely. Not only

the technical instrument, not only the form-language, but also *the choice of art-genus itself* is seen to be a means of expression. What the creation of a masterpiece means for an individual artist—the "Night Watch" for Rembrandt or the *Meistersinger* for Wagner—the creation of a *species* of art, comprehended as such, means for the life-history of a Culture. It is epochal. Apart from the merest externals, each such art is an individual organism without predecessor or successor. Its theory, technique and convention all belong to its character, and contain nothing of eternal or universal validity. When one of these arts is born, when it is spent, whether it dies or is transmuted into another, why this or that art is dominant in or absent from a particular Culture—all these are questions of Form in the highest sense, just as is that other question of why individual painters and musicians unconsciously avoid certain shades and harmonies or, on the contrary, show preferences so marked that authorship-attributions can be based on them.

The importance of these groups of questions has not yet been recognized by theory, even by that of the present day. Having assumed as self-evident the existence of a number of constant and well-defined provinces of art, one proceeded to order the history of these several provinces according to the—equally self-evident—scheme of ancient-mediaeval-modern. A futile up-and-down course was stolidly traced out. Static times were described as "natural pauses," it was called "decline" when some great art in reality died, and "renaissance" where an eye really free from prepossessions would have seen another art being born in another landscape to express another humanity.

And yet it is precisely in this problem of the end, the impressively sudden end, of a great art—the end of the Attic drama in Euripides, of Florentine sculpture with Michelangelo, of instrumental music in Liszt, Wagner and Bruckner—that the organic character of these arts is most evident. If we look closely enough we shall have no difficulty in convincing ourselves that no *one* art of any greatness has ever been "reborn."

Of the Pyramid style *nothing* passed over into the Doric. *Nothing* connects the Classical temple with the basilica of the Middle East. To believe genuinely in a rebirth of Classical art of whatsoever kind in the Western fifteenth century requires a rare stretch of the imagination.

APOLLINIAN AND FAUSTIAN ART

The temple of Poseidon at Paestum and the Minster of Ulm, works of the ripest Doric and the ripest Gothic, differ precisely as the Euclidean geometry of bodily bounding-surfaces differs from the analytical geometry of the position of points in space referred to spatial axes. All Classical building begins from the outside, all Western from the inside. The Arabian also begins with the inside, but it stays there. The exterior of the basilica and the domical building may be a *field for ornamentation,* but *architecture* it is not. The impression that meets the beholder as he approaches is that of something shielding, something that hides a secret. The form-language in the cavern-twilight exists for the faithful only—that is the factor common to the highest examples of the style and to the simplest Mithraea and Catacombs, the prime powerful utterance of a new soul. Now, as soon as the Germanic spirit takes possession of the basilical type, there begins a wondrous mutation of all structural parts, as to both position and significance. Here in the Faustian North the outer form of the building, be it cathedral or mere dwelling-house, begins to be brought into relation with the meaning that governs the arrangement of the interior. The Faustian building has a *visage* and not merely a façade—whereas the front of a peripteros is, after all, only one of four sides and the centre-domed building in principle has not even a front. The *motive of the façade,* which greets the beholder and tells him the inner meaning of the house, dominates not only individual major buildings but also the whole aspect of our streets, squares and towns with their characteristic wealth of windows.

The great architecture of the early period is ever the mother of all following arts; it determines the choice of them and the spirit of them. Accordingly, we find that the history of the Classical shaping art is one untiring effort to accomplish one single ideal, viz., the conquest of the free-standing human body as the vessel of the pure real present. The temple of the naked body was to it what the "cathedral" of music was to the Faustian from earliest counterpoint to the orchestral writing of the eighteenth century. We have failed hitherto to understand the emotional force of this secular tendency of the Apollinian, because we have not felt how the *purely material, soulless body* (for the Temple of the Body, too, has no "interior"!) is the object which archaic relief, Corinthian painting on clay, and Attic fresco were all striving to obtain until Polycletus and Phidias showed how to achieve it in full.

The evolution of this rigorously *non-spatial* art occupies the three centuries from 650 to 350, a period extending from the completion of the Doric to the coming of the Hellenistic and its illusion-painting which closed-off the grand style. This sculpture will never be rightly appreciated until it is regarded as the last and highest Classical, as *springing from a plane art, first obeying and then overcoming the fresco.* But as a *form-ideal* the statue goes back through relief to the archaic clay-painting in which fresco also originated. Relief, like fresco, is tied to the bodily wall. The change is completed about 460 with Polycletus, and thenceforward plastic groups become the model for strict painting. But it is with Lysippus that a completely all-round treatment is carried thoroughly into effect. Till then, even in the case of Praxiteles, we have still a lateral or planar development of the subject, with a clear outline that is only fully effective in respect of one or two standpoints.

The corresponding stage of Western art occupies the three centuries 1500–1800, between the end of late Gothic and the decay of Rococo, which marks the end of the great Faustian style. In this period, conformably to the persistent growth into consciousness of the will to spatial transcendence, it is instrumental music that develops into the ruling art. At the beginning, in the seventeenth century, music uses the characteristic tone-colours of the instruments, and the contrasts of strings and wind, human voices and instrumental voices, as means wherewith to *paint*. Its (quite unconscious) ambition is to parallel the great masters from Titian to Velásquez and Rembrandt. It makes pictures (in the sonata from Gabrieli [d. 1612] to Corelli [d. 1713] every movement shows a theme embellished with graces and set upon the background of a *basso continuo*), paints heroic landscapes (in the pastoral cantata), and draws a portrait in lines of melody (in Monteverde's *Lament of Ariadne*, 1608). With the German masters, all this goes. Painting can take music no further. Music becomes itself *absolute*: it is music that (quite unconsciously again) dominates both painting and architecture in the eighteenth century. And, ever more and more decisively, sculpture fades out from among the deeper possibilities of this form-world. But the serious music of the Classical was nothing but a *plastic for the ear*. This music was single-voiced. West Europe has an *ornamental music of the grand style* which is associated with the architectural history of the cathedral. Counterpoint developed simultaneously with the flying-buttress system, and its source was the "Romanesque" style of the faux-bourdon and the descant with their simple parallel and contrary motion.[1] It is an architecture of human voices and, like the statuary-group and the glass-paintings, is only conceivable in the setting of these stone vaultings.

Along with this there came into being in castle and village a secular *imitative* music, that of troubadours, *Minnesänger* and minstrels. It consisted of simple melodies that appealed to the heart with their major and minor, of canzoni, madrigals and caccias. After 1400, these forms give rise to forms of collective singing—the rondeau and the ballade. All this is "art" for a public.[2] It is the distinction between waking-consciousness and living-existence, between the spiritual and the knightly singer. Imitation stands nearest to life and direction and therefore begins with melody, while the symbolism of counterpoint belongs to extension and through polyphony signifies infinite space. The evolution of strict musical form from the Motet to the four-voice Mass through Dunstaple, Binchois and Dufay (c. 1430) proceeded wholly within the magic circle of Gothic architecture. From Fra Angelico to Michelangelo the great Netherlanders ruled alone in ornamental music.

The transition into the "Late" age was heralded in Rome and Venice. With Baroque the leadership in music passes to Italy. But at the same time architecture ceases to be the ruling art and there is formed a group of Faustian special-arts in which oil-painting occupies the central place. About 1560 the empire of the human voice comes to an end in the *a cappella* style of Palestrina and Orlando Lasso (both d. 1594). Its powers could no longer express the passionate drive into the infinite, and it made way

---

[1] See articles *fauxbourdon, descant* and *Goudimel* in *Grove's Dictionary of Music.—At.*

[2] Even the first great troubadour, Guilhem of Poitiers, though a reigning sovereign, made it his ambition to be regarded as a "professional," as we should say.—*At.*

for the chorus of instruments, wind and string. The music of the Gothic is architectural and vocal, that of the Baroque pictorial and instrumental. The one builds, the other operates by means of motives. For all the arts have become urban and therefore secular. We pass from super-personal Form to the personal expression of the Master, and shortly before 1600 Italy produces the *basso continuo* which requires virtuosi and not pious participants.

Thenceforward, the great task was to extend the tone-corpus into the infinity, or rather to *resolve it into an infinite space of tone*. Gothic had developed the instruments into families of definite timbre. But the new-born "orchestra" no longer observes limitations imposed by the human voice, but treats it as a voice to be combined with other voices—at the same moment as our mathematic proceeds from the geometrical analysis of Fermat to the purely functional analysis of Descartes. To the vocal masses and motets the Baroque opposes its grand, orchestrally conceived forms of the oratorio (Carissimi), the cantata (Viadana) and the opera (Monteverde).

From out of these forms of the early Baroque there proceeded, in the seventeenth century, the sonata-like forms of suite, symphony and *concerto grosso*. The inner structure and the sequence of movements, the thematic working out and modulation became more and more firmly established. And thus was reached the great, immensely dynamic form in which music—now completely bodiless—was raised by Corelli and Handel and Bach to be the ruling art of the West. When Newton and Leibniz, about 1670, discovered the Infinitesimal Calculus, the fugal style was fulfilled. And when, about 1740, Euler began the definitive formulation of functional Analysis, Stamitz and his generation were discovering the last and ripest form of musical ornamentation, the four-part movement as vehicle of pure and unlimited motion. For, at that time, there was still this one step to be taken. The theme of the fugue "is," that of the new sonata-movement "becomes," and the issue of its working out is in the one case a picture, in the other a drama. Instead of a series of pictures we get a cyclic succession, and the real source of this tone-language was in the possibilities, realized at last, of our deepest and most intimate kind of music—the music of the strings. Certain it is that the violin is the noblest of all instruments that the Faustian soul has imagined and trained for the expression of its last secrets, and certain it is, too, that it is in string quartets and violin sonatas that it has experienced its most transcendent and most holy moments of full illumination. Here, *in chamber-music, Western art as a whole reaches its highest point.* Here our prime symbol of endless space is expressed as completely as the Spearman of Polycletus expresses that of intense bodiliness.

With this, the Faustian music becomes dominant among the Faustian arts. It banishes the plastic of the statue and tolerates only the minor art—an entirely musical, refined, un-Classical and counter-Renaissance art—of porcelain, which is contemporary with the rise of chamber-music to full effectiveness. Whereas the statuary of Gothic is through-and-through architectural ornamentation, human espalier-work, that of the Rococo remarkably exemplifies the pseudo-plastic that results from entire subjection to the form-language of music, and shows to what degree the technique governing the presented foreground can be in contradiction with the real expression-language that is hidden behind it. Music transmuted also the architecture of Bernini's Baroque into accord with its own spirit, and made of it Rococo, a style of transcendent ornamentation upon which lights (or rather "tones") play to dissolve ceilings, walls and everything else constructional and actual into polyphonies and harmonies, with architectural trills and cadences and runs to complete the identification of the form-language of these halls and galleries with that of the music imagined for them. Dresden and Vienna are the homes of this late and soon-extinguished fairyland of *visible* chamber music, of curved furniture and mirror-halls, and shepherdesses in verse and porcelain. It is the last supreme expression, lit by an autumnal sun, of the Western soul. And in the Vienna of the Congress-time it faded and died.

THE RENAISSANCE REGARDED AS AN ANTI-GOTHIC (ANTI-MUSICAL) MOVEMENT

The Art of the Renaissance, considered from this particular one of its many aspects, is *a revolt against the spirit of the Faustian forest-music* of counterpoint, which at that time was preparing to dominate the whole form-language of Western Culture. It never disavowed its Gothic origin and it maintained the character of a simple *counter-movement;* necessarily, therefore, it remained dependent upon the forms of the original movement, and represented simply the effect of these upon a hesitant soul. Hence, it was without true depth, either in idea or in performance. We have only to think of the bursting passion with which the Gothic world-feeling discharged itself upon the whole Western landscape, and we shall see at once what sort of a movement it was that the handful of select spirits—scholars, artists and humanists—initiated about 1420. What had been an issue of life and death for a new-born soul became a point of—taste. The Gothic gripped life in its entirety, penetrated its most hidden corners. It created new men and a new world. But the Renaissance, when it had mastered some arts of word and picture, had shot its bolt. It altered the ways of thought and the life-feeling of West Europe not one whit. The Renaissance as an anti-Gothic movement and a reaction against the spirit of polyphonic music has its Classical equivalent in the Dionysiac movement. This was a reaction against Doric and against the sculptural-Apollinian world-feeling. It did *not* "originate" in the Thracian Dionysus-cult, but merely took this up as a weapon against and counter-symbol to the Olympian religion, precisely as in Florence the cult of the antique was called in for the justification and confirmation of a feeling already there. The period of the great protest was the seventh century in Greece and the fifteenth in West Europe.

It follows from the very character of a counter-movement that it is far easier for it to define what it is opposing than what it is aiming at. This is the difficulty of all Renaissance research. Renaissance art is nothing more nor less than anti-Gothic art. Renaissance music, too, is a contradiction in itself; the music of the Medicean court was the Southern French *ars nova,* that of the Florentine Duomo was the Low-German counterpoint, both alike essentially *Gothic* and the property of the *whole* West.

In the actual birth of the Gothic style Italy had indeed no inward share. At the epoch of 1000 the country was still absolutely under the domination of Byzantine taste in the East and Moorish taste in the South. When Gothic first took root here it was the mature Gothic, and it implanted itself with an intensity and force for which we look in vain in any of the great Renaissance creations—think of the *Stabat Mater,* the *Dies Irae,* Catherine of Siena, Giotto and Simone Martini!

If the Renaissance had been a "renewal" (whatever that may

mean) of the Classical *world-feeling*, then, surely, would it not
have had to replace the symbol of encompassed rhythmically
ordered *space* by that of closed structural *body*? But there was
never any question of this. On the contrary, the Renaissance
practised wholly and exclusively an architecture of space prescribed for it by Gothic, from which it differed *only* in that in
lieu of the Northern *Sturm und Drang* it breathed the clear
equable calm of the sunny, carefree and unquestioning South. It
produced *no* new building-idea.

If we take away from the models of the Renaissance all
elements that originated later than the Roman Imperial Age—
that is to say, those belonging to the Magian form-world—nothing is left. Most conclusive of all, though, is that motive which
actually *dominates* the Renaissance, which because of its South-
ernness we regard as the noblest of the Renaissance characters,
viz., *the association of round-arch and column*. This association,
no doubt, is very un-Gothic, but in the Classical style it simply
does not exist, and in fact it represents the leitmotif of the
Magian architecture that originated in Syria.

But it was just then that the South received from the North
those decisive impulses which helped it first of all to emancipate
itself entirely from Byzantium and then to step from Gothic
into Baroque. In the region comprised between Amsterdam,
Köln and Paris [3] counterpoint and oil-painting had been created
in association with the Gothic architecture. Thence Dufay in
1428 and Willaert in 1516 came to the Papal Chapel, and in
1527 the latter founded that Venetian school which was decisive
for Baroque music. The successor of Willaert was De Rore of
Antwerp. A Florentine commissioned Hugo van der Goes to exe-
cute the Portinari altar for Santa Maria Nuova, and Memling to
paint a Last Judgment. And over and above this, numerous pictures (especially Low Countries portraits) were acquired and
exercised an enormous influence. In 1450 Rogier van der Wey-
den himself came to Florence, where his art was both admired
and imitated. In 1470 Justus van Gent introduced oil-painting
to Umbria, and Antonello da Messina brought what he had

---

[3] Inclusive of Paris itself. Even as late as the fifteenth century Flemish
was as much spoken there as French, and the architectural appearance of
the city in its oldest parts connects it with Bruges and Ghent and not with
Troyes and Poitiers.

learned in the Netherlands to Venice. How much "Dutch" and how little "Classical" there is in the pictures of Filippino Lippi, Ghirlandaio and Botticelli and especially in the engravings of Pollaiuolo! Or in Leonardo himself.

The high period of the Renaissance is a moment of *apparent* expulsion of music from Faustian art. And in fact, for a few decades, in the only area where Classical and Western landscapes touched, Florence did uphold—with one grand effort that was essentially metaphysical and essentially defensive—an image of the Classical so convincing that, although its deeper characters were without exception mere anti-Gothic, it lasted beyond Goethe and, if not for our criticism, yet for our feelings, is valid to this day. The great achievement of Giotto and Masaccio in creating a fresco-art is only *apparently* a revival of the Apollinian way of feeling; but the depth-experience and idea of extension that underlies it is not the Apollinian unspatial and self-contained body, but the *Gothic* space picture. However recessive the backgrounds are, they exist. Yet here again there was the fullness of light, the clarity of atmosphere, the great noon-calm, of the South; dynamic space was changed in Tuscany, and only in Tuscany, to the static space of which Piero della Francesca was the master. The hidden dynamic is equally unmistakable in the sculpture of Florence—it would be perfectly hopeless to look for an Attic companion for Verrocchio's equestrian statue.[4] The indescribable inward purity of Gothic form often causes us to forget what an excess of native strength and depth it possessed. Gothic, it must be repeated again, is the *only* foundation of the Renaissance. The Renaissance never even touched the real Classical, let alone understood it or "revived" it. The consciousness of the Florentine group, wholly under literary influences, fashioned the deceptive name to positivize the negative element of the movement—thereby demonstrating how little such currents are aware of their own nature. Classical motives are a matter of indifference if the method of treatment has an un-Classical effect—significance lies not in the thing but in the way in which it is used. But even in Donatello such motives are far fewer than in mature Baroque. As for a strict Classical capital, no such thing is to be found.

And yet, at moments, Renaissance art succeeded in achieving

[4] The colossal statue of Bartolommeo Colleoni at Venice.—*At.*

something wonderful that music *could not* reproduce—a feeling for the bliss of perfect *nearness*, for pure, restful and *liberating* space-effects, bright and tidy and free from the passionate movement of Gothic and Baroque. It is not Classical, but it is a dream of Classical existence, the only dream of the Faustian soul in which it was able to forget itself.

CHARACTER OF THE BAROQUE

And now, with the sixteenth century, the decisive epochal turn begins for Western painting. The trusteeship of architecture in the North and that of sculpture in Italy expire, and painting becomes polyphonic, "picturesque," infinity-seeking. The colours become tones. The background, hitherto casually put in, regarded as a fill-up and, as space, almost shuffled out of sight, gains a preponderant importance. A development sets in that is paralleled in no other Culture, not even in the Chinese, which in many other respects is so near to ours. The background as symbol of the infinite conquers the sense-perceptible foreground, and at last (herein lies the distinction between the depicting and the delineating styles) the depth-experience of the Faustian soul is captured in the kinesis of a picture. The space-relief of Mantegna's plane layers dissolves in Tintoretto into directional energy, and there emerges in the picture the great symbol of an unlimited space-universe which comprises the individual things within itself as incidentals—the *horizon*. There is not a hint of it, either in Egyptian relief or in Byzantine mosaic or in vase-paintings and frescoes of the Classical age, or even in those of the Hellenistic in spite of its spatial treatment of foregrounds. This line, in the unreal vapour of which heaven and earth melt, the sum and potent symbol of the far, contains the painter's version of the "infinitesimal" principle. It is out of the remoteness of this horizon that the *music* of the picture flows, and for this reason the great landscape-painters of Holland paint only backgrounds and atmospheres, just as for the contrary reason "anti-musical" masters like Signorelli, and especially Mantegna, paint *only* foregrounds and "reliefs." It is in the horizon, then, that Music triumphs over Plastic, the *passion* of extension over its *substance*. It is not too much to say that no picture by Rembrandt has a foreground at all.

The same symbolic meaning attaches to clouds. Classical art concerns itself with them no more than with horizons, and the painter of the Renaissance treats them with a certain playful superficiality. But very early the Gothic looked at its cloud-masses, and through them, with the long sight of mysticism; and the Venetians (Giorgione and Paolo Veronese above all) discovered the full magic of the cloud-world, of the thousand-tinted Being that fills the heavens with its sheets and wisps and mountains. Grünewald and the Netherlanders heightened its significance to the level of tragedy. El Greco brought the grand art of cloud-symbolism to Spain.

It was at the same time that along with oil-painting and counterpoint the *art of gardens* ripened. Here, expressed on the canvas of Nature itself by lengthy stretches of water, avenues, vistas and galleries, is the same tendency that is represented in painting by the effort towards the linear perspective that the early Flemish artists felt to be the basic problem of their art and Brunelleschi, Alberti and Piero della Francesca formulated. The point at which the perspective lines coalesce is at infinity. It was just because it avoided infinity and rejected distance that Classical painting possessed no perspective. *Consequently* the Park, the deliberate manipulation of Nature so as to obtain space and distance effects, is an impossibility in Classical art.

The most significant element in the Western garden-art is thus the *point de vue* of the great Rococo park, upon which all its avenues and clipped-hedge walks open and from which vision may travel out to lose itself in the distances. This element is wanting even in the Chinese garden-art. But it is exactly matched by some of the silver-bright distance-pictures of the pastoral music of that age (in Couperin for example). It is the *point de vue* that gives us the key to a real understanding of this remarkable mode of making nature itself speak the form-language of a human symbolism. It was *we* and not the Hellenes or the men of the high Renaissance that prized and sought out high mountaintops for the sake of the limitless range of vision that they afford. This is a Faustian craving—to be *alone* with endless space. The great achievement of Lenôtre and the landscape-gardeners of Northern France, beginning with Fouquet's epoch-making creation of Vaux-le-Vicomte, was that they were able to render this symbol with such high emphasis. Compare the Renaissance park of the Medicean age—all within range of vision, gay, cosy, well-rounded—with these parks in which the narrow lakes, statue-rows, hedges and labyrinths are instinct with the suggestion of distance. It is the Destiny of Western oil-painting told over again in a bit of garden-history.

A feeling for the faraway is at the same time one for history. At a distance, space becomes time and the horizon signifies the future. *The Baroque park is the park of the Late season,* of the approaching end, of the falling leaf. A Renaissance park brings us a vision of a midsummer noon. It is timeless, and nothing in its form-language reminds us of mortality. It is perspective that begins to awaken a premonition of something passing, fugitive and final. The very words of distance possess, in the lyric poetry of all Western languages, a plaintive autumnal accent that one looks for in vain in the Greek and Latin. It is there in Macpherson's *Ossian* and Hölderlin, and in Nietzsche's Dionysus-Dithyrambs, and lastly in Baudelaire, Verlaine, George and Droem. The Late poetry of the withering garden avenues, the unending lines in the streets of a megalopolis, the ranks of pillars in a cathedral, the peak in a distant mountain chain—all tell us that the depth-experience which constitutes our space-world for us is in the last analysis our inward certainty of a Destiny, of a prescribed direction, of *time,* of the irrevocable. Here, in the experience of horizon as future, we become directly and surely conscious of the identity of Time with the "third dimension" of that experienced space which is living self-extension.

Oil-painting and instrumental music evolve organically towards aims that were comprehended in the Gothic and achieved in the Baroque. Both arts—Faustian in the highest sense—are within those limits *prime phenomena.* They have a soul, a physiognomy and therefore a history. And in this they are alone. All that sculpture could thenceforward achieve was a few beautiful incidental pieces in the shadow of painting, garden-art or architecture. The art of the West had no real need of them. There was no longer a *style* of plastic in the sense that there were styles of painting or music. What there is in a Rembrandt portrait simply cannot be rendered in a bust. Now and then a sculptor of power arises, like Bernini or the masters of the contemporary Spanish school, or Pigalle or Rodin (none of whom, naturally, transcended the decorative and attained the level of grand symbolism), but such an artist is always visibly either a belated imitator of the Renaissance like Thorwaldsen, a disguised painter like Houdon or Rodin, an architect like Bernini and Schlüter or a decorator like Coysevox. And his very appearance on the scene only shows the more clearly that this art, incapable of carrying the Faustian burden, has no longer a mission—and therefore no longer a soul or a life-history of specific style-development—in the Faustian world.

SYMBOLISM OF THE COLOURS

The strict style in Classical painting limited its palette to yellow, red, black and white. This singular fact was observed long ago, and, since the explanation was only sought for in superficial and definitely material causes, wild hypotheses were brought forward to account for it, e.g. a supposed colour-blindness in the Greeks.

Blue and green are the colours of the heavens, the sea, the fruitful plain, the shadow of the Southern noon, the evening, the remote mountains. They are essentially atmospheric and not substantial colours. They are *cold*, they disembody and they evoke impressions of expanse and distance and boundlessness.

And for this reason an atmospheric blue-green is the space-creating element throughout the history of our perspective oil-painting, from the Venetians right into the nineteenth century; it is the basic and supremely important tone which *supports* the ensemble of the intended colour-effect, as the *basso continuo* supports the orchestra, whereas the warm yellow and red tones are put on sparingly and in dependence upon this basic tone. It is not the full, gorgeous and *familiar* green that Raphael and Dürer sometimes—and seldom at that—use for draperies, but an indefinite blue-green of a thousand nuances into white and grey and brown; something deeply musical, into which (notably in Gobelin tapestry) the whole atmosphere is plunged. That quality which we have named aerial perspective in contrast to linear—and might also have called *Baroque* perspective in contrast to Renaissance—rests almost exclusively upon this. Wé find it with more and more intense depth-effect in Leonardo, Guercino, Albani in the case of Italy, and in Ruysdael and Hobbema in that of Holland, but, above all, in the great French painters, from Poussin and Claude Lorrain and Watteau to Corot. Blue, equally a perspective colour, always stands in relation to the dark, the unillumined, the unactual. It does not press in on us, it pulls us out into the remote.

Blue and green are transcendent, spiritual, non-sensuous colours. Yellow and red, the Classical colours, are the colours of the material, the near, the full-blooded. Red is the characteristic colour of sexuality.

Yellow and red are the *popular* colours, the colours of the crowd, of children, of women and of savages. Amongst the Venetians and the Spaniards high personages affected a splendid black or blue, with an unconscious sense of the aloofness inherent in these colours. For red and yellow, the *Apollinian, Euclidean-polytheistic* colours, belong to the foreground even in respect of social life; the noisy hearty market-days and holidays. But blue and green—the Faustian, monotheistic colours—are those of loneliness, of care, of a present that is related to a past and a future, of destiny as the dispensation dwelling in the universe.

The most significant use of dusky green as the colour of destiny is Grünewald's. The indescribable power of space in his *nights* is equalled only by Rembrandt's. And the thought suggests itself here, is it possible to say that his bluish-green, the colour in which the interior of a great cathedral is so often clothed, is the specifically *Catholic* colour?—it being understood that we mean by "Catholic" strictly the Faustian Christianity (with the Eucharist as its centre) that was founded in the Lateran Council of 1215 and fulfilled in the Council of Trent. This colour with its silent grandeur is as remote from the resplendent gold-ground of early Christian-Byzantine pictures as it is from the gay, loquacious "pagan" colours of the painted Hellenic temples and statues. It is to be noted that the effect of this colour, entirely unlike that of yellow and red, depends upon work being exhibited *indoors*. Classical painting is emphatically an open-air art, Western just as emphatically a studio-art. The whole of our great oil-painting, from Leonardo to the end of the eighteenth century, is not meant for the bright light of day. Here once more we meet the same opposition as that between chamber-music and the statue. The climatic explanation of the difference is merely superficial; the example of Egyptian painting would suffice to disprove it if disproof were necessary at all.

GOLD BACKGROUND AND STUDIO-BROWN

Arabian art expressed the feeling of the Magian world by means of the *gold background* of its mosaics and pictures.

In this instance we can study the soul of three Cultures working upon very similar tasks in very dissimilar ways. The Apollinian Culture recognized as actual only that which was immediately present in time and place—and thus it repudiated the background as pictorial element. The Faustian strove through all sensuous barriers towards infinity—and it projected the centre of gravity of the pictorial idea into the distance by means of perspective. The Magian felt all happening as an expression of mysterious powers that filled the world-cavern with their spiritual substance—and it shut off the depicted scene with a gold background, that is, by something that stood beyond and outside all nature-colours. Gold is not a colour. Colours are natural; but the metallic gleam, which is practically never found in natural conditions, is unearthly.[5] It recalls impressively the other symbols of the Culture, Alchemy and Kabbala, the Philosophers' Stone, the Holy Scriptures, the Arabesque, the inner form of the tales of the *Thousand and One Nights*. The gleaming gold takes away from the scene, the life and the body their substantial being. The gold background possesses, in the iconography of the Western Church, an explicit dogmatic significance. It is an express assertion of the existence and activity of the divine spirit. When "natural" backgrounds, with their blue-green heavens, far horizons and depth perspective, began to appear in early Gothic, they had at first the appearance of something profane and worldly. The change of dogma that they implied was, if not acknowledged, at any rate felt, witness the tapestry backgrounds with which the real depth of space was covered up by a pious awe that disguised what it dared not exhibit. The final schism took place almost at the same moment in Church and in Art. The landscape-background of the depicted

---

[5] The brilliant *polish* of the stone in Egyptian art has a deep symbolic significance of much the same kind. Its effect is to dematerialize the statue by causing the eye to glide along its exterior. Hellas on the contrary manifests, by its progress from "Poros" stone, through Naxian, to the translucent Parian and Pentelic marbles, how determined it is that the look shall sink right into the material essence of the body.

scene and the *dynamic* infiniteness of God were comprehended at the same moment; and, simultaneously with the gold ground of the sacred picture, there vanished from the Councils of the West that Magian, ontological problem of Godhead which had so passionately agitated Nicaea, Ephesus, Chalcedon and all the Councils of the East.

The Venetians discovered, and introduced into oil-painting as a space-forming and quasi-musical motive, the handwriting of the *visible brush-stroke*. It is only in the brush-work, which remains permanently visible and, in a way, perennially fresh, that the *historical* feeling comes out. Our desire is to see in the work of the painter not merely something that *has become* but something that *is becoming*. And this is precisely what the Renaissance wanted to avoid. The individual brush-strokes—first met with as a complete new form-language in the later work of Titian—are accents of a personal temperament, characteristic in the orchestra-colours of Monteverde, melodically flowing as a contemporary Venetian madrigal: streaks and dabs, immediately juxtaposed, cross one another, cover one another, entangle one another, and bring unending movement into the plain element of colour. The physiognomy of this script of the brush—an ornamentation that is entirely new, infinitely rich and personal, and peculiar to the Western Culture—is purely and simply *musical*. Henceforward the notion of *tempo* is introduced into painting. The aery web of brush-strokes at once dissolves surfaces. Contours melt into chiaroscuro.

At the same time with this, there appeared in Western painting another symbol of highest significance, which subdued more and more the actuality of all colour—the "studio-brown" (*Atelierbraun*). This was unknown to the early Florentines and the older Flemish and Rhenish masters alike. Pacher, Dürer, Holbein, passionately strong as their tendency towards spatial depth seems, are quite without it, and its reign begins only with the last years of the sixteenth century. This brown does not repudiate its descent from the atmospheric greens of Leonardo's, Schöngauer's and Grünewald's backgrounds, but it possesses a mightier power over things than they, and it carries the battle of Space against Matter to a decisive close. It even prevails over the more primitive linear perspective, which is unable to shake off its Renaissance association with architectural motives. Between it and the Impressionist technique of the visible brush-stroke there is an enduring and deeply suggestive connexion. Ultimately both dissolve the tangible presences of the sense-world—the foreground at a given moment—into ethereal semblances. Its discovery marks the zenith of the Western style. *As contrasted with the preceding green, this colour has something Protestant in it.* The atmosphere of Lear and the atmosphere of Macbeth are akin to it. The contemporary striving of instrumental music towards freer and ever freer chromatics corresponds exactly with the new tendency of oil-painting to create *pictorial chromatics* out of pure colours, by means of these unlimited brown shadings and the contrast-effect of immediately juxtaposed colour-strokes. Thereafter both the arts spread through their worlds of tones and colours—colour-tones and tone-colours— an atmosphere of the purest spatiality, which enveloped and rendered, no longer body—the human being as a shape—but the soul unconfined. This atmospheric brown, which was entirely alien to the Renaissance, is the unrealest colour that there is. It is the one major colour that *does not exist in the rainbow.* A pure brown light is outside the possibilities of the Nature that we know. All the greenish-brown, silvery, moist brown and deep gold tones that appear in their splendid variety with Giorgione, grow bolder and bolder in the great Dutch painters and lose themselves towards the end of the eighteenth century, have the common quality that they strip nature of her tangible actuality. They contain, therefore, what is almost a religious profession of faith; we feel that here we are not very far from Port Royal, from Leibniz. With Constable—who is the founder of the painting of *Civilization*—it is a different will that seeks expression; and the very brown that he had learnt from the Dutch meant to him not what it had meant to them—Destiny, God, the meaning of life—but simply romance, sensibility, yearning for something that was gone, memorial of the great past of the dying art. In the last German masters too—Lessing, Marées, Spitzweg, Diez, Leibl—whose belated art is a romantic retrospect, an epilogue, the brown tones appear simply as a precious heirloom. Unwilling in their hearts to part with this last relic of the great style, they preferred to set themselves against the evident tendency of their generation—the soulless and soul-killing generation of *plein-air* and Haeckel.

It was the masters who were inwardly greatest—Rembrandt above all—who best understood this colour. It is the enigmatic brown of his most telling work, and its origin is in the deep lights of Gothic church-windows and the twilight of the high-vaulted Gothic nave.

Brown, then, became the characteristic colour of the *soul*, and more particularly of a historically disposed soul. Nietzsche has, I think, spoken somewhere of the "brown" music of Bizet, but the adjective is far more appropriate to the music which Beethoven wrote for strings [6] and to the orchestration that even as late as Bruckner so often fills space with a browny-golden expanse of tone. All other colours are relegated to ancillary functions—thus the bright yellow and the vermilion of Vermeer intrude into the spatial almost as though from another world and with an emphasis that is truly metaphysical, and the yellow-green and blood-red lights of Rembrandt seem at most to play with the symbolism of space.

PATINA

I have called brown a historical colour. By this is meant that it makes the atmosphere of the pictured space signify directedness and *future*. The other colours of distance have also this significance, and they lead to an important, considerable and distinctly bizarre extension of the Western symbolism. The Hellenes had in the end come to prefer bronze and even gilt-bronze to the painted marble, the better to express (by the radiance of this phenomenon against a deep blue sky) the idea of the individualness of any and every corporeal thing.[7] Now, when the Renaissance dug these statues up, it found them black and green with the patina of many centuries. The historic spirit, with its piety and longing, fastened onto this—and from that time forth our form-feeling has canonized this black and green

~~~~~~~~

[6] The strings in the Orchestra represent, as a class, the colours of the distance. The bluish-green of Watteau is found already in the Neapolitan *bel canto* of about 1700, in Couperin, in Mozart and Haydn; and the brown of the Dutch in Corelli, Handel and Beethoven. The woodwind, too, calls up illumined distances. Yellow and red, on the other hand, the colours of nearness, the *popular* colours, are associated with the brass timbre, the effect of which is corporeal often to the point of vulgarity. The tone of an old fiddle is entirely bodiless.

(The horn is an exception, and is always treated as an exception, to the brass generally. Its place is with the woodwind, and its colours are those of the distance.—*At.*)

[7] The use of gold in this way, viz., to add brilliancy to bodies standing freely in the open, has nothing in common with its employment in Magian art to provide glittering backgrounds for figures seen in dim interiors.

of distance. Patina is a symbol of *mortality* and hence related in a remarkable way to the symbols of time-measurement and the funeral rite. It corresponds to the wistful regard of the Faustian soul for ruins and evidences of the distant past, its proneness to the collection of antiquities and manuscripts and coins, to pilgrimages to the Forum Romanum and to Pompeii, to excavations and philological studies, which appears as early as the time of Petrarch. We are moved by a secret piety to preserve the aqueducts of the Campagna, the Etruscan tombs, the ruins of Luxor and Karnak, the crumbling castles of the Rhine, the Roman Limes, Hersfeld and Paulinzella from becoming mere rubbish—but we keep them *as ruins*, feeling in some subtle way that reconstruction would deprive them of something, indefinable in terms, that can never be reproduced. Nothing was further from the Classical mind than this reverence for the weather-beaten evidences of a once and a formerly. It cleared out of sight everything that did not speak of the present; never was the old preserved because it was old. The heroic landscape of the Claude Lorrain type is inconceivable without ruins. The English park with its atmospheric suggestion, which supplanted the French about 1750 and abandoned the great perspective idea of the latter in favour of the "Nature" of Addison, Pope and sensibility, introduced into its stock of motives perhaps the most astonishing bizarrerie ever perpetrated, the *artificial ruin,* in order to deepen the historical character in the presented landscape.[8] Again, it is not the Classical statue, but the Classical *torso* that we really love. It has had a destiny: something suggestive of the past as past envelops it, and our imagination delights to fill the empty space of missing limbs with the pulse and swing of invisible lines. A good restoration—and the secret charm of endless possibilities is all gone. I venture to maintain that it is only by way of this *transposition into the musical* that the remains of Classical sculpture can really reach us. Would not the towers and domes of our old cities lose their deep metaphysical charm if they were sheathed in new copper? Age, for us as for the Egyptian, ennobles all things. For Classical man, it depreciates them.

---

[8] Home, an English philosopher of the eighteenth century, declared in a lecture on English parks that Gothic ruins represented the triumph of *time over power*, Classical ruins that of barbarism over taste. It was that age that first discovered the beauty of the ruin-studded Rhine, which was thenceforward the *historic* river of the Germans.

VII

MUSIC AND PLASTIC:
ACT[1] AND PORTRAIT

IF the environment of a man (whatever else it may be) is with respect to him a macrocosm with respect to a microcosm, an immense aggregate of symbols, then the man himself, insofar as he belongs to the fabric of actuality, insofar as he is *phenomenal,* must be comprised in the general symbolism. But, in the impress of him made upon men like himself, what is it that possesses the force of Symbol, viz., the capacity of summing within itself and intelligibly presenting the essence of that man and the signification of his being? Art gives the answer.

The Apollinian soul, Euclidean and confined to a point, felt the empirical visible body as the complete expression of its own way of being; the Faustian, wandering far away, found this expression not in *person, σῶμα,* but in *personality, character,* call it what you will. While Gluck expresses the woe of Armida by a melody combined with drear gnawing tones in the instrumental accompaniment, the same is achieved in Pergamene sculptures by making every muscle speak. The Hellenistic portraiture tries to draw a spiritual *type* in the structure of its heads. In China the heads of the Saints of Lin-yan-si tell of a *wholly personal* inner life by their look and the play of the corners of the mouth. What Apollinian man and Apollinian art can claim as their very own is simply the apotheosis of the bodily *phenomenon,* taking the word perfectly literally—the rhythmic proportioning of limbs

~~~~~~~~

[1] The word *Akt* means "pose" and, in art language, "nude." In this work it must be understood in a widened connotation—viz., as expressing the instantaneous-become as against the historically-becoming, the presentation in the perfect as against the imperfect sense, the act as against the action. It has therefore been retained, "nude" however being substituted in certain cases.—*At.*

and harmonious build of muscles. This is *not* Pagan as against Christian, it is Attic as against Baroque.

Thus the Classical plastic art, after liberating the form completely from the actual or imaginary back-wall and setting it up in the open, free and unrelated, to be seen as a body among bodies, moved on logically till the *naked* body became its only subject. And, moreover, it is unlike every other kind of sculpture recorded in art-history in that its treatment of the bounding surfaces of this body is *anatomically convincing*. Just as Classical man properly meant, with his perfected working out of *superficial* body, to exhaust the whole essence of the living phenomenon in and by the rendering of its bounding surfaces, so Faustian man no less logically found the most genuine, the only exhaustive, expression of his life-feeling in the *Portrait*. The Hellenic treatment of the nude is the great exceptional case; in this and in this only has it led to an art of the high order.[2]

Act and *Portrait* have never hitherto been felt as constituting an opposition and consequently the full significance of their appearances in art-history has never been appreciated. But in order to grasp the significance of the portraiture of the West more specifically in contrast with that of Egypt and that of China, we have to consider the deep change in the language of the West that began in Merovingian times to foreshadow the dawn of a new life-feeling. This change extended *equally* over the old German and the vulgar Latin, but it affected only the tongues spoken in the countries of the coming Culture (for instance, Norwegian and Spanish, but not Rumanian). The change would be inexplicable if we were to regard merely the spirit of these languages and their "influence" of one upon another; the explanation is in the spirit of the mankind that raised a mere way of using words to the level of a symbol. Instead of *sum*, Gothic *im*, we say *ich bin, I am, je suis;* instead of *fecisti*, we say *tu habes factum, tu as fait, du habes gitân;* and again, *daz wîp, un homme, man hat*. The coming of this specific "I" is the

---

[2] In other countries, e.g. Old Egypt and Japan (to anticipate a particularly foolish and shallow assertion), the sight of naked men was a far more ordinary and commonplace thing than it was in Athens, but the Japanese art-lover feels emphasized nudity as ridiculous and vulgar. The nude is depicted (as for that matter it is in the "Adam and Eve" of Bamberg Cathedral), but merely as an object without any significance of potential whatsoever.

first dawning of that personality-idea which was so much later to create the sacrament of Contrition and *personal* absolution. And this "I" and "Thou" is the key to Gothic portraiture.

It has been shown how the experience of the extended has its origin in the living *direction, time, destiny.* In the perfected "being" of the all-round nude body the depth-experience has been cut away, but the "look" of a portrait leads this experience into the supersensuous infinite. Therefore the Ancient art is an art of the near and tangible and timeless. The Classical statue is a piece of present "Nature" and nothing besides. The Classical poetry is statuary in verse. Herein is the root of our feeling that ascribes to the Greek an unreserved devotion to Nature. We shall never entirely shake off the idea that the Gothic style as compared with the Greek is "unnatural." Of course it is, for it is *more than Nature;* only we are unnecessarily loath to realize that it is a deficiency in the Greek that our feeling has detected. The Western form-language is richer—portraiture belongs to Nature *and* to history. Any monument by the Netherlands sculptors who worked on the Royal tombs of St. Denis from 1260, a portrait by Holbein or Titian or Rembrandt or Goya, is a *biography,* and a self-portrait is a historical *confession.* To make one's confession is not to avow an act but to lay before the Judge the inner history of that act. The whole of Northern poetry is one outspoken confession. So are the portrait of Rembrandt and the music of Beethoven. What Raphael and Calderon and Haydn told to the priests, these men put into the language of their works. Western man lives in the *consciousness* of his becoming and his eyes are constantly upon past and future. The Greek lives pointwise, ahistorically, somatically. No Greek would have been capable of a genuine self-criticism. As the phenomenon of the nude statue is the completely ahistoric copy of a man, so the Western self-portrait is the exact equivalent of the *Werther* or *Tasso* autobiography. To the Classical both are equally and wholly alien. There is nothing so impersonal as Greek art. Myron's Discobolus renders the exterior form purely as itself, without relation of any sort to the inner organs, let alone to any "soul." One has only to take the best work of this period and compare it with the old Egyptian statues, say the "Village Sheikh" [3] or King Phiops

───────

[3] A cast of this is in the British Museum.—*At.*

(Pepi), or again with Donatello's "David," [4] to understand at once what it means to recognize a body purely with reference to its material boundaries. Everything in a head that might allow something intimate or spiritual to become phenomenal the Greeks (and markedly this same Myron) most carefully avoid. Once this characteristic has struck us, the best heads of the great age sooner or later begin to pall. Seen in the perspective of our world-feeling, they are stupid and dull, wanting in the biographical element, devoid of any *destiny*. Right down to Lysippus there is not one single character-head, but only masks. Again, considering the figure as a whole, with what skill the Greeks avoid giving any impression that the head is the favoured part of the body! That is why these heads are so small, so un-significant in their pose, so un-thoroughly modelled. Always they are formed as a part of the body like arms and legs, never as the seat and symbol of an "I."

At last, even, we come to regard the feminine (not to say effeminate) look of many of these heads of the fifth, and still more of the fourth, century [5] as the—no doubt unintentional—outcome of an effort to get rid of personal character entirely.

The portraiture of the great age of Baroque, on the contrary, applies to historical distance all those means of pictorial counterpoint that we already know as the fabric of their spatial distance—the brown-dipped atmosphere, the perspective, the dynamic brush-stroke, the quivering colour-tones and lights— and with their aid succeeds in treating body as something intrinsically non-material, as the highly expressive envelope of a space-commanding ego. (This problem the fresco-technique, Euclidean that it is, is powerless to solve.) The whole painting has only one theme, a soul. Observe the rendering of the hands and the brow in Rembrandt (e.g. in the etching of Burgomaster Six or the portrait of an architect at Cassel), and again, even so late, in Marées and Leibl—spiritual to the point of dematerialization, visionary, lyrical. Compare them with the hand and brow of an Apollo or a Poseidon of the Periclean Age!

[4] In the Bargello, Florence. Replica in Victoria and Albert Museum, London.—*At.*

[5] The "Apollo with the lyre" at Munich was admired by Winckelmann and his time as a Muse. Till quite recently a head of Athene (a copy of Praxiteles) at Bologna passed as that of a general. Such errors would be entirely impossible in dealing with a physiognomic art, e.g. Baroque.

The Gothic, too, had deeply and sincerely felt this. It had draped body, not for its own sake but for the sake of developing in the ornament of the drapery a form-language consonant with the language of the head and the hands in a living fugue. So, too, with the relations of the voices in counterpoint and, in Baroque, those of the *continuo* to the upper voices of the orchestra. In Rembrandt there is always interplay of bass melody in the costume and motives in the head.

The opposition of Apollinian and Faustian ideals of Humanity may now be stated concisely. Act and Portrait are to one another as body and space, instant and history, foreground and background, Euclidean and analytical number, proportion and relation. The Statue is rooted in the ground, Music (and the Western portrait *is* music, soul woven of colour-tones) invades and pervades space without limit. The Apollinian form-language reveals only the become, the Faustian shows above all a becoming.

It is for this reason that child-portraits and family groups are amongst the finest and most intimately right achievements of Western art. The child links past and future. In every art of human representation that has a claim to symbolic import, it signifies duration in the midst of phenomenal change, the endlessness of life. But the Classical Life exhausted itself in the completeness of the moment. The individual shut his eyes to time-distances; he comprehended in his thought the men like himself whom he saw around him, but not the coming generations; and therefore there has never been an art that so emphatically ignored the intimate representation of children as the Greek art did.

Endless Becoming is comprehended in the idea of *Motherhood*, Woman as Mother *is* Time and *is* Destiny. All symbols of Time and Distance are also symbols of maternity. *Care* is the root-feeling of future, and all care is motherly.

In the religious art of the West, the representation of Motherhood is the noblest of all tasks. As Gothic dawns, the Theotokos of the Byzantine changes into the Mater Dolorosa, the Mother of God. In German mythology she appears (doubtless from Carolingian times only) as Frigga and Frau Holle. The same feeling comes out in beautiful Minnesinger fancies like Lady Sun, Lady World, Lady Love. The whole panorama of early Gothic mankind is pervaded by something maternal, something caring and patient, and Germanic-Catholic Christianity—when it had ripened into full consciousness of itself and in one impulse settled its sacraments and created its Gothic style—placed *not the suffering Redeemer but the suffering Mother* in the centre of its world-picture. About 1250, in the great epic of statuary of Reims Cathedral, the principal place in the centre of the main porch, which in the cathedrals of Paris and Amiens was still that of Christ, was assigned to the Madonna; and it was about this time, too, that the Tuscan school at Arezzo and Siena (Guido da Siena) began to infuse a suggestion of mother-love into the conventional Byzantine theotokos. And after that the Madonnas of Raphael led the way to the purely human type of the Baroque, the mother in the sweetheart—Ophelia, Gretchen—whose secret reveals itself in the glorious close of *Faust II* and in its fusion with the early Gothic Mary.

As against these types, the imagination of the Greeks conceived goddesses who are either Amazons like Athene or hetaerae like Aphrodite. In the root-feeling which produced the Classical type of womanhood, fruitfulness has a vegetal character—in this connexion as in others the word $\sigma\tilde{\omega}\mu\alpha$ exhaustively expresses the meaning of the phenomenon. Think of the masterpieces of this art, the three mighty female bodies of the East Pediment of the Parthenon,[6] and compare with them that noblest image of a mother, Raphael's Sistine Madonna. In the latter, all bodiliness has disappeared. She is all distance and space. The Helen of the *Iliad*, compared with Kriemhild, the motherly comrade of Siegfried, is a courtesan, while Antigone and Clytaemnestra are Amazons. When the Classical sculpture, *late* art that it is,[7] arrives at secularizing [8] the pictures of the god, it creates the antique ideal of female form in a Cnidian Aphrodite—merely a very beautiful object, not a character or an ego but a piece of Nature.

---

[6] The so-called "Three Fates" in the British Museum.—*At.*

[7] The Orphic springtime *contemplates* the Gods and does not *see* them.

[8] There was indeed a beginning of this in the aristocratic epic of Homer—so nearly akin to the courtly narrative art of Boccaccio. But throughout the Classical age strictly religious people felt it as a profanation; the worship that shines through the Homeric poems is quite without idolatry, and a further proof is the anger of thinkers who, like Heraclitus and Plato, were in close touch with the temple tradition. It will occur to the student that the unrestricted handling of even the highest divinities in this very late art is not unlike the theatrical Catholicism of Rossini and Liszt, which is already foreshadowed in Corelli and Handel and had, earlier even, almost led to the condemnation of Church music in 1564.

And in the end Praxiteles finds the hardihood to represent a goddess entirely naked. This innovation met with severe criticism, for it was felt to be a sign of the decline of the Classical world-feeling; suitable as it was to erotic symbolism, it was in sharp contradiction with the dignity of the older Greek religion.

HELLENISTIC PORTRAITURE

It was at this time that an art of portraiture appeared simultaneously with the invention of a form that has never since been forgotten, the *bust*. Unfortunately (here as elsewhere) art-research has made the mistake of discovering in this the "beginnings" of "the" portrait. This "portrait" is distinguishable not by personal traits but by the label only. This is the general custom amongst children and primitive men, and it is connected with name-magic. But now, in the later phase, there was an additional factor—the tendency of the time towards genre and applied art, which produced also the Corinthian column. What the sculptors worked out was the *types* of life's stage, the $\tilde{\eta}\theta o\varsigma$ which we mistranslate by "character" but which is really the kinds and modes of public behaviour and attitude; thus there is "the" grave Commander, "the" tragic poet, "the" passion-torn actor, "the" absorbed philosopher. Here is the real key to the understanding of the celebrated Hellenistic portraiture, for which the quite unjustifiable claim has been set up that its products are expressions of a deep spiritual life. It was only in the fourth century that Demetrius of Alopeke began to emphasize individual traits in the *external build* of the man and Lysistratus the brother of Lysippus to copy (as Pliny tells us) a plaster-of-paris cast of the subject's face without much subsequent modification. And how little such portraiture is portraiture in Rembrandt's sense should surely have been obvious to anyone. The *soul* is missing. The brilliant fidelity of Roman busts especially has been mistaken for physiognomic depth. But what really distinguishes the higher work from this craftsman's and virtuoso's work is that in such work the important and significant is not *brought out*, it is *put in*. An example of this is seen in the Demosthenes statue,[9] the artist of which possibly saw the orator in life. Here the particulars of the body-surface are em-

---

[9] In the Vatican Museum.—*At.*

phasized, perhaps over-emphasized ("true to Nature," they called this then), but upon a foundation so conceived he introduces the character-type of the Serious Orator which we meet again on different bases in the portraits of Aeschines and Lysias at Naples.

BAROQUE PORTRAITURE

In the oil-painting age that followed the end of the Renaissance, the depth of an artist can be accurately measured by the content of his portraits. To this rule there is hardly an exception. All forms in the picture (whether single, or in scenes, groups or masses) [1] are fundamentally felt as portraits; whether they are meant to be so or not is immaterial, for the individual painter has no choice in the matter. Nothing is more instructive than to observe how under the hands of a Faustian artist even the Act transforms itself into a portrait-study. A Faustian nude is a contradiction in itself—hence the character-heads that we so often see on feeble representations of the nude (as far back as the Job of old French cathedral-sculpture) and hence also the laborious, forced, equivocal character that arouses our dislike in too manifest efforts to placate the Classical ideal—sacrifices offered up not by the soul but by the cultivated understanding. In the whole of painting after Leonardo there is not one important or distinctive work that derives its meaning from the Euclidean being of the nude body. It is mere incomprehension to quote Rubens here, and to compare his unbridled dynamism of swelling bodies in any respect whatever with the art of Praxiteles and even Scopas. It is owing precisely to his splendid sensuality that he is so far from the *static* of Signorelli's bodies. If there ever was an artist who could put a maximum of "becoming" into the beauty of naked bodies, who could treat bodily floridness *historically* and convey the (utterly un-Hellenic) idea of an inexhaustible outflowing from within, it was Rubens. In Rubens (recalling once more the characteristic opposition of Apollinian and Faustian mathematics) the body is not magnitude but relation. What matters is the fullness of life that streams

------

[1] Even the landscape of the Baroque develops from composed backgrounds to portraits of definite localities, representations of the soul of these localities which are thus endowed with *faces*.

out of it and the stride of its life along the road from youth to age, where the Last Judgment that turns bodies into flames takes up the motive and intertwines it in the quivering web of active space. Such a synthesis is entirely un-Classical; but even nymphs, when it is Corot who paints them, are likewise shapes ready to dissolve into colour-patches reflecting endless space. Such was *not* the intention of the Classical artist when he depicted the nude.

At the same time, the Greek form-ideal—the self-contained unit of being expressed in sculpture—has equally to be distinguished from that of the merely beautiful bodies on which painters from Giorgione to Boucher were always exercising their cleverness, which are fleshly still-life, genre-work expressing merely a certain gay sensuousness (e.g. "Rubens's Wife in a Fur Cloak" [2]) and in contrast with the high ethical significance of the Classical Act have almost no symbolic force.[3] The episode of Florence amounts to an attempt to replace the Portrait of the Gothic style by the Act as a symbol of humanity. Logically, therefore, the entire art of the Renaissance should be wanting in the physiognomic traits, but the whole of the portrait-work of A. Rossellino, Donatello, Benedetto de Maiano, Mino da Fiesole, stands so near in spirit to that of Van Eyck, Memling and the early Rhenish masters as to be often indistinguishable from theirs. In architecture, little as the new work was Apollinian in spirit, it was possible to create anti-Gothically, but in portraiture —no. It was too specifically Faustian a symbol. However highly we may value the Uzzano bust of Donatello—which is perhaps the most important achievement of that age and that circle—it will be admitted that by the side of the portraits of the Venetians it hardly counts.

LEONARDO, RAPHAEL AND MICHELANGELO—
AS VANQUISHERS OF THE RENAISSANCE

The Renaissance was born of defiance. In Gothic, and again in Baroque, an entirely great artist was fulfilling his art in deepen-

---

[2] Art Gallery, Vienna.—*At.*

[3] Nothing more clearly displays the decadence of Western art since the middle of the nineteenth century than its absurd mass-wise rendering of nudes; the deeper meaning of study of the nude and the importance of the motive have been entirely forgotten.

ing and completing its language, but in Renaissance he was necessarily only destroying it.

So it was in the cases of Leonardo, Raphael and Michelangelo, the only really great men of Italy after Dante. Is it not curious that between the masters of the Gothic—who were nothing but silent workers in their art and yet achieved the very highest that could be achieved within its convention and its field—and the Venetians and Dutch of 1600—who again were purely workers—there should be these three men who were not only "sculptors" or "painters" but *thinkers,* and thinkers who of necessity busied themselves not merely with all the available means of artistic expression but with a thousand other things besides, ever restless and dissatisfied, in their effort to get at the real essence and aim of their being? Does it not mean—that in the Renaissance they could not "find themselves"? Each in his own fashion, each under his own tragic illusion, these three giants strove to be "Classical" in the Medicean sense; and yet it was they themselves who in one and another way—Raphael in respect of the line, Leonardo in respect of the surface, Michelangelo in respect of the body—shattered the dream. In them the misguided soul is finding its way back to its Faustian starting-points. What they *intended* was to substitute proportion for relation, drawing for light-and-air effect, Euclidean body for pure space. But neither they nor others of their time produced a Euclidean-static sculpture—for that was possible once only, in Athens. In all their work one feels a secret music, in all their forms the movement-quality and the bias towards distance and depth. They are on the way, not to Phidias but to Palestrina, and they have come thither not from Roman ruins but from the still music of the cathedral. The majestic spirit of the Counter Reformation, massive, animated, gorgeous, lives already in Michelangelo. The question of form was for him a religious matter; for him (and only for him) it was all or nothing. And this is the explanation of the lonely fearful wrestlings of this man, surely the unhappiest figure in our art; of the fragmentary, the tortured, the unsatisfied, the *terrible* in his forms that frightened his contemporaries.

His was the last effort, repeated again and again, to put the entirety of the artist-personality into the language of marble. But the Euclidean material failed him. For Phidias, marble is the cosmic stuff that is crying for form. The story of Pygmalion and Galatea expresses the very essence of that art. But for Michelangelo marble was the foe to be subdued, the prison out of which he must deliver his idea as Siegfried delivered Brunhilde. Everyone knows his way of setting to work. He did not approach the rough block coolly from every aspect of the intended form, but attacked it with a passionate frontal attack, hewing into it as though into space, cutting away the material layer by layer and driving deeper and deeper until his form emerged, while the members slowly developed themselves out of the quarry. Never perhaps has there been a more open expression of world-dread in the presence of the become—Death—of the will to overpower and capture it in vibrant form. There is no other artist of the West whose relation to the stone has been that of Michelangelo—at once so intimate and so violently masterful. It is his symbol of Death. In it dwells the hostile principle that his daemonic nature is always striving to overpower, whether he is cutting statues or piling great buildings out of it. He produced acts—a sacrifice to the Hellenic idol—but the soul in them denies or overmasters the visible form. The Classical eye absorbs plastic form into itself, but Michelangelo saw with the spiritual eye and broke through the foreground-language of immediate sensuousness. And inevitably, in the long run, he destroyed the conditions for this art. Marble became too trivial for his will-to-form. He ceased to be sculptor and turned architect. In his old age, when he was producing only wild fragments like the Rondanini Madonna and leaving his figures almost in the rough, the *musical* tendency of his artistry broke through. In the end the impulse towards contrapuntal form was no longer to be repressed and, dissatisfied through and through with the art upon which he had spent his life, yet dominated still by the unquenchable will to self-expression, he shattered the canon of Renaissance architecture and created the Roman Baroque. For relations of material and form he substituted the contest of force and mass. He grouped the columns in sheaves or else pushed them away into niches. He broke up the stories with huge pilasters and gave the façade a sort of surging and thrusting quality. Measure yielded to melody, the static to the dynamic. And thus Faustian music enlisted in its service the chief of all the other arts.

With Michelangelo the history of Western sculpture is at an end. What of it there was after him was mere misunderstanding or reminiscence. His real heir was *Palestrina*.

Leonardo does not speak the language of his contemporaries. He alone had neither the ambition to be sculptor nor the ambition to be architect. It was a strange illusion of the Renaissance that the Hellenic feeling and the Hellenic cult of the exterior structure be achieved through anatomy. But when Leonardo studied anatomy it was not, as in Michelangelo's case, foreground anatomy, the *topography* of human surfaces, studied for the sake of plastic, but *physiology* studied for the inward secrets. While Michelangelo tried to force the whole meaning of human existence into the language of the living body. Leonardo's studies show the exact opposite. His much-admired *sfumato* is the first sign of the repudiation of corporeal bounds, in the name of *space,* and as such it is the starting-point of Impressionism. Leonardo begins with the spiritual space, not with defined outlines, and when he ends (that is, if he ends at all and does not leave the picture unfinished), the substance of colour lies like a mere tinge over the real structure of the picture, which is something incorporeal and indescribable. Raphael's paintings fall into planes in which he disposes his well-ordered groups, and he closes off the whole with a well-proportioned background. But Leonardo knows only one space, wide and eternal, and his figures, as it were, float therein. The one puts inside a frame a sum of individual near things, the other a portion cut out of the infinite.

Leonardo discovered the circulation of the blood. It was no Renaissance spirit that brought him to that—on the contrary, the whole course of his thought took him right outside the conceptions of his age. Neither Michelangelo nor Raphael could have done it, for their painter's anatomy regarded only the form and position, not the function, of the parts. But Leonardo investigated the *life* in the body as Rubens did, and not the body-in-itself like Signorelli. The Baroque is truly the *period of the great discoveries*.

Leonardo was a discoverer through and through, and discovery was the sum in one word of his whole nature. He was the first, too, who set his mind to work on aviation. To fly, to free oneself from earth, to lose oneself in the expanse of the universe—is not this ambition Faustian in the highest degree? Is it not in fact the fulfilment of our dreams? Has it never been observed how the Christian legend became in Western painting a glorious transfiguration of this motive? All the pictured ascents into heaven and falls into hell, the divine figures floating above the clouds, the blissful detachment of angels and saints, the insistent emphasis upon freedom from earth's heaviness, are emblems of soul-flight, peculiar to the art of the Faustian, utterly remote from that of the Byzantine.

The transformation of Renaissance fresco-painting into Venetian oil-painting is a matter of *spiritual history*. We have to appreciate very delicate and subtle traits to discern the process of change. In almost every picture from Masaccio's "Peter and the Tribute Money" in the Brancacci Chapel, through the soaring background that Piero della Francesca gave to the figures of Federigo and Battista of Urbino, to Perugino's "Christ Giving the Keys," the fresco manner is contending with the invasive new form. It was, as always, the struggle between hand and soul, between eye and instrument, between the form willed by the artist and the form willed by time—the struggle between Plastic and Music.

In the light of this, we can at last understand that gigantic effort of Leonardo, the cartoon of the "Adoration of the Magi" in the Uffizi. It is the most daring painting of the Renaissance. Nothing like it was even imagined till Rembrandt. Transcending all optical measures, everything then called drawing, outline, composition and grouping, he pushes fearlessly on to challenge eternal space; everything bodily floats like the planets in the Copernican system and the tones of a Bach organ-fugue in the dimness of old churches. In the technical possibilities of the time, so dynamic an image of distance could only remain a torso.

In the Sistine Madonna, which is the very summation of the Renaissance, Raphael causes the outline to draw into itself the entire content of the work. It is the *last grand line* of Western art. Already (and it is this that makes Raphael the least intelligible of Renaissance artists) convention is strained almost to breaking-point by the intensity of inward feeling. He did not indeed wrestle with problems. He had not even an inkling of them. But he brought art to the brink where it could no longer shirk the plunge, and he lived to achieve the utmost possibilities *within* its form-world. The ordinary person who thinks him flat simply fails to realize *what is going on* in his scheme. We do understand Perugino at a glance, we merely think we understand Raphael. His very line—that drawing-character that at first sight seems so Classical—is something that floats in space, unearthly, Beethoven-like. In this work Raphael is the least obvious of all artists, much less obvious even than Michelangelo, whose intention is manifest through all the fragmentariness of his works.

Leonardo *is* over the frontier. The sketch for "Adoration of the Magi" *is* already music. It is not a casual but a deeply significant circumstance that in this work, as also in his "St. Jerome," he did not go beyond the brown underpainting, the "Rembrandt" stage, the atmospheric brown of the following century. For him, entire fullness and clearness of intention was attained with the work in that state, and one step into the domain of colour (for that domain was still under the metaphysical limitations of the fresco style) would have destroyed the soul of what he had created. It was reserved for the Venetians, who stood outside the Florentine convention, to achieve what he strove for here, to fashion a colour-world subserving space instead of things.

The men of this time were not ripe for portraiture as Rembrandt understood the word, the building up of a soul-history out of dynamic brush-strokes and lights and tones. But only Leonardo was great enough to experience this limitation as a Destiny. Others merely set themselves to paint heads (in the modes prescribed by their respective schools) but Leonardo—the first, here, to make the *hands* also speak, and that with a physiognomic *maestria*—had an infinitely wider purpose. His soul was lost afar in the future, though his mortal part, his eye and hand, obeyed the spirit of the age. Assuredly he was the freest of the three great ones. Deeper than Dürer, bolder than Titian, more comprehensive than any single man of his time, he was essentially the *artist of torsos*.[4] Michelangelo the belated sculptor was so, too, but in another sense, while in Goethe's day that which had been unattainable for the painter of "The Last Supper" had already been reached and overpassed. Michelangelo strove to force life once more into a dead form-world, Leonardo felt a new form-world in the future, Goethe divined that there could be

---

[4] In Renaissance work the finished product is often quite depressingly complete. The absence of "infinity" is palpable. No secrets, no discoveries.

no more new form-worlds. Between the first and the last of these men lie the ripe centuries of the Faustian Culture.

THE VICTORY OF INSTRUMENTAL MUSIC IN 1670 AND A CLASSICAL PARALLEL

It remains now to deal with the major characters of Western art during the phase of accomplishment. In this the inexorable progress of Necessity is apparent. We have learned to understand arts as prime phenomena. We no longer look to the operations of cause and effect to give unity to the story of development. Instead, we have set up the idea of the *Destiny* of an art, and admitted arts to be *organisms* of the Culture, organisms which are born, ripen, age and *forever* die.

As a "late" period, the Baroque knows, just as the Ionic had known, what the form-language of its arts has to mean. From being a philosophical religion, art has to be a religious philosophy. Great masters come forward in the place of anonymous schools. At the culmination of every Culture we have the spectacle of a splendid *group of great arts,* well ordered and linked as a unit by the unity of the prime symbol underlying them all. The *Apollinian group,* to which belong vase-painting, fresco relief, the architecture of ranked columns, the Attic drama and the dance, centres upon the naked statue. The *Faustian group* forms itself round the ideal of pure spatial infinity and its centre of gravity is instrumental music. The nearer the grand style comes to its point of fulfilment, the more decisive the tendency to an ornamental language of inexorable clarity of symbolism. The group of great arts is further simplified. About 1670, just when Newton and Leibniz were discovering the Differential Calculus, oil-painting had reached the limits of its possibilities. Its last great masters were dead or dying—Velásquez, 1660; Poussin, 1665; Frans Hals, 1666; Rembrandt, 1669; Vermeer, 1675; Murillo, Ruysdael and Claude Lorrain, 1682—and one has only to name the few successors of any importance (Watteau, Hogarth, Tiepolo) to feel at once the descent, the end, of an art. In this time also, the great forms of *pictorial* music expired. Heinrich Schütz died in 1672, Carissimi in 1674, and Purcell in 1695—the last great masters of the Cantata, who had played around image-themes with infinite variety of vocal and instrumental colour and had painted veritable pictures of fine landscape and grand legend-scene. With Lully (1687) the heart of the heroic Baroque opera of Monteverde ceased to beat. It was the same with the old "classical" sonata for orchestra, organ and string trio, which was a development of image-themes in the fugal style. Thereafter, the forms become those of final maturity, the *concerto grosso,* the suite and the three-part sonata for solo instruments. Music frees itself from the relics of bodiliness inherent in the human voice and becomes absolute. The theme is no longer an image but a pregnant *function,* existent only in and by its own evolution, for the fugal style as Bach practised it can only be regarded as a ceaseless process of differentiation and integration. The victory of pure music over painting stands recorded in the Passions which Heinrich Schütz composed in his old age—the visible dawn of the new form-language—in the sonatas of Dall'Abaco and Corelli, the oratorios of Handel and the Baroque polyphony of Bach. Henceforth this music is *the* Faustian art, and Watteau may fairly be described as a painter-Couperin, Tiepolo as a painter-Handel.

In the Classical world the corresponding change occurred about 460, when Polygnotus, the last of the great fresco-painters, ceded the inheritance of the grand style to Polycletus and to sculpture in the round. Till then—as late even as Polygnotus' contemporaries Myron and the masters of the Olympia pediment —the form-language of a purely planar art had dominated that of statuary also; for, just as painting had developed its form more and more towards the ideal of the *silhouette of colour with internal drawing superposed*—to such an extent that at last there was almost no difference between the painted relief and the flat picture—so also the sculptor had regarded the frontal *outline* as it presented itself to the beholder as the true symbol of the Ethos, the cultural type, that he meant his figure to represent. The field of the temple-pediment constitutes a *picture;* seen from the proper distance, it makes exactly the same impression as its contemporary the red-figure vase-painting. In Polycletus' generation the monumental wall-painting gives place to the board-picture, the "picture" proper, in tempera or wax—a clear indication that the great style has gone to reside elsewhere. The ambition of Apollodorus' shadow-painting was not in any sense what we call chiaroscuro and atmosphere, but sheer *modelling in the round* in the sculptor's sense; and of Zeuxis, Aristotle says expressly that his work lacked "Ethos." Thus, this newer Classical painting with its cleverness and human charm is the equivalent of our eighteenth-century work. Both lacked inner greatness, and both tried by force of virtuosity to speak in the language of that single and final Art which in each case stood for ornamentation in the higher sense. Hence Polycletus and Phidias aline themselves with Bach and Handel; as the Western masters liberated strict musical form from the executive methods of the Painting, so the Greek masters finally delivered the statue from the associations of the Relief.

And with plastic and music at this stage of development the two Cultures reach their respective ends. A pure symbolism of mathematical rigour had become possible. Polycletus could produce his "canon" of the proportions of the human body, and his contemporary Bach the *Kunst der Fuge* and *Wohltemperiertes Klavier*. In the two arts that ensued, we have the last perfection of achievement that pure form saturated with meaning can give. The mathematics of beauty and the beauty of mathematics are henceforth inseparable. The unending space of tone and the all-round body of marble or bronze are *immediate* interpretations of the extended. They belong to number-as-relation and to number-as-measure. In fresco and in oil-painting, in the laws of proportion and those of perspective, the mathematical is only indicated, but the two final arts *are* mathematics, and on these peaks Apollinian art and Faustian art are seen entire.

With the exit of fresco and oil-painting, the great masters of absolute plastic and absolute music file on to the stage, man after man. Polycletus is followed by Phidias, Paeonius, Alcamenes, Scopas, Praxiteles, Lysippus. Behind Bach and Handel come Gluck, Stamitz, the younger Bachs, Haydn, Mozart, Beethoven—in their hands an armoury of wonderful and now long-forgotten instruments, a whole magician's world created by the discovering and inventing spirit of the West in the hope of getting more and more tones and timbres for the service and enhancement of musical expression—visualizing an abundance of grand, solemn, ornate, dainty, ironic, laughing and sobbing forms of perfectly regular structure, forms that no one now understands. In those days, in eighteenth-century Germany especially, there was actually and effectively a *Culture of Music* that suffused all Life. Its type was Hoffmann's Kapellmeister Kreisler. Today it is hardly even a memory.

And with the eighteenth century, too, architecture died at last, submerged and choked in the music of Rococo. On that last wonderful fragile growth of Western architecture criticism has blown mercilessly, failing to realize that its origin is in the spirit of the fugue and that its non-proportion and non-form, its evanescence and instability and sparkle, its destruction of surface and visual order, are nothing else than a victory of tones and melodies over lines and walls, the triumph of pure space over material, of absolute becoming over the become. They are no longer buildings, these abbeys and castles and churches with their flowing façades and porches and "gingerbread" courts and their splendid staircases, galleries, salons and cabinets; they are sonatas, minuets, madrigals in stone, chamber-music in stucco, marble, ivory and fine woods, cantilene of volutes and cartouches, cadences of fliers and copings. The Dresden Zwinger is the most completely musical piece in all the world's architecture, with an ornamentation like the tone of an old violin, an *allegro fugitivo* for small orchestra.

IMPRESSIONISM

"Impressionism," which only came into general use in Manet's time (and then, originally, as a word of contempt like Baroque and Rococo), very happily summarizes the special quality of the Faustian way of art that has evolved from oil-painting. Impressionism is the inverse of the Euclidean world-feeling. It tries to get as far as possible from the language of plastic and as near as possible to that of music. The effect that is made upon us by things that receive and reflect light is made not because the things *are* there, but as though they "in themselves" *are not* there. The things are not even bodies, but light-resistances in space, and their illusive density is to be unmasked by the brush-stroke. What is received and rendered is the *impression* of such resistances, which are tacitly evaluated as simple functions of a transcendent extension. The artist's inner eye penetrates the body, breaks the spell of its material bounding surfaces and sacrifices it to the majesty of Space. And with this impression, under its influence, he feels an endless *movement-quality* in the sensuous element that is in utter contrast to the statuesque "Ataraxia" of the fresco. Therefore, there was not and could not be any Hellenic impressionism; if there is one art that *must* exclude it on principle, it is Classical sculpture.

Impressionism is the comprehensive expression of a world-feeling, and it must obviously therefore permeate the whole physiognomy of our "Late" Culture. There is an impressionistic mathematic, which frankly and with intent transcends all optical limitations. It is Analysis, as developed after Newton and Leibniz, and to it belong the visionary images of number-"bodies," aggregates, and the multi-dimensional geometry. There is again an impressionistic physics which "sees" in lieu of bodies systems of mass-points—units that are evidently no more than constant relations between variable efficients. There are impressionistic ethics, tragedy and logic, and even (in Pietism) an impressionistic Christianity.

Be the artist painter or musician, his art consists in creating with a few strokes or spots or tones an image of inexhaustible content, a microcosm meet for the eyes or ears of Faustian man; that is, in laying the actuality of infinite space under enchantment by fleeting and incorporeal indications of something objective which, so to say, forces that actuality to become phenomenal. The daring of these arts of moving the immobile has no parallel. Right from the later work of Titian to Corot and Menzel, matter quivers and flows like a solution under the mysterious pressure of brush-stroke and broken colours and lights. It was in pursuit of the same object that Baroque music became "thematic" instead of melodic and—reinforcing the "theme" with every expedient of harmonic charm, instrumental colour, rhythm and tempo—developed the tone-picture from the imitative piece of Titian's day to the leitmotiv-fabric of Wagner, and captured a whole new world of feeling and experience. When German music was at its culmination, this art penetrated also into lyric poetry. On a small scale, it continually repeats the achievements of Copernicus and Columbus. No other Culture possesses an ornament-language of such dynamical impressiveness relatively to the means it employs. Every point or stroke of colour, every scarcely audible tone, releases some surprising charm and continually feeds the imagination with fresh elements of space-creating energy.

Is Impressionism (in the current narrow sense) a creation of the nineteenth century? Has painting lived, after all, two centuries more? Is it still existing? But we must not be deceived in the character of the new *episode*, that in the nineteenth century (i.e. beyond the 1800 frontier and in "Civilization") succeeded in awakening some illusion of a great culture of painting, choosing the word *Plein-air* (*Freilicht*) to designate its special characteristic. The materialism of a Western cosmopolis blew into the ashes and rekindled this curious brief flicker—a brief flicker of two generations, for with the generation of Manet all was ended again. I have characterized the noble green of Grünewald and Claude and Giorgione as the Catholic space-colour and the transcendent brown of Rembrandt as the colour of the Protestant world-feeling. On the other hand, *Plein-air* and its new colour scale stand for irreligion.[5] From the spheres of Beethoven and the stellar expanses of Kant, Impressionism has come down again to the crust of the earth. Its space is cognized, not experienced, seen, not contemplated; there is tunedness in it, but not Destiny. Rousseau's tragically correct prophecy of a "return to Nature" fulfils itself in this dying art—the senile, too, return to Nature day by day. The modern artist is a workman, not a creator. He sets unbroken spectrum-colours side by side. The subtle script, the dance of brush-strokes, give way to crude commonplaces, pilings and mixings and daubings of points, squares, broad inorganic masses. The whitewasher's brush and the trowel appear in the painter's equipment; the oil-priming of the canvas is brought into the scheme of execution and in places left bare. It is a risky art, meticulous, cold, diseased—an art for overdeveloped nerves, but scientific to the last degree, energetic in everything that relates to the conquest of technical obstacles, acutely assertive of programme. It is the "satyric pendant" of the great age of oil-painting that stretches from Leonardo to Rembrandt; it could be at home only in the Paris of Baudelaire. Corot's silvern landscapes, with their grey-greens and browns, dream still of the spiritual of the Old Masters; but Courbet and Manet conquer bare physical space, "factual" space. The meditative discoverer represented by Leonardo gives way to the paint-

~~~~~~~

[5] Hence the impossibility of achieving a genuinely religious painting on *plein-air* principles. The world-feeling that underlies it is so thoroughly irreligious, so worthless for any but a "religion of reason" so called, that every one of its efforts in that direction, even with the noblest intentions (Uhde, Puvis de Chavannes), strikes us as hollow and false. One instant of *plein-air* treatment suffices to secularize the interior of a church and degrade it into a showroom.

ing experimentalist. Corot, the eternal child, French but not Parisian, finds his transcendent landscapes anywhere and everywhere; Courbet, Manet, Cézanne, portray over and over again, painfully, laboriously, soullessly, the Forest of Fontainebleau, the bank of the Seine at Argenteuil, or that remarkable valley near Arles. Rembrandt's mighty landscapes lie essentially in the universe, Manet's near a railway station.

In Germany it was otherwise. After Beethoven, music, without change of inward essence, was diverted (one of the modalities of the German Romantic movement) back into painting. And it was in painting that it flowered longest and bore its kindliest fruits, for the portraits and landscapes are suffused with a secret wistful music, and there is a breath of Eichendorff and Mörike left even in Thoma and Böcklin.

The studio-brown of the seventeenth century had had by its side a second art, the intensely Faustian art of etching. In this, as in the other, Rembrandt is the greatest master of all time; this, like the other, has something Protestant in it that puts it in a quite different category from the work of the Southern Catholic painters of blue-green atmospheres and the Gobelin tapestries. And Leibl, the last artist in the brown, was the last great etcher whose plates possess that Rembrandtesque infinity that contains and reveals secrets without end. In Marées, lastly, there was all the mighty intention of the great Baroque style, but, though Géricault and Daumier were not too belated to capture it in positive form, he—lacking just that strength that a tradition would have given him—was unable to force it into the world of painter's actuality.

PERGAMUM AND BAYREUTH: THE END OF ART

The last of the Faustian arts died in *Tristan*. This work is the giant keystone of Western music. Painting achieved nothing like this as a finale.

"Contemporaneously," Apollinian art came to its end in Pergamene sculpture. *Pergamum is the counterpart of Bayreuth.* The famous altar itself,[6] indeed, is later, and probably not the most important work of the epoch at that; we have to assume a cen-

---

[6] State Museum, Berlin.—*At.*

tury (330–220 B.C.) of development now lost in oblivion. Nevertheless, all Nietzsche's charges against Wagner and Bayreuth, *The Ring* and *Parsifal*—decadence, theatricalness and the like—could have been levelled in the same words at the Pergamene sculpture. A masterpiece of this sculpture—a veritable *Ring*—has come down to us in the Gigantomachia frieze of the great altar. Here is the same theatrical note, the same use of motives from ancient discredited mythology, the same ruthless bombardment of the nerves, and also (though the lack of inner power cannot altogether be concealed) the same fully self-conscious force and towering greatness. To this art the Farnese Bull and the older model of the Laocoön group certainly belong.

The symptom of decline in creative power is the fact that to produce something round and complete the artist now requires to be emancipated from form and proportion. Its most obvious, though not its most significant, manifestation is the taste for the gigantic. Here size is not, as in the Gothic and the Pyramid styles, the expression of inward greatness, but the dissimulation of its absence. This swaggering in *specious* dimensions is common to all nascent Civilizations—we find it in the Zeus altar of Pergamum, the Helios of Chares called the "Colossus of Rhodes," the architecture of the Roman Imperial Age, the New Empire work in Egypt, the American skyscraper of today. But what is far more indicative is the arbitrariness and immoderateness that tramples on and shatters the conventions of centuries. In the time of Rembrandt or Bach the ambitious "failures" that we know only too well were quite unthinkable. The Destiny of the form lay in the race or the school, not in the private tendencies of the individual. Under the spell of a great tradition full achievement is possible even to a minor artist, because the living art brings him in touch with his task and the task with him. Today, these artists can no longer perform what they intend, for intellectual operations are a poor substitute for the trained instinct that has died out. All of them have experienced this. Manet was exhausted after he had painted thirty pictures, and his "Shooting of the Emperor Maximilian," in spite of the immense care that is visible in every item of the picture and the studies for it, hardly achieved as much as Goya managed without effort in its prototype the "shootings of the 3rd of May." Bach, Haydn, Mozart and a thousand obscure musicians of the eighteenth century could rapidly turn out the most finished work as a matter of routine, but Wagner knew full well that he could only reach the heights by concentrating all his energy upon "getting the last ounce" out of the best moments of his artistic endowment.

Between Wagner and Manet there is a deep relationship, which is not, indeed, obvious to everyone but which Baudelaire with his unerring flair for the decadent detected at once. For the Impressionists, the end and the culmination of art was the conjuring up of a world in space out of strokes and patches of colour, and this was just what Wagner achieved with three bars. A whole world of soul could crowd into these three bars. Colours of starry midnight, of sweeping clouds, of autumn, of the day dawning in fear and sorrow, sudden glimpses of sunlit distances, world-fear, impending doom, despair and its fierce effort, hopeless hope—all these impressions which no composer before him had thought it possible to catch, he could paint with entire distinctness in the few tones of a motive. Here the contrast of Western music with Greek plastic has reached its maximum. Everything merges in bodiless infinity, no longer even does a linear melody wrestle itself clear of the vague tone-masses that in strange surgings challenge an imaginary space. The motive comes up out of dark terrible deeps. It is flooded for an instant by a flash of hard bright sun. Then, suddenly, it is so close upon us that we shrink. It laughs, it coaxes, it threatens, and anon it vanishes into the domain of the strings, only to return again out of endless distances, faintly modified and in the voice of a single oboe, to pour out a fresh cornucopia of spiritual colours.

All that Nietzsche says of Wagner is applicable, also, to Manet. Ostensibly a return to the elemental, to Nature, as against contemplation-painting (*Inhaltsmalerei*) and abstract music, their art really signifies a concession to the barbarism of the Megalopolis, the beginning of dissolution sensibly manifested in a mixture of brutality and refinement. As a step, it is necessarily the last step. An artificial art has no further organic future, it is the mark of the end.

And the bitter conclusion is that it is all irretrievably over with the arts of form of the West. The crisis of the nineteenth century was the death-struggle. Like the Apollinian, the Egyptian and every other, the Faustian art dies of senility, having actualized its inward possibilities and fulfilled its mission within the course of its Culture.

What is practised as art today—be it music after Wagner or

painting after Manet, Cézanne, Leibl and Menzel—is impotence and falsehood. One thing is quite certain, that today every single art-school could be shut down without art being affected in the slightest. We can learn all we wish to know about the art-clamour which a megalopolis sets up in order to forget that its art is dead from the Alexandria of the year 200. There, as here in our world-cities, we find a pursuit of illusions of artistic progress, of personal peculiarity, of "the new style," of "unsuspected possibilities," theoretical babble, pretentious fashionable artists, weight-lifters with cardboard dumb-bells—the "Literary Man" in the Poet's place, the unabashed farce of Expressionism, which the art-trade has organized as a "phase of art-history," thinking and feeling and forming as industrial art. Alexandria, too, had problem-dramatists and box-office artists whom it preferred to Sophocles, and painters who invented new tendencies and successfully bluffed their public. The final result is that endless industrious repetition of a stock of fixed forms which we see today in Indian, Chinese and Arabian-Persian art. Pictures and fabrics, verses and vessels, furniture, dramas and musical compositions—all is pattern-work. We cease to be able to date anything within centuries, let alone decades, by the language of its ornamentation. So it has been in the Last Act of all Cultures.

VIII

SOUL-IMAGE AND
LIFE-FEELING:
ON THE FORM OF THE SOUL

THE SOUL-IMAGE, A FUNCTION OF THE WORLD-IMAGE

WHAT is not the world around us we do not see, but we do divine
"its" presence in ourselves and in others, and by virtue of "its"
physiognomic impressive power it evokes in us the anxiety and
the desire to know; and thus arises the meditated or pondered
image of a counterworld which is our mode of visualizing that
which remains eternally alien to the physical eye. The image of
the soul is mythic and remains objective in the field of spiritual
religion so long as the image of Nature is contemplated in the
spirit of religion; and it transforms itself into a scientific notion
and becomes objective in the field of scientific criticism as soon
as "Nature" comes to be observed critically. As "Time" is a counter-concept to space, so the "soul" is a counterworld to "Nature"
and therefore variable in dependence upon the notion of Nature
as this stands from moment to moment. *Every psychology is a
counter-physics.*

I maintain, then, that scientific psychology has, in its inability
to discover or even to approach the essence of the soul, simply
added one more to the symbols that collectively make up the Macrocosm of the culture-man. Like everything else that is no longer
becoming but become, it has put a *mechanism* in place of an *organism.*

This *imaginary soul-body* (let it be called so outright for the
first time) is never anything but the exact mirror-image of the
form in which the matured culture-man looks on his outer world.
In the one as in the other, the depth-experience actualizes the
extension-world. Alike out of the perception of the outside and
the conception of the inside, the secret that is hinted at in the

root-word "Time" creates Space. The soul-image like the world-image has its directional depth, its horizon, and its boundedness or its unboundedness.

This being so, everything that has been said in this work regarding the phenomenon of the high Cultures combines to demand an immensely wider and richer sort of soul-study than anything worked upon so far. For everything that our present-day psychologist has to tell us—and here we refer not only to systematic science but also in the wider sense to the physiognomic knowledge of men—relates to the *present* condition of the *Western* soul, and not, as hitherto gratuitously assumed, to "the human soul" at large.

A soul-image is never anything but the image of one quite definite soul.

In reality, every Culture possesses its own systematic psychology just as it possesses its own style of knowledge of men and experience of life; and just as even each separate stage—the age of Scholasticism, that of the Sophists, that of Enlightenment—forms special ideas of number and thought and Nature that pertain to itself only, so even each separate century mirrors itself in a soul-image of its own.

THE GOTHIC WILL

The separation of its ultimate elements is a task that the Gothic world-outlook and its philosophy leaves to the courage of the future. Just as the ornamentation of the cathedral and the primitive contemporary painting still shirk the decision between gold and wide atmosphere in backgrounds, so this early, timid, immature soul-image as it presents itself in this philosophy mingles characters derived from the Christian-Arabian metaphysic and its dualism of Spirit and Soul with Northern inklings of functional soul-forces not yet avowed. This is the discrepancy that underlies the conflict concerning the primacy of will or reason, the *basic problem of the Gothic philosophy,* which men tried to solve now in the old Arabian, now in the new Western sense.

Will and thought in the soul-image correspond to Direction and Extension, History and Nature, Destiny and Causality in the image of the outer world. The direction-feeling as "Will" and the space-feeling as "Reason" are imagined as entities, almost as legend-figures; and out of them comes the picture that our psychologists of necessity abstract from the inner life.

To call the Faustian Culture a *Will-Culture* is only another way of expressing the eminently historical disposition of its soul. Our first-person idiom, our *"ego habeo factum"*—our dynamic syntax, that is—faithfully renders the "way of doing things" that results from this disposition and, with its positive directional energy, dominates not only our picture of the World-as-History but our own history to boot. This first person towers up in the Gothic architecture; the spire is an "I," the flying buttress is an "I." And therefore the *entire Faustian ethic,* from Thomas Aquinas to Kant, *is an "excelsior"*—fulfilment of an "I," ethical work upon an "I," justification of an "I" by faith and works; respect of the neighbour "Thou" for the sake of one's "I" and its happiness; and, lastly and supremely, immortality of the "I."

Now this, precisely this, the genuine Russian regards as contemptible vainglory. The Russian soul, will-less, having the limitless *plane* as its prime symbol, seeks to grow up—serving, anonymous, self-oblivious—in the brother-world of the plane. To take "I" as the starting-point of relations with the neighbour, to elevate "I" morally through "I's" love of near and dear, to repent for "I's" own sake, are to him traits of Western vanity as presumptuous as is the upthrusting challenge to heaven of our cathedrals, which he compares with his plane church-roof and its sprinkling of cupolas. Tolstoi's hero Nechludov looks after his moral "I" as he does after his finger-nails; this is just what betrays Tolstoi as belonging to the pseudomorphosis of Petrinism. But Raskolnikov is only something in a "we." His fault is the fault of all, and even to regard his sin as special to himself is pride and vanity. Something of the kind underlies the Magian soul-image also. "If any man come to me," says Jesus (Luke: xiv, 26), "and hate not his father and mother, and wife, and children, and brethren, *yea, and his own life* [τὴν ἑαυτοῦ ψυχήν] *also*,[1] he cannot be my disciple"; and it is the same feeling that makes him call himself by the title that we mistranslate "Son of Man."[2] The contest of thinking and willing that is the hidden theme of every serious

~~~~~~

[1] In the German: *"Vor allem aber sein eignes Ich."* (But in Luther's Bible, characteristically: *"Auch dazu sein eigen Leben."*)—*At.*

[2] *Barnasha.* The underlying idea is not the filial relation, but an impersonal coming up in the field of mankind.

portrait from Jan van Eyck to Marées is impossible in Classical portraiture, for in the Classical soul-image thought (νοῦς), the inner Zeus, is accompanied by the wholly ahistoric entities of animal and vegetative impulse (θυμός and ἐπιθυμία), wholly somatic and wholly destitute of conscious direction and drive towards an end. The actual designation of the Faustian principle, which belongs to us and to us alone, is a matter of indifference. It is not the notion of "Will," but the circumstance that we possess it while the Greeks *were entirely ignorant of it,* that gives it high symbolic import. At the very bottom, there is no distinction between space-as-depth and will. For the one, and *therefore* for the other also, the Classical languages had no expression.[3] We shall see how the identity of space and will comes to expression in the acts of Copernicus and Columbus—as well as in those of the Hohenstaufen and Napoleon—but it underlies also, in another way, the physical notions of fields of force and potential, ideas that it would be impossible to convey to the comprehension of any Greek. "Space as *a priori* form of perception," the formula in which Kant finally enunciated that for which Baroque philosophy had so long and tirelessly striven, implies an assertion of supremacy of soul over the alien; the ego, through the form, is to rule the world.[4]

This is brought to expression in the depth-perspective of oil-painting, which makes the space-field of the picture, conceived as infinite, dependent on the observer, who in choosing his dis-

---

[3] ἐθέλω and βούλομαι imply, to have the intention, or wish, or inclination (βουλή means counsel, council, plan, and ἐθέλω has no equivalent noun). *Voluntas* is not a psychological concept but, like *potestas* and *virtus,* a thoroughly Roman and matter-of-fact designation for a practical, visible and outward asset—substantially, the *mass* of an individual's being. In like case, we use the word "energy." The "will" of Napoleon is something very different from the energy of Napoleon, being, as it were, lift in contrast to weight. We must not confuse the outward-directed intelligence, which distinguishes the Romans as civilized men from the Greeks as cultured men, with "will" as understood here. Caesar is *not* a man of will in the Napoleonic sense. The idioms of Roman law, which represent the root-feeling of the Roman soul far better than those of poetry, are significant in this regard. Intention in the legal sense is *animus* (*animus occidendi*); the wish, directed to some criminal end, is *dolus* as distinct from the unintended wrongdoing (*culpa*). *Voluntas* is nowhere used as a technical term.

[4] The Chinese soul "wanders" in its world. This is the meaning of the East Asiatic perspective, which places the vanishing point in the *middle* of the picture instead of in the depth as we do. The function of perspective is to subject things to the "I," which in ordering comprehends them.

tance asserts his dominion. It is this attraction of distance that produces the type of the *heroic and historically felt* landscape that we have alike in the picture and the park of the Baroque period, and that is expressed also in the mathematico-physical concept of the vector. For centuries painting fought passionately to reach this symbol, which contains all that the words "space," "will" and "force" are capable of indicating. And correspondingly we find in our metaphysic the steady tendency to formulate pairs of concepts (such as phenomena and things-in-themselves, will and idea, ego and non-ego) all of the same purely dynamic content, and—in utter contrast to Protagoras' conception of man as the measure, not the creator, of things—to establish a functional dependence of things upon spirit.

THE INNER MYTHOLOGY

For every man, whatever the Culture to which he belongs, the elements of the soul are the deities of an *inner mythology*. What Zeus was for the outer Olympus, νοῦς was for the inner world that every Greek was entirely conscious of possessing—the throned lord of the other soul-elements. What "God" is for us, God as Breath of the world, the Universal Power, the ever-present doer and provider, that also—reflected from the space of world into the imaginary space of soul and necessarily felt as an actual presence—is "Will." In the Baroque age the pantheism of the outer world immediately resulted in one of the inner world also; and the word "God" in antithesis to "world" has always—however interpreted in this or that case—implied exactly what is implied in the word "will" with respect to soul, viz., the power that moves all that is within its domain.[5] Thought no sooner leaves Religion for Science than we get the double myth of concepts, in physics and psychology. The concepts "force," "mass," "will," passion," rest not on objective experience but on a life-feeling. Darwinism is nothing but a specially shallow formulation of this feeling. No Greek would have used the word "Nature" as our biology employs it, in the sense of an absolute and methodical activity. "The will

---

[5] Obviously, atheism is no exception to this. When a Materialist or Darwinian speaks of a "Nature" that orders everything, that effects selections, that produces and destroys anything, he differs only to the extent of one word from the eighteenth-century Deist. The *world-feeling* has undergone no change.

of God" for us is a pleonasm—God (or "Nature," as some say) is nothing but will. Zeus emphatically does *not* possess full powers over the world, but is simply *primus inter pares,* a body amongst bodies, as the Apollinian world-feeling requires. Blind necessity, the *ananke* immanent in the cosmos of Classical consciousness, is in no sense dependent upon him; on the contrary, the Gods are subordinate to It. Aeschylus says so outright in a powerful passage of the *Prometheus,* but it is perceptible enough even in Homer, e.g. in the Strife of the Gods and in that decisive passage in which Zeus takes up the scales of destiny, not to settle, but to learn, the fate of Hector. The Classical soul, therefore, with its parts and its properties, imagines itself as an Olympus of little gods, and to keep these at peace and in harmony with one another is the ideal of the Greek life-ethic of σωφροσύνη and ἀταραξία. More than one of the philosophers betrays the connexion by calling νοῦς, the highest part of the soul, Zeus. Aristotle assigns to his deity the single function of θεωρία, contemplation, and this is Diogenes' ideal also—a completely matured static of life in contrast to the equally ripe dynamic of our eighteenth-century ideal.

The enigmatic Something in the soul-image that is called "will," the *passion of the third dimension,* is therefore quite specially a creation of the Baroque, like the perspective of oil-painting and the force-idea of modern physics and the tone-world of instrumental music.

Baroque architecture began, as we have seen, when Michelangelo replaced the tectonic elements of the Renaissance, support and load, by those of dynamics, force and mass. While Brunelleschi's chapel of the Pazzi in Florence expresses a bright composedness, Vignola's façade of the Gesú in Rome is *will become stone.* The new style in its ecclesiastical form has been designated the "Jesuit," and indeed there is an inward connexion between the achievement of Vignola and Giacomo della Porta and the creation by Igatius Loyola of the Order that stands for the pure and abstract will of the Church,[6] just as there is between the invisible operations and the unlimited range of the Order and the arts of Calculus and Fugue.

[6] The great part played by learned Jesuits in the development of theoretical physics must not be overlooked. Father Boscovich, with his system of atomic forces (1759), made the first serious advance beyond Newton. The idea of the equivalence of God and pure space is even more evident in Jesuit work than it is in that of the Jansenists of Port Royal with whom Descartes and Pascal were associated.

Henceforward, then, the reader will not be shocked if we speak of *a Baroque, and even of a Jesuit, style in psychology, mathematics, and pure physics.* The form-language of dynamics, which puts the energetic contrast of capacity and intensity in place of the volitionless somatic contrast of material and form, is one common to all the mind-creations of those centuries.

CLASSICAL BEHAVIOUR-DRAMA AND FAUSTIAN CHARACTER-DRAMA

The question is now: How far is the man of this Culture himself fulfilling what the soul-image that he has created requires of him?

What will is in the soul-image, character is in the picture of life as we see it, the Western life that is self-evident to Western men. It is the fundamental postulate of all our ethical systems, differ otherwise as they may in their metaphysical or practical precepts, that man has character. Character, which forms itself *in the stream of the world—the personality, the relation of living to doing*—is a Faustian impression of Man. The conception of mankind as an active, fighting, progressing whole is (and has been since Joachim of Floris and the Crusades) so necessary an idea for us that we find it hard indeed to realize that it is an exclusively Western hypothesis, living and valid only for a season. The *carpe diem*, the saturated being, of the Classical standpoint is the most direct contrary of that which is felt by Goethe and Kant and Pascal, by Church and Freethinker, as alone possessing value—*active, fighting and victorious being.*[7]

It is character—the form in virtue of which an eventful existence can combine the highest constancy in the essential with the

---

[7] Luther placed practical activity (the day's demands, as Goethe said) at the very centre of morale, and that is one of the main reasons why it was to the deeper natures that Protestantism appealed most cogently. Works of piety devoid of directional energy (in the sense that we give the words here) fell at once from the high esteem in which they had been sustained (as the Renaissance was sustained) by a relic of *Southern feeling.* On ethical grounds monasticism thenceforth falls into ever-increasing disrepute. In the Gothic age entry into the cloister, the renunciation of care, deed and will, had been an act of the loftiest ethical character—the highest sacrifice that it was possible to imagine, that of *life.* But in the Baroque even Roman Catholics no longer felt thus about it. And the institutions, no longer of renunciation but merely of inactive comfort, went down before the spirit of the Enlightenment.

maximum variability in the details—which is essential to a good biography. Plutarch's truly Classical biographies are by comparison mere collections of anecdotes strung together chronologically and not ordered pictures of historical development.

It goes without saying that we, when we turn to look into the Classical life-feeling, must find there some basic element of ethical values that is antithetical to "character" in the same way as the statue is antithetical to the fugue, Euclidean geometry to Analysis, and body to space. We find it in the *Gesture*. It is this that provides the necessary foundation for a spiritual static. The word that stands in the Classical vocabulary where "personality" stands in our own is πρόσωπον, *persona*—namely, *role* or *mask*. In late Greek or Roman speech it means *the public aspect and mien* of a man, which for Classical man is tantamount to the essence and kernel of him. An orator was described as speaking in the πρόσωπον of a priest or a soldier. The slave was ἀπρόσωπος —that is, he had *no* attitude or figure in the public life—but not ἀσώματος—that is, he did have a *soul*. The idea that Destiny had assigned the role of king or general to a man was expressed by Romans in the words *persona regis, imperatoris*.[8] The Apollinian cast of life is manifest enough here. What is indicated is not the personality (that is, an unfolding of inward possibilities in *active striving*), but a permanent and self-contained *posture* strictly adapted to a so-to-say plastic ideal of being. The significance of Aristotle's phrase ζῷον πολιτίκον—quite untranslatable and habitually translated with a Western connotation—is that it refers to men who are nothing when single and lonely and only count for anything when in a plurality, in agora or forum, where each reflects his neighbour and thus, only thus, acquires a genuine reality. It is all implicit in the phrase σώματα πόλεως, used for the burghers of the city.

This opposition, further, has produced forms of tragedy that differ from one another radically in every respect. The Faustian *character-drama* and the Apollinian *drama of noble gesture* have in fact nothing but name in common. It is not enough to distinguish Classical and Western tragedy merely as action-drama and event-drama. Faustian tragedy is *biographical*, Classical *anecdo-*

---

[8] πρόσωπον meant in the older Greek "visage," and later, in Athens, "mask." As late as Aristotle the word is not yet in use for "person." *Persona*, originally also a theatre-mask, came to have a juristic application, and in Roman Imperial times the pregnant Roman sense of this word affected the Greek πρόσωπον also.

tal; that is, the one deals with the sense of a whole life and the other with the content of the single moment. What relation, for instance, has the entire *inward* past of Oedipus or Orestes to the shattering event that suddenly meets him on his way? There is not the smallest trait in the past existence of Othello—that masterpiece of psychological analysis—that has not some bearing on the catastrophe. Race-hatred, the isolation of the upstart amongst the patricians, the Moor as soldier and as child of Nature, the loneliness of the aging bachelor—all these things have their significance. "Psychology" in fact is the proper designation for the *Western* way of fashioning men; the word holds good for a portrait by Rembrandt as for the music of *Tristan,* for Stendhal's Julien Sorel as for Dante's *Vita Nuova.* The like of it is not to be found in any other Culture. If there is anything that the Classical arts scrupulously exclude it is this, for psychology is the form in which art handles man as incarnate will and not as σῶμα. To call Euripides a psychologist is to betray ignorance of what psychology is.

Of deep necessity, therefore, we Faustians understand drama as a maximum of activity; and, of deep necessity also, the Greek understood it as a maximum of passivity.[9] Speaking generally, the Attic tragedy had no "action" at all. The Mysteries were purely δράματα or δρώμενα, i.e. ritual performances, and it was from the Mystery-form with its *peripeteia* that Aeschylus (himself an Eleusinian) derived the high drama that he created. Aristotle describes tragedy as the *imitation* of an occurrence. This imitation is identical with the "profanation" of the mysteries; and we know that Aeschylus went further and made the sacral vestments of the Eleusinian priesthood the regular costume of the Attic stage, and was accused on that account.[1] For the δράμα proper, with its

---

[9] The evolution of meaning in the Classical words *pathos* and *passio* corresponds with this. The second was formed from the first only in the Imperial period, and carried its original sense in the "Passion" of Christ. It was in the early Gothic times, and particularly in the language of the Franciscan "Zealots" and the disciples of Joachim of Floris, that its meaning underwent the decisive reversal. Expressing thenceforward a condition of profound excitement which strained to discharge itself, it became finally a generic name for all spiritual dynamic; in this sense of strong will and directional energy it was brought into German as *Leidenschaft* by Zesen in 1647.

[1] The Eleusinian mysteries contained no secrets at all. Everyone knew what went on. But upon the believers they exercised a strange and overpowering effect, and the "betrayal" consisted in profaning them by imitating their holy forms outside the temple-precinct.

reversal from lamentation to joy, consisted not in the fable that was narrated but in the ritual action that lay behind it, and was understood and felt by the spectator as deeply symbolic. With this element of the non-Homeric early religion there became associated another, a boorish—the burlesque (whether phallic or dithyrambic) scenes of the spring festivals of Demeter and Dionysus. The beast-dances and the accompanying song were the germ of the tragic Chorus which is the accompaniment to the actor or "answerer" of Thespis (534).

The genuine tragedy grew up out of the solemn death-lament (*threnos, naenia*). At some time or other the gay Dionysus festival (which also was a soul-feast) became a mourners' chorus of men, the Satyr-play being relegated to the end. It was Aeschylus' introduction of the second actor that accomplished the essential of Classical tragedy; the lament as *given theme* was thenceforward subordinated to the visual presentation of a great human suffering as *present motive*. The foreground-story ($\mu\hat{\upsilon}\theta o\varsigma$) is not "action" but the occasion for the songs of the Chorus, which still constitutes the $\tau\rho\alpha\gamma\wp\delta\acute{\iota}\alpha$ proper. But presently there emerges high above the lament the grandeur of human endurance, the attitude, the $\hat{\eta}\theta o\varsigma$ of the Hero. The theme is, not the heroic Doer whose will surges and breaks against the resistance of alien powers or the demons in his own breast, but the will-less Patient whose somatic existence is—gratuitously—destroyed. The Prometheus trilogy of Aeschylus begins just where Goethe would in all probability have left off. King Lear's madness is the *issue* of the tragic action, but Sophocles' Ajax is *made* mad by Athene before the drama opens—here is the difference between a character and an operated figure. Fear and compassion, in fact, are, as Aristotle says, the necessary effect of Greek tragedy upon the Greek (and only the Greek) spectator, as is evident from his choice of the most effective scenes depicting either abrupt reversals of fortune or else virtue rewarded. In the first, the ruling impression is $\phi\acute{o}\beta o\varsigma$ (terror) and in the second it is $\dot{\epsilon}\lambda\epsilon\acute{o}\varsigma$ (pity), and the $\kappa\alpha\theta\acute{\alpha}\rho\sigma\iota\varsigma$ in the spectator presupposes his existence-ideal to be that of $\dot{\alpha}\tau\alpha\rho\alpha\xi\acute{\iota}\alpha$. The Greek "soul" is the "here and now," the $\sigma\hat{\omega}\mu\alpha$, static, "fixed point," being. To see this imperilled by the jealousy of the gods or by that blind chance that may crash upon any man's head without reason and without warning, is the most fearful of all experiences. The very roots of Greek being are struck at by what for the challenging Faustian is the first stimulus to living activity. And then—to find one's self *delivered*, to see the sun come out again and the dark thunder clouds huddle themselves away on the remote horizon, to rejoice profoundly in the admired grand gesture, to see the tortured mythical soul breathe again—that is the καθάρσις. But it presupposes a kind of life-feeling that is entirely alien to us, the very word being hardly translatable into our languages and our sensations. It took all the aesthetic industry and assertiveness of the Baroque and of Classicism, backed by the meekest submissiveness before ancient texts, to persuade us that this is the spiritual basis of our own tragedy as well. And no wonder. For the fact is that the effect of our tragedy is precisely the opposite. It does not deliver us from dead-weight pressure of events, but evokes active dynamic elements in us, stings us, stimulates us. It awakens the primary feelings of an energetic human being, the fierceness and the joy of tension, danger, violent deed, victory, crime, the triumph of overcoming and destroying—feelings that have slumbered in the depths of every Northern soul since the days of the Vikings, the Hohenstaufen and the Crusades. *That* is Shakespearian effect. A Greek would not have tolerated Macbeth, nor, generally, would he have comprehended the meaning of this mighty art of directional biography at all.

SYMBOLISM OF THE DRAMA

There are corresponding differences between the Apollinian and the Faustian outlook in the forms of dramatic presentation, which are the complement of the poetic idea. The antique drama is a piece of plastic, a group of dramatic scenes conceived as reliefs, a pageant of gigantic marionettes disposed against the definitive plane of the back-wall. Presentation is entirely that of grandly imagined gestures, the meagre facts of the fable being solemnly recited rather than presented. The technique of Western drama aims at just the opposite—unbroken movement and strict exclusion of flat static moments. The famous "three unities" of place, time and action, as unconsciously evolved (though not expressly formulated) in Athens, are a paraphrase of the type of the Classical marble statue and, like it, an indication of what Classical man, the man of the Polis and the pure present and the gesture, felt about life. The unities are all, effectively, *negative,* denials of past and future, repudiation of all spiritual action-at-a-distance. The Spanish theatre of the sixteenth century bowed itself to the authority of "Classical" rules; the great Spanish dramatists, Tirso da Molina above all, fashioned the "unities" of the Baroque, not as metaphysical negations however, but purely as expressions of the spirit of high courtesy, and it was as such that Corneille, the docile pupil of Spanish *grandezza,* borrowed them. It was a fateful step. Here there was the possibility of a mighty drama, purely Faustian, of unimagined forms and daring. That this did *not* appear, that for all the greatness of Shakespeare the Teutonic drama never quite shook off the spell of misunderstood convention, was the consequence of blind faith in the authority of Aristotle. What might not have come out of Baroque drama had it remained under the impression of the knightly epic and the Gothic Easter-play and Mystery, in the near neighbourhood of Oratorios and Passions, without ever hearing of the Greek theatre! A tragedy issuing from the spirit of contrapuntal music, free of limitations proper to plastic but here meaningless, a dramatic poetry that from Orlando Lasso and Palestrina could develop— side by side with Heinrich Schütz, Bach, Handel, Gluck and Beethoven, but entirely free—to a pure form of its own: that was what was possible, and that was what did not happen.

The unities were not sufficient for the Attic drama. It demanded, further, the rigid mask in lieu of facial play, thus forbidding spiritual characterization in the same spirit as Attic sentiment forbade likeness-statuary. It demanded more-than-life-sized figures and got them by means of the cothurnus and by padding and draping the actor till he could scarcely move, thus eliminating all his individuality. Lastly, it required monotonous sing-song delivery, which it ensured by means of a mouthpiece fixed in the mask.

And here our attention is drawn to a feature of Greek tragedy that any true tragedy of the Faustian style must find intolerable, the continual presence of the Chorus. This Chorus as crowd (the ideal opposite to the lonely or inward man and the monologue of the West), this Chorus which is always there, the witness of every "soliloquy," this Chorus by which, in the stage-life as in the real life, fear before the boundless and the void is banished, is truly Apollinian. Self-review as a *public* action, pompous public mourning in lieu of the solitary anguish of the bedchamber, the tears and lamentations that fill a whole series of dramas like the *Philoctetes* and the *Trachiniae*, the impossibility of being alone, the feeling of the Polis, all the feminine of this Culture that we see idealized in the Belvedere Apollo, betrays itself in this symbol of the Chorus. In comparison with this kind of drama, Shakespeare's is a single monologue. Even in the conversations, even in the group-scenes, we are sensible of the immense *inner* distance between the persons, each of whom at bottom is only talking with himself. Nothing can overcome this spiritual remoteness. It is felt in Hamlet as in Tasso and in Don Quixote as in Werther, but even Wolfram von Eschenbach's Parzeval is filled with and stamped by the sense of infinity. The distinction holds for all Western poetry against all Classical. All our lyric verse from Walther von der Vogelweide to Goethe and from Goethe to the poems of our dying world-cities is monologue, while the Classical lyric is a choral lyric, a singing before witnesses.

THE ART OF THE DAY AND OF THE NIGHT

Thus, although the Eleusinian Mysteries and the Thracian festival of the epiphany of Dionysus had been nocturnal celebrations, the art of Thespis developed, as its inmost nature required, as a scene of the morning and the full sunlight. On the contrary, our Western popular and Passion plays, which originated in the sermon of allocated parts and were produced first by priests in the church, and then by laymen in the open square, on the *mornings* of high festivals, led almost unnoticed to an art of evening and night. Already in Shakespeare's time performances took place in the late afternoon, and by Goethe's this mystical sense of a proper relation between art and light-setting had attained its object. In general, every art and every Culture has its significant times of day. The music of the eighteenth century is a music of the darkness and the inner eye, and the plastic of Athens is an art of cloudless day. That this is no superficial contrast we can see by comparing the Gothic plastic, wrapped eternally in "dim religious light," and the Ionic flute, the instrument of high noon. The candle affirms and the sunlight denies space as the opposite of things. At night the universe of space triumphs over matter, at midday the surroundings assert themselves and space is repudiated. The same contrast appears in Attic fresco and Northern oil-painting, and in the symbols of Helios and Pan and those of the starry night and red sunset.

The Classical vase-painting and fresco has no time-of-day. No shadow indicates the state of the sun, no heaven shows the stars. There is neither morning nor evening, neither spring nor autumn, but *pure timeless brightness*. For equally obvious reasons our oil-painting developed in the opposite direction, towards an imaginary darkness, also independent of time-of-day, which forms the characteristic atmosphere of the Faustian soul-space. There are early mornings, sunset-clouds, the last gleams upon the sky-line of distant mountains, the candle-lighted room, the spring meadows and the autumn woods, the long and short shadows of bushes and furrows. But they are all penetrated through and through with a subdued darkness that is *not* derived from the motion of the heavenly bodies. In fact, steady brightness and steady twilight are the respective hallmarks of the Classical and the Western, alike in painting and in drama; and may we not also describe Euclidean geometry as a mathematic of the day and Analysis as a mathematic of the night?

Change of scene, undoubtedly regarded by the Greeks as a sort of profanation, is for us almost a religious necessity, a postulate of our world-feeling. We *inwardly* need a drama of perspectives and wide backgrounds, a stage that shakes off sensuous limitations and draws the whole world to itself. In Shakespeare, who was born when Michelangelo died and ceased to write when Rembrandt came into the world, dramatic infinity, the passionate overthrow of all static limitations, attained the maximum. His woods, seas, alleys, gardens, battlefields, lie in the afar, the boundless. Years fly past in the space of minutes. The mad Lear between fool and reckless outcast on the heath, in the night and the storm, the unutterably lonely ego lost in space—here is the Faustian life-feeling!

POPULAR AND ESOTERIC CHARACTER. THE IMAGE OF ASTRONOMY. THE GEOGRAPHICAL HORIZON

Every Culture has its own quite definite sort of esoteric or popular character that is immanent in all its doings, so far as these have symbolic importance. We find everywhere in the Western what we find nowhere in the Classical—the exclusive form. Whole periods—for instance, the Provençal Culture and the Rococo—are in the highest degree select and exclusive, their ideas and forms having no existence except for a small class of higher men. Even the Renaissance is no exception, for though it purports to be the rebirth of that Antique which is so utterly *non*-exclusive and caters so frankly for all, it is in fact, through and through, the creation of a circle or of individual chosen souls, a taste that rejects popularity from the outset. On the contrary, *every* Attic burgher belonged to the Attic Culture, which excluded nobody; and consequently, the distinction of deep and shallow, which is so decisively important for us, did not exist at all for it. For us, popular and shallow are synonymous—in art as in science—but for Classical man it was not so.

From Titian painting becomes more and more esoteric. So, too, poetry. So, too, music. And the Gothic *per se* had been esoteric from its very beginnings—witness Dante and Wolfram. The Masses of Okeghem and Palestrina, or of Bach for that matter, were never intelligible to the average member of the congregation. Ordinary people are bored by Mozart and Beethoven, and regard music generally as something for which one is or is not in the mood. A certain degree of interest in these matters has been induced by concert room and gallery since the age of enlightenment invented the phrase "art for all." But Faustian art is not, and by very essence cannot be, "for all." If modern painting has ceased to appeal to any but a small (and ever decreasing) circle of connoisseurs, it is because it has turned away from the painting of things that the man in the street can understand. It has transferred the property of actuality from contents to space— the space *through* which alone, according to Kant, things *are*.

Consider our sciences too. Every one of them, without exception, has besides its elementary groundwork certain "higher" regions that are inaccessible to the layman—symbols, these also, of our will-to-infinity and directional energy. Indeed, we may take the craving for wide effect as a sufficient index by itself of the commencing and already perceptible decline of Western science. That the severe esoteric of the Baroque age is felt now as a burden, is a symptom of sinking strength and of the dulling of that distance-sense which *confessed* the limitation with humility. For us, the polarity of expert and layman has all the significance of a high symbol, and when the tension of this distance is beginning to slacken, there the Faustian life is fading out.

THE WILL TO POWER

[*The will to power—in contrast to the Moral of Behaviour —finds its expression also in the astronomical picture. The telescope, a truly Faustian discovery, penetrates into space which is hidden from the naked eye, and thereby increases the universe that we "possess." What we see are merely light indices; what we understand are symbols of ourselves. World signifies, above all, space and the stars are hardly more than tiny balls in the immensity, which as material no longer affect the world-feeling. While Democritus, who tried (as on behalf of the Apollinian Culture he was bound to try) to lay down some limit of a bodily kind to it all, imagined a layer of hook-shaped atoms over the Cosmos, an insatiable hunger drives us further and ever further into the remote.*

The same holds good for the geographical horizon. Apollinian man felt the Columbus longing as little as he did the Copernican. In the tenth century, which heralded the Faustian birth, the spirit of the Norsemen drove their cockle boats to the coasts of America but Classical man was totally indifferent to the circumnavigation of Africa, which had already been achieved by Egyptians and Carthaginians. Athens shut its eyes to this, as it did to the knowledge of the old East.]

The discoveries of Columbus and Vasco da Gama extended the geographical horizon without limit, and the world-sea came into the same relation with land as that of the universe of space with earth. And then the first political tension within the Faustian world-consciousness discharged itself. For the Greeks, Hellas was and remained the important part of the earth's surface, but with the discovery of America, West Europe became a province in a gigantic whole. Thenceforward the history of the Western Culture has a *planetary* character.

Every Culture possesses its own conception of home and fatherland, which is hard to comprehend, scarcely to be expressed in words, full of dark metaphysical relations, but nevertheless unmistakable in its tendency. The Classical home-feeling which tied the individual corporally and Euclidean-ly to the Polis is the very antithesis of that enigmatic *Heimweh* of the Northerner, which has something of the musical, soaring and unearthly. Classical man felt as "home" just what he could see from the Acropolis of his native city. Where the horizon of Athens ended, the alien, the hostile, the "fatherland" of another began.

If, in fine, we look at the whole picture—the expansion of the Copernican world into that aspect of stellar space that we possess today; the development of Columbus's discovery into a world-wide command of the earth's surface by the West; the perspective of oil-painting and the theatre; the sublimation of the idea of home; the passion of our Civilization for swift transit, the conquest of the air, the exploration of the Polar regions and the climbing of almost impossible mountain-peaks—we see, emerging everywhere, the prime symbol of the Faustian soul, Limitless Space. And those specially Western creations of the soul-myth called "Will," "Force" and "Deed" must be regarded as derivatives of this prime symbol.

IX

SOUL-IMAGE AND
LIFE-FEELING:
BUDDHISM, STOICISM, SOCIALISM

EVERY CULTURE POSSESSES ITS OWN ETHIC

WESTERN mankind, without exception, is under the influence of an immense optical illusion. Everyone *demands* something of the rest. We say "thou shalt" in the conviction that so-and-so in fact will, can and must be changed or fashioned or arranged conformably to the order, and our belief both in the efficacy of, and in our title to give, such orders is unshakable. *That,* and nothing short of it, *is,* for us, morale. In the ethics of the West everything is direction, claim to power, will to affect the distant. Here Luther is completely at one with Nietzsche, Popes with Darwinians, Socialists with Jesuits; for one and all, the beginning of morale is a claim to general and permanent validity. It is a necessity of the Faustian soul that this should be so. He who thinks or teaches "otherwise" is sinful, a back-slider, a *foe,* and he is fought down without mercy. You "shall," the State "shall," society "shall"—this form of morale is to us self-evident; it represents the only real meaning that we can attach to the word. But it was not so either in the Classical, or in India, or in China. Buddha, for instance, gives a pattern to take or to leave, and Epicurus offers counsel. Both undeniably are forms of high morale, and neither contains the will-element.

What we have entirely failed to observe is the peculiarity of moral *dynamic*. If we allow that Socialism (in the ethical, not the economic, sense) is that world-feeling which seeks to carry out its own views on behalf of all, then we are all without exception, willingly or no, wittingly or no, Socialists. Even Nietzsche, that most passionate opponent of "herd morale," was perfectly incapable of limiting his zeal to himself in the Classical way. He thought only of "mankind," and he attacked everyone who differed from himself. Epicurus, on the contrary, was heartily indifferent to others' opinions and acts. But the Nietzschean Zarathustra—though professedly standing beyond good and evil—breathes from end to end the pain of seeing men to be other than as he would have them be, and the deep and utterly un-Classical desire to devote a life to their reformation—his own sense of the word, naturally, being the only one. It is just this, the *general* transvaluation, that makes ethical monotheism and—using the word in a novel and deep sense—socialism. All world-improvers are Socialists. And consequently there are no Classical world-improvers.

The moral imperative as the form of morale is Faustian and only Faustian. It is quite wrong to associate Christianity with the moral imperative. It was not Christianity that transformed Faustian man, but Faustian man who transformed Christianity—and he not only made it a new religion but also gave it a new moral direction. The "it" became "I," the passion-charged centre of the world, the foundation of the great Sacrament of *personal* contrition. Will-to-power even in ethics, the passionate striving to set up a proper morale as a universal truth, and to enforce it upon humanity, to reinterpret or overcome or destroy everything otherwise constituted—nothing is more characteristically our own than this is. And in virtue of it the Gothic springtime proceeded to a profound—and never yet appreciated—*inward transformation* of the morale of Jesus. A quiet spiritual morale welling from Magian feeling—a morale or conduct recommended as potent for salvation, a morale the knowledge of which was communicated as a special act of grace—was recast as a *morale of imperative command.*[1]

There are as many morales as there are Cultures, no more and no fewer. Just as every painter and every musician has something in him which, by force of inward necessity, never emerges into consciousness but dominates *a priori* the form-language of his work and differentiates that work from the work of every other Culture, so every conception of Life held by a Culture-man possesses *a priori* (in the very strictest Kantian sense of the

---

[1] "He who hath ears to hear, let him hear"—there is no claim to power in these words. But the Western Church never conceived its mission thus. The "Glad Tidings" of Jesus, like those of Zoroaster, of Mani, of Mahomet, of the Neo-Platonists and of all the cognate Magian religions were mystic benefits *displayed* but in nowise imposed.

phrase) a constitution that is deeper than all momentary judgments and strivings and impresses the *style* of these with the hallmark of the particular Culture. The individual may act morally or immorally, may do "good" or "evil" with respect to the primary feeling of his Culture, but the theory of his actions is not a result but a datum. Each Culture possesses its own standards, the validity of which begins and ends with it. There is no general morale of humanity. A morale, like a sculpture, a music, a painting-art, is a self-contained form-world expressing a life-feeling; it is a datum, fundamentally unalterable, an inward necessity.

FAUSTIAN MORALE

Every Classical ethic that we know or can conceive of constitutes man an individual static entity, a body among bodies, and all Western valuations relate to him as a centre of effect in an infinite generality. Ethical Socialism is neither more nor less than the sentiment of action-at-a-distance, the moral pathos of the third dimension; and the root-feeling of Care—care for those who are with us, and for those who are to follow—pervades the atmosphere of our time. Consequently there is for us something socialistic in the aspect of the Egyptian Culture, while the opposite tendency to immobile attitude, to non-desire, to static self-containedness of the individual, recalls the Indian ethic and the man formed by it. The seated Buddha-status ("looking at its navel") and Zeno's *ataraxia* are not altogether alien to one another. The ethical ideal of Classical man was that which is led up to in his tragedy, and revealed in its *katharsis*. This in its last depths means the purgation of the Apollinian soul from its burden of what is *not* Apollinian, not free from the elements of distance and direction, and to understand it we have to recognize that Stoicism is simply the mature form of it. The Stoa wished to spread over the whole field of life the solemn theme of the Greek tragedy—statuesque steadiness and will-less ethos. Now, is not this conception of καθάρσις closely akin to the Buddhist ideal of Nirvana, which as a formula is no doubt very "late" but as an essence is thoroughly Indian and traceable even from Vedic times? When one thinks of it, there is nothing preposterous in the idea of Socrates, Epicurus, and especially Diogenes, sitting by the

Ganges, whereas Diogenes in a Western megalopolis would be an unimportant fool. Nor, on the other hand, is Frederick William I of Prussia, the prototype of the Socialist in the grand sense, unthinkable in the polity of the Nile, whereas in Periclean Athens he is impossible.

Had Nietzsche regarded his own times with fewer prejudices and less disposition to romantic championship of certain ethical creations, he would have perceived that a specifically Christian morale of compassion in his sense does not exist on West European soil. We must not let the words of humane formulae mislead us as to their real significance. Between the morale that one has and the morale that one thinks one has, there is a relation which is very obscure and very unsteady, and it is just here that an incorruptible psychology would be invaluable. The *text* of a conviction is never a test of its *reality*, for man is rarely conscious of his own beliefs. Our theoretical reverence for the propositions of the New Testament is in fact of the same order as the theoretical reverence of the Renaissance and of Classicism for antique art; the one has no more transformed the spirit of men than the other has transformed the spirit of works. The oft-quoted cases of the Mendicant Orders, the Moravians and the Salvation Army prove by their very rarity, and even more by the slightness of the effects that they have been able to produce, that they are exceptions in a quite different generality—namely, the *Faustian-Christian* morale. That morale will not indeed be found formulated, either by Luther or by the Council of Trent, but all Christians of the great style—Innocent III and Calvin, Loyola and Savonarola, Pascal and St. Theresa—have had it in them, even in unconscious contradiction to their own formal teachings.

We have only to compare the purely Western conception of the manly virtue that is designated by Nietzsche's *"moralinfrei" virtù,* the *grandezza* of Spanish and the *grandeur* of French Baroque, with that very feminine ἀρετή of the Hellenic ideal, of which the practical application is presented to us as capacity for enjoyment (ἡδονή), placidity of disposition (γαλήνη, ἀπάθεια), absence of wants and demands, and, above all, the so typical ἀταραξία. What Nietzsche called the Blond Beast and conceived to be embodied in the type of Renaissance Man that he so overvalued (for it is really only a jackal counterfeit of the great Hohenstaufen Germans) is the utter antithesis of the type that is presented in every

Classical ethic without exception and embodied in every Classical man of worth. The Faustian Culture has produced a long series of granite-men, the Classical never a one. But in the North the great Saxon, Franconian and Hohenstaufen emperors appear on the very threshold of the Culture, surrounded by giant-men like Henry the Lion and Gregory VII. Then came the men of the Renaissance, of the struggle of the two Roses, of the Huguenot Wars, the Spanish Conquistadores, the Prussian electors and kings, Napoleon, Bismarck, Rhodes. What other Culture has exhibited the like of these? Where, on the heights of Faustian morale, from the Crusades to the World War, do we find anything of the "slave-morale," the meek resignation, the deaconess's *caritas*? Only in pious and honoured words, nowhere else. The type of the very priesthood is Faustian; think of those magnificent bishops of the old German empire who on horseback led their flocks into battle,[2] or those Popes who could force submission on a Henry IV and a Frederick II, of the Teutonic Knights in the Ostmark, of Luther's challenge in which the old Northern heathendom rose up against old Roman, of the great Cardinals (Richelieu, Mazarin, Fleury) who shaped France. *That* is Faustian morale, and one must be blind indeed if one does not see it efficient in the whole field of West European history. And it is only through such grand instances of worldly passion which express the consciousness of a *mission* that we are able to understand those of grand spiritual passion, of the upright and forthright *caritas* which nothing can resist, the dynamic charity that is so utterly unlike Classical moderation and early-Christian mildness. There is a *hardness* in the sort of com-passion that was practised by the German mystics, the German and Spanish military Orders, the French and English Calvinists. In the Russian, the Raskolnikov, type of charity a soul melts into the fraternity of souls; in the Faustian it arises out of it. Here too *"ego habeo factum"* is the formula. Personal charity is the justification before God of the Person, the individual.

---

[2] The battle of Tusculum in 1167 was won by the Archbishops of Köln and Mainz. English history, too, contains the figures of warlike prelates— not only leaders of national movements like Stephen Langton but strong-handed administrators and fighters. The great Scots invasion of 1346 was met and defeated by the Archbishop of York. The Bishops of Durham were for centuries "palatines"; we find one of them serving *on pay* in the King's army in France, 1348. The line of these warlike Bishops in our history extends from Odo, the brother of William the Conqueror, to Scrope, archbishop and rebel in Henry IV's time.—*At.*

THE MORALE OF DAWNING "CIVILIZATION"

When Nietzsche wrote down the phrase "transvaluation of all values" for the first time, the spiritual movement of the centuries in which we are living found at last its formula. Transvaluation of all values is the most fundamental character of *every* civilization. For it is the beginning of a Civilization that it remoulds all the forms of the Culture that went before, understands them otherwise, practises them in a different way. It begets no more, but only reinterprets, and herein lies the negativeness common to all periods of this character. It assumes that the genuine act of creation has already occurred, and merely enters upon an inheritance of big actualities. In the late-Classical, we find the same taking place inside Hellenistic-Roman Stoicism, that is, the long death-struggle of the Apollinian soul. In the interval from Socrates—who was the spiritual father of the Stoa and in whom the first signs of inward impoverishment and city-intellectualism became visible—to Epictetus and Marcus Aurelius, every existence-ideal of the old Classical underwent transvaluation. In the case of India, the transvaluation of Brahman life was complete by the time of King Asoka (250 B.C.), as we can see by comparing the parts of the Vedanta put into writing before and after Buddha. And ourselves? Even now the ethical socialism of the Faustian soul, its fundamental ethic, as we have seen, is being worked upon by the process of transvaluation as that soul is walled up in the stone of the great cities. *Rousseau is the ancestor of this Socialism; he stands, like Socrates and Buddha, as the representative spokesman of a great Civilization.* Rousseau's rejection of all great Culture-forms and all significant conventions, his famous "Return to the state of Nature," his practical rationalism, are unmistakable evidences. Each of the three buried a millennium of spiritual depth. Each proclaimed his gospel to mankind, but it was to the mankind of the city intelligentsia, which was tired of the town and the Late Culture, and whose "pure" (i.e. soulless) reason longed to be free from them and their authoritative form and their severity, from the symbolism with which it was no longer in living communion and which therefore it detested. The Culture was annihilated by dialectic. Socrates was a nihilist, and Buddha. There was an Egyptian or an Arabian or a Chinese de-souling of the human being, just as there is a Western. This is a matter not of mere political and economic, nor even of religious and artistic, transformations, nor of any tangible or factual change whatsoever, but of the condition of a soul after it has actualized its possibilities in full.

Culture and Civilization—the living body of a soul and the mummy of it. For Western existence the distinction lies at about the year 1800—on the one side of that frontier life in fullness and sureness of itself, formed by growth from within, in one great uninterrupted evolution from Gothic childhood to Goethe and Napoleon, and on the other the autumnal, artificial, rootless life of our great cities, under forms fashioned by the intellect. Culture-man lives inwards, Civilization-man outwards in space and amongst bodies and "facts." That which the one feels as Destiny the other understands as a linkage of causes and effects, and thenceforward he is a materialist—in the sense of the word valid for, and only valid for, Civilization—whether he wills it or no, and whether Buddhist, Stoic or Socialist doctrines wear the garb of religion or not.

Only the sick man feels his limbs. When men construct an unmetaphysical religion in opposition to cults and dogmas; when a "natural law" is set up against historical law; when, in art, styles are invented in place of *the* style that can no longer be borne or mastered; when men conceive of the State as an "order of society" which not only can be but must be altered—then it is evident that something has definitely broken down. The Cosmopolis itself, the supreme Inorganic, is there, settled in the midst of the Culture-landscape, whose men it is uprooting, drawing into itself and using up.

So long as the man of a Culture that is approaching its fulfilment still continues to follow straight onwards naturally and unquestioningly, his life has a settled conduct. This is the *instinctive* morale, which may disguise itself in a thousand controversial forms but which he himself does not controvert, because he *has* it. As soon as Life is fatigued, as soon as a man is put on to the artificial soil of great cities—which are intellectual worlds to themselves—and needs a theory in which suitably to present Life to himself, morale turns into a *problem*. As late as Plato and as late as Kant ethics are still mere dialectics, a game with concepts, or the rounding off of a metaphysical system, something that at bottom would not be thought really necessary. The Categorical Imperative is merely an abstract statement of what, for Kant, was not in question at all. But with Zeno and with Schopenhauer this is no longer so. It had become necessary to discover, to invent or to squeeze into form, as a rule of being, that which was no longer anchored in instinct; and at this point therefore begin the civilized ethics that are no longer the reflection of Life but the reflection of Knowledge upon Life. One feels that there is something artificial, soulless, half-true in all these *considered* systems that fill the first centuries of all the Civilizations. They are not those profound and almost unearthly creations that are worthy to rank with the great arts. All metaphysic of the high style, all pure intuition, vanishes before the one need that has suddenly made itself felt, the need of a *practical* morale for the governance of a Life that can no longer govern itself. Up to Kant, up to Aristotle, up to the Yoga and Vedanta doctrines, philosophy had been a sequence of grand world-systems in which *formal* ethics occupied a very modest place. But now it became "moral philosophy" with a metaphysic as background. The enthusiasm of epistemology had to give way to hard practical needs. Socialism, Stoicism and Buddhism are philosophies of this type.

IRRELIGION

Each Culture, further, has *its own mode of spiritual extinction,* which is that which follows of necessity from its life as a whole. And hence Buddhism, Stoicism and Socialism are morphologically equivalent as end-phenomena.

For Buddhism too is such. Hitherto the deeper meaning of it has always been misunderstood. It was *not* a Puritan movement like, for instance, Islamism and Jansenism, *not* a Reformation as the Dionysiac wave was for the Apollinian world, and, in fact, *not* a religion at all in the sense of the religions of the Vedas or the religion of the Apostle Paul.[3] It was the basic feeling of the Indian Civilization and as such both equivalent to and "contemporary" with Stoicism and Socialism. The quintessence of this thoroughly worldly and unmetaphysical thought is to be found in the famous

[3] It was many centuries later that the Buddhist ethic of life gave rise to a religion for simple peasantry, and it was only enabled to do so by reaching back to the long-stiffened theology of Brahmanism and, further, back still, to very ancient popular cults.

sermon near Benares, the Four Noble Truths that won the prince-philosopher his first adherents. Its roots lay in the rationalist-atheistic Sankhya philosophy, the world-view of which it tacitly accepts, just as the social ethic of the nineteenth century comes from the Sensualism and Materialism of the eighteenth, and the Stoa (in spite of its superficial exploitation of Heraclitus) is derived from Protagoras and the Sophists. In each case it is the all-power of Reason that is the starting-point from which to discuss morale, and religion (in the sense of belief in anything metaphysical) does not enter into the matter. Nothing could be more irreligious than these systems in their original forms—and it is these, and not derivatives of them belonging to later stages of the Civilizations, that concern us here.

What we have before us is three forms of Nihilism, using the word in Nietzsche's sense. In each case, the ideals of yesterday, the religious and artistic and political forms that have grown up through the centuries, are discarded; yet even in this last act, this self-repudiation, each several Culture employs the prime symbol of its whole existence. The Faustian nihilist—Ibsen or Nietzsche, Marx or Wagner—shatters the ideals. The Apollinian —Epicurus or Antisthenes or Zeno—watches them crumble before his eyes. And the Indian withdraws from their presence into himself. Stoicism is directed to *individual self-management,* to statuesque and purely present being, without regard to future or past or neighbour. Socialism is the dynamic treatment of the same theme; it is defensive like Stoicism, but is concerned not with conduct but procedure, and more, it is offensive-defensive, for it projects itself into the future and plans to bring the whole of mankind under a single regimen. Buddhism, which only a mere dabbler in religious research could compare with Christianity, is hardly reproducible in words of the Western languages. But it is permissible to speak of a Stoic Nirvana and point to the figure of Diogenes, and even the notion of a Socialist Nirvana has its justification insofar that European weariness covers its flight from the struggle for existence under the catchwords World-Peace, Humanity and the Brotherhood of Man. Still, none of this comes anywhere near the strange profundity of the Buddhist conception of Nirvana.

Every soul has religion, which is only another word for its existence. All living forms in which it expresses itself—all arts, doctrines, customs, all metaphysical and mathematical form-worlds, all ornament, every column and verse and idea—are ultimately religious, and *must* be so. But from the setting in of Civilization they *cannot* be so any longer. As the essence of every Culture is religion, so—and *consequently*—the essence of every Civilization is irreligion—the two words are synonymous. Megalopolis itself, as against the old Culture-towns—Alexandria as against Athens, Paris as against Bruges, Berlin as against Nürnberg—is irreligious [4] down to the last detail, down to the look of the streets, the dry intelligence of the faces.[5] And, correspondingly, the ethical sentiments belonging to the form-language of the megalopolis are irreligious and soulless also. Socialism is the Faustian world-feeling become irreligious; "Christianity" so called (and qualified even as "true Christianity") is always on the lips of the English Socialist, to whom it seems to be something in the nature of a "dogma-less morale."

Stoicism also was irreligious as compared with Orphic religion, and Buddhism as compared with Vedic, and it is of no importance whatever that the Roman Stoic approved and conformed to Emperor-worship, that the later Buddhist sincerely denied his atheism, or that the Socialist calls himself an earnest Freethinker or even goes on believing in God.

It is this extinction of living inner religiousness, which gradually tells upon even the most insignificant element in a man's being, that becomes phenomenal in the historical world-picture at the turn from Culture to Civilization.

ETHICAL SOCIALISM

Let us, once more, review Socialism (independently of the economic movement of the same name) as the Faustian example of Civilization-ethics. Its friends regard it as the form of the future, its enemies as a sign of downfall, and both are equally right. We are all Socialists, wittingly or unwittingly, willingly or unwillingly. Even resistance to it wears its form.

Socialism—in its highest and not its street-corner sense—is,

[4] The term must not be confused with *anti*-religious.

[5] Note the striking similarity of many Roman portrait-busts to the matter-of-fact modern heads of the American style, and also (though this is not so distinct) to many of the portrait-heads of the Egyptian New Empire.

like every other Faustian ideal, exclusive. It owes its popularity only to the fact that it is completely misunderstood even by its exponents, who present it as a sum of rights instead of as one of duties, an abolition instead of an intensification of the Kantian imperative, a slackening instead of a tautening of directional energy. The trivial and superficial tendency towards ideals of "welfare," "freedom," "humanity," the doctrine of the "greatest happiness of the greatest number," are mere negations of the Faustian ethic—a very different matter from the tendency of Epicureanism towards the ideal of "happiness," for the condition of happiness was the actual sum and substance of the Classical ethic. Here precisely is an instance of sentiments to all outward appearance much the same, but meaning in the one case everything and in the other nothing.

Similarly, and equally necessarily, all Classical men of the Late period were Stoics unawares. The whole Roman people, as a body, had a Stoic soul. The genuine Roman, the very man who fought Stoicism hardest, was a Stoic of a stricter sort than ever a Greek could be.

The directional movement of Life that is felt as Time and Destiny, when it takes the form of an intellectual machinery of means and ends, stiffens in death. Ethical Socialism is the most exalted expression possible of life's aims.

In spite of its foreground appearances, ethical Socialism is *not* a system of compassion, humanity, peace and kindly care, but one of will-to-power. Any other reading of it is illusory. The Stoic takes the world as he finds it, but the Socialist wants to organize and recast it in form and substance, to fill it with *his own* spirit. The Stoic adapts himself, the Socialist commands. He would have the whole world take the shape he desires, thus transferring the idea of the *Critique of Pure Reason* into the ethical field. This is the ultimate meaning of the Categorical Imperative, which he brings to bear in political, social and economic matters alike—act as though the maxims that you practise *were to become by your will the law for all.* And this tyrannical tendency is not absent from even the shallowest phenomena of the time. It is not attitude and mien, but activity that is to be given form. As in China and in Egypt, life only counts insofar as it is deed. And it is the mechanicalizing of the organic concept of Deed that leads to the concept of *work* as commonly understood, *the civilized form of Faustian effecting.* Apollinian man looked *back* to a Golden

Age; this relieved him of the trouble of thinking upon what was still to come. The Socialist feels the Future as his task and aim, and accounts the happiness of the moment as worthless in comparison. The Classical spirit, with its oracles and its omens, wants only to *know* the future, but the Westerner would *shape* it. *The Third Kingdom is the Germanic ideal.* From Joachim of Floris to Nietzsche and Ibsen—arrows of yearning to the other bank, as the Zarathustra says—every great man has linked his life to an eternal *morning.*

And here Socialism becomes tragic. It is of the deepest significance that Nietzsche, so completely clear and sure in dealing with what should be destroyed, what transvalued, loses himself in nebulous generalities as soon as he comes to discuss the Whither, the Aim. His criticism of decadence is unanswerable, but his theory of the Superman is a castle in the air. And therein lies a deep necessity; for, from Rousseau onwards, Faustian man has nothing more to hope for in anything pertaining to the grand style of Life. Something has come to an end. The Northern soul has exhausted its inner possibilities, and of the dynamic force and insistence that had expressed itself in world-historical visions of the future—visions of millennial scope—nothing remains but the mere pressure, the passionate desire to create, the form without the content. This soul was Will and nothing but Will. It needed an aim for its Columbus-longing; it *had* to give its inherent activity at least the illusion of a meaning and an object. And so the keener critic will find a trace of Hjalmar Ekdal in all modernity, even its highest phenomena. Ibsen called it the lie of life. For deep down beneath it all is the gloomy feeling, not to be repressed, that all this hectic zeal is the despairing self-deception of a soul that may not and cannot rest. This is the tragic situation —the inversion of the Hamlet motive—and a thread of it runs through the entire fabric of Socialism, political, economic and ethical, which forces itself to ignore the annihilating seriousness of its own final implications, so as to keep alive the illusion of the historical necessity of its own existence.

X

FAUSTIAN AND APOLLINIAN
NATURE-KNOWLEDGE

EVERY SCIENCE IS DEPENDENT UPON A RELIGION

HELMHOLTZ observed, in a lecture of 1869 that has become famous, that "the final aim of Natural Science is to discover the motions underlying all changes, and the motive forces thereof; that is, to resolve itself into Mechanics." What this resolution into mechanics means is the reference of all qualitative impressions to fixed quantitative base-values, that is, to the *extended* and to *change of place* therein. It means, further—if we bear in mind the opposition of becoming and become, form and law, image and notion—the referring of the seen Nature-picture to the imagined picture of a single numerically and structurally measurable Order. The specific tendency of all Western mechanics is towards an intellectual *conquest by measurement,* and it is therefore obliged to look for the essence of the phenomenon in a system of constant elements that are susceptible of full and inclusive appreciation by measurement, of which Helmholtz distinguishes *motion* (using the word in its everyday sense) as the most important.

To the physicist this definition appears unambiguous and exhaustive, but to the sceptic who has followed out the history of this scientific conviction, it is very far from being either. To the physicist, present-day mechanics is a logical system of clear, uniquely significant concepts and of simple, necessary relations; while to the other it is a *picture* distinctive of the structure of the West European spirit, though he admits that the picture is consistent in the highest degree and most impressively convincing. It is self-evident that no *practical* results and discoveries can prove anything as to the "truth" of the *theory,* the *picture.*

Modern physics, as a science, is an immense system of indications in the form of names and numbers whereby we are enabled to work with Nature as with a machine. As such, it may have an exactly definable end. But as a piece of *history,* all made up of destinies and incidents in the lives of the men who have worked in it and in the course of research itself, physics is, in point of object, methods and results, alike an expression and actualization of a Culture, an organic and evolving element in the essence of that Culture, and every one of its results is a symbol. Its discoveries, in virtue of their imagined content (as distinguished from their printable formulae), have been of a purely mythic nature, even in minds so prudent as those of J. R. Mayer, Faraday and Hertz. In every Nature-law, physically exact as it may be, we are called upon to distinguish between the nameless number and the naming of it, between the plain fixation of limits and their theoretical interpretation. The formulae represent general logical values, pure numbers—that is to say, objective space—and boundary-elements. But formulae are dumb. The expression $s = \frac{1}{2}gt^2$ means nothing at all unless one is able mentally to connect the letters with particular words and their symbolism. But the moment we clothe the dead signs in such words, give them flesh, body and life, and, in sum, a perceptible significance in the world, we have overstepped the limits of a mere *order.* Θεωρία means image, vision, and it is this that makes a Nature-law out of a figure-and-letter formula. Everything exact is in itself *meaningless,* and every physical observation is so constituted that it *proves the basis of a certain number of imaged presuppositions;* and the effect of its successful issue is to make these presuppositions more convincing than ever. Apart from these, the result consists merely of empty figures. But in fact we do not and cannot get apart from them. Even if an investigator puts on one side every hypothesis that he knows as such, as soon as he sets his *thought* to work on the supposedly clear task, he is not controlling but being controlled by the unconscious form of it, for in living activity he is always a man of his Culture, of his age, of his school and of his tradition. Faith and "knowledge" are only two species of inner certitude, but of the two faith is the older and it dominates all the conditions of knowing, be they never so exact. And thus it is theories and not pure numbers that are the support of all natural science. The unconscious longing for that genuine knowledge which (be it repeated) is peculiar to the spirit of Culture-man sets itself to apprehend, to penetrate, and to comprise within its grasp the world-image of Nature. Mere industrious measuring for measuring's sake is not and never has been more than a delight for little minds. Every savant's experiment, be it what it may, is at the same time an instance of the *kind* of symbolism that rules in the savant's ideation. All Laws formulated in words are derived from experiences, typical of the one—and only the one—Culture. As to the "necessity" which is a postulate in all exact research, here too we have to consider two kinds of necessity, viz., a necessity within the spiritual and living (for it is Destiny that the history of every individual research-act takes its course when, where and how it does) and a necessity within the known (for which the current Western name is Causality). If the pure numbers of a physical formula represent a causal necessity, the existence, the birth and the life-duration of a theory are a Destiny.

The pure mechanics that the physicist has set before himself as the end-form to which it is his task (and the purpose of all this imagination-machinery) to reduce Nature, presupposes a *dogma* —namely, the religious world-picture of the Gothic centuries. For it is from this world-picture that the physics peculiar to the Western intellect is derived. There is no science that is without unconscious presuppositions of this kind, over which the researcher has no control and which can be traced back to the earliest days of the awakening Culture. *There is no Natural science without a precedent Religion.*

Every critical science, like every myth and every religious belief, rests upon an inner certitude. Various as the creations of this certitude may be, both in structure and in repute, they are not different in basic principle. Any reproach, therefore, levelled by Natural science at Religion is a boomerang. We are presumptuous and no less in supposing that we can ever set up "the Truth" in the place of "anthropomorphic" conceptions, for no other conceptions but these exist at all. Every idea that is possible at all is a mirror of the being of its author. The statement that "man created God in his own image," valid for every historical religion, is not less valid for every physical theory, however firm its reputed basis of fact.

Each Culture has made its own set of images of physical processes, which are true only for itself and only alive while it is itself alive. The "Nature" of Classical man found its highest artistic emblem in the nude statue, and out of it logically there grew up a *static of bodies, a physics of the near*. The Arabian Culture can be symbolized by the arabesque and the cavern-vaulting of the mosque, and out of this world-feeling there issued *Alchemy* with its ideas of mysterious substances like the "philosophical mercury," which is neither a material nor a property but by magic can transmute one metal into another. And the outcome of Faustian man's Nature idea was *a dynamic of unlimited span, a physics of the distant.* To the Classical therefore belong the conceptions of *matter and form,* to the Arabian (quite Spinozistically) the idea of *substances* with visible or secret *attributes,* and to the Faustian the idea of *force and mass.*

As with the formulation of problems and the methods of dealing with them, so also with the basic concepts. They are symbols in each case of one and only the one Culture. The Classical root-words ἄπειρον, ἀρχή, μορφή, ὕλη, are not translatable into our speech. To render ἀρχή by "prime-stuff" is to eliminate its Apollinian connotation, to make the hollow shell of the word sound an alien note. That which Classical man saw before him as "motion" in space, he understood as ἀλλοίωσις, change of position of bodies; we, from the way in which we experience motion, have deduced the concept of a *process,* a "going forward," thereby expressing and emphasizing that element of directional energy which our thought necessarily predicates in the courses of Nature. In Alchemy there is deep scientific doubt as to the plastic actuality of things—of the "somata" of Greek mathematicians, physicists and poets—and it dissolves and destroys the soma in the hope of finding its essence. The conflict concerning the person of Christ which manifested itself in all the early Councils and led to the Nestorian and Monophysite secessions is an *alchemistic* problem. It would never have occurred to a Classical physicist to investigate things while at the same time denying or annihilating their perceivable form. And for that very reason there was no Classical chemistry.

The rise of a chemical method of the Arabian style betokens a new world-consciousness. The discovery of it, which at one blow made an end of Apollinian natural science, of mechanical statics, is linked with the enigmatic name of Hermes Trismegistus, who is supposed to have lived in Alexandria *at the same time as Plotinus and Diophantus.* Similarly it was just at the time of the definite emancipation of the Western mathematic by Newton and Leibniz that the Western chemistry was freed from Arabic form by Stahl (1660–1734) and his Phlogiston theory. Chemistry and mathematic alike became pure analysis. Then Robert Boyle

(1626–91) devised the analytical method and *with it the Western conception of the Element.* That is in fact the *end* of genuine chemistry, its dissolution into the comprehensive system of pure dynamic, its assimilation into the mechanical outlook which the Baroque Age had established through Galileo and Newton.

What we call Statics, Chemistry and Dynamics—words that as used in modern science are merely traditional distinctions without deeper meaning—are really the *respective physical systems of the Apollinian, Magian and Faustian souls,* each of which grew up in its own Culture and was limited as to validity to the same. Corresponding to these sciences, each to each, we have the mathematics of Euclidean geometry, Algebra and Higher Analysis, and the arts of statue, arabesque and fugue.

THE ATOMIC THEORY

Now, the tendency of human thought (which is always causally disposed) to reduce the image of Nature to the simplest possible quantitative form-units that can be got by causal reasoning, measuring and counting—in a word, by mechanical differentiation—leads necessarily in Classical, Western and every other possible physics, to an atomic theory. Of the Indian and Chinese theories we know hardly more than the fact they once existed, and the Arabian is so complicated that even now it seems to defy presentation. But we do know our own and the Apollinian sciences well enough to observe, here too, a deeply symbolical opposition.

The Classical atoms are *miniature forms,* the Western *minimal quanta,* and quanta, too, of energy. The atoms of Leucippus and Democritus were different in form and magnitude, that is to say, they were purely plastic units, "indivisible," as their name asserts, but only plastically indivisible. The atoms of Western physics, for which "indivisibility" has quite another meaning, resemble the figures and themes of music; their being or essence consisting in vibration and radiation, and their relation to the processes of Nature being that of the "motive" to the "movement." On the one hand—Democritus' multitude of confused atoms, victims, hunted like Oedipus, of blind Chance, which he as well as Sophocles called ἀνάγκη. On the other hand—systems of abstract force-points working in unison, aggressive, energetically dominating space (as "field"), overcoming resistances like Macbeth. According to Leucippus the atoms fly about in the void "of themselves"; Democritus merely regards shock and counter-shock as a form of change of place. Aristotle explains individual movements as accidental; Empedocles speaks of love and hate, Anaxagoras of meetings and partings. All these are elements also of Classical tragedy; the figures on the Attic stage are related to one another just so. Further, and logically, they are the elements of Classical politics.

But the inner relationship between atom-theory and ethic goes further. It has been shown how the Faustian soul—whose being consists in the overcoming of the visible, whose feeling is loneliness and whose yearning is infinity—puts its need of solitude, distance and abstraction into all its actualities, into its public life, its spiritual and its artistic form-worlds alike. This pathos of distance (to use Nietzsche's expression) is peculiarly alien to the Classical, in which everything human demanded nearness, support and community. It is this that distinguishes the spirit of the Baroque from that of the Ionic, the culture of the *ancien régime* from that of Periclean Athens. And this pathos, which distinguishes the heroic doer from the heroic sufferer, appears also in the picture of Western physics as *tension*. It is tension that is missing in the science of Democritus; for in the principle of shock and counter-shock it is denied by implication that there is a force commanding space and identical with space. And, correspondingly, the element of Will is absent from the Classical soul-image. The principle of tension (developed in the potential theory), which is wholly untranslatable into Classical tongues and incommunicable to Classical minds, has become for Western physics fundamental. Its content follows from the notion of energy, *the Will-to-Power in Nature,* and therefore it is for us just as necessary as for the Classical thought it is impossible.

THE PROBLEM OF MOTION

Every atomic theory, therefore, is a myth and not an experience. In it the Culture, through the contemplative-creative power of its great physicists, reveals its inmost essence and very self.

We have already shown [1] the decisive importance of the *depth-*

[1] See pages 90–1.

experience, which is identical with the awakening of a soul and therefore with the creation of the outer world belonging to that soul. The mere sense-impression contains only length and breadth, and it is the living and necessary art of interpretation—which, like everything else living, possesses direction, motion and irreversibility (the qualities that our consciousness synthesizes in the word "time")—that *adds* depth and thereby fashions actuality and world. Life itself enters into experience as third dimension. The perfected extension of the Classical consciousness is one of sensuous and bodily presence. The Western consciousness achieves extension, after its own fashion, as transcendental space, and as it thinks its space more and more transcendentally it develops by degrees the abstract polarity of Capacity and Intensity that so completely contrasts with the Classical visual polarity of Matter and Form.

But it follows from this that in the known there can be no reappearance of living time. For this has already passed into the known, into constant "existence," as Depth, and hence duration (i.e. timelessness) and extension are identical. Only knowing possesses the mark of direction. The application of the word "time" to the imaginary and measurable time-dimension of physics is a mistake. The only question is whether it is possible or not to avoid the mistake. If one substitutes the word "Destiny" for "time" in any physical enunciation, one feels at once that pure Nature does not contain Time. The form-world of physics extends just as far as the cognate form-world of number and notion extend, and we have seen that (notwithstanding Kant) there is not and cannot be the slightest relation of any sort between mathematical number and Time. And yet this is controverted *by the fact of motion* in the picture of the world-around. It is the unsolved and unsolvable problem of the Eleatics—being (or thinking) and motion are incompatible; motion "is" not (is only "apparent").

And here, for the second time, Natural science becomes dogmatic and mythological. The words "time" and "Destiny," for anyone who uses them instinctively, touch Life itself in its deepest depths—life as a whole, which is not to be separated from lived-experience. Physics, on the other hand—i.e. the observing Reason—*must* separate them. The livingly-experienced "in-itself," mentally emancipated from the act of the observer and become object, dead, inorganic, rigid, is now "Nature," something open to exhaustive mathematical treatment. In this sense the knowledge of Nature is an activity of *measurement*. All the same, we live even when we are observing and therefore the thing we are observing *lives with us*. The element in the Nature-picture in virtue of which it not merely from moment to moment *is*, but in a continuous flow with and around us *becomes*, is the copula of the waking-consciousness and its world. This element is *called* movement, and it contradicts Nature as a picture, but it represents the *history* of this picture. And therefore, as precisely as Understanding is abstracted (by means of words) from feeling, and mathematical space from light-resistances ("things"), so also physical "time" is abstracted from the impression of motion.

"Physics," says Kirchhoff, "is the complete and simple description of motions." That indeed has always been its object. But the question is not one of motion *in* the picture but of motion *of* the picture. Motion, in the Nature of physics, is nothing else but that *metaphysical* something which gives rise to the consciousness of a succession. The known is timeless and alien to motion; its state of becomeness implies this. It is the *organic sequence* of knowns that gives the impression of a motion. The physicist receives the word as an impression not upon "reason" but upon the whole man, and the function of that man is not "Nature" only but the whole world. And that is the world-as-history. "Nature," then, is an expression of the Culture in each instance. All physics is treatment of the motion-problem—in which the life-problem is implicit—not as though it could one day be solved, *but in spite of, nay because of, the fact that it is insoluble.*

Let the reader conceive of the motion *within* a physical system as the *aging* of that system (as in fact it is, as lived-experience of the observer), and he will feel at once and distinctly the fatefulness immanent in, the unconquerably organic content of, the word "motion" and all its derivative ideas. But Mechanics, having nothing to do with aging, should have nothing to do with motion either, and consequently, since no scientific system is conceivable without a motion-problem in it, a complete and self-contained mechanics is an impossibility. Somewhere or other there is always an organic starting-point in the system where immediate Life enters it—an umbilical cord that connects the mind-child with the life-mother, the thought with the thinker.

This puts the fundamentals of Faustian and Apollinian Nature-science in quite another light. No "Nature" is pure—there is always something of history in it. If man is ahistorical, like the Greek, so that the totality of his impressions of the world is absorbed in a pure point-formed present, his Nature-image is static, self-contained. Time as magnitude figures in Greek physics as little as it does in Aristotle's entelechy-idea. If, on the other hand, Man is historically constituted, the image formed is dynamic.

History is eternal becoming and therefore eternal future; Nature is become and therefore eternally past. And here a strange inversion seems to have taken place—the Becoming has lost its priority over the Become. When the intellect looks back from *its* sphere, the Become, the aspect of life is reversed, the idea of Destiny which carries aim and future in it having turned into the mechanical principle of cause-and-effect of which the centre of gravity lies in the past. The spatially-experienced is promoted to rank above the temporal living, and time is replaced by a length in a spatial world-system. And, since in the creative experience extension follows from direction, the spatial from life, the human understanding imports life *as a process* into the inorganic space of its imagination. While life looks on space as something functionally belonging to itself, intellect looks upon life as something *in* space. To establish scientifically means, starting from the become and actualized, to search for "causes" by going back along a mechanically conceived course, that is to say, by treating becoming as a length. But it is not possible to live backwards, only to think backwards. Not Time and Destiny are reversible, but only that which the physicist calls "time" and admits into his formulae as divisible, and preferably as negative or imaginary quantities.

The perplexity is always there, though it has rarely been seen to be originally and necessarily inherent. In the Classical science the Eleatics, declining to admit the necessity of thinking of Nature as in motion, set up against it the logical view that thinking is a being, with the corollary that known and extended are identical and knowledge and becoming therefore irreconcilable. Their criticisms have not been, and cannot be, refuted. But they did not hinder the evolution of Classical physics, which was a necessary expression of the Apollinian soul and as such superior to logical difficulties. In the "classical" mechanics so-called of the Baroque, founded by Galileo and Newton, an irreproachable solution of the motion-problem on dynamic lines has been sought again and again. The last serious attempt—which failed like the rest, and of necessity—was Hertz's. Hertz tried to eliminate the notion of force entirely—rightly feeling that error in all mechanical systems has to be looked for in one or another of the basic concepts—and to build up the whole picture of physics on the quantities of time, space and mass. But he did not observe that it is Time itself (which as direction-factor is present in the force-concept) that is the organic element without which a dynamic theory cannot be expressed and with which a clean solution cannot be got. Moreover, quite apart from this, the concepts force, mass and motion constitute a dogmatic unit. They so condition one another that the application of one of them tacitly involves both the others from the outset. The notion of mass is only the complement of that of force. Newton, a deeply religious nature, was only bringing the Faustian world-feeling to expression when, to elucidate the words "force" and "motion," he said that masses are points of attack for force and carriers for motion. So the thirteenth-century Mystics had conceived of God and his relation to world. *Force is to the mechanical Nature-picture of Western man what Will is to his soul-picture and infinite Godhead in his world-picture.* The primary ideas of this physics stood firm long before the first physicist was born, for they lay in the earliest religious world-consciousness of our Culture.

THE INTERPRETATION OF "EXPERIENCE"

Nature-laws are forms of the known in which an aggregate of individual cases are brought together as a unit of higher degree. Living Time is ignored—that is, it does not matter whether, when or how often the case arises, for the question is not of chronological sequence but of mathematical consequence. But in the consciousness that no power in the world can shake this calculation lies our will to command over Nature. That is Faustian. It is only from this standpoint that miracles appear as breaches of the laws of Nature. Magian man saw in them merely the exercise of a power that was not common to all, not in any way a contradiction of the laws of Nature. And Classical man, according to Protagoras, was only the measure and not the creator of things—a view that unconsciously forgoes all conquest of Nature through the discovery and application of laws.

We see, then, that the causality-principle, in the form in which it is self-evidently necessary for us—the agreed basis of truth for our mathematics, physics and philosophy—is a Western and, more strictly speaking, a Baroque phenomenon. It cannot be proved, for every proof set forth in a Western language and every experiment conducted by a Western mind presupposes itself. In every problem, the enunciation contains the proof in germ. The method of a science is the science itself. Beyond question, the notion of laws of Nature and the conception of physics as *"scientia experimentalis,"* which has held ever since Roger Bacon, contain *a priori* this specific kind of necessity. The Classical mode of regarding Nature—the alter ego of the Classical mode of being—on the contrary, does *not* contain it, and yet it does not appear that the scientific position is weakened in logic thereby. If we work carefully through the utterances of Democritus, Anaxagoras, and Aristotle (in whom is contained the whole sum of Classical Nature-speculation), and, above all, if we examine the connotations of key-terms like ἀλλοίωσις, ἀνάγκη, ἐντελέχεια, we look with astonishment into a world-image totally unlike our own. This world-image is self-sufficing and therefore, for this definite sort of mankind, unconditionally true. And causality in our sense plays no part therein.

The principle of the Conservation of Energy, which since its enunciation by J. R. Mayer has been regarded in all seriousness as a plain conceptual necessity, is in fact a redescription of the *dynamic* principle of causality by means of the physical concept of force. The appeal to "experience," and the controversy as to whether judgment is necessary or empirical—i.e., in the language of Kant (who greatly deceived himself about the highly fluid boundaries between the two), whether it is *a priori* or *a posteriori* certain—are characteristically Western. But no one has noticed that a whole world-view is implicit in such a concept of "experience" with its aggressive dynamic connotation, and that there is not and cannot be "experience" in this pregnant sense for men of other Cultures. When we decline to recognize the scientific results of Anaxagoras or Democritus as experiential results, it does not mean that these Classical thinkers were incapable of interpreting and merely threw off fancies, but that we miss in their generalizations that causal element which for us *constitutes* experience in our sense of the word. Experience means to us an *activity* of the intellect, which does not resignedly confine itself to receiving, acknowledging and arranging momentary and purely present impressions, but seeks them out and calls them up in order to overcome them in their sensuous presence and to bring them into an unbounded unity in which their sensuous discreteness is dissolved. Experience in our sense possesses the tendency *from particular to infinite*. And for that very reason it is in contradiction with the feeling of Classical science. What for us is the way to acquire experience is for the Greek the way to lose it. And therefore he kept away from the drastic method of experiment. Our exact Natural science is imperative, the Classical is θεωρία in the literal sense, the result of passive contemplativeness.

THE "GOD-FEELING" AND NATURE

We can now say without any hesitation that the form-world of a Natural science corresponds to those of the appropriate mathematic, the appropriate religion, the appropriate art. A deep mathematician—by which is meant not a master-computer, but a man, any man, who feels the spirit of numbers living within him—realizes that through it he "knows God." Pythagoras and Plato were as well aware of this as Pascal and Leibniz.

The word "God" has a different sound under the vaulting of Gothic cathedrals or in the cloisters of Maulbronn and St. Gallen and in the basilicas of Syria and the temples of Republican Rome. The character of the Faustian cathedral is that of the *forest*. It is the architectural actualizing of a world-feeling that had found the first of all its symbols in the high forest of the Northern plains, the deciduous forest with its mysterious tracery, its whispering of ever-restless foliage high over the watcher's head, its treetops struggling to escape from earth. Think of Romanesque ornamentation and its deep affinity to the sense of the woods.

Cypresses and pines, with their corporeal and Euclidean effect, could never have become symbols of unending space. But the oaks, beeches and limes with the fitful light-flecks playing in their shadow-filled volume are felt as bodiless, boundless, spiritual. The rustle of the woods, a charm that no Classical poet ever felt—for it lies beyond the possibilities of Apollinian Nature-feeling—stands with its secret questions "whence?" "whither?" its

merging of presence into eternity, in a deep relation with
Destiny, with the feeling of History and Duration, with the
quality of Direction that impels the anxious, Faustian soul towards infinitely distant Future. And for that reason the organ,
which roars deep and high through our churches in tones that,
compared with the plain solid notes of aulos and cithara, seem
to know neither limit nor restraint, is the instrument of instruments in Western devotions. Cathedral and organ form a symbolic unity like temple and statue. Orchestra-tone strove tirelessly
in the eighteenth century towards a nearer kinship with the
organ-tone. The word *schwebend* [2]—meaningless as applied to
Classical things—is important alike in the theory of music, in
oil-painting, in architecture and in the dynamic physics of the
Baroque. Stand in a high wood of mighty stems while the storm
is tearing above, and you will comprehend instantly the full
meaning of the concept of a force which moves mass.

Out of such a primary feeling there arises, then, an idea of the
Divine immanent in the world-around, and this idea becomes
steadily more definite. The percipient receives the impression of
motion in Nature. He feels about him an almost indescribable
alien life of unknown powers, and traces the origin of these effects to "numina," to the Other, inasmuch as this Other also possesses Life. Astonishment at *alien motion* is the source of religion
and of physics both; respectively, they are the elucidations of
Nature (world-around) by the soul and by the reason. The "powers" are the first object both of fearful or loving reverence and
of critical investigation. There is a religious experience *and* a
scientific experience.

Now it is important to observe how the consciousness of
each Culture intellectually condenses its primary "numina." It
imposes significant words—*names*—on them and thereby conjures (seizes or bounds) them. By virtue of the Name they are
subject to the intellectual power of the man who possesses the
Name. The pronouncement of the right name (in physics, the
right concept) is an incantation. Deities and basic notions of
science alike come into being first as invocable names, representing an idea that tends to become more and more sensuously
definite. The outcome of a *Numen* is a *Deus,* the outcome of a

---

[2] It is used in the phrase "The spirit of God *schwebte* upon the face of
the waters."

notion is an idea. In the mere naming of "thing-in-itself," "atom," "energy," "gravitation," "cause," "evolution" and the like is for most learned men the same sense of deliverance as there was for the peasant of Latium in the words "Ceres," "Consus," "Janus," "Vesta." [3]

THE GREAT MYTH. FAUSTIAN, CLASSICAL, MAGIAN NUMINA

Scientists are wont to assume that myths and God-ideas are creations of primitive man, and that as spiritual culture "advances," this myth-forming power is shed. In reality it is the exact opposite, and had not the morphology of history remained to this day an almost unexplored field, the supposedly universal mythopoetic power would long ago have been found to be limited to particular periods. It would have been realized that this ability of a soul to fill its world with shapes, traits and symbols—like and consistent amongst themselves—belongs most decidedly not to the world-age of the primitives but exclusively to the springtimes of *great* Cultures. Every myth of the great style stands at the beginning of an awakening spirituality. It is the first formative act of that spirituality. Nowhere else is it to be found. There—it *must* be.

There are as many form-worlds of great myth as there are Cultures and early architectures. It was in the Homeric age (1100–800 B.C.) and in the corresponding age of chivalry (A.D. 900–1200), that is, the *epic* ages, and neither before nor after them, that the great world-image of a new religion came into being. The corresponding ages in India and Egypt are the Vedic and the Pyramid periods; one day it will be discovered that Egyptian mythology did in fact ripen into *depth* during the Third and Fourth Dynasties.

Only in this way can we understand the immense wealth of religious-intuitive creations that fills the three centuries of the Imperial Age in Germany. What came into existence then was *the Faustian mythology*. Hitherto, owing to religious and learned

---

[3] And it may be asserted that the downright faith that Haeckel, for example, pins to the names atom, matter, energy, is not essentially different from the fetishism of Neanderthal Man.

preconceptions, either the Catholic element has been treated to the exclusion of the Northern-Heathen or vice versa, and consequently we have been blind to the breadth and the unity of this form-world. In reality there is no such difference. The deep change of meaning in the Christian circle of ideas is identical, as a creative act, with the consolidation of the old heathen cults of the Migrations. To this lore belong the great God-legends of the Edda and many motives in the gospel-poetry of learned monks; the German hero-tales of Siegfried and Gudrun, Dietrich and Wayland; the vast wealth of chivalry-tales, derived from ancient Celtic fables, that was simultaneously coming to harvest on French soil, concerning King Arthur and the Round Table, the Holy Grail, Tristan, Percival and Roland. And with these are to be counted—beside the spiritual transvaluation, unremarked but all the deeper for that, of the Passion-Story—the Catholic hagiology of which the richest floraison was in the tenth and eleventh centuries and which produced the Lives of the Virgin and the histories of SS. Roch, Sebald, Severin, Francis, Bernard, Odilia. The *Legenda Aurea* was composed about 1250—this was the blossoming-time of courtly epic and Icelandic skald-poetry alike. Nowhere is the final meaning of these religious creations more clearly indicated than in the history of Valhalla. It was not an original German idea, and even the tribes of the Migrations were totally without it. It took shape just at *this* time, instantly and as an inward necessity, in the consciousness of the peoples newly arisen on the soil of the West. Thus it is "contemporary" with Olympus, which we know from the Homeric epos and which is as little Mycenaean as Valhalla is German in origin. As to the meaning of a myth, its provenance proves *nothing*. The "numen" itself, the primary form of the world-feeling, is a pure, necessary and unconscious creation, and it is not transferable.

In the Classical, Arabian and Western Cultures, the myth of the springtime is in each case that which we should expect; in the first static, in the second Magian, in the third dynamic. Examine every detail of form, and see how in the Classical it is an attitude and in the West a deed, there a being and here a will that underlies them; how in the Classical the bodily and tangible, the sensuously saturated, prevails and how therefore in the mode of worshipping the centre of gravity lies in the sense-impressive *cult,* whereas in the North it is space, force and therefore a religiousness that is predominantly dogmatic in colouring that rule. These very earliest creations of the young soul tell us that there is relationship between the Olympian figures, the statue and the corporeal Doric temple; between the domed basilica, the "Spirit" of God and the arabesque; between Valhalla and the Mary myth, the soaring nave and instrumental music.

Classical polytheism, consequently, has a style of its own which puts it in a different category from the conceptions of any other world-feelings, whatever the superficial affinities may be. This mode of possessing gods without godhead has existed only once, and it was in the one Culture that made the statue of naked Man the whole sum of its art.

Nature, as Classical man felt and knew it about him, viz., a sum of well-formed bodily things, could not be deified in any other form but this. The Roman felt that the claim of Yahweh to be recognized as sole God had something atheistic in it. One God, for him, was no God, and to this may be ascribed the strong dislike of popular feeling, both Greek and Roman, for the philosophers insofar as they were pantheists and godless. Gods are bodies, $\sigma\acute{\omega}\mu\alpha\tau\alpha$ of the highest type, and plurality was an attribute of bodies alike for mathematicians, lawyers and poets. The concept of $\zeta\tilde{\omega}o\nu$ $\pi o\lambda\iota\tau\iota\kappa\acute{o}\nu$ was valid for gods as well as for men. It is a deeply significant fact that in Hellas of all countries, star-gods, the numina of the Far, are wanting. Helios was worshipped only in half-Oriental Rhodes and Selene had no cult at all. The old Roman religion, in which the Classical world-feeling was expressed with special purity, knew neither sun nor moon, neither storm nor cloud as deities. The forest stirrings and the forest solitude, the tempest and the surf, which completely dominated the Nature of Faustian man (even that of pre-Faustian Celts and Teutons) and imparted to their mythology its peculiar character, left Classical man unmoved. Only concretes—hearth and door, the coppice and the plot-field, this particular river and that particular hill—condensed into Being for him.

The bases of the Apollinian and the Faustian Nature-images respectively are in all contexts the two opposite symbols of *individual thing* and *unitary space*. Olympus and Hades are perfectly sense-definite places, while the kingdom of the dwarfs, elves and goblins, and Valhalla and Niflheim, are all somewhere or other in the universe of space. In the old Roman religion "Tellus Mater" is not the all-mother but the visible arable field itself. Faunus *is* the wood and Vulturnus *is* the river, the name of the seed *is* Ceres and that of the harvest *is* Consus. Horace is a true Roman when he speaks of *"sub Jove frigido,"* under the cold sky. In these cases there is not even the attempt to reproduce the God in any sort of image at the places of worship, for that would be tantamount to duplicating him. Even in very late times the instinct not only of the Romans but of the Greeks also is opposed to idols, as is shown by the fact that plastic art, as it became more and more profane, came into conflict more and more with popular beliefs and the devout philosophy. In the house, Janus is the door as god, Vesta the hearth as goddess, the two functions of the house are objectivized and deified at once. A Hellenic river-god (like Acheloüs, who appears as a bull,) is definitely understood as being the river and not as, so to say, dwelling in the river. The Pans [4] and Satyrs are the fields and meadows as noon defines them. Dryads and Hamadryads *are* trees. On the contrary, not a trace of this localized materiality clings to the elves, dwarfs, witches, Valkyries and their kindred, the armies of departed souls that sweep round o' nights. Naiads *are* sources: nixies and tree-spirits and brownies are souls that are only bound to sources, trees and houses, from which they long to be released into the freedom of roaming. A nymph—a spring, that is—assumes human form when she would visit a handsome shepherd, but a nixie is an enchanted princess with nenuphars in her hair who comes up at midnight from the depths of the pool wherein she dwells. Kaiser Barbarossa sits in the Kyffhäuser cavern and Frau Venus in the Hörselberg. It is as though the Faustian universe abhorred anything material and impenetrable. In things, we suspect other worlds. Their hardness and thickness is merely appearance, and—a trait that would be impossible in Classical myth, because fatal to it—some favoured mortals are accorded the power to see through cliffs and crags into the depths. But is not just this the secret intent of our physical theories, of each new hypothesis? No other Culture knows so many fables of treasures lying in mountains and pools, of secret subterranean realms, palaces, gardens, wherein other beings dwell. The whole substantiality of the visible world is denied by the Faustian Nature-feeling, for which in the end

---

[4] The pantheistic idea of Pan, familiar in European poetry, is a conception of later Classical ages, acquired in principle from Egypt.—*At.*

nothing is of earth and the only actual is Space. The fairy-tale dissolves the matter of Nature, as the Gothic style dissolves the stone-mass of our cathedrals, into a ghostly wealth of forms and lines that have shed all weight and acknowledge no bounds.

The ever-increasing emphasis with which Classical polytheism somatically individualized its deities is peculiarly evident in its attitude to "strange gods." For Classical man the gods of the Egyptians, the Phoenicians and the Germans, insofar as they could be imagined as figures, were as real as his own gods. If a man were sojourning in Babylon, for instance, and Zeus and Apollo were far away, all the more reason for *particularly* honouring the local gods. This is the meaning of the altars dedicated "to the unknown gods," such as that which Paul so significantly misunderstood in a Magian monotheistic sense at Athens. These were gods not known by name to the Greek but worshipped by the foreigners of the great seaports (Piraeus, Corinth or other) and therefore entitled to their due of respect from him. Rome expressed this with Classical clearness in her religious law and in carefully preserved formulae like, for example, the *generalis invocatio.* As the universe is the sum of things, and as gods are things, recognition had to be accorded even to those gods with whom the Roman had not yet practically and historically come into relations.

In the first generations of the Imperial Age, the antique polytheism gradually dissolved, often without any alteration of outward ritual and mythic form, into the Magian monotheism. A new soul had come up, and it lived the old forms in a new mode. The names continued, but they covered other numina.

In all late-Classical cults, those of Isis and Cybele, of Mithras and Sol and Serapis, the divinity is no longer felt as a localized and formable being in an identifiable shape. In early-Christian times Jupiter Dolichenus or Sol Invictus [5] could be worshipped "wheresoever two or three were gathered together in his name." All these deities more and more came to be felt as a single

---

[5] Jupiter Dolichenus was a local deity of Doliche in Commagene, whose worship was spread over all parts of the Empire by soldiers recruited from that region; the tablet dedicated to him which is in the British Museum was found, for example, near Frankfurt-am-Main.

Sol Invictus is the Roman official form of Mithras. Troop-movements and trade spread his worship, like that of Jupiter Dolichenus, over the Empire.—*At.*

numen, though the adherents of a particular cult would believe that they in particular knew the numen in its true shape. Hence it is that Isis could be spoken of as the "million-named." Hitherto, names had been the designations of so many gods different in body and locality; now they are *titles* of the One whom every man has in mind.

This Magian monotheism reveals itself in all the religious creations that flooded the Empire from the East—the Alexandrian Isis, the Sun-god favoured by Aurelian (the Baal of Palmyra), the Mithras protected by Diocletian (whose Persian form had been completely recast in Syria), the Baalath of Carthage (Tanit, Dea Caelestis [6]) honoured by Septimius Severus. The importation of these figures no longer increases as in Classical times the number of concrete gods. On the contrary, they absorb the old gods into themselves, and do so in such a way as to deprive them more and more of picturable shape. Alchemy is replacing statics. Correspondingly, instead of the image we more and more find symbols—e.g. the Bull, the Lamb, the Fish, the Triangle, the Cross—coming to the front. In Constantine's *in hoc signo vinces* scarcely an echo of the Classical remains. Already there is setting in that aversion to human representation that ended in the Islamic and Byzantine prohibitions of images.

ATHEISM

Atheism is a subject that the psychologist and the student of religion have hitherto regarded as scarcely worth careful investigation. Much has been written and argued about it, and very roundly, by the free-thought martyr on the one hand and the religious zealot on the other. But no one has had anything to say about the *species* of atheism; or has treated it analytically as an *individual and definite* phenomenon, positive and necessary and intensely symbolic; or has realized how it is limited in time.

Atheism, rightly understood, is the necessary expression of a spirituality that has accomplished itself and exhausted its religious possibilities, and is declining into the inorganic. It is entirely compatible with a living wistful desire for real religious-

---

[6] To whom the inhabitants of "Roman" Carthage managed to attach even Dido.—*At.*

ness [7]—therein resembling Romanticism, which likewise would recall that which has irrevocably gone, namely, the Culture —and it may quite well be in a man as a creation of his feeling without his being aware of it, without its ever interfering with the habits of his thought or challenging his convictions. We can understand this if we can see what it was that made the devout Haydn call Beethoven an atheist after he had heard some of his music. Atheism comes not with the evening of the Culture but with the dawn of Civilization.

But, if this late form of world-feeling and world-image which preludes our "second religiousness" is universally a negation of the religious in us, the structure of it is different in each of the Civilizations. There is no religiousness that is without an atheistic opposition belonging uniquely to itself and directed uniquely against itself. Men continue to experience the outer world that extends around them as a cosmos of well-ordered bodies or a world-cavern or eternally active space, as the case may be, but they no longer livingly experience the sacred causality in it. They only perceive a profane causality that is, or is desired to be, inclusively mechanical. There are atheisms of Classical, Arabian and Western kinds and these differ from one another in meaning and in matter. Nietzsche formulated the dynamic atheism on the basis that "God is dead," and a Classical philosopher would have expressed the static and Euclidean by saying that the "gods who dwell in the holy places are dead," the one indicating that boundless space has, the other that countless bodies have, become godless. But *dead* space and *dead* things are the "facts" of physics. The atheist is unable to experience any difference between the Nature-picture of physics and that of religion. Language, with a fine feeling, distinguishes wisdom and intelligence—the early and the late, the rural and the megalopolitan conditions of the soul.

The spiritual in every living Culture is religious, has religion, whether it be conscious of it or not. It is not open to a spirituality to be irreligious; at most it can play with the idea of irreligion as Medicean Florentines did. But the megalopolitan *is* irreligious;

---

[7] Diagoras, who was condemned to death by the Athenians for his "godless" writings, left behind him deeply pious dithyrambs. Read, too, Hebbel's diaries and his letters to Elise. He "did not believe in God," but he prayed.

this is part of his being, a mark of his historical position. The degree of piety of which a period is capable is revealed in its attitude towards toleration. One tolerates something either because it seems to have some relation to what according to one's experience is the divine or else because one is no longer capable of such experience and is indifferent.

What we moderns have called "Toleration" in the Classical world is an expression of the *contrary* of atheism. Plurality of numina and cults is inherent in the conception of Classical religion. But to the Faustian soul *dogma* and not visible ritual constitutes the essence. What is regarded as godless is opposition to doctrine. Here begins the spatial-spiritual conception of heresy. A Faustian religion by its very nature cannot allow any freedom of conscience; it would be in contradiction with its space-invasive dynamic. Even free-thinking itself is no exception to the rule. Amongst us there is no faith without leanings to an Inquisition of some sort. Expressed in *appropriate* electrodynamic imagery, the field of force of a conviction adjusts all the minds within it according to its own intensity. Failure to do so means absence of conviction—in ecclesiastical language, ungodliness. For the Apollinian soul, on the contrary, it was contempt of the cult—$\dot{\alpha}\sigma\acute{\epsilon}\beta\epsilon\iota\alpha$ in the literal sense—that was ungodly, and here its religion admitted no freedom of *attitude*. In both cases there was a line drawn between the toleration demanded by the god-feeling and that forbidden by it.

The *histories* of the gods could be made fun of in Satyric drama and comedy—even that did not impugn their Euclidean existence. But the statue of the god, the cult, the plastic embodiment of piety—it was not permitted to any man to touch these. It was not out of hypocrisy that the fine minds of the earlier Empire, who had ceased to take a myth of any kind seriously, punctiliously conformed to the public cults and, above all, to the cult—deeply real for all classes—of the Emperor. And, on the other hand, the poets and thinkers of the mature Faustian Culture were at liberty "not to go to Church," to avoid Confession, to stay at home on procession-days and (in Protestant surroundings) to live without any relations with the church whatever. But they were not free to touch points of dogma, for that would have been dangerous within any confession and any sect, including, once more and expressly, free-thought. The Roman Stoic, who without faith in the mythology piously observed the ritual forms, has his counterpart in those men of the Age of Enlightenment, like Lessing and Goethe, who disregarded the rites of the Church but never doubted the "fundamental truths of faith."

FAUSTIAN PHYSICS AS THE DOGMA OF FORCE

If we turn back from Nature-feeling become form to Nature-knowledge become system, we know God or the gods as the origin of the images by which the intellect seeks to make the world-around comprehensible to itself. Goethe once remarked (to Riemer): "Reason is as old as the World; even the child has reason. But it is not applied in all times in the same way or to the same objects. The earlier centuries obtained their ideas from imaginative contemplation, but ours reduces them to concepts. Then the productive force was greater, now the destructive force or art of distinguishing." The strong religiousness of Newton's mechanics [8] and the almost complete atheism of the formulations of modern dynamics are of like colour, positive and negative of the same primary feeling. A physical system of necessity has all the characteristics of the soul to whose world-form it belongs. The Deism of the Baroque goes together with its dynamics and its analytical geometry; its three basic principles, God, Freedom and Immortality, are in the language of mechanics the principles of inertia (Galileo), least action (D'Alembert) and the conservation of energy (J. R. Mayer).

Western physics is by its inward form dogmatic and not ritualistic (*kultisch*). Its content is the *dogma of Force,* which is identical with space and distance.

That this "force" or "energy" is really a numen stiffened into a concept (and in nowise the result of scientific experience) is shown by the often overlooked fact that the basic principle known as the First Law of Thermodynamics [9] says nothing whatever about the nature of energy, and it is properly speaking an

---

[8] In the famous conclusion of his *Optics* (1706), which made a powerful impression and became the starting-point of quite new enunciations of theological problems, Newton limits the domain of mechanical causes as against the Divine First Cause, whose perception-organ is necessarily infinite space itself.

[9] The law of the equivalence of heat and work.—*At.*

incorrect (though psychologically most significant) assumption that the idea of the "Conservation of Energy" is part of it. Experimental measurement can in the nature of things only establish a *number,* which number we have (significantly, again) named *work.* But the dynamical cast of our thought demanded that this should be conceived as a *difference* of energy, although the absolute value of energy is only a figment and can never be rendered by a definite number. There always remains, therefore, an undefined additive constant, as we call it; in other words, we always strive to maintain the image of an energy that our inner eye has formed, although actual scientific practice is not concerned with it.

This being the provenance of the force-concept, it follows that we can no more define it than we can define those other un-Classical words "will" and "space." There remains always a felt and intuitively perceived remainder which makes every personal definition an almost religious *creed* of its author. Laplace called it an unknown of which the workings are all that we know, and Newton imagined immaterial forces at a distance. Leibniz spoke of *Vis viva* as a quantum which together with matter formed the unit that he called the monad, and Descartes, with certain thinkers of the eighteenth century, was equally unwilling to draw fundamental distinctions between motion and the moved. Beside *potentia, virtus, impetus,* we find even in Gothic times periphrases such as *conatus* and *nisus,* in which the force and the releasing cause are obviously not separated. Spinoza, a Jew and therefore, spiritually, a member of the Magian Culture, could not absorb the Faustian force-concept at all, and it has no place in his system. And it is an astounding proof of the secret power of root-ideas that Heinrich Hertz, the only Jew amongst the great physicists of the recent past, was also the only one of them who tried to resolve the dilemma of mechanics by *eliminating* the idea of force.

The force-dogma is the one and only theme of Faustian physics. There *is* no Western statics—that is, no interpretation of mechanical facts that is natural to the Western spirit bases itself on the ideas of form and substance, or even, for that matter, on the ideas of space and mass otherwise than in connexion with those of time and force. The reader can test this in any department that he pleases.

The Late Renaissance imagined that it had revived the Archimedean physics just as it believed that it was continuing the

Classical sculpture. Even Galileo was still under the influence of
the Renaissance feeling. He therefore limited the idea of force
to contact-force (impact) and his formulation did not go beyond
conservation of momentum (quantity of motion). He held fast
to mere "moved-ness" and fought shy of any emphasis on space,
and it was left to Leibniz to develop—first in the course of
controversy and then positively by the application of his mathematical discoveries—the idea of genuine *free and directional
forces* (living force, *activum thema*). The notion of conservation
of momentum then gave way to that of conservation of living
forces, as quantitative number gave way to functional number.
Newton it was who first got completely away from Renaissance
feeling and formed the notion of distant forces, the attraction
and repulsion of bodies across space itself. Distance is already
in itself a force. The very idea of it is so free from all sense-
perceptible content that Newton himself felt uncomfortable with
it—in fact it mastered him and not he it. To this day no one has
produced an adequate definition of these forces-at-a-distance. No
one has ever yet understood what centrifugal force really is. Is
the force of the earth rotating on its axis the cause of this motion or vice versa? Or are the two identical?

This *symbolic* difficulty of modern mechanics is in no way removed by the potential theory that was founded by Faraday
when the centre of gravity of physical thought had passed from
the dynamics of matter to the electro-dynamics of the aether.
The famous experimenter, who was a visionary through and
through—alone amongst the modern masters of physics he was
not a mathematician—observed in 1846: "I assume nothing to be
true in any part of space (whether this be empty as is commonly
said, or filled with matter) except forces and the lines in which
they are exercised." Here Faraday is metaphysically at one with
Newton, whose forces-at-a-distance point to a mythic background
that the devout physicist declined to examine. The possible alternative way of reaching an unequivocal definition of force—
viz., that which starts from World and not God, from the object
and not the subject of natural motion-state—was leading at the
very same time to the formulation of the concept of Energy.
Now, this concept represents, as distinct from that of force, a
quantum of directedness and not a direction, and is in so far
akin to Leibniz's conception of "living force" unalterabie in quantity. It will not escape notice that essential features of the mass-
concept have been taken over here; indeed, even the bizarre no-

tion of an atomic structure of energy has been seriously discussed.

This rearrangement of the basic words has not, however, altered the feeling that a world-force with its substratum does exist. The motion-problem is as insoluble as ever. All that has happened on the way from Newton to Faraday—or from Berkeley to Mill—is that the religious deed-idea has been replaced by the irreligious work-idea. In the Nature-picture of modern physics *Nature is doing work;* for every "process" within the meaning of the First Law of Thermodynamics is or should be measurable by the expenditure of energy to which a quantity of work corresponds in the form of "bound energy."

Naturally, therefore, we find the decisive discovery of J. R. Mayer coinciding in time with the birth of the Socialist theory. Even economic systems wield the same concepts; the value-problem has been in relation with quantity of work ever since Adam Smith, who *vis-à-vis* Quesney and Turgot marks the change from an organic to a mechanical structure of the economic field. Phrases could be found in the language of economists which correspond exactly to the physical propositions of conservation of energy, entropy and least action.

If, then, we review the successive stages through which the central idea of force has passed since its birth in the Baroque, and its intimate relations with the form-worlds of the great arts and of mathematics, we find that (1) in the seventeenth century (Galileo, Newton, Leibniz) it is pictorially formed and in unison with the great art of oil-painting that died out about 1630; (2) in the eighteenth century (the "classical" mechanics of Laplace and Lagrange) it acquires the abstract character of the fugue-style and is in unison with Bach; and (3) with the Culture at its end and the civilized intelligence victorious over the spiritual, it appears in the domain of pure analysis, and in particular in the theory of functions of several complex variables, without which it is, in its most modern form, scarcely understandable.

THE LIMITS OF FURTHER THEORETICAL— NOT TECHNICAL—DEVELOPMENT

But with this, it cannot be denied, Western physics is drawing near to the limit of its possibilities. At bottom, its mission as a historical phenomenon has been to transform the Faustian Nature-feeling into an intellectual knowledge, the faith-forms of springtime into the machine-forms of exact science. And, though for the time being it will continue to quarry more and more practical and even "purely theoretical" results, results as such, whatever their kind, belong to the superficial history of a science. To its deeps belong only the history of its symbolism and its style, and it is almost too evident to be worth the saying that in those deeps the essence and nucleus of our science is in rapid disintegration. Up to the end of the nineteenth century every step was in the direction of an inward fulfilment, an increasing purity, rigour and fullness of the dynamic Nature-picture—and then, that which has brought it to an optimum of theoretical clarity, suddenly becomes a *solvent*. This is not happening intentionally—the high intelligences of modern physics are, in fact, unconscious that it is happening at all—but therein lies an inherent historic necessity. Just so, at the same relative stage, the Classical science inwardly fulfilled itself about 200 B.C. Analysis reached its goal with Gauss, Cauchy and Riemann, and today it is only filling up the gaps in its structure.

This is the origin of the sudden and annihilating doubt that has arisen about things that even yesterday were the unchallenged foundation of physical theory, about the meaning of the energy-principle, the concepts of mass, space, absolute time, and causality-laws generally. This doubt is no longer the fruitful doubt of the Baroque, which brought the knower and the object of his knowledge together; it is a doubt affecting the very possibility of a Nature-science. To take one instance alone, what a depth of unconscious Skepsis there is in the rapidly increasing use of enumerative and statistical methods, which aim only at *probability* of results and forgo in advance the absolute scientific exactitude that was a creed to the hopeful earlier generations.

The moment is at hand now when the possibility of a self-contained and self-consistent mechanics will be given up for good. Every physics, as I have shown, must break down over the motion-problem, in which the living person of the knower methodically intrudes into the inorganic form-world of the known. But today, not only is this dilemma still inherent in all the newest theories but three centuries of intellectual work have brought it so sharply to focus that there is no possibility more of ignoring it. The theory of gravitation, which since Newton has been an impregnable truth, has now been recognized as a temporally limited and shaky hypothesis. The principle of the Conservation of Energy has no meaning if energy is supposed to be infinite in an infinite space. The acceptance of the principle is incompatible with any three-dimensional structure of space, whether infinite or Euclidean or (as the non-Euclidean geometries present it) spherical and of "finite, yet unbounded" volume. Its validity therefore is restricted to "a system of bodies self-contained and not externally influenced" and such a limitation does not and cannot exist in actuality. But symbolic infinity was just what the Faustian world-feeling had meant to express in this basic idea, which was simply *the mechanical and extensional re-ideation of the idea of immortality of the world-soul*. In fact it was a feeling out of which knowledge could never succeed in forming a clear system. The luminiferous aether, again, was an ideal postulate of modern dynamics whereby every motion required a something-to-be-moved, but every conceivable hypothesis concerning the constitution of this aether has broken down under inner contradictions; more, Lord Kelvin has proved mathematically that there *can* be no structure of this light-transmitter that is not open to objections. As, according to the interpretation of Fresnel's experiments, the light-waves are transversal, the aether would have to be a rigid body (with truly quaint properties), but then the laws of elasticity would have to apply to it and in that case the waves would be longitudinal. The Maxwell-Hertz equations of the Electromagnetic Theory of Light, which in fact are pure nameless numbers of indubitable validity, exclude the explanation of the aether by any mechanics whatsoever. Therefore, and having regard also to the consequences of the Relativity theory, physicists now regard the aether as pure vacuum. But that, after all, is not very different from demolishing the dynamic picture itself.

Since Newton, the assumption of constant mass—the counterpart of constant force—has had uncontested validity. But the Quantum theory of Planck, and the conclusions of Niels Bohr therefrom as to the fine structure of atoms, which experimental experience had rendered necessary, have destroyed this assumption. Every self-contained system possesses, besides kinetic energy, an energy of radiant heat which is inseparable from it and therefore cannot be represented purely by the concept of mass. For if mass is defined by living energy it is *ipso facto* no longer constant with reference to thermodynamic state. Nevertheless, it is impossible to fit the theory of quanta into the group of hypotheses constituting the "classical" mechanics of the Baroque; moreover, along with the principle of causal continuity, the basis of the Infinitesimal Calculus founded by Newton and Leibniz is threatened. But, if these are serious enough doubts, the ruthlessly cynical hypothesis of the Relativity theory strikes to the very heart of dynamics. Supported by the experiments of A. A. Michelson, which showed that the velocity of light remains unaffected by the motion of the medium, and prepared mathematically by Lorentz and Minkowski, its specific tendency is to *destroy the notion of absolute time.* Astronomical discoveries (and here present-day scientists are seriously deceiving themselves) can neither establish nor refute it. "Correct" and "incorrect" are not the criteria whereby such assumptions are to be tested; the question is whether, in the chaos of involved and artificial ideas that has been produced by the innumerable hypotheses of Radioactivity and Thermodynamics, it can hold its own as a *usable* hypothesis or not. But however this may be, *it has abolished the constancy of those physical quantities into the definition of which time has entered,* and unlike the antique statics, the Western dynamics knows *only* such quantities. Absolute measures of length and rigid bodies are no more. And with this the possibility of absolute quantitative delimitations and therefore the "classical" concept of mass as the constant ratio between force and acceleration fell to the ground—when the quantum of action, a product of energy and time, had been set up as a new constant.

If we make it clear to ourselves that the atomic ideas of Rutherford and Bohr [1] signify nothing but this, that the numerical results of observations have suddenly been provided with a picture of a planetary world within the atom, instead of that of atom-swarms hitherto favoured; if we observe how rapidly card-houses of hypothesis are run up nowadays, every contradiction being immediately covered up by a new hurried hypothesis; if we reflect on how little heed is paid to the fact that these images

---

[1] Which in many cases have led to the supposition that the "actual existence" of atoms has now at last been proved—a singular throw-back to the materialism of the preceding generation.

contradict one another and the "classical" Baroque mechanics alike, we cannot but realize that the *great style of ideation is at an end* and that, as in architecture and the arts of form, a sort of craft-art of hypothesis-building has taken its place. Only our extreme maestria in experimental technique—true child of its century—hides the collapse of the symbolism.

THE SELF-DESTRUCTION OF DYNAMIC PHYSICS; HISTORICAL IDEAS APPEAR

Amongst these symbols of decline, the most conspicuous is the notion of Entropy, which forms the subject of the Second Law of Thermodynamics. The First Law, that of the conservation of energy, is the plain formulation of the essence of dynamics—not to say of the constitution of the West European soul, to which Nature is necessarily visible only in the form of a contrapuntal-dynamic causality (as against the static-plastic causality of Aristotle). The basic element of the Faustian world-picture is not the Attitude but the Deed and, mechanically considered, the Process, and this law merely puts the mathematical character of these processes in the form of variables and constants. But the Second Law goes deeper, and shows a *bias* in Nature-happenings which is in no wise imposed *a priori* by the conceptual fundamentals of dynamics.

Mathematically, Entropy is represented by a quantity which is fixed by the momentary state of a self-contained system of bodies and under all physical and chemical alterations can only increase, never diminish; in the most favourable conditions it remains unchanged. Entropy, like Force and Will, is something which (to anyone for whom this form-world is accessible at all) is inwardly clear and meaningful, but is formulated differently by every different authority and never satisfactorily by any. Here again, the intellect breaks down where the world-feeling demands expression.

Nature-processes in general have been classified as irreversible and reversible, according as entropy is increased or not. In any process of the first kind, free energy is converted into bound energy, and if this dead energy is to be turned once more into living, this can only occur through the simultaneous binding of a further quantum of living energy in some second process; the best-known example is the combustion of coal—that is, the conversion of the living energy stored up in it into heat bound by the gas form of the carbon dioxide, if the latent energy of water is to be translated into steam-pressure and thereafter into motion. It follows that in the world as a whole entropy continually increases; that is, the dynamic system is manifestly approaching to some final state, whatever this may be.[2] Examples of the irreversible processes are conduction of heat, diffusion, friction, emission of light and chemical reactions; of reversible, gravitation, electric oscillations, electromagnetic waves and sound-waves.

What has never hitherto been fully felt, and what leads me to regard the Entropy theory (1850) as the beginning of the destruction of that masterpiece of Western intelligence, the old dynamic physics, is the deep opposition of theory and actuality which is here for the first time introduced into theory itself. The First Law had drawn the strict picture of a causal Nature-happening, but the Second Law by introducing irreversibility has for the first time brought into the mechanical-logical domain a tendency belonging to immediate life and thus in fundamental contradiction with the very essence of that domain.

If the Entropy theory is followed out to its conclusion, it results, *firstly*, that in theory all processes must be reversible—which is one of the basic postulates of dynamics and is reasserted with all rigour in the law of the Conservation of Energy [3]—but, *secondly*, that in actuality processes of Nature in their entirety are irreversible. Not even under the artificial conditions of laboratory experiment can the simplest process be exactly reversed, that is, a state once passed cannot be re-established. Nothing is more significant of the present condition of systematics than the introduction of the hypothesis of "elementary disorder" for the purpose of smoothing out the contradiction between intellectual postulate and actual experience. The "smallest particles" of a body

[2] Spengler was severely attacked for this formulation, which is derived from Clausius, one of the founders of the theory of Entropy. Up to now, however, it has not been confuted. At least it can be argued that every finite part of the world has a finite supply of energy and to this extent the Second Law applies.—H.W.

[3] As it was conceived by J. R. Mayer, and to this extent the law of energy is a more exact formulation of part of the general principle of causality. The First and Second Laws do not contradict one another in the modern interpretation of the theory of causality.—H.W.

(an image, no more) throughout perform reversible processes, but in actual things the smallest particles are in disorder and mutually interfere; and so the irreversible process that alone is experienced by the observer is linked with increase of entropy by taking the mean probabilities of occurrences. And thus theory becomes a chapter of the Calculus of Probabilities, and in lieu of exact we have statistical methods.

Evidently, the significance of this has passed unnoticed. Statistics belong, like chronology, to the domain of the organic, to fluctuating Life, to Destiny and Incident, and not to the world of laws and timeless causality. As everyone knows, statistics serve above all to characterize political and economic, that is, historical, developments. In the "classical" mechanics of Galileo and Newton there would have been no room for them. And if, now, suddenly the contents of that field are supposed to be understood and understandable only statistically and under the aspect of Probability—instead of under that of the *a priori* exactitude which the Baroque thinkers unanimously demanded—what does it mean? It means that the object of understanding is ourselves. The Nature "known" in this wise is the Nature that we know by way of living experience, that we live in ourselves. What *theory* asserts (and, being itself, must assert)—to wit, this ideal irreversibility that never happens in actuality—represents a relic of the old severe intellectual form, the great Baroque tradition that had contrapuntal music for twin sister. But the resort to statistics shows that the force that that tradition regulated and made effective is exhausted. Becoming and Become, Destiny and Causality, historical and natural-science elements, are beginning to be confused. Formulae of life, growth, age, direction and death are crowding up.

That is what, from this point of view, irreversibility in world-processes has to mean. It is the expression, no longer of the physical t but of genuine *historical,* inwardly experienced Time, which is identical with Destiny.[4] The critical form-world of Na-

---

[4] As entropic loss is regarded only in one sense—that of increase—so this corresponds with the course of time. Thus one can say that our measurement of time is actually a measure of the probability of change of the situation in the direction towards the final state of absolute equilibrium.

The latest development is to regard the process of life on the earth in its entirety as excluded from the operation of entropy. Here qualitative suppositions and biological theories have been introduced into physics. This

ture-*knowledge* started in the opposite direction to Nature-*feeling*, God-feeling. Here, at the end of the Late period, it has reached the maximal distance and is turning to come home. The more dynamics exhausts its inner possibilities as it nears the goal, the more decidedly the historical characters in the picture come to the front and the more insistently the organic necessity of Destiny asserts itself side by side with the inorganic necessity of Causality, and Direction makes itself felt along with capacity and intensity, the factors of pure extension. The course of this process is marked by the appearance of whole series of daring hypotheses, all of like sort, which are only apparently demanded by experimental results and which in fact world-feeling and mythology imagined as long ago as the Gothic age.

Above all, this is manifested in the bizarre hypotheses of atomic disintegration which elucidate the phenomena of radioactivity, and according to which uranium atoms that have kept their essence unaltered, in spite of all external influences, for millions of years, quite suddenly without assignable cause explode, scattering their smallest particles over space with velocities of thousands of kilometers per second. Only a few individuals in an aggregate of radioactive atoms are struck by Destiny thus, the neighbours being entirely unaffected. Here too, then, is a picture of history and not "Nature," and although statistical methods here also prove to be necessary, one might almost say that in them mathematical number has been replaced by chronological.[5]

With ideas like these, the mythopoetic force of the Faustian soul is returning to its origins. Force, Will, has an aim, and where there is an aim there is for the inquiring eye an end. That which the perspective of oil-painting expressed by means of the vanishing point, the Baroque park by its *point de vue,* and analysis by

〰〰〰

entails a sacrifice of strict physical thinking or rather the relation of physics to biology.

It can be regarded as certain that the development of "forms" does not conflict with the Second Law. All life in the Cosmos, great and small, can be looked upon as a development of perpetually differentiating stages between the initial Chaos and final congelation; compare *Die Theorie von der Cosmogenie,* by C. F. von Weizsäcker. The Second Law and the development of forms follow from the same structure of the historical world.—H.W.

[5] The application of the idea of "lifetime" to elements has in fact produced the conception of "half-transformation times" [such as 3.85 days for radium emanation—*At.*].

the nth term of an infinite series—the conclusion, that is, of a willed directedness—assumes here the form of the concept. The Faust of the Second Part is dying, for he has reached his goal. What the myth of Götterdämmerung signified of old, the irreligious form of it, the theory of Entropy,[6] signifies today.

THE LAST STAGE. DISSOLUTION IN A SYSTEM OF MORPHOLOGICAL RELATIONSHIPS

It remains now to sketch the last stage of Western science. From our standpoint of today, the gently sloping route of decline is clearly visible.

This too, the power of looking ahead to inevitable Destiny, is part of the historical capacity that is the peculiar endowment of the Faustian. The Classical died, as we shall die, but it died unknowing. It believed in an eternal Being and to the last it lived its days with frank satisfaction, each day spent as a gift of the gods. But we know our history. Before us there stands a last

---

[6] Today the idea is openly expressed that the science of physics has reached the limit of possible knowledge. Opinions differ as to how the difficulty can be overcome. On the one hand, R. B. Lindsay maintains that in the nature of things every measurement carries in itself the possibility of error. At the same time Lindsay attacks the Heisenberg Uncertainty-Relation insofar as a general principle of renunciation of knowledge is derived from it.

The Vienna school holds that man's thinking powers are the bar: that the world as represented is purely conventional: that it remains to be seen whether causal thought can be replaced by another but equally exact form of thought. Finally Sir E. Whittaker suggests the application of the notion of "Postulates of Impotence." The theoretical meaning of these is the idea that in due course every branch of physics can be closed like Euclidean geometry. The controversy discloses a state of affairs which Spengler had foreseen better than his scientific contemporaries. Actually what Spengler tried to point out regarding the theory of Entropy and the movements of atoms in relation to the macro-state of an object has been followed by present-day atom-physicists. Entropy is still causally deducible, the elements of Quantum-Mechanics are no longer so. Admitting that the decisive break comes later, all the more important is the service rendered by Spengler in diagnosing the tendency in advance. Regarding his own observations on the subject of Entropy, C. F. von Weizsäcker says that they show "how little we are in a position to think about the objects of physics unconnected with a subject who perceives. This fact is revealed to us by atom-physics" (1946) and: "The metaphysical hope of the classical physicists to obtain a hold over 'Being in itself' collapses. The physics of today force the physicist to consideration of himself as subject" (1948).—H.W.

spiritual crisis that will involve all Europe and America. What its course will be, Late Hellenism tells us. The tyranny of the Reason—of which we are not conscious, for we are ourselves its apex —is in every Culture an epoch between man and old-man, and no more. Its most distinct expression is the cult of exact sciences, of dialectic, of demonstration, of causality. Of old the Ionic and in our case the Baroque were its rising limb, and now the question is: What form will the down-curve assume?

In this very century, I prophesy, the century of scientific-critical Alexandrianism, of the great harvests, of the final formulations, a change of feeling (*neuer Zug von Innerlichkeit*) will overcome the will-to-victory of science. Exact science must presently fall upon its own keen sword. First, in the eighteenth century, its methods were tried out, then, in the nineteenth, its powers, and now its historical role is critically reviewed. But from Skepsis there is a path to "second religiousness," which is the sequel and not the preface of the Culture. Men dispense with proof, desire only to believe and not to dissect.

Science exists only in the living thought of great savant-generations, and books are nothing if they are not living and effective in men worthy of them. Scientific results are merely items of an intellectual tradition. An orgy of two centuries of exact scientific-ness brings satiety. The great century of the Classical science was the third, after the death of Aristotle; when Archimedes died and the Romans came, it was already almost at its end. Our great century has been the nineteenth. Savants of the calibre of Gauss and Humboldt and Helmholtz were already no more by 1900. In physics as in chemistry, in biology as in mathematics, the great masters are dead, and we are now experiencing the *decrescendo* of brilliant gleaners who arrange, collect and finish off like the Alexandrian scholars of the Roman age. Everything that does not belong to the matter-of-fact side of life —to politics, technics or economics—exhibits the common symptom.

But before the curtain falls, there is one more task for the historical Faustian spirit, a task not yet specified, hitherto not even imagined as possible. There has still to be written a *morphology of the exact sciences,* which shall discover how all laws, concepts and theories inwardly hang together as forms and what they have meant as such in the life-course of the Faustian Culture. The re-treatment of theoretical physics, of chemistry, of mathematics as a sum of symbols—this will be the definitive conquest of the mechanical world-aspect by an intuitive, once more religious world-outlook, a last master-effort of physiognomic to break down even systematic and to absorb it, as expression and symbol, into its own domain. One day we shall no longer ask, as the nineteenth century asked, what are the valid laws underlying chemical affinity or diamagnetism—rather, we shall be amazed indeed that minds of the first order could ever have been completely preoccupied by questions such as these. We shall inquire whence came these forms that were prescribed for the Faustian spirit, why they had to come exclusively to this one Culture and what deep meaning there is in the fact that the figures we have obtained appeared in just this picture-like disguise. And, be it said, we have today hardly yet an inkling of how much in our reputedly objective values and experiences is only disguise, only image and expression.

The separate sciences—epistemology, physics, chemistry, mathematics, astronomy—are approaching one another with acceleration, converging towards a complete identity of results. The issue will be a fusion of the form-worlds, which will present on the one hand a system of numbers, functional in nature and reduced to a few ground-formulae, and on the other a small group of theories, denominators to those numerators, which in the end will be seen to be myths of the springtime under modern veils, reducible therefore—and at once of necessity reduced—to picturable and physiognomically significant basic characteristics. This convergence has not yet been observed, for the reason that since Kant—indeed, since Leibniz—there has been no philosopher who commanded the problems of *all* the exact sciences.

While fifty years ago the essence of chemistry could still be described almost without mathematics, today the chemical elements are in course of volatilizing themselves into the mathematical constants of variable relation-complexes. Physiology is becoming a chapter of organic chemistry and is making use of the methods of the Infinitesimal Calculus. The latest views on epistemology are now associated with those of higher analysis and theoretical physics to occupy an almost inaccessible domain, the domain to which, for example, the theory of Relativity belongs or ought to belong. The sign-language in which the emanation-theory of radioactivity expresses itself is completely de-sensualized.

Chemistry, once concerned with defining as sharply as possible the qualities of elements, such as valency, weight, affinity and reactivity, is setting to work to get rid of these sensible traits. The elements are held to differ in character according to their derivation from this or that compound. They are represented to be complexes of different units which indeed behave ("actually") as units of a higher order and are not practically separable but show deep differences in point of radioactivity. Through the emanation of radiant energy degradation is always going on, so that we can speak of the *lifetime* of an element, in formal contradiction with the original concept of the element and the spirit of modern chemistry as created by Lavoisier. All these tendencies are bringing the ideas of chemistry very close to the theory of Entropy, with its suggestive opposition of causality and destiny, Nature and History. And they indicate the paths that our science is pursuing—on the one hand, towards the discovery that its logical and numerical results are identical with the structure of the reason itself, and, on the other, towards the revelation that the whole theory which clothes these numbers merely represents the symbolic expression of Faustian life.

And here we must mention finally the truly Faustian theory of "aggregates," one of the weightiest in all this form-world of our science. In sharpest antithesis to the older mathematic, it deals, not with singular quantities, but with the aggregates constituted by all quantities [or objects] having this or that specified morphological similarity—for instance all square numbers or all differential equations of a given type. Such an aggregate it conceives as a new unit, a new *number of higher order,* and subjects it to criteria of new and hitherto quite unsuspected kinds such as "potency," "order," "equivalence," "computability," [7] and devises laws and operative methods for it in respect of these criteria. Thus is being actualized a last extension of the function-theory. Little by little this absorbed the whole of our mathematic, and now it is dealing with variables by the principles of

---

[7] The "Aggregate" of rational numbers is computable, that of real numbers is not. The aggregate of complex numbers is two-dimensional; from this follows the theory of n-dimensional aggregates, which also includes geometrical fields in the aggregate theory.

the Theory of Groups in respect of the character of the function and by those of the Theory of Aggregates in respect of the values of the variables. Mathematical philosophy is well aware that these ultimate meditations on the nature of number are fusing with those upon pure logic, and an algebra of logic is talked of. The study of geometrical axioms has become a chapter of epistemology.[8]

The aim to which all this is striving, and which in particular every Nature-searcher feels in himself as an impulse, is the achievement of a pure numerical transcendence, the complete and inclusive conquest of the visibly apparent and its replacement by a language of imagery unintelligible to the layman and impossible of sensuous realization—but a language that the great Faustian symbol of Infinite space endows with the dignity of inward necessity. The deep scepticism of these final judgments links the soul anew to the forms of early Gothic religiousness. The inorganic, known and dissected world, the World as Nature and System, has deepened itself until it is a pure sphere of functional numbers. But, as we have seen, number is one of the most primary symbols in every Culture; and consequently the way to pure number is the return of the waking-consciousness to its own secret, the revelation of its own formal necessity. The goal reached, the vast and ever more meaningless and threadbare fabric woven around natural science falls apart. It was, after all, nothing but the "word-bound" structure of the "Reason," the grammar by which it believed it could overcome the Visible and extract therefrom the True. But what appears under the fabric is once again the earliest and deepest, the Myth, the immediate Becoming, Life itself. The less anthropomorphic science believes itself to be, the more anthropomorphic it is. One by one it gets rid of the *separate* human traits in the Nature-picture, only to find at the end that the supposed pure Nature which it holds in its hand is—humanity itself, pure and com-

---

[8] The notion of "Order" is carried still further today, particularly in the investigation of infinite aggregates. Fixed relations, namely their positions in relation to their surroundings, are regarded as invariable (the hypothesis of Stability). These properties of Order are transferred into systems which are neither planes nor continua in the sense of classical mathematics. This new branch of mathematical science is called topology. In this modern sense it cannot have been known to Spengler. All the more impressive is its confirmation of his conclusions. In fact topology can be regarded as a general morphology of mathematical operations.—H.W.

plete. Out of the Gothic soul grew up, till it overshadowed the religious world-picture, the spirit of the City, the alter ego of irreligious Nature-science. But now, in the sunset of the scientific epoch and the rise of victorious Skepsis, the clouds dissolve and the quiet landscape of the morning reappears in all distinctness.

The final issue to which the Faustian wisdom tends—though it is only in the highest moments that it has seen it—is the dissolution of all knowledge into a vast system of morphological relationships. Dynamics and Analysis are, in respect of meaning, form-language and substance, identical with Romanesque ornament, Gothic cathedrals, Christian-German dogma and the dynastic state. One and the same world-feeling speaks in all of them. They were born with, and they aged with, the Faustian Culture, and they present that Culture in the world of day and space as a historical drama. The uniting of the several scientific aspects into one will bear all the marks of the great art of counterpoint. *The eternal music of the boundless world-space* —that is the deep unresting longing of this soul, as the orderly statuesque and Euclidean Cosmos was the satisfaction of the Classical. This union, a necessity of the Faustian understanding of the world, following the formula of a dynamic-imperative causality, will develop into a single world-transforming science, which will be the grand legacy of the Faustian soul to the souls of Cultures yet to be, a bequest of immensely transcendent forms that the heirs will possibly ignore. And then, weary after its striving, Western science returns to its spiritual home.

XI

ORIGIN AND LANDSCAPE:
THE COSMIC AND THE MICROCOSM

REGARD the flowers at eventide as, one after the other, they close in the setting sun. Strange is the feeling that then presses in upon you—a feeling of enigmatic fear in the presence of this blind dreamlike earth-bound existence. The dumb forest, the silent meadows, this bush, that twig, do not stir themselves, it is the wind that plays with them. Only the little gnat is free—he dances still in the evening light, he moves whither he will.

A plant is nothing on its own account. It forms a part of the landscape in which a chance made it take root. The twilight, the chill, the closing of every flower—these are not cause and effect, not danger and willed answer to danger. They are a single process of nature, which is accomplishing itself near, with, and in the plant. The individual is not free to look out for itself, will for itself, or choose for itself.

An animal, on the contrary, can choose. It is emancipated from the servitude of all the rest of the world. This midget swarm that dances on and on, that solitary bird still flying through the evening, the fox furtively approaching the nest—these are *little worlds of their own within another great world*. An animalcule in a drop of water, too tiny to be perceived by the human eye, though it lasts but a second and has but a corner of this drop as its field—nevertheless is *free and independent in the face of the universe*. The giant oak, upon one of whose leaves the droplet hangs, is not.[1]

Servitude and freedom—this is in last and deepest analysis the differentia by which we distinguish vegetable and animal[2]

[1] In what follows I have drawn upon a metaphysical work that I hope shortly to be able to publish.

[2] When in the following passages mention is made of the "animal" in man, it must be taken in this metaphysical sense.—H.W.

existence. Yet only the plant is wholly and entirely what it is; in the being of the animal there is something dual. A vegetable is only a vegetable; an animal is a vegetable and something more besides. A herd that huddles together trembling in the presence of danger, a child that clings weeping to its mother, a man desperately striving to force a way into his God—all these are seeking to return out of the life of freedom into the vegetal servitude from which they were emancipated into individuality and loneliness.

[*The plant is something cosmic; the animal has an additional quality, it is a microcosm in relation to a macrocosm. All that is cosmic bears the trademark of periodicity. It has beat-rhythm. Everything microcosmic possesses polarity. We talk of tense thought, but all wakeful states are in their nature tension—subject and object, I and You. To become aware of the cosmic beat we call to* feel; *microcosmic tensions we call perceptions. The ambiguity of the word* Sinnlichkeit—*sensitive faculty, sensuousness—has obscured the difference between the plant and the animal sides of life; the former always bears the mark of periodicity, beat: the latter consists in tensions, polarity of light and object illuminated, of cognition and that which it cognized. We use the word "touch" quite generally of contacts: to "establish" means to fix the position of something relatively to its surroundings. All senses are* positive. *The blood is for us the symbol of the living. The blood of ancestors flows through the chain of generations and binds them in a great linkage of destiny, beat and time.*

The word "consciousness" is ambiguous; it contains the meaning Being ("Dasein") and Waking-consciousness (Wachsein). *Being possesses beat and direction: waking-consciousness is tension and extension. The plant exists without waking-consciousness.*

The opposite pole of the eye is light. The picture of life is taken in through the light world of the eye. In man's waking-consciousness nothing disturbs the lordship of the eye. The idea of an invisible *God is the highest expression of human transcendence. Where the boundaries of the light world are lies the beyond. Music is the only art whose means lie outside the light world. Hence it can take us be-*

yond the tyranny of light. Even in the higher animals there are differences between mere sensation and understanding sensation. The development of language brought about the emancipation of understanding from sensation. Understanding detached from sensation is called thought.]

The development of theoretical thought within the human waking-consciousness gives rise to a kind of activity that makes inevitable a fresh conflict—that between Being (existence) and Waking-Being (waking-consciousness). The animal microcosm, in which existence and consciousness are joined in a self-evident unit of living, knows of consciousness *only as the servant* of existence. The animal "lives" simply and does not reflect upon life. Owing, however, to the unconditional monarchy of the eye, life is presented as the life of a visible entity in the light; understanding, then, when it becomes interlocked with speech, promptly forms a *concept* of thought and with it a *counter-concept* of life, and in the end it distinguishes life as it is from that which might be. Instead of straight, uncomplicated living, we have the antithesis represented in the phrase "thought and action." That which is not possible at all in the beasts becomes in every man not merely a possibility but a fact, and in the end an alternative. The entire history of mature humanity with all its phenomena has been formed by it, and the higher the form that a Culture takes, the more fully this opposition dominates the significant moments of its conscious being.

[*Human waking-consciousness consists of sensation and understanding and to that extent is equivalent to "ascertainment." It thus encounters the epistemological problem. Waking-consciousness is synonymous with the existence of oppositions; whereas the world of tensions is necessarily rigid and dead, namely "eternal truth," something beyond all time, something that is a state, the actual world of waking-consciousness is full of changes. Rest and movement, duration and change, become and becoming, are oppositions denoting something that in its very nature "passeth all understanding" and must therefore from the point of view of the understanding contain an absurdity. If the will to know breaks down on the problem of motion, it may well be because life's purpose has at that point been achieved. In spite of this, and indeed because of this, the motion problem remains the centre of gravity of all higher thought.]*

The problem of motion touches, at once and immediately, the secrets of existence, which are alien to the waking-consciousness and yet inexorably press upon it. In posing motion as a problem we affirm our will to comprehend the incomprehensible, the when and wherefore, Destiny, blood, all that our intuitive processes touch in our depths. Born to see, we strive to set it before our eyes in the light, so that we may in the literal sense grasp it, assure ourselves of it as of something tangible.

For this is the decisive fact, of which the observer is unconscious—his whole effort of seeking is aimed not at life, but at the seeing of life, and not at death, but at the seeing of death.

That we do not merely live but *know* about "living" is a consequence of our bodily existence in the light. But the beast knows only life, not death. Were we pure plantlike beings, we should die unconscious of dying, for to feel death and to die would be identical. But animals, even though they hear the death-cry, see the dead body, and scent putrefaction, behold death without comprehending it. Only when understanding has become, through language, detached from visual awareness and pure, does death appear to man as the great enigma of the light-world about him.

Then, and only then, life becomes the short span of time between birth and death, and it is in relation to death that that other great mystery of generation arises also. Only then does the diffuse animal fear of everything become the definite human fear of death. It is *this* that makes the love of man and woman, the love of mother and child, the tree of the generations, the family, the people, and so at last world-history itself the infinitely deep facts and problems of destiny that they are. To death, as the common lot of every human being born into the light, adhere the ideas of guilt and punishment, of existence as a penance, of a new life beyond the world of this light, and of a salvation that makes an end of the death-fear. In the knowledge of death is originated that world-outlook which we possess as being men and not beasts.

XII

ORIGIN AND LANDSCAPE:
THE GROUP OF THE HIGHER CULTURES

[*MAN, no matter whether it is for life or thought that he is born, so long as he is acting or thinking, is awake and therefore* in focus—*adjusted to the one significance that for the moment his light-world holds for him.*

In the picture of the world as history, knowledge is simply an auxiliary; in what we call memory things present themselves as bathed in an inner light swept by the pulsation of our existence. In the Nature (or Science) world-picture, it is the ever-present subjective that is alien and illusive. Thought itself rules, though thought, as soon as it becomes thought-history, is no longer immune from the basic conditions of all waking-consciousness.

Every period has its own historical horizon, and it is the mark of the genuine historical thinker that he actualizes the picture of history that his time demands. Every Culture and every period has its own way of regarding history. There is no such thing as history in itself.]

Even the history of plants and animals, even that of the earth's crust or that of the stars, is a *fable convenue* and mirrors in outward actuality the inward tendency of the ego's being. The student of the animal world or of stratification is a man, living in a period and having a nationality and a social status, and it is no more possible to eliminate his subjective standpoint from his treatment of these things than it would be to obtain a perfectly abstract account of the French Revolution or the World War.

The picture that we possess of the history of the earth's crust and of life is at present still dominated by the ideas which civilized English thought has developed, since the Age of Enlightenment, out of the English habit of life—Lyell's "phlegmatic" theory of the formation of the geological strata, and Darwin's of the origin of species, are actually but derivatives of the development of England herself. In place of the incalculable catastrophes and metamorphoses such as von Buch and Cuvier admitted, they put a methodical evolution over very long periods of time and recognize as causes only *scientifically calculable* and indeed *mechanical utility-causes.*

It will be the characteristic task of the twentieth century, as compared with the nineteenth, to get rid of this system of superficial causality, whose roots reach back into the rationalism of the Baroque period, and to put in its place a pure physiognomic. For the nineteenth century the word "evolution" meant progress in the sense of increasing fitness of life to purposes. For Leibniz—whose *Protogaea* (1691), a work full of significant thought, outlines, on the basis of studies made in the Harz silvermines, a picture of the world's infancy that is Goethian through and through—and for Goethe himself it meant fulfilment in the sense of increasing connotation of the form. The two concepts, Goethe's form-fulfilment and Darwin's evolution, are in as complete opposition as destiny to causality, and (be it added) as German to English thought, and German to English history.

There is no more conclusive refutation of Darwinism than that furnished by palaeontology. Simple probability indicates that fossil hoards can only be test samples. Each sample, then, should represent a different stage of evolution, and there ought to be merely "transitional" types, no definition and no species. Instead of this we find perfectly stable and unaltered forms persevering through long ages, forms that have not developed themselves on the fitness principle, but *appear suddenly and at once in their definitive shape;* that do not thereafter evolve towards better adaptation, but become rarer and finally disappear, while quite different forms crop up again. What unfolds itself, in ever-increasing richness of form, is the great classes and kinds of living beings which *exist aboriginally and exist still, without transition types,* in the grouping of today. We see how, amongst fish, the Selachians, with their simple form, appear first in the foreground of history and then slowly fade out again, while the Teleostians slowly bring a more perfected fish-type to predominance. The same applies to the plant-world of the ferns and horsetails, of which only the last species now linger in the fully developed kingdom of the flowering plants. But the assumption of utility-causes or other visible causes for these phenomena has no support of actuality.[1] It is a Destiny that evoked into the world life as life, the ever-sharper opposition between plant and animal, each single type, each genus, and each species. And along with this existence there is given also a definite *energy* of the form—by virtue of which in the course of its self-fulfilment it keeps itself pure or, on the contrary, becomes dull and unclear or evasively splits into numerous varieties— and finally a *life-duration of this form,* which (unless, again, incident intervenes to shorten it) leads naturally to a senility of the species and finally to its disappearance.

As for mankind, discoveries of the Diluvial age indicate more and more pointedly that the man-forms existing then correspond to those living now; there is not the slightest trace of evolution towards a race of greater utilitarian "fitness." And the continued failure to find man in the Tertiary discoveries indicates more and more clearly that the human life-form, like every other, originates in a sudden mutation (*Wandlung*) of which the "whence," "how" and "why" remain an impenetrable secret. If, indeed, there were evolution in the English sense of the word, there could be neither defined earth-strata nor specific animal-classes, but only a single geological mass and a chaos of living singular forms which we may suppose to have been left over from the struggle for existence. But all that we see about us impels us to the conviction that again and again profound and very sudden changes take place in the being of plants and animals, changes which are of a cosmic kind and nowise restricted to the earth's surface, which are beyond the ken of human sense and understanding in respect of causes, if not indeed in all respects. So, too, we observe that swift and deep changes assert themselves in the history of the great Cultures, without assignable causes, influences or purposes of any kind. The Gothic and the Pyramid styles come into full being as suddenly as do the Chinese imperialism of Shih Huang Ti and the Roman of Augustus, as Hellenism and Buddhism and Islam. It is exactly the same with the events in the individual life of every person who counts at all, and he who is ignorant of this knows nothing

[1] The first proof that the basic forms of plants and animals did not evolve, but were suddenly there, was given by Hugo de Vries in his *Mutation Theory* (1886). In the language of Goethe, we see how the "impressed form" works itself out in the individual samples, but not how the die was cut for *the whole genus.*

of men and still less of children. Every being, active or contemplative, strides on to its fulfilment by *epochs* and we have to assume just such epochs in the history of solar systems and the world of the fixed stars. The origins of the earth, of life, of the free-moving animal, *are* such epochs, and, therefore, mysteries that we can do no more than accept.[2]

That which we know of man divides clearly into two great ages of his being. The first is, as far as our view is concerned, limited on the one side by that profound fugue of planetary Destiny which we call the beginning of the Ice Age—and about which we can (within the picture of world-history) say no more than *that* a cosmic change took place—and on the other by the beginnings of high Cultures on Nile and Euphrates, with which the whole meaning of human existence became suddenly different. We discover everywhere the sharp frontier of Tertiary and Diluvial, and on the hither side of it we see man as a completely formed type, familiar with custom, myth, wit, ornament and technique and endowed with a bodily structure that has not materially altered up to the present day.

In all primitive existence the "it," the Cosmic, is at work with such immediacy of force that all microcosmic utterances, whether in myth, custom, technique or ornament, obey only the pressures of the very instant. For us, there are no ascertainable rules for the duration, tempo and course of development of these utterances. No necessary connexions come to light between ornament and organization by age-classes, or between the cult of a god and the kind of agriculture practised. Development in these cases means always some development of one or another individual aspect or trait of the primitive Culture, never of that Culture itself. This, as I have said before, is essentially chaotic; the primitive Culture is neither an organism nor a sum of organisms.

But with the type of the higher Culture this "it" gives way to a strong and undiffused *tendency*. Within the primitive Culture, tribes and clans are the only quickened (*beseelte*) beings—other than the individual men of course. *Here, however, the Culture itself is such a being.* Everything primitive is a sum—a sum of

---

[2] It is perhaps not unnecessary to remark that the word "epoch" is used throughout this book in its proper sense of "turning point" or "moment of change" and *not* in the loose sense of "period" which it has acquired.—*At.*

the expression-forms of primitive groupings. The high Culture, on the contrary, is the waking-being of a single huge organism which makes not only custom, myths, technique and art, but the very peoples and classes incorporated in itself the vessels of one single form-language and one single history. It was an incident, the sense of which cannot now be scrutinized, that the type of the higher Culture appeared suddenly in the field of human history. Quite possibly, indeed, it was some sudden event in the domain of earth-history that brought forth a new and different form into phenomenal existence. But the fact that we have before us eight such Cultures, all of the same build, the same development and the same duration, justifies us in *looking at them comparatively,* and therefore justifies our treating them as comparable, studying them comparatively and obtaining from our study a knowledge which we can extend backwards over lost periods and forwards over the future—provided always that a Destiny of a different order does not replace this form-world, suddenly and basically, by another. Our licence to proceed thus comes from general experience of organic being. As in the history of the Raptores or the Coniferae we cannot prophesy whether and when a new species will arise, so in that of Cultural history we cannot say whether and when a new Culture shall be. But from the moment when a new being is conceived in the womb, or a seed sinks into the earth, we do know *the inner form of this new life-course;* and we know that the quiet course of its development and fulfilment may be disturbed by the pressure of external powers, but never altered.

The group of the high Cultures is not, as a group, an organic unit. That they have happened in just this number, at just these places and times, is, for the human eye, an incident without deeper intelligibility. The ordering of the individual Cultures, on the contrary, has stood out so distinctly that the historical technique of the Chinese, the Magian and the Western worlds— often, indeed, the mere common consent of the educated in these Cultures—has been able to fashion a set of names upon which it would be impossible to improve.[3]

About 3000–2600 after a long "Merovingian" period, which is still distinctly perceptible in Egypt, the two oldest Cultures be-

---

[3] Goethe, in his little essay "Geistesepochen," has characterized the four parts of a Culture—its preliminary, early, late and civilized stages—with such a depth of insight that even today there is nothing to add.

gan, in exceedingly limited areas on the lower Nile and the lower Euphrates. In these cases the distinctions between early and late periods have long ago been labelled as Old and Middle Kingdom, Sumer and Akkad. The outcome of the Egyptian feudal period marked by the establishment of a hereditary nobility and the decline (from Dynasty VI) of the older Kingship, presents so astounding a similarity with the course of events in the Chinese springtime from I-Wang (934–909) and that in the Western from the Emperor Henry IV (1056–1106) that a unified comparative study of all three might well be risked. At the beginning of the Babylonian "Baroque" we see the figure of the great Sargon (2500), who pushed out to the Mediterranean coast, conquered Cyprus, and styled himself, like Justinian I and Charles V, "lord of the four parts of the earth." And in due course, about 1800 on the Nile and rather earlier in Sumer-Akkad, we perceive the beginnings of the first Civilizations. Of these the Asiatic displayed immense expansive power. The "achievements of the Babylonian Civilization" (as the books say), many things and notions connected with measuring, numbering and accounting, travelled probably as far as the North and Yellow Seas. Many a Babylonian trademark upon a tool may have come to be honoured out there in the Germanic wild, as a magic symbol, and so may have originated some "early-German" ornament. But meantime the Babylonian realm itself passed from hand to hand. Kassites, Assyrians, Chaldeans, Medes, Persians, Macedonians—all of these small warrior-hosts under energetic leaders—successively replaced one another in the capital city without any serious resistance on the part of its people.

It is a first example—soon paralleled in Egypt—of the "Roman Empire" style. Under the Kassites rulers were set up and displaced by praetorians; the Assyrians, like the later soldier-emperors of Rome (after Commodus), maintained the old constitutional forms; the Persian Cyrus and the Ostrogoth Theodoric regarded themselves as managers of the Empire, and the warrior bands, Mede and Lombard, as master-peoples in alien surroundings. But these are constitutional rather than factual distinctions.

After 1500 three new Cultures begin—first, the Indian, in the upper Punjab; then, a hundred years later, the Chinese, on the middle Hwang Ho; and then, about 1100, the Classical, on the Aegean Sea. The Chinese historians speak of the three great dynasties of Hsia, Shang, and Chou in much the same way as Napoleon regarded himself as a fourth dynasty following the Merovingians, the Carolingians and the Capetians—in reality, the third coexisted with the Culture right through its course in each case. When in 441 B.C. the titular Emperor of the Chou dynasty became a state pensioner of the "Eastern Duke" and when in A.D. 1793 "Louis Capet" was executed, the Culture in each case passed into the Civilization. There are some bronzes of very great antiquity preserved from late Shang times, which stand towards the later art in exactly the same relation as Mycenaean to early-Classical pottery and Carolingian to Romanesque art. In the Vedic, Homeric and Chinese springtimes, with their *"Pfalzen"* and *"Burgen,"* their knighthood and feudal rulership, can be seen the whole image of our Gothic, and the "period of the Great Protectors" (Ming Chu, 691–685) corresponds precisely to the time of Cromwell, Wallenstein and Richelieu and to the First Tyrannis of the Greek world.

The period 480–230 is called by the Chinese historians the "Period of the Contending States"; it culminated in a century of unbroken warfare between mass-armies with frightful social upheavals, and out of it came the "Roman" state of Tsin as founder of a Chinese Imperium. This phase Egypt experienced between 1780 and 1580, of which the last century was the "Hyksos" time. The Classical experienced it from Chaeronea (338), and, at the high pitch of horror, from the Gracchi (133) to Actium (31 B.C.). And it is the destiny of the West European–American world for the nineteenth and twentieth centuries.

During this period the centre of gravity changes—as from Attica to Latium, so from the Hwang Ho (at Honan-fu) to the Yangtze (modern province of Hupeh). The Si-kiang was as vague for the Chinese savants of those days as the Elbe for the Alexandrian geographer, and of the existence of India they had as yet no notion.

As on the other side of the globe there arose the *principes* of the Julian-Claudian house, so here in China there arose the mighty figure of Wang Cheng, who led Tsin through the decisive struggle to sole supremacy and in 221 assumed the title of Ti (literally equivalent to "Augustus") and the Caesar-name Huang Ti. He founded the *"Pax Serica,"* as we may call it, carried out a grand social reform in the exhausted Empire and—as promptly as Rome—began to build his *"Limes,"* the famous

Great Wall, for which in 214 he annexed a part of Mongolia. He was the first, too, to subdue the barbarians south of the Yangtze, in a series of large-scale campaigns followed and confirmed by military roads, castles and colonies. But "Roman," too, was his family history—a Tacitean drama with Lui Ti (Chancellor and stepfather of the Emperor) and Li Szu, the great statesman (the Agrippa of his day, and unifier of the Chinese script), playing parts, and one that quickly closed in Neronic horrors. Followed then the two Han dynasties (Western, 206 B.C.–A.D. 23; Eastern, A.D. 25–220), under which the frontiers extended more and more, while in the capital eunuch-ministers, generals and soldiery made and unmade the rulers at their pleasure. At certain rare moments, as under Wu Ti (140–86) and Ming Ti (58–76), the Chinese-Confucian, the Indian-Buddhist and the Classical-Stoic world-forces approached one another so closely in the region of the Caspian that they might easily have come into actual touch.[4]

Chance decreed that the heavy attacks of the Huns should break themselves in vain upon the Chinese *Limes*, which at each crisis found a strong emperor to defend it. The decisive repulse of the Huns took place in 124–119 under the Chinese Trajan, Wu Ti; and it was he, too, who finally incorporated Southern China in the Empire, with the object of obtaining a route into India, and built a grand embattled road to the Tarim. And so the Huns turned westward, and in due course they appear, impelling a swarm of Germanic tribes, in face of the *Limes* of the Roman world. This time they succeeded. The Roman Imperium collapsed, and thus only two of the three empires continued, and still continue, as desirable spoil for a succession of different powers. Today it is the "red-haired barbarian" of the West who is playing before the highly civilized eyes of Brahman and Mandarin the role once played by Mogul and Manchu, playing it neither better nor worse than they, and certain like them to be superseded in due course by other actors. But in the colonization-field of foundering Rome, on the other hand, the future Western Culture was ripening underground in the northwest, while in the east the Arabian Culture had flowered already.

~~~~~~~~

[4] For at that time imperialistic tendencies found expression even in India, in the Maurya and Sunga dynasty; these, however, could only be confused and ineffective, Indian nature being what it was.

The Arabian Culture is a discovery. Its unity was suspected by late Arabians, but it has so entirely escaped Western historical research that not even a satisfactory name can be found for it. Conformably to the dominant languages, the seed-time and the spring might be called the Aramaic and the later time the Arabian, but there is no really effectual name. In this field the Cultures were close to one another, and the extension of the corresponding Civilizations led to much overlaying. The pre-Cultural period of the Arabian, which we can follow out in Persian and Jewish history, lay completely within the area of the old Babylonian world, but the springtime was under the mighty spell of the Classical Civilization, which invaded from the West with all the power of a just-attained maturity, and the Egyptian and Indian Civilizations also made themselves distinctly felt. And then in turn the Arabian spirit—under late-Classical disguises for the most part—cast its spell over the nascent Culture of the West. The Arabian Civilization stratified over a still-surviving Classical in the popular soul of Southern Spain, Provence and Sicily, and became the model upon which the Gothic soul educated itself. The proper landscape of this Culture is remarkably extended and singularly fragmented. Let one put oneself at Palmyra or Ctesiphon, and, musing, look outwards all round. In the north is Osrhoene; Edessa became the Florence of the Arabian spring. To the west are Syria and Palestine—the home of the New Testament and of the Jewish Mishna, with Alexandria as a standing outpost. To the east Mazdaism experienced a mighty regeneration, which corresponded to the birth of Jesus in Jewry and about which the fragmentary state of Avesta literature enables us to say only *that* it happened. Here, too, were born the Talmud and the religion of Mani. Deep in the south, the future home of Islam, an age of chivalry was able to develop as fully as in the realm of the Sassanids; even today there survive, unexplored, the ruins of castles and strongholds whence the decisive wars were waged between the Christian state of Axum and the Jewish state of the Himyarites on the two shores of the Red Sea, with Roman and Persian diplomacy poking the fire. In the extreme north was Byzantium, that strange mixture of sere, civilized, Classical, with vernal and *chevaleresque* which is manifested above all in the bewildering history of the Byzantine army system. Into this world Islam at last—and far too late —brought a consciousness of unity, and this accounts for the self-evident character of its victorious progress and the almost unresisting adhesion of Christians, Jews and Persians alike. Out of Islam in due course arose the Arabian Civilization, which was at the peak of its intellectual completeness when the barbarians from the West broke in for a moment, marching on Jerusalem. How, we may ask ourselves, did this inroad appear in the eyes of cultivated Arabians of the time? Somewhat like Bolshevism perhaps? For the statecraft of the Arabian World the political relations of "Frankistan" were something on a lower plane.

Meantime yet another new Culture developed in Mexico. This lay so remote from the rest that no word even passed between them. All the more astonishing, therefore, is the similarity of its development to that of the Classical. No doubt the archaeologist standing before a teocalli would be horrified to think of his Doric temple in such a connexion; yet it was a thoroughly Classical trait —feebleness of the will-to-power in the matter of technics— that kept the Aztecs ill armed and so made possible their catastrophe.

For, as it happens, this is the one example of a Culture ended by violent death. It was not starved, suppressed or thwarted, but murdered in the full glory of its unfolding, destroyed like a sunflower whose head is struck off by one passing. All these states—including a world-power and more than one federation—with an extent and resources far superior to those of the Greek and Roman states of Hannibal's day; with a comprehensive policy, a carefully ordered financial system and a highly developed legislation; with administrative ideas and economic tradition such as the ministers of Charles V could never have imagined; with a wealth of literature in several languages, an intellectually brilliant and polite society in great cities to which the West could not show one single parallel—all this was not broken down in some desperate war, but washed out by a handful of bandits in a few years, and so entirely that the relics of the population retained not even a memory of it all. Of the giant city Tenochtitlán [5] not a stone remains aboveground. The cluster of great Mayan cities in the virgin forests of Yucatán succumbed swiftly to the attack of vegetation, and we do not know

[5] Mexico City, or, better, the agglomeration of towns and villages in the valley of Mexico.—*At.*

the old name of any one of them. Of the literature three books survive, but no one can read them.

The most appalling feature of the tragedy was that it was not in the least a necessity of the Western Culture that it should happen. It was a private affair of adventurers, and at the time no one in Germany, France or England had any idea of what was taking place. This instance shows, as no other shows, that *the history of humanity has no meaning whatever* and that deep significances reside only in the life-courses of the separate Cultures. Their interrelations are unimportant and accidental. In this case the accident was so cruelly banal, so supremely absurd, that it would not be tolerated in the wildest farce. A few cannon and hand-guns began and ended the drama.[6]

Events as important as our Crusades and Reformation have vanished without leaving a trace. Only in recent years has research managed to settle the outline, at any rate, of the later course of development, and with the help of these data comparative morphology may attempt to widen and deepen the picture by means of those of other Cultures. On this basis the epochal points of this Culture lie about two hundred years later than those of the Arabian and seven hundred years before those of our own. There was a pre-Cultural period which, as in China and Egypt, developed script and calendar, but of this we now know nothing. The time-reckoning began with an initial date which lies far behind the birth of Christ, but it is impossible now to fix it with certainty relative to that event. In any case, it shows an extraordinarily strongly developed history-sense in Mexican mankind.

The springtime of the "Hellenic" Maya states is evidenced by the dated relief-pillars of the old cities of Copán (in the south), Tikal and somewhat later Chichén Itzá (in the north), Naranjo and Seibal [7]—about 160–450. At the end of this period Chichén Itzá was a model of architecture that was followed for centuries. The full glory of Palenque and Piedras Negras (in the west) may

---

[6] According to Prescott, Cortez's force on landing had thirteen hand-fire-arms and fourteen cannon, great and small, altogether. The whole of these were lost in the first defeat at Mexico. Later a pure accident gave Cortez the contents of a supply-ship from Europe. In a military sense horses contributed to the Spanish victories nearly if not quite as much as firearms, but these, too, were in small numbers, sixteen at the outset.—*At.*

[7] These are the names of near-by villages serving as labels; the true names are lost.

correspond to our Late Gothic and Renaissance (450–600 = European 1250–1400?). In the Baroque or Late period Champotón appears as the centre of style-formation, and now the "Italic" Nahua peoples of the high plateau of Anáhuac began to come under the cultural influence. Artistically and spiritually these peoples were mere recipients, but in their political instincts, they were far superior to the Maya (about 600–960 = Classical 750–400 = Western 1400–1750?). And now Maya entered on the "Hellenistic" phase. About 960 Uxmal was founded, soon to be a cosmopolis of the first rank, an Alexandria or Baghdad, founded like these on the threshold of the Civilization. With it we find a series of brilliant cities like Labná, Mayapán, Chacmultun and a revived Chichén Itzá. These places mark the culminating point of a grandiose architecture, which thereafter produced no new style, but applies the old motives with taste and discrimination to mighty masses. Politically this is the age of the celebrated League of Mayapán, an alliance of three leading states, which appears to have maintained the position successfully—if somewhat artificially and arbitrarily—in spite of great wars and repeated revolutions (960–1165 = Classical 350–150 = Western 1800–2000).

The end of this period was marked by a great revolution, and with it the definitive intervention of the ("Roman") Nahua powers in the Maya affair. With their aid Hunac Ceel brought about a general overthrow and destroyed Mayapán (about 1190 = Classical 150). The sequel was typical of the history of the overripened Civilization in which different peoples contend for military lordship. The great Maya cities sink into the same bland contentment as Roman Athens and Alexandria, but out of the horizon of the Nahua lands was developing the last of these peoples, the Aztecs—young, vigorous, barbaric and filled with an insatiable will-to-power. In 1325 (= the Age of Augustus) they founded Tenochtitlán, which soon became the paramount and capital city of the whole Mexican world. About 1400 military expansion began on the grand scale. Conquered regions were secured by military colonies and a network of military roads, and a superior diplomacy kept the dependent states in check and separated. Imperial Tenochtitlán grew enormous and housed a cosmopolitan population speaking every tongue of this world-empire. The Nahua provinces were politically and militarily secure, the southward thrust was developing rapidly and a hand was about to be laid on the Maya states; there is no telling what the course of the next centuries would have been. And suddenly—the end.

At that date the West was at a level which the Maya had already overpassed by 700; nothing short of the age of Frederick the Great would have been ripe enough to comprehend the politics of the Mayapán League, and what the Aztecs of A.D. 1500 were organizing lies for us well in the future. But that which distinguished Faustian man, even then, from the man of any other Culture was his irrepressible urge into distance. It was this, in the last resort, that killed and even annihilated the Mexican and Peruvian Culture—the unparalleled drive that was ready for service in any and every domain. Certainly the Ionic style was imitated in Carthage and in Persepolis, and Hellenistic taste in the Gandara art of India found admirers. Future investigation will probably find some Chinese in the primitive German wood-architecture. The Mosque style ruled from Farther India to North Russia, to West Africa, and to Spain. But all that amounts to nothing as compared with the expansion-power of the Western Soul. The true style-history of that soul, it need hardly be said, accomplished itself only on the mother soil, but its resultant effects knew no bounds. On the spot where Tenochtitlán had stood, the Spaniards erected a Baroque cathedral adorned with masterpieces of Spanish painting and plastic. Already at that date the Portuguese had got to work in Hither India and late-Baroque architects from Spain and Italy in the heart of Poland and Russia. The English Rococo, and especially Empire, made for themselves a broad province in the Plantation States of North America, whose wonderful rooms and furniture are far less well known in Germany than they ought to be. Classicism was at work already in Canada and at the Cape, and presently there were no limits at all. It was just the same in every other domain of form; the relation between this forceful young Civilization and the still-remaining old ones—is that it covers them, all alike, with ever-thickening layers of West European–American life-forms under which, slowly, the ancient native form disappears.

What is History? [8] The scheme of ancient-mediaeval-modern history, as understood by the nineteenth century, contained only

---

[8] Spengler here means higher history.—H.W.

a selection of the more obvious relations. But the influence that old Chinese and Mexican history are beginning to exercise on us today is of a subtler and more intellectual kind. There we are sounding the last necessities of life itself. We are learning out of another life-course to know ourselves what we are, what we must be, what we shall be. It is the great school of our future. We who have history still, are making history still, find here on the extreme frontiers of historical humanity what history *is*.

A battle between two Negro tribes in the Sudan, or between the Cherusci and Chatti of Caesar's time, or—what is substantially the same—between ant-communities, is merely a drama of "living Nature." But when the Cherusci beat the Romans, as in the year 9,[9] or the Aztecs the Tlascalans, it is *history*. Here the "when" is of importance and each decade, or even year, matters, for here one is dealing with the march of a grand life-course, in which every decision takes rank as an epoch. Here there is an object towards which every happening impels, a being that strives to fulfil its predestination, a tempo, an organic duration—and not the disorderly ups and downs of Scythians, Gauls or Caribs, of which the particular detail is as unimportant as that of doings in a colony of beavers or a steppe-herd of gazelles. And here I would protest against two assumptions that have so far vitiated all historical thought: the assertion of an ultimate aim of mankind as a whole and the denial of there being ultimate aims at all. Life *has* an aim. It is the fulfilment of that which was ordained at its conception. But the individual belongs by birth either to a particular high Culture or only to the human type in general—there is no third unit of being for him. His destiny must lie either in the zoological or in the world-historical field. "Historical" man, as I understand the word and as all great historians have meant it to be taken, is the man of a Culture that is in full march towards self-fulfilment. Before this, after this, outside this, man is *historyless*.

From this there follows the fact that man not only is history-less before the birth of the Culture, but again becomes so as soon as a Civilization has worked itself out fully to the definitive form which betokens the end of the living development of the Culture and the exhaustion of the last potentialities of its significant existence. That which we see in the Egyptian Civilization after

[9] Varus's disaster in the Teutoburger Wald.—*At.*

Seti I (1300) and in the Chinese, the Indian, the Arabian to this day is—notwithstanding all the cleverness of the religious, philosophical and, especially, political forms in which it is wrapped—just the old zoological up and down of the primitive age again.

In the history, the genuine history, of higher men the stake fought for and the basis of the animal struggle to prevail is ever —even when driver and driven are completely unconscious of the symbolic force of their doings, purposes and fortunes—the actualization of something that is essentially spiritual, the translation of an idea into a living historical form. This applies equally to the struggle of big style-tendencies in art, of philosophy, of political ideals and of economic forms. But the post-history is void of all this. All that remains is the struggle for mere power, for animal advantage *per se*. Whereas previously power, even when to all appearance destitute of any inspiration, was always serving the Idea somehow or other, in the late Civilization even the most convincing illusion of an idea is only the mask for purely zoological strivings.

The distinction between Indian philosophy before and after Buddha is that the former is a grand movement towards attaining the aim of Indian thought by and in the Indian soul, and the latter the perpetual turning up of new facets of a now crystallized and undevelopable thought-stock. The solutions are there, for good, though the fashions of expressing them change. The same is true of Chinese painting before and after the Han dynasties—whether we know it or not—and of Egyptian architecture before and after the beginning of the New Empire. So also with technics. This it is that confers upon these very Late conditions—which to the people living in them seem almost self-evident—that character of changeless pageantry which the genuine Culture-man—e.g. Herodotus in Egypt and the Western successors of Marco Polo in China—has found so astonishing in comparison with his own vigorous pulse of development. It is the changelessness of non-history.

XIII

CITIES AND PEOPLES

THE TWO SOULS

[*WHAT the house is to the peasant, a symbol of "the settled," the town is to the man of culture. The town is plantlike, and like every development of a higher speech-form tied to the landscape. Only Civilization with its giant towns despises this soul-root and frees itself from it. The silhouette of a town speaks the language of its own soul. Town and country differ in soul; there is a difference in the great epochs of a Culture between one town and another, as well as between one Culture and another.*

The peasant is eternal man, independent of all Cultures. The piety of the real peasant is older than Christianity, his gods are older than those of any of the higher religions. World-history is town-history, though to a certain extent the countryside falls under the influence of the higher Cultures, and is then no longer historyless.

The town means intellect and money; compared with it the country is provincial. Eventually the town itself, whether large or small, becomes provincial when compared to Megalopolis.]

These stone visages that have incorporated in their light-world the humanness of the citizen himself and, like him, are all eye and intellect—how distinct the language of form that they talk, how different from the rustic drawl of the landscape! The silhouette of the great city, its roofs and chimneys, the towers and domes on the horizon! What a language is imparted to us through *one* look at Nürnberg or Florence, Damascus or Moscow, Peking or Benares. What do we know of the Classical cities, seeing that we do not know the lines that they presented under the Southern noon, under clouds in the morning, in the starry night? The courses of the streets, straight or crooked, broad or narrow; the houses, low or tall, bright or dark, that in all Western cities turn their façades, *their faces,* and in all Eastern cities turn their backs, blank wall and railing, towards the street; the spirit of squares and corners, impasses and prospects, fountains and monuments, churches or temples or mosques, amphitheatres and railway stations, bazaars and town-halls! The suburbs, too, of neat garden-villas or of jumbled blocks of flats, rubbish-heaps and allotments; the fashionable quarter and the slum area, the Subura of Classical Rome and the Faubourg Saint-Germain of Paris, ancient Baiae and modern Nice, the little town-picture like Bruges and Rothenburg and the sea of houses like Babylon, Tenochtitlán, Rome and London! All this has history and *is* history. One major political event—and the visage of the town falls into different folds. Napoleon gave to Bourbon Paris, Bismarck gave to worthy little Berlin, a new mien.

In the earliest time the *landscape-figure alone* dominates man's eyes. It gives form to his soul and vibrates in tune therewith. Feelings and woodland rustlings beat together; the meadows and the copses adapt themselves to its shape, to its course, even to its dress. The village, with its quiet hillocky roofs, its evening smoke, its wells, its hedges and its beasts, lies completely fused and embedded in the landscape. The country town *confirms* the country, is an intensification of the picture of the country. It is the Late city that first defies the land, contradicts Nature in the lines of its silhouette, *denies* all Nature. It wants to be something different from and higher than Nature. These high-pitched gables, these Baroque cupolas, spires and pinnacles, neither are, nor desire to be, related with anything in Nature. And then begins the gigantic megalopolis, the *city-as-world,* which suffers nothing beside itself and sets about *annihilating* the country picture. The town that once upon a time humbly accommodated itself to that picture now insists that it shall be the same as itself. *Extra muros, chaussées* and woods and pastures become a park, mountains become tourists' viewpoints; and *intra muros* arises an imitation Nature, fountains in lieu of springs, flower-beds, formal pools and clipped hedges in lieu of meadows and ponds and bushes. In a village the thatched roof is still hill-like and the street is of the same nature as the baulk of earth between fields. But here the picture is of deep, long gorges between high, stony houses filled with coloured dust and strange uproar, and men dwell in these houses, the like of which no nature-being has ever conceived. Costumes, even faces, are adjusted to a background of stone. By day there is a street traffic of strange colours and tones, and by night a new light that outshines the moon. And the yokel stands helpless on the pavement, understanding nothing and understood by nobody, tolerated as a useful type in farce and provider of this world's daily bread.

It follows, however—and this is the most essential point of any—that we cannot comprehend political and economic history at all unless we realize that the city, with its gradual detachment from the final bankrupting of the country, is the determinative form to which the course and sense of higher history generally conforms. *World-history is city-history.*

But, quite apart from this instance, we find in every Culture (and very soon) the type of the *capital city*. The Classical forum, the Western press, are, essentially, intellectual engines of the ruling City. Any country-dweller who really understands the meaning of politics in such periods, and feels himself on their level, moves into the City, not perhaps in the body, but certainly in the spirit.[1] The sentiment and public opinion of the peasant's countryside—so far as it can be said to exist—is prescribed and guided by the print and speech of the city. Egypt is Thebes, the *orbis terrarum* is Rome, Islam is Baghdad, France is Paris.

Finally, there arises the monstrous symbol and vessel of the completely emancipated intellect, the world-city, the centre in which the course of a world-history ends by winding itself up. The earliest of all world-cities were Babylon and the Thebes of the New Empire—the Minoan world of Crete, for all its splendour, belonged to the Egyptian "provinces." In the Classical the first example is Alexandria, which reduced old Greece at one stroke to the provincial level, and which even Rome, even the resettled Carthage, even Byzantium, could not suppress. In India the giant cities of Ujjain, Kanauj and above all Pataliputra were renowned even in China and Java, and everyone knows the fairy-tale reputation of Baghdad and Granada in the West.

It should not be forgotten that the word "province" first ap-

---

[1] The phenomenon is perhaps too well known in our day to need exemplification. But it is worth while recalling that the usual form of disgrace for a minister or courtier of the seventeenth or eighteenth century was to be commanded to "retire to his estates," and that a student expelled from the universities is said to be "rusticated."—*At.*

pears as a constitutional designation given by the Romans to Sicily; the subjugation of Sicily, in fact, is the first example of a once pre-eminent Culture-landscape sinking so far as to be purely and simply an object. Syracuse, the first real great-city of the Classical world, had flourished when Rome was still an unimportant country town, but thenceforward, *vis-à-vis* Rome, it becomes a provincial city. In just the same way Habsburg Madrid and Papal Rome, leading cities in the Europe of the seventeenth century, were from the outset of the eighteenth depressed to the provincial level by the world-cities of Paris and London. And the rise of New York to the position of world-city during the Civil War of 1861–5 may perhaps prove to have been the most pregnant event of the nineteenth century.

The stone Colossus, "Cosmopolis," stands at the end of the life-course of every great Culture. Its image, as it appears with all its grandiose beauty in the light-world of the human eye, contains the whole noble death-symbolism of the definitive thing-become. The spirit-pervaded stone of Gothic buildings, after a millennium of style-evolution, has become the soulless material of this daemonic stone-desert.

Now the old mature cities with their Gothic nucleus of cathedral, town-halls and high-gabled streets, with their old walls, towers and gates, ringed about by the Baroque growth of brighter and more elegant patricians' houses, palaces and hall-churches, begin to overflow in all directions in formless masses, to eat into the decaying countryside with their multiplied barrack-tenements and utility buildings, and to destroy the noble aspect of the old time by clearances and rebuildings. Looking down from one of the old towers upon the sea of houses, we perceive in this petrification of a historic being the exact epoch that marks the end of organic growth and the beginning of an inorganic and therefore unrestrained process of agglomerations. And now, too, appears that artificial, mathematical, utterly land-alien product of a pure intellectual satisfaction in the appropriate, the city of the city-architect. In all Civilizations alike, these cities aim at the chessboard form, which is the symbol of soullessness. Regular rectangle-blocks astounded Herodotus in Babylon and Cortez in Tenochtitlán. In the Classical world the series of "abstract" cities begins with Thurii, which was "planned" by Hippodamus of Miletus in 441. Priene, whose chessboard scheme entirely ignores the ups and downs of the site, Rhodes and Alexandria follow, and become in turn models for innumerable provincial cities of the Imperial Age. The Islamic architects laid out Baghdad from 762, and the giant city of Samarra a century later, according to plan.[2] In the West European and American world the layout of Washington in 1791 is the first big example. There can be no doubt that the world-cities of the Han period in China and the Maurya dynasty in India possessed this same geometrical pattern. Even now the world-cities of the Western Civilization are far from having reached the peak of their development. I see, long after A.D. 2000, cities laid out for ten to twenty million inhabitants, spread over enormous areas of countryside, with buildings that will dwarf the biggest of today's and notions of traffic and communications that we should regard as fantastic to the point of madness.[3]

The synoecism that in the early Classical had gradually drawn the land-folk into the cities, and so created the type of the Polis, repeated itself at the last in absurd form; everyone wanted to live in the middle of the city, in its densest nucleus, for otherwise he could not feel himself to be the urban man that he was. All these cities are only *cités*, inner towns. The new synoecism formed, instead of suburban zones, *the world of the upper floors*. In the year 74 Rome, in spite of its immense population, had the ridiculously small perimeter of nineteen and a half kilometres [twelve miles].[4] Consequently these city-bodies extended in general not in breadth, but more and more upward. The block-tenements of Rome, such as the famous Insula Feliculae, rose with a street breadth of only three to five metres [ten to seven-

~~~~~~~~

[2] Samarra exhibits, like the Imperial Fora of Rome and the ruins of Luxor, truly American proportions. The city stretches for 33 km. [20 miles] along the Tigris. The Balkuwara Palace, which the Caliph Muta-wakil built for one of his sons, forms a square of 1250 m. [say, three-quarters of a mile] on each side. One of the giant mosques measures in plan 260 × 180 m. [858 × 594 ft.]. Schwarz, *Die Abbasidenresidenz Samarra* (1910); Herzfeld, *Ausgrabungen von Samarra* (1912). Pataliputra, in the days of Chandragupta and Asoka, measured *intra muros* 10 miles × 2 miles (equal to Manhattan Island or London along the Thames from Greenwich to Richmond).—*At.*

[3] In the case of Canada, not merely great regions but the *whole country* had been picketed out in equal rectangles for future development.—*At.*

[4] The "Late Classical city of Arabian soil was un-Classical in this respect as in others. The garden suburb of Antioch was renowned throughout the East."

teen feet] to heights that have never been seen in Western Europe [5] and are seen in only a few cities of America. Near the Capitol, the roofs already reached to the level of the hill-saddle.

What makes the man of the world-cities incapable of living on any but this artificial footing is that the cosmic beat in his being is ever decreasing, while the tensions of his waking-consciousness become more and more dangerous. It must be re-membered that in a microcosm the animal, waking side super-venes upon the vegetable side, that of being, and not vice versa. Beat and tension, blood and intellect, Destiny and Causality, are to one another as the countryside in bloom is to the city of stone, as something existing *per se* to something existing dependently. Tension without cosmic pulsation to animate it is the transition to nothingness. But Civilization is nothing but tension. The head, in all the outstanding men of the Civilizations, is dominated exclusively by an expression of extreme tension. Intelligence is only the capacity for understanding at high tension, and in every Culture these heads are the types of its final men—one has only to compare them with the peasant heads, when such happen to emerge in the swirl of the great city's street-life. The advance, too, from peasant wisdom—"slimness," mother wit, instinct, based as in other animals upon the sensed beat of life—through the city-spirit to the cosmopolitan intelligence—the very word with its sharp ring betraying the disappearance of the old cosmic foundation—can be described as a steady diminution of the Destiny-feeling and an unrestrained augmentation of needs according to the operation of a Causality. Intelligence is the re-placement of unconscious living by the exercise of thought, masterly, but bloodless and jejune. The intelligent visage is similar in all races—what is recessive in them is, precisely, race.

The abundant proliferation of primitive peoples is a *natural phenomenon*, which is not even thought about, still less judged as to its utility or the reverse. When reasons have to be put forward at all in a question of life, life itself has become question-able. At that point begins prudent limitation of the number of births. The primary woman, the peasant woman, is *mother*. The whole vocation towards which she has yearned from childhood

～～～～

[5] The city which the Egyptian "Julian the Apostate," Amenophis IV (Akhenaton) built himself in Tell-el-Amarna had streets up to 45 m. [149 ft.] wide.

is included in that one word. But now emerges the Ibsen woman, the comrade, the heroine of a whole megalopolitan literature from Northern drama to Parisian novel. Instead of children, she has soul-conflicts; marriage is a craft-art for the achievement of "mutual understanding." It is all the same whether the case against children is the American lady's who would not miss a season for anything, or the Parisienne's who fears that her lover would leave her, or an Ibsen heroine's who "belongs to herself"—they all belong to themselves and they are all unfruitful. The same fact, in conjunction with the same arguments, is to be found in the Alexandrian, in the Roman and, as a matter of course, in every other civilized society—and conspicuously in that in which Buddha grew up. And in Hellenism and in the nineteenth century, as in the times of Lao-tzu and the Charvaka doctrine, there is an ethic for childless intelligences, and a literature about the inner conflicts of Nora and Nana.

At this level all Civilizations enter upon a stage, which lasts for centuries, of appalling depopulation. The whole pyramid of cultural man vanishes. It crumbles from the summit, first the world-cities, then the provincial forms and finally the land itself, whose best blood has incontinently poured into the towns, merely to bolster them up awhile. At the last, only the primitive blood remains, alive, but robbed of its strongest and most promising elements. This residue is the *Fellah type*.

If the Maya population literally vanished within a very short time after the Spanish conquest, and their great empty cities were reabsorbed by the jungle, this does not prove merely the brutality of the conqueror—which in this regard would have been helpless before the self-renewing power of a young and fruitful Culture-mankind—but an extinction from within that no doubt had long been in progress. And if we turn to our own civilization, we find that the old families of the French *noblesse* were not, in the great majority of cases, eradicated in the Revolution, but have died out since 1815, and their sterility has spread to the bourgeoisie and, since 1870, to the peasantry which that very Revolution almost re-created.

Consequently we find everywhere in these Civilizations that the provincial cities at an early stage, and the giant cities in turn at the end of the evolution, stand empty, harbouring in their stone masses a small population of fellaheen who shelter in them as the men of the Stone Age sheltered in caves and pile-dwellings. Samarra was abandoned by the tenth century; Pataliputra, Asoka's capital, was an immense and completely uninhabited waste of houses when the Chinese traveller Hsüan Tsang visited it about A.D. 635, and many of the great Maya cities must have been in that condition even in Cortez's time. In a long series of Classical writers from Polybius onward we read of old, renowned cities in which the streets have become lines of empty, crumbling shells, where the cattle browse in forum and gymnasium, and the amphitheatre is a sown field, dotted with emergent statues and hermae. Rome had in the fifth century of our era the population of a village, but its Imperial palaces were still habitable.

This, then, is the conclusion of the city's history; growing from primitive barter-centre to Culture-city and at last to world-city, it sacrifices first the blood and soul of its creators to the needs of its majestic evolution, and then the last flower of that growth to the spirit of Civilization—and so, doomed, moves on to final self-destruction.

FORM-LANGUAGES OF "CIVILIZATION"

Not now Destiny, but Causality, not now living Direction, but Extension, rules. It follows from this that whereas every form-language of a Culture, together with the history of its evolution, adheres to the original spot, civilized forms are at home anywhere and are capable, therefore, of unlimited extension as soon as they appear. It is quite true that the Hansa Towns in their northern-Russian staples built Gothically, and the Spaniards in South America in the Baroque style, but that even the smallest chapter of Gothic style-*history* should *evolve* outside the limits of West Europe was impossible, as impossible as that Attic or English drama, or the art of fugue, or the Lutheran or the Orphic religion, should be propagated, or even inwardly assimilated, by men of alien Cultures. But the essence of Alexandrinism and of our Romanticism is something which belongs to all urban men without distinction. Romanticism marks the beginning of that which Goethe, with his wide vision, called world-literature— the literature of the leading world-*city*, against which a provincial literature, native to the soil but negligible, struggles everywhere with difficulty to maintain itself. The state of Venice, or that of Frederick the Great, or the English Parliament (as an effective reality), cannot be reproduced, but "modern constitutions" can be "introduced" into any African or Asiatic state as Classical Poleis could be set up amongst Numidians and ancient Britons. Consequently, in all Civilizations the "modern" cities assume a more and more uniform type. Go where we may, there are Berlin, London and New York for us, just as the Roman traveller would find his columnar architecture, his fora with their statuary and his temples in Palmyra or Trier or Timgad or the Hellenistic cities that extended out to the Indus and the Aral. But that which was thus disseminated was no longer a style but a taste, not genuine custom but mannerism, not national costume but the fashion. This, of course, makes it possible for remote peoples not only to accept the "permanent" gains of a Civilization, but even to re-radiate them in an independent form. Such regions of "moonlight" civilization are South China and especially Japan (which were first Sinized at the close of the Han period, about A.D. 220); Java as a relay of the Brahman Civilization; and Carthage, which obtained its forms from Babylon.

All these are forms of a waking-consciousness now acute to excess, mitigated or limited by no cosmic force, purely intellectual and extensive, but on that very account capable of so powerful an output that their last flickering rays reach out and superpose effects over almost the whole earth. Fragments of the forms of Chinese Civilization are probably to be found in Scandinavian wood-architecture, Babylonian measures probably in the South Seas, Classical coins in South Africa, Egyptian and Indian influences probably in the land of the Incas.

But while this process of extension was overpassing all frontiers, the development of inner form of the Civilization was fulfilling itself with impressive consistency. Three stages are clearly to be distinguished—the release from the Culture, the production of the thoroughbred Civilization-form and the final hardening. For us this development has now set in. Style, in the Cultures has been the *rhythm of the process of self-implementing.* But the Civilized style (if we may use the word at all) arises as the *expression of the state of completeness.* It attained—in Egypt and China especially—to a splendid perfection, and imparts this perfection to all the utterances of a life inwardly un-alterable, to its ceremonial and mien as to the superfine and studied forms of its art-practice.

RACE IS STYLE

A race has roots. Race and landscape belong together. Where a plant takes root, there it dies also. There is certainly a sense in which we can, without absurdity, work backwards from a race to its "home," but it is much more important to realize that the race adheres permanently to this home with some of its most es-sential characters of body and soul. If in that home the race can-not now be found, this means that the race has ceased to exist. A race does not migrate. Men migrate, and their successive generations are born in ever-changing landscapes; but the land-scape exercises a secret force upon the plant-nature in them, and eventually the race-expression is completely transformed by the extinction of the old and the appearance of a new one. English-men and Germans did not migrate to America, but human beings migrated thither *as* Englishmen and Germans, and their de-scendants are there *as* Americans. It has long been obvious that the soil of the Indians has made its mark upon them—genera-tion by generation they become more and more like the people they eradicated. Gould and Baxter have shown that whites of all races, Indians and Negroes have come to the same average in size of body and time of maturity—and that so rapidly that Irish immigrants, arriving young and developing very slowly, come under this power of the landscape within the same generation. Boas has shown that the American-born children of long-headed Sicilian and short-headed German Jews at once conform to the same head-type. This is not a special case, but a general phe-nomenon, and it should serve to make us very cautious in dealing with those migrations of history about which we know nothing more than some names of vagrant tribes and relics of languages (e.g. Danai, Etruscans, Pelasgi, Achaeans and Dorians). As to the race of these "peoples" we can conclude nothing whatever. That which flowed into the lands of southern Europe under the diverse names of Goths, Lombards and Vandals was without doubt a race in itself. But already by Renaissance times it had completely grown itself into the root characters of the Provençal, Castilian and Tuscan soil.

Not so with language. The home of a language means merely the accidental place of its formation, and this has no relation to its inner form. Languages migrate in that they spread by carriage from tribe to tribe. Above all, they are capable of being, and are, exchanged—indeed, in studying the early history of races we need not, and should not, feel the slightest hesitation about postulating such speech-changes. It is, I repeat, the form-content and not the speaking of a language that is taken over, and it is taken over (as primitives are forever taking over ornament-motives) in order to be used with perfect sureness as elements of their own form-language. In early times the fact that a people has shown itself the stronger, or the feeling that its language possesses superior efficacy, is enough to induce others to give up their own language and—with genuinely religious awe—to take its language to themselves. Follow out the speech-changes of the Normans, whom we find in Normandy, England, Sicily and Constantinople with different languages in each place, and ever ready to exchange one for another. Piety towards the mother tongue—the very term testifies to deep ethical forces, and accounts for the bitterness of our ever-recurring language-battles—is a trait of the *Late* Western soul, almost unknowable for the men of other Cultures and entirely so for the primitive.

Science has completely failed to note that race is not the same for rooted plants as it is for mobile animals, that with the microcosmic side of life a fresh group of characteristics appear and that for the animal world it is decisive. Nor again has it perceived that a completely different significance must be attached to "races" when the word denotes subdivisions *within the integral race "Man."* With its talk of adaptation and of inheritance it sets up a soulless causal concatenation of superficial characters, and blots out the fact that here the blood and there the power of the land over the blood are expressing themselves—secrets that cannot be inspected and measured, but only livingly experienced and felt from eye to eye. Nor are scientists at one as to the relative rank of these superficial characters.

Obviously, the *chaotic* in the total expression of the human body is not in the least realized. Quite apart from smell (which for the Chinese, for example, is a most characteristic mark of race) and sound (the sound of speech, song and, above all, laughter, which enables us accurately to sense deep differences inaccessible to scientific method) the profusion of images before the eye is so embarrassingly rich in details, either actually visible or sensible to the inner vision, that the possibility of marshalling them under a few aspects is simply unthinkable. And all these sides to the picture, all these traits composing it, are independent of one another and have each their individual history. There are cases in which the bony structure (and particularly the skull-form) completely alters without the expression of the fleshy parts—i.e. the face—becoming different. The brothers and sisters of the same family may all present almost every differentia posited by Blumenbach, Müller and Huxley, and yet the identity of their living race-expression may be patent to anyone who looks at them. But besides the energy of the blood—which coins the same living features ("family" traits) over and over again for centuries—and the power of the soil—evidenced in its stamp of man—there is that mysterious cosmic force of the syntony of close human connexions. What is called the "*Versehen*" of a pregnant woman is only a particular and not very important instance of the workings of a very deep and powerful formative principle inherent in all that is of the race side. It is impossible to exaggerate the formative power of this living pulse, this strong inward feeling for the perfection of one's own type. Comradeship breeds races. French *noblesse* and Prussian *Landadel* are genuine race-denotations. But it is just this, too, that has bred the types of the European Jew, with his immense race-energy and his thousand years of ghetto life; and it always will forge a population into a race whenever it has stood for long together spiritually firm and united in the presence of its Destiny. Where a race-ideal exists, as it does, supremely, in the Early period of the Culture—the Vedic, the Homeric, the knightly times of the Hohenstaufen—the yearning of a ruling class towards this ideal, its will to be just *so* and not otherwise, operates (quite independently of the choosing of wives) towards actualizing this ideal and eventually achieves it.

In reality, the race-expression of a human head can associate itself with any conceivable skull-form, the decisive element being not the bone, but the flesh, the look, the play of feature. Since the days of Romanticism we have spoken of an "Indogermanic" race. But is there such a thing as an Aryan or a Semitic skull?

Can we distinguish Celtic and Frankish skulls, or even Boer and Kaffir? As to race, and the race-wanderings of primitive men, the famous finds of prehistoric bones, Neanderthal to Aurignacian, prove nothing. Apart from some conclusions from the jaw-bone as to the kinds of food eaten, they merely indicate the basic land-form that is found there to this day.

Once more, it is the mysterious power of the soil, demonstrable at once in every living being as soon as we discover a criterion independent of the heavy hand of the Darwinian age. The Romans brought the vine from the South to the Rhine, and there it has certainly not visibly—i.e. botanically—changed. But in this instance "race" can be determined in other ways. There is a soil-born difference not merely between Southern and Northern, between Rhine and Moselle wines, but even between the products of every different site on every different hill-side; and the same holds good for every other high-grade vegetable "race," such as tea and tobacco. There is a like element, only sensible to the finest perceptions, a faint aroma in every form, that underneath all higher Culture connects the Etruscans and the Renaissance in Tuscany, and the Sumerians, the Persians of 500 B.C. and the Persians of Islam on the Tigris.

None of this is accessible to a science that measures and weighs. It exists for the feelings—with a plain certainty and at the first glance—but not for the savant's treatment. And the conclusion to which I come is that Race, like Time and Destiny, is a decisive element in every question of life, something which everyone knows clearly and definitely so long as he does not try to set himself to comprehend it by way of rational—i.e. soulless —dissection and ordering. Race, Time and Destiny belong together. Race, in contrast to speech, is unsystematic through and through. In the last resort every individual man and every individual moment of his existence have their own race. And therefore the only mode of approach is not classification, but physiognomic fact.

He who would penetrate into the essence of language should begin by putting aside all the philologist's apparatus and observe how a hunter speaks to his dog. The dog follows the outstretched finger. He listens, tense, to the sound of the word, but shakes his head—this kind of man-speech he does not understand. Then he makes one or two sentences to indicate *his* idea; he stands still and barks, which in his language is a sentence containing the question: "Is that what Master means?" Then, still in dog language, he expresses his pleasure at finding that he was right. In just the same way two men who do not really possess a single word in common seek to understand one another. When a country parson explains something to a peasant-woman, he looks at her keenly, and, unconsciously, he puts into his look the essence that she would certainly never be able to understand from a parsonic mode of expression. The locutions of today, without exception, are capable of comprehension only in association with other modes of speech—adequate by themselves they are not, and never have been.

If the dog, now, wants something, he wags his tail; impatient of Master's stupidity in not understanding this perfectly distinct and expressive speech, he adds a vocal expression—he barks—and finally an expression of attitude—he mimes or makes signs. Here the man is the obtuse one who has not yet learned to talk.

Finally something very remarkable happens. When the dog has exhausted every other device to comprehend the various speeches of his master, he suddenly plants himself squarely, and his eye bores into the eye of the human. Something deeply mysterious is happening here—the immediate contact of Ego and Tu. The look emancipates from the limitations of waking-consciousness. Being understands itself without signs. Here the dog has become a "judge" of men, looking his opposite straight in the eye and grasping, behind the speech, the speaker.

Languages of these kinds we habitually use without being conscious of the fact. The infant speaks long before it has learned its first word, and the grown-up talks with it without even thinking of the ordinary meanings of the words he or she is using—that is, the sound-forms in this case subserve a language that is quite other than that of words. Such languages also have their groups and dialects; they, too, can be learned, mastered and misunderstood, and they are so indispensable to us that verbal language would mutiny if we were to attempt to make it do all the work without assistance from tone- and gesture-language. Even our script, which is verbal language for the eye, would be almost incomprehensible but for the aid that it gets from gesture-language in the form of punctuation.

A race-character is involved, *a priori*, in the way in which the matter to be communicated is set in sentences. Sentences are not the same for Tacitus and Napoleon as for Cicero and

Nietzsche. The Englishman orders his material syntactically in a different way from the German. Not the ideas and thoughts, but the thinking, the kind of life, *the blood*, determine in the primitive, Classical, Chinese and Western speech-communities the type of the sentence-unit, and with it the *mechanical* relation of the word to the sentence. The boundary between grammar and syntax should be placed at the point where the mechanical of speech ceases and the organic of speaking begins —usages, custom, the *physiognomy* of the way that a man employs to express himself. The other boundary lies where the mechanical structure of the word passes into the organic factors of sound-formation and expression. Even the children of immigrants can often be recognized by the way in which the English "th" is pronounced—a race-trait of the land. Only that which lies between these limits is the "language," properly so called, which has system, is a technical instrument and can be invented, improved, changed and worn out; enunciation and expression, on the contrary, adhere to the *race*. We recognize a person known to us, without seeing him, by his pronunciation, and not only that, but we can recognize a member of an alien race even if he speaks perfectly correct German.

Words are the relatively smallest mechanical units in the sentence. There is probably nothing that is so characteristic of the thinking of a human species as the way in which these units are acquired by it. For the Bantu Negro a thing that he sees belongs first of all to a very large number of categories of comprehension. Correspondingly the word for it consists of a kernel or root and a number of monosyllabic prefixes. When he speaks of a woman in a field, his word is something like this: "living, one, big, old, female, outside, *human*"; this makes seven syllables, but it denotes a single, clear-headed and to us quite alien act of comprehension.[6] There are languages in which the word is almost coextensive with the sentence.

The gradual replacement of bodily or sonic by grammatical gestures is thus the decisive factor in the formation of sentences, but it has never been completed. There are no purely verbal languages. The activity of speaking, in words, as it emerges more and more precise, consists in this, that through word sounds we

[6] See the article "Bantu Languages," by Sir H. H. Johnston, *Ency. Brit.*, 11th ed.—*At.*

awaken significance-feelings, which in turn through the sound of the word-connexions evoke further relation-feelings. Our schooling in speech trains us to understand in this abbreviated and indicative form not only light-things and light-relations but also thought-things and thought-relations. Words are only named, not used definitively, and the hearer has to feel what the speaker means. This and this alone amounts to speech, and hence mien and tone play a much greater part than is generally admitted in the understanding of modern speech. Substantive signs may conceivably exist for many of the animals even, but verb-signs never.

This instrument of communication between Ego and Tu has, by reason of its perfection, fashioned out of the animal understanding of sensation, a thinking-in-words which stands proxy for sensation. Subtle thinking—"splitting hairs," as it is called—is conversing with oneself in word-significances. It is the activity that no kind of language but the language of words can subserve, and it becomes, with the perfection of the language, distinctive of the life-habit of whole classes of human beings. The divorce of speech, rigid and devitalized, from speaking, which makes it impossible to include the whole truth in a verbal utterance, has particularly far-reaching consequences in the sign-system of words. Abstract thinking consists in the use of a finite word-framework into which it is sought to squeeze the whole infinite content of life. Concepts kill Being and falsify Waking-Being. Long ago in the springtime of language-history, while understanding had still to struggle in order to hold its own with sensation, this mechanization was without importance for life. But now, from a being who occasionally thought, man has become a thinking being, and it is the ideal of every thought-system to subject life, once and for all, to the domination of intellect. This is achieved in theory by according validity only to the known and branding the actual as a sham and a delusion. It is achieved in practice by forcing the voices of the blood to be silent in the presence of universal ethical principles.[7]

Both logic and ethics alike are systems of absolute and eternal truths for the intellect, and correspondingly untruths for history.

---

[7] Only technics are entirely true, for here the words are merely the key to actuality, and the sentences are continually modified until they are, not "true," but actuality. A hypothesis claims, not rightness, but usefulness.

However completely the inner eye may triumph over the outer in the domain of thought, in the realm of facts the belief in eternal truths is a petty and absurd stage-play that exists only in the heads of individuals. A true system of thoughts emphatically cannot exist, for no sign can replace actuality. Profound and honest thinkers are always brought to the conclusion that all cognition is conditioned *a priori* by its own form and can never reach that which the words mean—apart, again, from the case of technics, in which the concepts are instruments and not aims in themselves. And this *ignorabimus* is in conformity also with the intuition of every true sage, that abstract principles of life are acceptable only as figures of speech, trite maxims of daily use underneath which life flows, as it has always flowed, onward. Race, in the end, is stronger than languages, and thus it is that, under all the great names, it has been thinkers—who are personalities—and not systems—which are mutable—that have taken effect upon life.

The inner history of word-languages shows three stages. In the first there appears, within highly developed but wordless communication-languages, the first names—units in a new sort of understanding. The world awakens *as a secret,* and religious thought begins. In the second stage, a complete communication-speech is gradually transformed into grammatical values. The gesture becomes the sentence, and the sentence transforms the names into words. Further, the sentence becomes the great school of understanding *vis-à-vis* sensation, and an increasingly subtle significance-feeling for abstract relations within the mechanism of the sentence evokes an immense profusion of inflexions, which attach themselves especially to the substantive and the verb, the space-word and the time-word. This is the blossoming time of grammar, the period of which we may probably (though under all reserves) take as the two millennia preceding the birth of the Egyptian and Babylonian Culture. The third stage is marked by a rapid decay of inflexions and a simultaneous replacement of grammar by syntax. The intellectualization of man's waking-consciousness has now proceeded so far that he no longer needs the sense-props of inflexion and, discarding the old luxuriance of word-forms, communicates freely and surely by means of the faintest nuances of idiom (particles, position of words, rhythm). By dint of speaking in words, the understanding has attained supremacy over the waking-consciousness, and today it is in process of liberating itself from the restrictions of sensible-verbal machinery and working towards pure mechanics of the intellect. Minds and not senses are making the contact.

In this third stage of linguistic history, which as such takes place in the biological plane and therefore belongs to *man as a type*, the history of the higher Cultures now intervenes with an entirely new speech, the speech of the distance—writing—an invention of such inward forcefulness that again there is a sudden decisive turn in the destinies of the word-languages.

The written language of Egypt is already by 3000 in a state of rapid grammatical decomposition; likewise the Sumerian literary languages called *eme-sal* (women's language). The written language of China—which *vis-à-vis* the vernaculars of the Chinese world has long formed a language apart—is, even in the oldest known texts, so entirely inflexionless that only recent research has established that it ever had inflexions at all. The Indogermanic system is known to us only in a state of complete breakdown. Of the Case in Old Vedic (about 1500 B.C.) the Classical languages a thousand years later retained only fragments. From Alexander the Great's time the dual disappeared from the declension of ordinary Hellenistic Greek, and the passive vanished from the conjugation entirely. The Western languages, although of the most miscellaneous provenance imaginable—the Germanic from primitive and the Romanic from highly civilized stock—modify in the same direction, the Romanic cases having become reduced to one, and the English, after the Reformation, to zero. Ordinary German definitely shed the genitive at the beginning of the nineteenth century and is now in process of abolishing the dative. Only after trying to translate a piece of difficult and pregnant prose—say of Tacitus or Mommsen— "back" into some very ancient language rich in inflexions does one realize how meantime the technique of signs has vaporized into a technique of thoughts, which now only needs to employ the signs—abbreviated, but replete with meaning—merely as the counters in a game that only the initiates of the particular speech-communion understand. This is why to a West European, the sacred Chinese texts must always be in the fullest sense a sealed book; but the same holds good also for the primary words of every other Culture-language—the Greek λογός and ἀρχή, the Sanskrit *Atman* and *Brahman*—indications of the world-outlook of their respective Cultures that no one not bred in the Culture can comprehend.

The external history of languages is as good as lost to us in just its most important parts. The tempo of linguistic history is immensely rapid; here a mere century signifies a great deal. I may refer to the gesture-language of the American Indians, which became necessary because the rapidity of changes in the tribal dialects made intertribal understanding impossible otherwise. Compare, too, the Latin of the recently discovered Forum inscription [8] (about 500) with the Latin of Plautus (about 200) and this again with the Latin of Cicero (about 50). If we assume that the oldest Vedic texts have preserved the linguistic state of 1200 B.C., then even that of 2000 may have differed from it far more completely than any Indogermanic philologists working by *a posteriori* methods can even surmise.[9] But *allegro* changes to *lento* in the moment when script, the language of duration, intervenes and ties down and immobilizes the systems at entirely different age-levels. This is what makes this evolution so opaque to research; all that we possess is remains of written languages. Of the Egyptian and Babylonian linguistic world we do possess originals from as far back as 3000, but the oldest Indogermanic relics are *copies*, of which the linguistic state is much younger than the contents.

Writing is above everything a matter of status, and more particularly an ancient privilege of priesthood. The peasantry is without history *and therefore without writing*. But, even apart from this, there is in Race an unmistakable antipathy to script. It is, I think, a fact of the highest importance to graphology that the more the writer has race (breed), the more cavalierly he treats the ornamental structure of the letters, and the more ready he is to replace this by personal line-pictures. Only the Taboo-man evidences a certain respect for the proper forms of the letters and ever, if unconsciously, tries to reproduce them. It is the distinction between the man of action, who makes history, and the scholar, who merely puts it down on paper, "eternalizes" it. In all Cultures the script is in the keeping of the priesthood, in which class we have to count also the poet and the scholar. The

---

[8] See *Ency. Brit.*, 11th ed., Vol. XVI, p. 251b.—*At.*

[9] See the articles "Sanskrit" and "Indo-European Languages," *Ency. Brit.*, 11th ed.—*At.*

nobility despises writing; it has people to write for it. From the remotest times this activity has had something intellectual-sacerdotal about it. Timeless truths came to be such, not at all through speech, but only when there came to be script for them. It is the opposition of castle and cathedral over again: which shall endure, deed or truth? The archivist's "sources" preserve facts; the holy scripture, truths. What chronicles and documents mean in the first-named, exegesis and library mean in the second. The art-history of all Cultural springtimes ought to begin with the script, and the cursive script even before the monumental. Here we can observe the essence of the Gothic style, or of the Magian, at its purest. No other ornament possesses the inwardness of a letter-shape or a manuscript page; nowhere else is arabesque as perfect as it is in the Koran texts on the walls of the mosque. And, then, the great art of initials, the architecture of the marginal picture, the plastic of the covers! In a Koran in the Kufi script every page has the effect of a piece of tapestry. A Gothic book of the Gospels is, as it were, a little cathedral. As for Classical art, it is very significant that the one thing that it did not beautify with its touch was the script and the book-roll—an exception founded in its steady hatred of that which endures, the contempt for a technique which insists on being more than a technique. Neither in Hellas nor in India do we find an art of monumental inscription as in Egypt. It does not seem to have occurred to anybody that a sheet of hand-writing of Plato was a relic, or that a fine edition of the dramas of Sophocles ought to be treasured up in the Acropolis.

PEOPLE AND NATION

For me, the "people" is a *unit of the soul.* The great events of history were not really achieved by peoples; *they themselves created the peoples.* Every act alters the soul of the doer. Even when the event is preceded by some grouping around or under a famous name, the fact that there is a people and not merely a band behind the prestige of that name is not a condition, but a result of the event. It was the fortunes of their migrations that made the Ostrogoths and the Osmanli what they afterwards were. The "Americans" did *not* immigrate from Europe; the name of the Florentine geographer Amerigo Vespucci designates today not only a continent but also a people in the true sense of the word, whose specific character was born in the spiritual upheavals of 1775 and, above all, 1861–5.

This is the one and only connotation of the word "people." Neither unity of speech nor physical descent is decisive. That which distinguishes a people from a population, raises it up out of the population and will one day let it find its level again in the population is always the inwardly lived experience of the "we." The deeper this feeling is, the stronger is the *vis viva* of the people. There are energetic and tame, ephemeral and indestructible, forms of peoples. They can change speech, name, race and land, but so long as their soul lasts, they can gather to themselves and transform human material of any and every provenance. The name Roman in Hannibal's day meant a people, in Trajan's time nothing more than a population.

Of course, it is often quite justifiable to align peoples with races, but "race" in this connexion must not be interpreted in the present-day Darwinian sense of the word. It cannot be accepted, surely, that a people were ever held together by the mere unity of physical origin, or, if it were, could maintain that unity for ten generations. It cannot be too often reiterated that this physiological provenance has no existence except for science—never for folk-consciousness—and that no people was ever yet stirred to enthusiasm for *this* ideal of blood-purity. In race (*Rasse haben*) there is nothing material but something cosmic and directional, the felt harmony of a Destiny, the single cadence of the march of historical Being. It is incoordination of this (wholly metaphysical) beat that produces race-hatred, which is just as strong between Germans and Frenchmen as it is between Germans and Jews, and it is resonance on this beat that makes the true love—so akin to hate—between man and wife. He who has not race knows nothing of this perilous love. If a part of the human multitude that now speaks Indogermanic languages cherishes a certain race-ideal, what is evidenced thereby is not the existence of the prototype-people so dear to the scholar, but the metaphysical force and power of the ideal.

Peoples are neither linguistic nor political nor zoological, but spiritual, units. And this leads at once to the further distinction between *peoples before, within and after a Culture*. It is a fact that has been profoundly felt in all ages that Culture-peoples are *more distinct* in character than the rest. Their predecessors

I will call primitive peoples. These are the fugitive and heterogeneous associations that form and dissolve without ascertainable rule, till at last, in the presentiment of a still-unborn Culture
(as, for example, in the pre-Homeric, the pre-Christian and the
Germanic periods), phase by phase, becoming ever more definite
in type, they assemble the human material of a population into
groups, though all the time little or no alteration has been occurring in the stamp of man. Such a superposition of phases
leads from the Cimbri and Teutones through the Marcomanni
and Goths to the Franks, Lombards and Saxons.

In the tenth century of our era the Faustian soul suddenly
awoke and manifested itself in innumerable shapes. Amongst
these, side by side with the architecture and the ornament, there
appears a distinctly characterized form of "people." Out of the
people-shapes of the Carolingian Empire—the Saxons, Swabians,
Franks, Visigoths, Lombards—arise suddenly the Germans, the
French, the Spaniards, the Italians. Hitherto (consciously and
deliberately or not) historical research has uniformly regarded
these Culture-peoples as something in being, as primaries, and
have treated the Culture itself as secondary, as their product.

I regard it, therefore, as a discovery of decisive importance
that the facts here set forth lead to the reverse conclusion. It
will be established in all rigour that the great Cultures are entities, primary or original, that arise out of the deepest foundations of spirituality, and that the peoples under the spell of a
Culture are, alike in their inward form and in their whole-
manifestation, its products and not its authors. These shapes in
which humanity is seized and moulded possess style and style-
history no less than kinds of art and modes of thought. The people of Athens is a symbol not less than the Doric temple, the
Englishman not less than modern physics. There are peoples
of Apollinian, Magian, Faustian cast. The Arabian Culture was
not created by "the Arabs"—quite the contrary, for the Magian
Culture begins in the time of Christ, and the Arabian people
represents its last great creation of that kind, a community
bonded by Islam as the Jewish and Persian communities before
it had been bonded by their religions. World-history is the history
of the great Cultures, and peoples are but the symbolic forms
and vessels in which the men of these Cultures fulfil their Destinies.

Peoples in the style of their Culture we will call *Nations*, the word itself distinguishing them from the forms that precede and that follow them. It is not merely a strong feeling of "we" that forges the inward unity of its most significant of all major associations; *underlying the nation there is an Idea.* This stream of a collective being possesses a very deep relation to Destiny, to Time and to History, a relation that is different in each instance and one, too, that determines the relation of the human material to race, language, land, state and religion. As the styles of the Old Chinese and the Classical peoples differ, so also the styles of their histories.

Life as experienced by primitive and by fellaheen peoples is just the zoological up and down, a planless happening without goal or cadenced march in time, wherein occurrences are many, but, in the last analysis, devoid of significance. The only historical peoples, the peoples whose existence *is world-history,* are the nations.

XIV

PROBLEMS OF
THE ARABIAN CULTURE:
HISTORIC PSEUDOMORPHOSES

THE IDEA

IN a rock-stratum are embedded crystals of a mineral. Clefts and cracks occur, water filters in and the crystals are gradually washed out, so that in due course only their hollow mould remains. Then come volcanic outbursts which explode the mountain; molten masses pour in, stiffen and crystallize out in their turn. But these are not free to do so in their own special forms. They must fill up the spaces that they find available. Thus there arise distorted forms, crystals whose inner structure contradicts their external shape, stones of one kind presenting the appearance of stones of another kind. The mineralogists call this phenomenon *Pseudomorphosis*.

By the term "historical pseudomorphosis" I propose to designate those cases in which an older alien Culture lies so massively over the land that a young Culture cannot get its breath and fails not only to achieve pure and specific expression-forms, but even to develop fully its own self-consciousness. All that wells up from the depths of the young soul is cast in the old moulds, young feelings stiffen in senile practices, and instead of expanding its own creative power, it can only hate the distant power with a hate that grows to be monstrous.

This is the case of the Arabian Culture. Its pre-history lies entirely within the ambit of the ancient Babylonian Civilization, which for two thousand years had been the prey of successive conquerors. Its "Merovingian period" is marked by the dictatorship of a small Persian clan, primitive as the Ostrogoths, whose domination of two hundred years, scarcely challenged, was founded on the infinite weariness of a fellah-world. But from

300 B.C. onwards there begins and spreads a great awakening in the young Aramaic-speaking [1] peoples between Sinai and the Zagros range. As at the epoch of the Trojan War and at that of the Saxon emperors, a new relation of man to God, a wholly new world-feeling, penetrated all the current religions, whether these bore the name of Ahuramazda, Baal or Yahweh, impelling everywhere to a great effort of creation. But precisely at this juncture there came the Macedonians—so appositely that some inner connexion is not altogether impossible, for the Persian power had rested on spiritual postulates, and it was precisely these that had disappeared. To Babylon these Macedonians appeared as yet another swarm of adventurers like the rest. They laid down a thin sheet of Classical Civilization stretching as far as Turkestan and India. The kingdoms of the Diadochi might indeed have become, insensibly, states of pre-Arabian spirit— the Seleucid Empire, which actually coincided geographically with the region of Aramaic speech, was in fact such a state by 200 B.C. But from the battle of Pydna onwards it was, in its western part, more and more embodied in the Classical Imperium and so subjected to the powerful workings of a spirit which had its centre of gravity in a distant region. And thus was prepared the Pseudomorphosis.

The Magian Culture, geographically and historically, is the midmost of the group of higher Cultures—the only one which, in point both of space and of time, was in touch with practically all others. The structure of its history as a whole in our world-picture depends, therefore, entirely on our recognizing the true inner form which the outer moulds distorted. In this instance the consequences of specialization have been graver perhaps than in any other. The historians proper stayed within the domain of Classical philology and made the Classical language-frontier their eastern horizon; hence they entirely failed to perceive the deep unity of development on both sides of their frontier, which spiritually had no existence. The result is a perspective of "Ancient," "Mediaeval" and "Modern" history, ordered and defined by the use of the Greek and Latin languages. For

---

[1] It is to be noted that the home of the Babylonian Culture, the ancient Sinear, plays no part of any importance in the coming events. For the Arabian Culture only the region north of Babylon, not that to the south, comes into question.

the experts of the old languages, with their "texts," Axum, Saba and even the realm of the Sassanids were unapproachable, and the consequence is that in "history" these scarcely exist at all. The literature-student (as a philologist) confuses the spirit of the language with the spirit of the work. Products of the Aramaean region, if they happen to be written in Greek or even merely preserved in Greek, he embodies in his "Late Greek literature" and proceeds to classify as a special period of that literature.

Theological research, in its turn, broke up its domain into subdivisions according to the different West European confessions, and so the "philological" frontier between West and East came into force, and still is in force, for Christian theology also. The Persian world fell to the student of Iranian philology, and as the Avesta texts were disseminated, though not composed, in an Aryan dialect, their immense problem came to be regarded as a minor branch of the Indologist's work and so disappeared absolutely from the field of vision of Christian theology. And lastly the history of Talmudic Judaism, since Hebrew philology became bound up in one specialism with Old Testament research, not only never obtained separate treatment, but has been *completely forgotten* by all the major histories of religions with which I am acquainted, although these find room for every Indian sect (since folk-lore, too, ranks as a specialism) and every primitive Negro religion to boot.

The Pseudomorphosis began with Actium; there *it should have been Antony who won.* It was not the struggle of Rome and Greece that came there to an issue—that struggle had been fought out at Cannae and Zama, where it was the tragic fate of Hannibal to stand as champion not for his own land, but for Hellenism. At Actium it was the unborn Arabian Culture that was opposed to iron-grey Classical Civilization; the issue lay between Principate and Caliphate. Antony's victory would have freed the Magian soul; his defeat imposed the impermeable layer of Roman Imperium.

THE RUSSIAN PSEUDOMORPHOSIS

A second pseudomorphosis is presented to our eyes today in Russia. The Russian hero-tales of the Bylini culminated in the epic cycle of Prince Vladimir of Kiev (*c.* A.D. 1000), with his Round Table, and in the popular hero Ilya Muromyets. The whole immense difference between the Russian and the Faustian soul is already revealed in the contrast of these with the "contemporary" Arthur, Ermanarich and Nibelungen sagas of the Migration period in the form of the *Hildebrandslied* and the *Waltharilied*. The Russian "Merovingian" period begins with the overthrow of the Tatar domination by Ivan III (1480) and passes, by the last princes of the House of Rurik and the first of the Romanovs, to Peter the Great (1689–1725). It corresponds exactly to the period between Clovis (481–511) and the battle of Testry (687), which effectively gave the Carolingians their supremacy. This Muscovite period of the great Boyar families and Patriarchs, in which a constant element is the resistance of an Old Russia party to the friends of Western Culture, is followed, from the founding of Petersburg in 1703, by the pseudomorphosis which forced the primitive Russian soul into the alien mould, first of full Baroque, then of the Enlightenment and then of the nineteenth century. The fate-figure in Russian history is Peter the Great. The primitive tsarism of Moscow is the only form which is even today appropriate to the Russian world, but in Petersburg it was distorted to the dynastic form of Western Europe. The pull of the sacred South—of Byzantium and Jerusalem—strong in every Orthodox soul, was twisted by the worldly diplomacy which set its face to the West. The burning of Moscow, that mighty symbolic act of a primitive people, that expression of Maccabaean hatred of the foreigner and heretic, was followed by the entry of Alexander I into Paris, the Holy Alliance and the concert of the Great Powers of the West. And thus a nationality, whose destiny should have been to continue without a history for some generations, was forced into a false and artificial history that the soul of Old Russia was simply incapable of understanding. Late-period arts and sciences, enlightenment, social ethics, the materialism of world-cities, were introduced, although in this pre-cultural time religion was the only language in which man understood himself and the world. In the townless land with its primitive peasantry, cities of alien type fixed themselves like ulcers—false, unnatural, unconvincing. "Petersburg," says Dostoievski, "is the most abstract and artificial city in the world." Born in it though he was, he had the feeling that one day it might vanish with the morning mist. Just so ghostly, so incredible, were the Hellenistic artifact-cities scattered in the Aramaic peasant-lands. Jesus in his Galilee knew this. St. Peter must have felt it when he set eyes on Imperial Rome.

After this everything that arose around it was felt by the true Russdom as lies and poison. A truly apocalyptic hatred was directed on Europe, and "Europe" was all that was not Russia, including Athens and Rome, just as for the Magian world in its time Old Egypt and Babylon had been antique, pagan, devilish. The contrast between Russian and Western, Jew-Christian and late-Classical nihilisms is extreme—the one kind is hatred of the alien that is poisoning the unborn Culture in the womb of the land, the other a surfeited disgust of one's own proper overgrowths. Depths of religious feeling, flashes of revelation, shuddering fear of the great awakening, metaphysical dreaming and yearning, belong to the beginning, as the pain of spiritual clarity belongs to the end of a history. In these pseudomorphoses they are mingled. Says Dostoievski: "Everyone in street and marketplace now speculates about the nature of Faith." So might it have been said of Edessa or Jerusalem. Those young Russians of the days before 1914—dirty, pale, exalted, moping in corners, ever absorbed in metaphysics, seeing all things with an eye of faith even when the ostensible topic is the franchise, chemistry or women's education—are the Jews and early Christians of the Hellenistic cities, whom the Romans regarded with a mixture of surly amusement and secret fear. In Tsarist Russia there was no bourgeoisie and, in general, no true class-system, but merely, as in the Frankish dominions, lord and peasant. There were no Russian towns. Moscow consisted of a fortified residency (the Kremlin) round which was spread a gigantic market. The imitation city that grew up and ringed it in, like every other city on the soil of Mother Russia, was there for the benefit of the Court and the administration. Its living elements were, on top, an Intelligentsia, literature become flesh, deep in intellectual problems; below, an uprooted peasantry, with all the metaphysical gloom, anxiety and misery of their own Dostoievski, perpetually homesick for the open land and bitterly hating the stony grey world into which Antichrist had tempted them. Moscow had no proper soul. The spirit of the upper classes was Western, and the lower had brought in with them the soul of the countryside. Between the two worlds there was no reciprocal comprehension, no communication, no charity. To understand the two spokesmen and victims of the pseudomorphosis, it is enough that Dostoievski is the peasant and Tolstoi the man of Western society. The one could never in his soul get away from the land; the other, in spite of his desperate efforts, could never get near it.

Tolstoi is the former Russia, Dostoievski the coming Russia. The inner Tolstoi is tied to the West. He is the great spokesman of Petrinism even when he is denying it. Rage as he might against Europe, Tolstoi could never shake it off. Hating it, he hates himself and so becomes the father of Bolshevism. The utter powerlessness of this spirit, and "its" 1917 revolution, stands confessed in his posthumously published *A Light Shines in the Darkness.* This hatred Dostoievski does not know. His passionate power of living is comprehensive enough to embrace all things Western as well—"I have two fatherlands, Russia and Europe." He has passed beyond both Petrinism and revolution, and from *his* future he looks back over them as from afar. His soul is apocalyptic, yearning, desperate, but of this future *certain.* "I will go to Europe," says Ivan Karamazov to his brother Alyosha; "I know well enough that I shall be going only to a churchyard, but I know too that that churchyard is dear, very dear to me. Beloved dead lie buried there, every stone over them tells of a life so ardently lived, so passionate a belief in its own achievements, its own truth, its own battle, its own knowledge, that I know—even now I know—I shall fall down and kiss these stones and weep over them." Tolstoi, on the contrary, is essentially a great understanding, "enlightened" and "socially minded." All that he sees about him takes the Late-period, megalopolitan and Western form of a *problem.* Tolstoi's hatred of property is an economist's, his hatred of society a social reformer's, his hatred of the State a political theorist's. Hence his immense effect upon the West—he belongs, in one respect as in another, to the school of Marx, Ibsen and Zola.

Dostoievski, on the contrary, belongs to no school, unless it be that of the Apostles of primitive Christianity. Such a soul as his can look beyond everything that we call social, for the things of this world seem to it so unimportant as not to be worth improving. What has the agony of a soul to do with Communism? A religion that has got as far as taking social problems in hand has ceased to be a religion. But the reality in which Dostoievski lives, even during this life, is a religious creation directly present to him. His Alyosha has defied all literary criticism, even Russian. His life of Christ, had he written it—as he always intended to do—would have been a genuine gospel like the Gospels of primitive Christianity, which stand completely outside Classical and Jewish literary forms. Tolstoi, on the other hand, is a master of the Western novel—*Anna Karenina* distances every rival—and even in his peasant's garb remains a man of polite society.

Here we have beginning and end chasing together. Dostoievski is a saint, Tolstoi only a revolutionary. From Tolstoi, the true successor of Peter, and from him only, proceeds Bolshevism, which is not the contrary, but the final issue of Petrinism, the last degradation of the metaphysical into the social, and *ipso facto* a new form of the Pseudomorphosis. If the building of Petersburg was the first act of Antichrist, the self-destruction of the society formed of that Petersburg is the second, and so the peasant soul must feel it. What gave this revolution its momentum was not the intelligentsia's hatred. It was the people itself, which, *without hatred,* urged only by the need of throwing off a disease, destroyed the old Westernism in one effort of upheaval, and will send the new after it in another. For what this townless people yearns for is its own life-form, its own religion, its own history. Tolstoi's Christianity was a misunderstanding. He spoke of Christ and he meant Marx. But to Dostoievski's Christianity will the next thousand years belong.[2]

~~~~~~~~

[2] The immeasurable difference between the Faustian and the Russian souls is disclosed in certain word-sounds. The Russian word for heaven is *nyebo,* which contains in its *n* a negative element. Western man looks up, the Russian looks horizontally into the broad plain. The death-impulse, too, of the respective souls is distinguishable, in that for the West it is the passion of drive all-ways into infinite space, whereas for Russians it is an expressing and expanding of self (*Sichentäussern*), till "it" in the man becomes identical with the boundless plain itself. It is thus that a Russian understands the words "man" and "brother." He sees even mankind as a plane. The idea of a Russian's being an astronomer! He does not see the stars at all, he sees only the horizon. Instead of the vault he sees the downhang of the heavens—something that somewhere combines with the plain to form the horizon. For him the Copernican system, be it never so mathematical, is spiritually contemptible.

While the German "*Schicksal*" rings like a trumpet call, "*Sud'bá*" is a genuflection. There is no room for the upstanding "I" beneath this almost flat-roofed heaven. That "*All are responsible for all*"—the "it" for the "it" in this boundlessly extended plain—is the metaphysical fundament of all

THE PERIOD OF ARABIAN FEUDALISM

Outside the Pseudomorphosis, and the more vigorously in proportion as the Classical influence is weaker over the country, there spring up all the forms of a genuine feudal age. In the Sassanid Empire, in Hauran, in southern Arabia, there dawned a pure feudal period. The exploits of a king of Saba, Shamir Juharish, are immortalized like those of a Roland or an Arthur, in the Arabic saga which tells of his advance through Persia as far as China. In Saba ruled the Hamdanids—who later became Christian. Behind them stood the Christian realm of Axum, in alliance with Rome, which about A.D. 300 stretched from the White Nile to the Somali coast and the Persian Gulf, and in 525 overthrew the Jewish-Himaryites. In 542 there was a diet of princes at Marib [3] to which both the Roman and the Sassanid Empire sent ambassadors. Even today the country is full of innumerable relics of mighty castles, which in Islamic times were popularly attributed to supernatural builders. The stronghold of Gomdan is a work of twenty tiers.

In the Sassanid Empire ruled the Dikhans, or local lords, while the brilliant court of these early-Eastern "Hohenstaufen" was in every respect a model for that of the Byzantines who followed Diocletian. Even much later the Abbassids in their new capital of Baghdad could think of nothing better than to imitate, on a grand scale, the Sassanid ideal of court-life. In northern

~~~~~~

Dostoievski's creation. This is why Ivan Karamazov must name himself murderer although another had done the murder. The criminal is the "unfortunate," the "wretch"—it is the utter negation of Faustian personal responsibility. Russian mysticism has nothing of that upstriving inwardness of Gothic, of Rembrandt, of Beethoven, which can swell up to a heaven-storming jubilation—its god is not the azure depth up above. Mystical Russian love is love of the plain, the love of brothers under equal pressure all along the earth, ever along and along; the love of the poor tortured beasts that wander on it, the love of plants—never of birds and clouds and stars. The Russian *"volya,"* our "will," means principally non-compulsion, freedom not *for* something but *from* something, and particularly freedom from compulsion to personal doing. Free-will is seen as a condition in which no one else can command "it," and in which, therefore, one may give way to one's own disposition. *"Geist," "esprit," "spirit,"* go thus: ↗ ; the Russian *"duch"* goes thus: ↘→. What sort of a Christianity will come forth one day from this world-feeling?

[3] The capital of Saba.—*At.*

Arabia, at the courts of the Ghassanids [4] and at those of the Lakhmids,[5] there sprang up a genuine troubadour and *Minne* poetry; and knightly poets, in the days of the Early Fathers, fought out their duels with "word, lance and sword."

For this young world of the first centuries of our era our antiquarians and theologians have had no eyes. Busied as they are with the state of Late Republican and Imperial Rome, the conditions of the Middle East seem to them merely primitive and void of all significance. But the Parthian bands that again and again rode at the legions of Rome were a chivalry exalted by Mazdaism; in their armies there was the spirit of crusade. Yet in spite of all this it was not, strictly speaking, a Parthian war, but a true crusade of Jewry that blazed out in 115 when Trajan marched into the East, and it was as a reprisal for the destruction of Jerusalem that the whole infidel ("Greek") population of Cyprus—traditionally 240,000 souls—was massacred. Nisibis, defended by Jews, made an illustrious resistance. Warlike Adiabene (the upper Tigris plain) was a Jewish state. In all the Parthian and Persian wars against Rome the gentry and peasantry, the feudal levy, of Jewish Mesopotamia fought in the front line.

The "Roman Army" in the East, meanwhile, was transformed in less than two centuries from an army of modern type to one of the feudal order. The Roman legion disappeared in the reorganization of the age of Severus, about A.D. 200. While in the West the army degenerated into hordes, in the East there arose in the fourth century a genuine, if belated, knighthood. Diocletian's *palatini* are not a substitute for the praetorians abolished by Septimius Severus, but a small, well-disciplined knight-army, while the *comitatenses*, the general levy, are organized in *"numeri"* or companies. The tactics are those of every Early period, with its pride of personal courage. The attack takes the

---

[4] The country of Ghassan extends east of the Jordan, parallel to and inland of Palestine and Syria, approximately from Petra to the middle Euphrates.—*At.*

[5] The Lakhmids were the ruling dynasty, from the third to the sixth century after Christ, of the realm of Hira, which ran in a strip between the Euphrates and the present Nejd coast on the one hand and the desert of Arabia on the other.—*At.*

Germanic form of the so-called "boar's head"—the deep mass technically called the *Gevierthaufe*.[6]

But there appeared also in these early centuries a brilliant Scholasticism and Mysticism of Magian type, domesticated in the renowned schools of the Aramaean region—the Persian schools of Ctesiphon, Resaina, Gundisapora, the Jewish of Sura, Nehardea, Kinnesrin.[7] These are flourishing headquarters of astronomy, philosophy, chemistry, medicine. But towards the west these grand manifestations, too, become falsified by the Pseudomorphosis. The characteristically Magian elements of this knowledge assume at Alexandria the forms of Greek philosophy and at Beyrout those of Roman jurisprudence; they are committed to writing in the Classical languages, squeezed into alien and long-petrified literary forms and perverted by the hoary logic of a Civilization of quite other structure. It is in this, and not in the Islamic, time that Arabian science began. In reality, practically everything that was produced on the "other" side— from Edessa's point of view—of the philologist's frontier, though seeming to the Western eye an offspring of a "late-Classical" spirit, is nothing but a reflection of early-Arabian contemplation. And so we come to consider what the Pseudomorphosis did for the Arabian religion.

SYNCRETISM

The Classical religion lived in its vast number of *separate cults;* the divinity is always *bound to and bounded by one locality,* in conformity with the static and Euclidean world-feeling. Correspondingly the relation of man to the divinity takes

---

[6] The typical form, for instance, of the Swiss in their independence-battles, and of Western infantry generally in the fifteenth and sixteenth centuries, during the transition from hand-arm to fire-arm warfare.—*At.*

[7] Nisibis and Edessa in the up-country between Euphrates and Tigris are represented today by Nasibin (Nezib) and Urfa, respectively; just to the west of them, east of the Euphrates above Sura, were the three Jewish academies, in which Talmudic Judaism took shape after the Dispersion. Kinnesrin lay just south of Aleppo. Ctesiphon is, of course, the classical city on the Tigris, still dominant under the Sassanids, and Resaina lies in the up-country southwest of Nisibis. Gundisapora is Gunder-Shapur (Jundaisapur), near the site of the old Elamite capital Susa in Arabistan.—*At.*

the shape of a local cult, in which the significances lie in the *form* of its ritual procedure and not in a dogma underlying them. Men could practise these cults without *belonging* to them. There were no communities of fellow-believers.

In the sharpest contrast to this stands the visible form of the Magian religion—the Church, the brotherhood of the faithful, which has no home and knows no earthly frontier, which believes the words of Jesus, "When two or three are gathered together in My name, there am I in the midst of them." It is self-evident that every such believer must believe that only one good and true God can be, and that the gods of the others are evil and false,[8] and therefore the centre of gravity of every Magian religion lies not in a cult, but in a doctrine, in *the creed*.

As long as the Classical remained spiritually strong, pseudomorphosis of all the Churches of the East into the style of the West continued. This is a most important aspect of Syncretism. The Persian religion enters in the shape of the Mithras cult, the Chaldean-Syrian element as the cults of the star-gods and Baals (Jupiter Dolichenus, Sabazius, Sol Invictus, Atargatis), the Jewish religion in the form of a Yahweh-cult (for no other name can be applied to the Egyptian communities of the Ptolemaic period), and primitive Early Christianity too—as the Pauline Epistles and the Catacombs of Rome clearly show—took substance as a Jesus-cult.

From the second century onwards, with the fading of the Apollinian and the flowering of the Magian soul, the relations are reversed. The consequences of the Pseudomorphosis continue, *but it is now cults of the West which tend to become a new Church of the East*—that is, from the sum of separate cults there evolves a community of those who believe in these gods and their rituals—and so there arises, by processes like those of

---

[8] Not "non-existent." It would be a misconception of the Magian world-feeling to attach a Faustian-dynamic meaning to the phrase "true God." In combatting the worship of godlings, the reality of godlings and daemons is presupposed. The Israelite prophets never dreamed of denying the Baals, and similarly Isis and Mithras for the Early Christians, Jehovah for the Christian Marcion, Jesus for the Manichaeans, are devilish, but perfectly real, powers. *Disbelieving in them* would have had no meaning for the Magian soul—what was required was that one should not *turn to them*. To use an expression now long current, it is "Henotheism" and not Monotheism.

the early-Persian and the early-Judaic, a Magian Greek nationality. Out of the rigorously established forms of detail-procedure in sacrifices and mysteries grows a sort of dogma concerning the inner significance of these acts. The cults can now represent each other, and men no longer practise or perform them in the old way, but become "adherents" of them. And the little god *of* the place becomes—without the gravity of the change being noticed by anyone—the great God really present in the place.

Carefully as Syncretism has been examined in recent years, the clue to its development—the transformation of Eastern Churches into Western cults, and then the reverse process of transformation of Western cults into Eastern Churches—has been missed.[9] The heaviest battle that Christianity had to fight, after it came itself under the influence of the Pseudomorphosis and began to develop spiritually with its face to the West, was not that against the true Classical deities. With these it was never face to face, for the public city-cults had long been inwardly dead and possessed no hold whatever on men's souls. The formidable enemy was Paganism, or Hellenism, emerging as *a powerful new Church* and born of the selfsame spirit as Christianity itself. In the end there were in the east of the Roman Empire not one cult-Church, but two, and if one of these comprised exclusively the followers of Christ, the other, too, was made up of communities which, under a thousand different labels, consciously worshipped one and the same divine principle.

Classical *cults* would have tolerated the Jesus-cult as one of their own number. But the cult-*Church* was bound to attack the Jesus-Church. All the great persecutions of Christians (corresponding therein exactly to the later persecutions of Paganism) came, not from the "Roman" State, but from this cult-Church, and they were only political inasmuch as the cult-Church was both nation and fatherland. The sacrifice for the Emperor was the most important *sacrament* of the Church—exactly corresponding to the baptism of the Christians—and it is easy, therefore, to understand the symbolic significance in the days of persecution of the command and the refusal to do these acts. *All*

[9] With the result that Syncretism is presented as a mere hotchpotch of every conceivable religion. Nothing is further from the truth. The process of taking shape moved first from East to West and then from West to East.

these Churches had their sacraments: holy meals like the Haoma-drinking of the Persians,[1] the Passover of the Jews, the Lord's Supper of the Christians, similar rites for Attis and Mithras, and baptismal ceremonies amongst the Mandaeans, the Christians and the worshippers of Isis and Cybele. The community of the Neopythagoreans, formed about 50 B.C. and closely related to the Jewish Essenes, is anything but a Classical "school of philosophy"; it is a pure monastic order, and it is not the only such order in the Syncretic movement that anticipated the ideals of the Christian hermits and the Mohammedan dervishes. The greatest of Plotinus' followers, Iamblichus, finally, about A.D. 300, evolved a mighty system of orthodox theology, ordered hierarchy and rigid ritual for the Pagan Church, and his disciple Julian devoted, and finally sacrificed, his life to the attempt to establish this Church for all eternity. He sought even to create cloisters for meditating men and women and to introduce ecclesiastical penance. This great work was supported by a great enthusiasm which rose to the height of martyrdom and endured long after the Emperor's death. Inscriptions exist which can hardly be translated but by the formula: "There is but one god and Julian is his Prophet." Ten years more, and this Church would have become a historic, permanent fact. In the end not only its power but also in important details its very form and content were inherited by Christianity. It is often stated that the Roman Church adapted itself to the structure of the Roman State; this is not quite correct. The latter structure was itself by hypothesis a Church. There was a period when the two were in touch—Constantine the Great acted simultaneously as convener of the Council of Nicaea and as Pontifex Maximus, and his sons, zealous Christians as they were, made him *Divus* and paid to him the prescribed rites. St. Augustine dared to assert that the true religion had existed before the coming of Christianity in the form of the Classical.[2]

~~~~~~~

[1] The Haoma plant symbolized the Tree of Life (Gaokerena) like the Soma plant of Brahmanism.—At.

[2] "*Res ipsa, quae nunc religio Christiana nuncupatur, erat apud antiquos nec defecit ab initio generis humani, quousque Christus veniret in carnem. Unde vera religio, quae jam erat coepit appellari Christiana*" (*Retractationes*, I, 13).

JEWS, CHALDEANS AND PERSIANS OF THE
"PRE-CULTURE"

The first heralds of the new soul were the *prophetic religions,* with their magnificent depth, which began to arise about 700 B.C. and challenged the primeval practices of the people and their rulers. They, too, are an essentially Aramaean phenomenon. The more I ponder Amos, Isaiah and Jeremiah on the one hand, Zarathustra on the other, the more closely related they appear to me to be. What seems to separate them is not their new beliefs, but the objects of their attack. The first battled with that savage old-Israel religion, which in fact is a whole bundle of religious elements. The second combatted the old Vedic beliefs of heroes and Vikings, similarly coarsened. And it is my belief that this great epoch brought forth yet a third prophetic religion, the Chaldean.

This, with its penetrating astronomy and its ever-amazing spirituality, was, I venture to guess, evolved at that time and by creative personalities of the Isaiah stature from relics of the old Babylonian religion.[3] About 1000, the Chaldeans were a group of Aramaic-speaking tribes like the Israelites, and lived in the south of Sinear—the mother tongue of Jesus is still sometimes called Chaldean. In Seleucid times the name was applied to a widespread religious community, and especially to its priests. The Chaldean religion was an astral religion, which before Hammurabi the Babylonian was *not.* It is the deepest of all interpretations of the Magian universe, the World-Cavern and Kismet working therein, and consequently it remained the foundation of Islamic and Jewish speculation to their very latest phases. It was by it, and not by the Babylonian Culture, that after the seventh century there was formed an astronomy worthy to be called an exact science—that is, a priestly technique of observation of marvellous acuteness. Finally, the henotheistic feeling announced itself; for Nebuchadnezzar the Great Marduk was the

[3] Research has treated the Chaldean, like the Talmudic, as a stepchild. The investigator's whole attention has been concentrated on the religion of the Babylonian Culture, and the Chaldean has been regarded as its dying echo. Such a view inevitably excludes any real understanding of it.

one true god, the god of mercy, and Nebo, the old god of Borsippa, was his son and envoy to mankind. The accession-prayer of Nebuchadnezzar, the contemporary of Jeremiah, to Marduk is still extant, and in depth and purity it is in nowise surpassed by the finest passages of Israelite prophecy.

The kernel of the prophetic teachings is already Magian. There is *one* god—be he called Yahweh, Ahuramazda or Marduk-Baal—who is the principle of good, and all other deities are either impotent or evil. To this doctrine there attached itself the hope of a Messiah, very clear in Isaiah, but also bursting out everywhere during the next centuries, under pressure of an inner necessity. It is the basic idea of Magian religion, for it contains implicitly the conception of the world-historical struggle between Good and Evil, with the power of Evil prevailing in the middle period, and the Good finally triumphant on the Day of Judgment. This moralization of history is common to Persians, Chaldeans and Jews. But with its coming, the idea of the localized people *ipso facto* vanished and the genesis of Magian nations without earthly homes and boundaries was at hand. The idea of the Chosen People emerged. But it is easy to understand that men of strong blood, and in particular the great families, found these too spiritual ideas repugnant to their natures and harked back to the stout old tribal faiths.

The Babylonian exile, however, did set up an important difference between the Jews and the Persians, in respect, not of the ultimate truths of conscious piety, but of all the facts of actuality and consequently men's inward attitude to these facts. It was the Yahweh believers who *were permitted* to go home and the adherents of Ahuramazda who *allowed* them to do so.

This is what made one religion so lordly, the other so humble. Let the student read, in contrast to Jeremiah, the great Behistun inscription [4] of Darius—what a splendid pride of the King in his

---

[4] The inscription and sculptures of Behistun (on an almost inaccessible cliff in the Zagros range on the Baghdad-Hamadan road) were reinvestigated by a British Museum expedition in 1904; see *The Inscription of Darius the Great at Behistun* (London, 1907). "Thus saith Darius the King. That what I have done I have done altogether by the grace of Ahuramazda. Ahuramazda and the other gods that be, brought aid to me. For this reason did Ahuramazda and the other gods that be bring aid to me because I was not hostile nor a liar nor a wrongdoer, neither I nor my family, but according to Rectitude have I ruled" (A. V. Williams Jackson, *Persia Past and Present*).—At.

victorious god! And how despairing are the arguments with which the Israelite prophets sought to preserve intact the image of their god. Here, in exile, with every Jewish eye turned by the Persian victory to the Zoroastrian doctrine, the pure Judaic prophecy (Amos, Hosea, Isaiah, Jeremiah) passes into *Apocalypse* (Deutero-Isaiah, Ezekiel, Zechariah). All the new visions of the Son of Man, of Satan, of archangels, of the seven heavens, of the last judgment, are *Persian presentations of the common world-feeling.* In Isaiah 41 appears Cyrus himself, hailed as Messiah. Did the great composer of Deutero-Isaiah draw his enlightenment from a Zoroastrian disciple?

We must not, however, forget to look at the "return from captivity" also from the point of view of Babylon. The majority were in reality far removed from these ideas, or regarded them as mere visions and dreams; and the solid peasantry, the artisans and no doubt the nascent land-aristocracy quietly remained in its holdings *under a prince of their own,* the Resh Galutha, whose capital was Nehardea.[5] Those who returned "home" were the small minority, the stubborn, the zealots. They numbered with their wives and children forty thousand, a figure which cannot be one-tenth or even one-twentieth of the total, and anyone who confuses these settlers and their destiny with Jewry as a whole must necessarily fail to read the inner meaning of all following events. The *little world of Judaism lived a spiritually separate life,* and the nation as a whole, while regarding this life with respect, certainly did not share in it. In the East, apocalyptic literature, the heiress of prophecy, blossomed richly. It was a genuine native poetry of the people, of which we still have the masterpiece, the Book of Job—a work in character Islamic and decidedly un-Jewish [6]—while a multitude of its other tales and sagas, such as Judith, Tobit, Achikar, are spread as motives over all the literatures of the "Arabian" world. In Judea only the Law flourished; the Talmudic spirit appears first in Ezekiel (chs. 40 ff.) and after 450 is made flesh in the scribes (Sopherim) headed by Ezra. From 300 B.C. to A.D. 200 the Tannaim ("Teach-

---

[5] This "King of the Banishment" (Exilarch) was long a conspicuous and politically important figure in the Persian Empire. He was removed only by Islam.

[6] Later it occurred to some Pharisee mind to Judaize it by interpolating chs. 32–37.

THE DECLINE OF THE WEST

ers") expounded the Torah and developed the Mishnah. Neither the coming of Jesus nor the destruction of the Temple interrupted this abstract scholarship. Jerusalem became for the rigid believer a Mecca. The "Law" and the "Prophets"—*these two nouns practically define the difference between Judea and Mesopotamia*. In the late-Persian and in every other Magian theology both tendencies are united; it is only in the case here considered that they were separated in space. The decisions of Jerusalem were recognized everywhere, but it is a question how widely they were obeyed.

One other subject must be considered. Jewry, like Persia, had since the Exile increased enormously beyond the old small clan-limits; this was owing to conversions and secessions—*the only form of conquest open to a landless nation and, therefore, natural and obvious to the Magian religions*.

But this movement *came out of Mesopotamia alone,* and the spirit in it was the Apocalyptic and not the Talmudic. Jerusalem was occupied in creating yet more legal barriers against the unbeliever. It was not enough even to abandon the practice of making converts. This is the same narrowness which in the primitive Christian brotherhood of Judea took the form of opposing the preaching of the Gospel to the heathen. In the East it would simply never have occurred to anyone to draw such barriers, which were contrary to the whole idea of the Magian nation. But in that very fact was based *the spiritual superiority* of the wide East.

The destruction of Jerusalem hits only a very small part of the nation, one moreover that was spiritually and politically by far the least important. It is not true that the Jewish people has lived "in the Dispersion" since that day, for it had lived for centuries (and so too had the Persian and others) in a form which was independent of country.

Vespasian's War, directed against Judea, was a liberation of Jewry. In the first place, it ended both the claim of the people of this petty district to be the genuine nation, and the pretensions of their bald spirituality to equivalence with the soul-life of the whole. The research, the scholasticism and the mysticism of the Oriental academies entered into possession of their rights. In the second place, it rescued this religion from the dangers of that pseudomorphosis to which Christianity in that same period was succumbing.

Apocalyptic, which is an expression-form of townless and town-fearing mankind, soon came to an end within the Synagogue, after a last wonderful reaction to the stimulus of the great catastrophe. When it had become evident that the teaching of Jesus would lead not to a reform of Judaism, but to a new religion, and when, about A.D. 100, the daily imprecation-formula against the Jew-Christians was introduced, Apocalyptic for the short remainder of its existence resided in the young Church.

JESUS

The incomparable thing which lifted the infant Christianity out above all religions of this rich springtime is the figure of Jesus. In all the great creations of those years there is nothing which can be set beside it. Tame and empty all the legends and holy adventures of Mithras, Attis and Osiris must have seemed to any man reading or listening to the still-recent story of Jesus' sufferings—the last journey to Jerusalem, the last anxious supper, the hours of despair in Gethsemane and the death on the cross.

Here was no matter of philosophy. Jesus' utterances, which stayed in the memory of many of the devoted, even in old age, are those of a child in the midst of an alien, aged and sick world. They are not sociological observations, problems, debatings. Like a quiet island of bliss was the life of these fishermen and craftsmen by the Lake of Gennesareth in the midst of the age of the great Tiberius, far from all world-history and innocent of all the doings of actuality, while round them glittered the Hellenistic towns with their theatres and temples, their refined Western society, their noisy mob-diversions, their Roman cohorts, their Greek philosophy. When the friends and disciples of the sufferer had grown grey and his brother was president of their group in Jerusalem, they put together, from the sayings and narratives generally current in their small communities, a biography so arresting in its inward appeal that it evolved a presentation-form of its own, of which neither the Classical nor the Arabian Culture has any example—the Gospel. Christianity is the one religion in the history of the world in which the fate of a man of the immediate present has become the emblem and the central point of the whole creation.

A strange excitement, like that which the Germanic world experienced about A.D. 1000, ran in those days through the whole Aramaean land. The Magian soul was awakened. That element which lay in the prophetic religions like a presentiment, and expressed itself in Alexander's time in metaphysical outlines, came now to the state of fulfilment. And this fulfilment awakened, in indescribable strength, the primitive feeling of Fear. In this dawn of Magian world-feeling, hesitant and apprehensive, the end of the world seemed close. All but the shallower souls trembled before revelations, miracles, a final insight into the genesis of things. Men now lived and thought only in apocalyptic images. Actuality became appearance. Strange and terrifying visions were told mysteriously by one to another, read out from fantastic veiled texts and grasped at once with an immediate inward certainty. These creations resemble the terrible figures of the Romanesque cathedral-porches in France, which also are not "art," but fear turned into stone. Everyone recognized those angels and devils, the ascent to heaven and descent to hell of divine Essence, the Second Adam, the Envoy of God, the Redeemer of the last days, the Son of Man, the eternal city and the last judgment. In this time of extreme, ever-increasing tension, and in the very years around Jesus' birth-year, there arose, besides endless communities and sects, another redemption-religion, the Mandaean, as to which we know nothing of founder or origins. In spite of its hatred of the Judaism of Jerusalem and its definite preference for the Persian idea of redemption, the Mandaean religion seems to have stood very close to the popular beliefs of Syrian Jewry. One after another, pieces of its wonderful documents are becoming available, and they consistently show us a "Him," a Son of Man, a Redeemer who is sent down into the depths, who himself must be redeemed and is the goal of man's expectations. In the Book of John, the Father high upraised in the House of Fulfilment, bathed in light, says to his only begotten Son: "My Son, be to me an ambassador; go into the world of darkness, where no ray of light is." And the Son calls up to him: "Father, in what have I sinned that thou hast sent me into the darkness?" And finally: "Without sin did I ascend and there was no sin and defect in me."

No doubt the beginnings of the new religion are lost irrevocably. But *one* historical figure of Mandaeanism stands forth with startling distinctness, as tragic in his purpose and his downfall as Jesus himself—John the Baptist. He, almost emancipated from Judaism, and filled with as mighty a hatred of the Jerusalem spirit as that of primitive Russia for Petersburg, preached the end of the world and the coming of the Barnasha, the Son of Man, *who is no longer the longed-for national Messiah of the Jews,* but the bringer of the world-conflagration.[7] To him came Jesus and was his disciple. He was thirty years old when the awakening came over him. Thenceforth the apocalyptic, and in particular the Mandaean, thought-world filled his whole being. The other world of historical actuality lying round him was to him as something sham, alien, void of significance. That "He" would now come and make an end of this unreal reality was his magnificent certainty, and like his master John, he stepped forth as its herald.

So he went, proclaiming his message without reservation, through his country. But this country was Palestine. He was born in the Classical Empire and lived under the eyes of the Judaism of Jerusalem, and when his soul, fresh from the awful revelation of its mission, looked about, it was confronted by the actuality of the Roman State and that of Pharisaism. His repugnance for the stiff and selfish ideal of the latter, a feeling which was shared by the Mandaeans and doubtless by the peasant Jewry of the wide East, is the hallmark of all his discourses from first to last. It angered him that this wilderness of cold-hearted formulae was reputed to be the only way to salvation. Still, thus far it was only another kind of piety that his conviction was asserting against Rabbinical logic. Thus far it is only the Law versus the Prophets.

But when Jesus was taken before Pilate, then *the world of facts and the world of truths were face to face in immediate and implacable hostility.* It is a scene appallingly distinct and overwhelming in its symbolism, such as the world's history had never before and has never since looked at. The discord that lies at the

[7] In the New Testament, of which the final redaction lies entirely in the sphere of Western-Classical thought, the Mandaean religion and the sects belonging thereto are no longer understood, and indeed everything Oriental seems to have dropped out. Acts 18–19, however, discloses a perceptible hostility between the then widespread John-communities and the Primitive Christians (see Dibelius, *Die Urchristliche Überlieferungen von Johannes dem Täufer*). The Mandaeans later rejected Christianity as flatly as they had rejected Judaism. Jesus was for them a false Messiah. In their Apocalypse of the Lord of Greatness the apparition of Enosh was also announced.

root of all human life from its beginning, in virtue of its very *being*, of its having both existence *and* awareness, took here the highest form that can possibly be conceived of human tragedy. In the famous question of the Roman Procurator: "What is truth?" lies *the entire meaning of history*, the exclusive validity of the deed, the prestige of the State and war and the all-powerfulness of success and the pride of ancestry in an exalted destiny. The silence of Jesus answers this question by that other which is decisive in all things of religion—*What is actuality?* For Pilate actuality was all; for Him nothing. Were it anything, indeed, pure religiousness could never stand up against history and the powers of history, or sit in judgment on active life; or if it does, it ceases to be religion and is subjected itself to the spirit of history.

My kingdom is not of this world. This is the final word which admits of no gloss and on which each must check the course wherein birth and nature have set him. There is no bridge between directional Time and timeless Eternity, between the *course* of history and the *existence* of a divine world-order, in the structure of which the word "Providence" or "dispensation" denotes the form of causality. *This is the final meaning of the moment in which Jesus and Pilate confronted each other.* In the one world, the historical, the Roman caused the Galilean to be crucified—that was his Destiny. In the other world, Rome was cast for perdition and the Cross became the pledge of Redemption—that was the "will of God." [8]

Religion is metaphysic and nothing else—"Credo quia absurdum"—and this metaphysic is not the metaphysic of knowledge, argument, proof (which is mere philosophy of learnedness), but *lived and experienced* metaphysic—that is, the unthinkable as a certainty, the supernatural as a fact, life as existence in a world that is non-actual, but true. Jesus never lived one moment in any other world but this. He was no moralizer, and to see in moralizing the final aim of religion is to be ignorant of what religion is. Moralizing is nineteenth-century Enlightenment, humane Philistinism. To ascribe social purposes to Jesus is a blasphemy. His

---

[8] The method of the present work is historical. It therefore recognizes the anti-historical as well as the historical as a *fact*. The religious method, on the contrary, necessarily looks upon itself as the *true* and the opposite as *false*. This difference is quite insuperable.

teaching was the proclamation, nothing but the proclamation, of those Last Things with whose images he was constantly filled, the dawn of the New Age, the advent of heavenly envoys, the last judgment, a new heaven and a new earth.[9] Any other conception of religion was never in Jesus, nor in any truly deep-feeling period in history. *Religion is, first and last, metaphysic,* other-worldliness (*Jenseitigkeit*), awareness of a world of which the evidence of the senses merely lights the foreground. It is life in and with the supersensible. And where the capacity for this awareness, or even the capacity for believing in its existence, is wanting, real religion is at an end.

"Consider the lilies" means: "Give no heed to riches *and poverty,* for both fetter the soul to cares of this world." "Man cannot serve both God and Mammon"—by Mammon is meant the *whole* of actuality. It is shallow, and it is cowardly, to argue away the grand significance of this demand. Between working for the increase of one's own riches, and working for the social ease of everyone, he would have felt no difference whatever. When wealth affrighted him, when the primitive community in Jerusalem—which was a strict Order and not a socialist club—rejected ownership, it was the most direct opposite of "social" sentiment that moved them. Their conviction was, not that the visible state of things was all, but that it was nothing: that it rested not on appreciation of comfort in this world, but on unreserved contempt of it.

THE TEACHING OF JESUS. PAUL

Amongst Jesus' friends and disciples, stunned as they were by the appalling outcome of the journey to Jerusalem, there spread

---

[9] Hence Mark 13, taken from an older document, is perhaps the purest example of his usual daily discourse. Paul (1 Thess. 4:15-17) quotes another, which is missing in the Gospels. With these, we have the priceless—but, by commentators dominated by the Gospel tone, misunderstood—contributions of Papias, who about 100 was still in a position to collect much oral tradition. The little that we have of his work suffices amply to show us the apocalyptic character of Jesus' daily discourses. It is Mark 13 and not the Sermon on the Mount that reproduces the real note of them. But as *his* teaching became modified into a teaching of *Him,* this material likewise was transformed and the record of his utterances became the narrative of his manifestation. In this one respect the picture given by the Gospels is inevitably false.

after a few days the news of his resurrection and reappearance. The impression of this news on such souls and in such a time can never be more than partially echoed in the sensibilities of a Late mankind. It meant the actual fulfilment of the entire Apocalyptic of that Magian springtime—the end of the present aeon marked by the ascension of the redeemed Redeemer, the Second Adam, the Saoshyant, Enosh, Barnasha or whatever other name man attached to "Him," into the light-realm of the Father. And therewith the foretold future, the new world-aeon, "the Kingdom of Heaven," became immediately present. They felt themselves at the decisive point in the history of redemption.

This certainty completely transformed the world-outlook of the little community. "His" teachings, as they had flowed from his mild and noble nature—his inner feeling of the relation between God and man and of the high meaning of the times, which were exhaustively comprised in and defined by the word "love"—fell into the background, and their place was taken by the *teaching of Him*. As the Arisen he became for his disciples a new figure, in and of the Apocalyptic, and (what was more) its most important and final figure. But therewith their image of the future took form as an image of memory.

> [*His oldest friends, who had established themselves as a community of the Last Days in Jerusalem and frequented the Temple, saw in Jesus the Messiah of the old holy books, who was to come for the Jews only. They remained one of the many sects within Judaism. But all the rest of the Aramaean world awaited the Redeemer of the world, the Saviour, the Son of Man of the apocalyptic writings, whether Jewish, Persian, Chaldean or Mandaean.*
>
> *Among the later disciples of Jesus were many who were purely Magian in feeling, and wholly free from the Pharisaic spirit; these had acted as missionaries long before Paul.*
>
> *The important question, much more important than the contest between Judea and the world, was: Should the gospel of Jesus be directed towards the East or the West? In close connection with the Persian or the Syncretic Church, both of which were then in process of formation?*]

This was the question decided by Paul—the first great personality in the new movement, and the first who had the sense not only of truths but of facts. After an awakening of the sort that often happened in those days, he turned to the numerous small cult-communities of the West and forged out of them a Church of *his own* modelling.

Paul was a rabbi in intellect and an apocalyptic in feeling. He recognized Judaism, but as a *preliminary* development. And thus there came to be two Magian religions with the same Scriptures (namely, the Old Testament), but a double Halakha, the one setting towards the Talmud—developed by the Tannaim at Jerusalem from 300 B.C. onwards—and the other, founded by Paul and completed by the Fathers, in the direction of the Gospel. But, further, Paul unified the prevalent profusion of apocalyptic ideas and the promises of a coming Redeemer into a salvation-*certainty,* the certainty immediately revealed to him and to him *alone* near Damascus. *"Jesus is the Redeemer and Paul is his Prophet"*— this is the whole content of his message.

With Paul, urban man and his "intelligence" come on the scene. Paul was the first by whom the Resurrection-experience was *seen as a problem;* the ecstatic awe of the young country-man changed in his brain into an intellectual conflict. For the old comrades it was simply not possible to understand him in the least—and mournfully and doubtfully they must have looked at him while he was addressing them. Their living image of Jesus (whom Paul had never seen) paled in this bright, hard light of concepts and propositions. Thenceforward the holy memory faded into a Scholastic system. But Paul had a perfectly exact feeling for the true home of his ideas. His missionary journeys were all directed westward, and the East he ignored. *He never left the domain of the Classical city.* Why did he go to Rome, to Corinth, and not to Edessa or Ctesiphon? And why was it that he worked *only in the cities, and never from village to village?*

That things developed thus was due to Paul *alone.* In the face of his practical energy the feelings of all the rest counted for nothing, and so the young Church took the urban and Western tendency decisively, so decisively that later it could describe the remaining heathen as *"pagani,"* country-folk. Thus arose an immense danger that only youth and vernal force enabled the growing Church to repel; the fellah-world of the Classical cities grasped at it with both hands, and the marks of that grasp are visible today. But—how remote already from the essence of Jesus, whose entire life had been bound to country and the country-folk! The Pseudomorphosis in which he was born he had simply not noticed; his soul contained not the smallest trace of its influence—and now, a generation after him, probably within the lifetime of his mother, that which had grown up out of his death had already become a centre of formative purpose for that Pseudomorphosis.

It was a second creation, then, that came out of Paul's immediate entourage, and it was this creation that, essentially, defined the form of the new Church. The personality and the story of Jesus cried aloud to be put into poetic form, and yet it is due to one man alone, Mark, that Gospels came into existence at all.[1] In any case, of course, serious documents would have come into existence some time or another, but their natural form as products of the spirit of those who had *lived* with Jesus (and of the spirit of the East generally) would have been a canonical collection of his sayings, amplified, conclusively defined and provided with an exegesis by the Councils and pivoting upon the Second Advent. But any tentatives in this direction were completely broken off by the Gospel of Mark, which was written down about A.D. 65, at the same time as the last Pauline Epistles, and, like them, in Greek. The work was the outcome of the wishes of Pauline, literate, circles that had never heard any of Jesus' companions discourse about him. It is *an apocalyptic life-picture from a distance;* lived experience is replaced by narrative, and narrative so plain and straightforward that the apocalyptic tendency passes quite unperceived.[2] And yet Apocalyptic is its condition precedent. It is not the words of Jesus, but the doctrine of Jesus in the Pauline form, that constitutes the substance of Mark. The first Christian book emanates from the Pauline creation. But very soon the latter itself becomes unthinkable without the book and its successors.

For presently there arose something which Paul, the born

---

[1] The researchers who argue with such over-learnedness about a proto-Mark, Source Q, the "Twelve"-source and so on, overlook the essential novelty of Mark, which is the *first "Book" of Christendom,* plan-uniform and entire. Work of this sort is never the natural product of an evolution, but the merit of an individual man, and it marks, here if anywhere, a historical turning-point.

[2] Mark is generally *the* Gospel; after him the partisan writings (Matthew, Luke) begin; the tone of narrative passes into that of legend and ends, beyond the Hebrew and John gospels, in Jesus-romances like the Gospels of Peter and James.

schoolman, had never intended, but which nevertheless had been made inevitable by the tendency of his work—the *cult-Church of Christian nationality*. Around the birth of Jesus, of which the Disciples knew nothing, grew up a story of his childhood. In the Mark Gospel it has not yet come into existence. Already in the old Persian apocalyptic, indeed, the Saoshyant as Saviour of the Last Day was said to be born of a virgin. But the new Western myth was of quite other significance and had incalculable consequences. For within the Pseudomorphosis-region there arose presently beside Jesus a figure to which he was Son, which transcended his figure—that of the Mother of God. She, like her Son, was a simple human destiny of such arresting and attractive force that she towered above all the hundred and one Virgins and Mothers of Syncretism—Isis, Tanit, Cybele, Demeter —and all the mysteries of birth and pain, and finally drew them into herself. For Irenaeus she is the Eve of a new mankind. Origen champions her continued virginity. By giving birth to Redeemer-God it is *she* really who has redeemed the world. Mary the *"Theotokos"* (she who bore God) was the great stumbling-block for the Christians outside the Classical frontier, and it was the doctrinal developments of this idea that led Monophysites and Nestorians to break away and re-establish the pure Jesus-religion. But the Faustian Culture, again, when it awoke and needed a symbol whereby to express its primary feeling for Infinity in time and to manifest its sense of the succession of generations, *set up the "Mater Dolorosa" and not the suffering Redeemer* as the pivot of the German-Catholic Christianity of the Gothic age; and for whole centuries of bright fruitful devotion this woman-figure was the very synthesis of Faustian world-feeling and the object of all art, poetry and piety.

Paul and Mark were decisive in yet another matter of inestimably wide import. It was a result of Paul's mission that, contrary to all the initial probabilities, Greek became the language of the Church and—following the lead of the first Gospel—of a sacred *Greek* literature. Touch with the folk-spirit of the Aramaean motherland was lost. Thenceforward both the cult-Churches possessed the same language, the same conceptual traditions, the same book-literature from the same schools. The far less sophisticated Aramaic literatures of the East—the truly Magian, written and thought in the language of Jesus and his companions—were excluded from the life of the Church and vanished from the field of view, to be replaced by Plato and Aristotle, both of whom were taken up, worked upon in common and misunderstood in common by the Schoolmen of the two cult-Churches.

JOHN, MARCION

A final step in this direction was attempted by a man who was the equal of Paul in organizing talent and greatly his superior in intellectual creativeness, but who was inferior to him in the feeling for possibilities and actualities, and consequently failed to achieve his grandly conceived schemes—Marcion. He saw in Paul's creation and its consequences only the basis on which to found the true religion of salvation. Paul the prophet had declared the Old Testament as fulfilled and concluded—Marcion the founder pronounced it defeated and cancelled. He strove to cut out everything Jewish, down to the last detail. From end to end he was fighting nothing but Judaism. Like every true founder, as in every religiously creative period, he transformed the old gods into defeated powers. Jehovah as the Creator-God, the Demiurge, is the "Just" *and therefore the Evil:* Jesus as the incarnation of the Saviour-God in this evil creation is the "alien" —that is, the Good Principle.[3]

But to the new doctrine properly belonged new Scriptures. The "Law and Prophets" which had hitherto been canonical for the whole of Christendom was the *Bible of the Jewish God.* Thus, it was a Devil's book that the Christian had in his hands, and Marcion, therefore, now set up against it the Bible of the Redeemer-God—likewise an assemblage and ordering of writings that had hitherto been current in the community as simple edification-books without canonical claims. In place of the Torah he puts the—*one and true*—Gospel, which he builds up uniformly out of various separate, and, in his view, corrupted and falsified, Gospels. In place of the Israelite prophets he sets up the Epistles of the *one prophet of Jesus,* who was Paul.

Thus Marcion became the real creator of the New Testament.

～～～～

[3] This is one of the profoundest ideas in all religious history, and one that must forever remain inaccessible to the pious average man. Marcion's identification of the "Just" with the Evil enables him in this sense to oppose the Law of the Old Testament to the Evangel of the New.

But for that reason it is impossible to ignore the mysterious personage, closely related to him, who not long before had written the Gospel "according to John." The intention of this writer was neither to amplify nor to supersede the Gospels proper; what he did—and, unlike Mark, consciously did—was to create something quite new, *the first sacred book* of Christianity, the Koran of the new religion.[4] The idea of the immediately impending end of the world, with which Jesus was filled through and through [5] and which even Paul and Mark in a measure shared, lies far behind "John" and Marcion. Apocalyptic is at an end, and Mysticism is beginning. Their content is not the teaching of Jesus, nor even the Pauline teaching about Jesus, but the enigma of the universe, the World-Cavern. There is here no question of a Gospel; not the figure of the Redeemer, but the principle of the Logos, is the meaning and the means of happening. The childhood story is rejected again; a god is not "born," he is "there," and wanders in human form over the earth. And this god is a Trinity —God, the Spirit of God, the Word of God. This sacred book of earliest Christianity contains, for the first time, the Magian problem of "Substance," which dominated the following centuries to the exclusion of everything else and finally led to the religion's splitting up into three churches. And—what is significant in more respects than one—the solution of that problem to which "John" stands closest is that which the Nestorian East stood for as the true one. It is, in virtue of the Logos idea (Greek though the word happens to be), the "easternmost" of the Gospels, and presents Jesus, emphatically not as the bringer of the final and total revelation, but as the second envoy, who is to be *followed by a third* (the Comforter, Paraclete, of John 14: 16, 26; 15: 26). This is the astounding doctrine that Jesus himself proclaims, and the decisive note of this enigmatic book. Here is unveiled, quite suddenly, the faith of the Magian East. If the Logos does not go,

---

[4] For the notions of Koran and Logos, see below. Again as in the case of Mark, the really important question is, not what the material before him was, but how this entirely novel idea for such a book, which anticipated and indeed made possible Marcion's plan for a Christian Bible, could arise. The book presupposes a great spiritual movement (in eastern Asia Minor?) that knew scarcely anything of Jewish Christianity and was yet remote from the Pauline, westerly thought-world. But of the region and type of this movement we know nothing whatever.

[5] See page 302 n.—*Tr.*

the Paraclete [6] cannot come (John 16:7), but between them lies the last Aeon, the rule of Ahriman (14:30). The Church of the Pseudomorphosis, ruled by Pauline intellect, fought long against the John Gospel and gave it recognition only when the offensive, darkly hinted doctrine had been covered over by a Pauline interpretation. About 245, Mani, who was intimately in touch with the currents of Eastern Christianity, cast out the Pauline, human Jesus as a demon and confessed the Johannine Logos as the true Jesus, but announced himself as the Paraclete of the fourth Gospel. In Carthage, Augustine became a Manichaean, and it is a highly suggestive fact that both movements finally fused with Marcionism.

To return to Marcion himself, it was he who carried through the idea of "John" and created a Christian Bible. He was, like Paul before him and Athanasius after him, the deliverer of Christianity at a moment when it threatened to break up, and the grandeur of his idea is in no wise diminished by the fact that union came about in opposition to, instead of through, him. The early Catholic Church—that is, the *Church of the Pseudomorphosis*—arose in its greatness only about 190, and then it was in self-defence against the Church of Marcion and with the aid of an organization taken from that Church. Further, it replaced Marcion's Bible by another of similar structure—Gospels and apostolic Epistles—which it then proceeded to combine with the Law and the Prophets in one unit. And finally, this act of linking the two Testaments having in itself settled the Church's attitude towards Judaism, it proceeded to combat Marcion's third creation, his Redeemer-doctrine, by making a start with a theology of its own on the basis of *his* enunciation of the problem.

THE HEATHEN AND CHRISTIAN CULT-CHURCHES

This development, however, took place on Classical soil. On the Western margin of the young Culture the Pagan cult-Church, the Jesus-Church (removed thither by Paul) and the Greek-speaking Judaism of the Philo stamp were in point of language and literature so interlocked that the last-named fell into Chris-

―――――

[6] Vohu Mano, the Spirit of Truth, in the shape of the Saoshyant.

tianity even in the first century, and Christianity and Hellenism combined to form a *common* early philosophy. In the Aramaic-speaking world from the Orontes to the Tigris, on the other hand, Judaism and Persism interacted constantly and intimately, each creating in this period its own strict theology and scholastic in the Talmud and the Avesta; and from the fourth century both these theologies exercised *the most potent influence upon the Aramaic-speaking Christendom that resisted the Pseudomorphosis,* so that finally it broke away in the form of the Nestorian Church.

On the other side, the Pseudomorphosis is single and whole both in its Magian believing acceptance (Pistis) and its metaphysical introversion (Gnosis). The Magian belief in its Westerly shape was formulated for the Christians by Irenaeus and, above all, by Tertullian, whose famous aphorism *"Credo quia absurdum"* is the very summation of this certainty in belief. The Pagan counterpart is Plotinus in his Enneads and even more so Porphyry in his treatise *On the Return of the Soul to God.* But for the great schoolmen of the Pagan Church too, there were Father (Nous), Son and the intermediate Being, just as already for Philo the Logos had been first-born Son and second God. Plotinus and Origen, both pupils of the same master, show that the scholasticism of the Pseudomorphosis consisted in the development of Magian concepts and thoughts, by systematic transvaluation of the texts of Plato and Aristotle.

The characteristic *central idea of the whole thought of the Pseudomorphosis is the Logos,* in use and development its faithful image. There is no possibility here of any "Greek," in the sense of Classical, influence; there was not a man alive in those days whose spiritual disposition could have accommodated the smallest trace of the Logos of Heraclitus and the Stoa. But, equally, the theologies that lived side by side in Alexandria were never able to develop in full purity the Logos-notion as they meant it, whereas both in Persian and Chaldean imaginings—as Spirit or Word of God—and in Jewish doctrine—as Ruach and Memra—it played a decisive part. What the Logos-teaching in the West did was to develop a Classical formula, by way of Philo and the John Gospel (the enduring effect of which on the West was its mark upon the Schoolmen), not only into an element of Christian mysticism, but, eventually, into a dogma. This was inevitable. This dogma which *both* the Western Churches held, corresponded, on the side of knowledge, to that which, on the side of faith, was represented *both* by the syncretic cults and by the cults of Mary and the Saints. And against the whole thing, dogma and cult, the feeling of the East revolted from the fourth century on.

For the eye the history of these thoughts and feelings is repeated in the history of Magian architecture.

XV

PROBLEMS OF
THE ARABIAN CULTURE:
THE MAGIAN SOUL

THE DUALISM OF THE WORLD-CAVERN

THE world, as spread out for the Magian waking-consciousness, possesses a kind of extension that may be called cavern-like,[1] though it is difficult for Western man to pick upon any word in his vocabulary that can convey anything more than a hint of the meaning of Magian "space." In the Classical Culture the opposition that universally dominates the waking-consciousness is the opposition of matter and form; in the West it is that of force and mass. In the former the tension loses itself in the small and particular, and in the latter it discharges itself in its characteristic activities. In the World-Cavern persistent and unresolved struggles become that "Semitic" primary-dualism which, ever the same under its thousand forms, fills the Magian world. The light shines through the cavern and battles against the darkness (John 1:5). Both are Magian substances. Above and below, heaven and earth become powers that have entity and contend with one another. But these polarities in the most primary sensations mingle with those of the refined and critical understanding, like good and evil, God and Satan. Death, for the author of the John Gospel as for the strict Moslem, is not the end of life, but a Something, a death-force, that contends with a life-force for the possession of man.

But still more important than all this is the opposition of Spirit and Soul (Hebrew *ruach* and *nephesh*, Persian *abu* and *urvan*, Mandaean *monuhmed* and *gyan*, Greek *pneuma* and *psyche*)

---

[1] The expression is Leo Frobenius's (Paideuma, 1920, p. 92).

which first comes out in the basic feeling of the prophetic religions, then pervades the whole of Apocalyptic and finally forms and guides the world-contemplations of the awakened Culture—Philo, Paul and Plotinus, Gnostics and Mandaeans, Augustine and the Avesta, Islam and the Kabbalah. *Ruach* means originally "wind" and *nephesh* "breath." The *nephesh* is always in one way or another related to the bodily and earthly, to the below, the evil, the darkness. Its effort is the "upward." The *ruach* belongs to the divine, to the above, to the light. Its effects in man when it descends are the heroism of a Samson, the holy wrath of an Elijah, the enlightenment of the judge (the Solomon passing judgment) and all kinds of divination and ecstasy. It is poured out. From Isaiah 11:2, the Messiah becomes the incarnation of the *ruach.* For Paul (I Cor. 15) the meaning of the Resurrection lies in the opposition of a psychic and a pneumatic body, which alike for him and Philo and the author of the Baruch apocalypse coincides with the opposition of heaven and earth, light and darkness. For Paul, the Saviour is the heavenly Pneuma. In the John Gospel he fuses as Logos with the Light; in Neoplatonism he appears as *Nous* or, in the Classical terminology, the All-One opposed to *Physis.* Paul and Philo, with their "Classical" (that is, Western) conceptual criteria, equated soul and body with good and bad respectively; Augustine, as a Manichaean with Persian-Eastern bases of distinction, lumps soul and body together as the naturally bad, in contrast to God as the sole Good, and finds in this opposition the source of his doctrine of Grace, which developed also, in the same form (though quite independently of him), in Islam.

But souls are at bottom discrete entities, whereas the Pneuma is one and ever the same. The man *possesses* a soul, but he only *participates* in the spirit of the Light and the Good; the divine descends into him, thus binding all the individuals of the Below together with the one in the Above.

Whereas the Faustian man is an "I" that in the last resort draws its own conclusions about the Infinite; the Magian man, with his spiritual kind of being, is only a *part of a pneumatic* "We" that, descending from above, is one and the same in all believers. All our epistemological methods, resting upon the *individual* judgment, are for him madness and infatuation, and its scientific results a work of the Evil One, who has confused and deceived the spirit as to its true dispositions and purposes. The idea of individual wills is simply meaningless, for "will" and "thought" in man are not prime, but already effects of the deity upon him. Out of this unshakable root-feeling, which is merely re-expressed, never essentially altered, by any conversions, illumination or subtilizing in the world—there emerges of necessity the idea of the Divine Mediator, of one who transforms this state from a torment into a bliss. All Magian religions are by this idea bound together, and separated from those of all other Cultures.

The Logos-idea in its broadest sense, an abstraction of the Magian light-sensation of the Cavern, is the exact correlative of this sensation in Magian thought. It meant that from the unattainable Godhead its Spirit, its "Word," is released as carrier of the light and bringer of the good, and enters into relation with human being to uplift, pervade and redeem it. This distinctness of three substances, which does not contradict their oneness in religious thought, was known already to the prophetic religions. The thought which the Chaldeans built up on the separation of God and His Word and the opposition of Marduk and Nabu, which breaks forth with power in the whole Aramaean Apocalyptic, remained permanently active and creative; by Philo and John, Marcion and Mani, it entered into the Talmudic teachings and thence into the Kabbalistic books Yesirah and Sohar, into the Church Councils and the works of the Fathers, into the later Avesta and finally into Islam, in which a Mohammed gradually became the Logos and, as the mystically present, *living* Mohammed of the popular religion, fused into the figure of Christ.[2] This conception is for Magian man so self-evident that it was able to break through even the strictly monotheistic structure of the original Islam and to appear with Allah as the Word of God (*kalimah*), the Holy Spirit (*ruh*) and the "light of Mohammed."

"WORLD-TIME." GRACE

The prime thing that the humanity of Magian Culture, from poor slaves and porters to the prophets and the caliphs themselves, feels as the Kismet above him is not a limitless flight of the ages

---

[2] By the Shiites the Logos-idea was transferred to Ali.

that never lets a lost moment recur, but a Beginning and an End of "This Day," which is irrevocably ordained and in which the human existence takes the place assigned to it from creation itself. Not only world-space but world-time also is cavern-like. Hence comes the thoroughly Magian certainty that *everything has "a" time,* from the origins of the Saviour, whose hour stood written in ancient texts, to the smallest detail of the everyday, in which Faustian hurry would be meaningless and unimaginable. Here, too, is the basis of the early-Magian (and in particular the Chaldean) astrology, which likewise presupposes that all things are written down in the stars and that the scientifically calculable course of the planets authorized conclusions as to the course of earthly things. The Classical oracle answered the only question that could perturb Apollinian man—the form, the "How?" of coming things. But the question of the Cavern is "When?" The whole of Apocalyptic, the spiritual life of Jesus, the agony of Gethsemane and the grand movement that arose out of his death are unintelligible if we have not grasped this primary question of Magian being and the presuppositions lying behind it.

The cavern-feeling postulates a surveyable history consisting in a beginning and an end to the world *that is also the beginning and the end of man*—acts of God of mighty magic—and between these terms, spellbound to the limits of the Cavern and the ordained period, the battle of light and darkness, of the angels and Jazatas with Ahriman, Satan and Eblis, in which Man, his Soul and his Spirit are involved. God can destroy and replace the existing cavern by a new creation. The Persian-Chaldean apocalyptic offers to the gaze a whole series of such aeons, and Jesus, along with his time, stood in expectation of the end of the existing one.[3]

Further, for the Magian human-existence, the issue of the feeling of *this* sort of Time and the view of *this* sort of space is a quite individual type of piety, which likewise we may put under the sign of the Cavern—a *will-less* resignation, to which the spiritual "I" is unknown, and which feels the spiritual "We" that

[3] That the Eastern world at that time was in a general state of apocalyptic expectation was confirmed by the rolls found in 1947 at Qumran on the Dead Sea. It is admitted today by theologians that the gospel of Jesus was eschatological. The question of issue is whether Jesus regarded the eschatological event as having already taken place with the appearance of Him himself or as an event to occur in the near future.—H.W.

has entered into the quickened body as simply a reflection of the divine Light. The Arab word for this is "Islam" (=submission) but this Islam was equally Jesus' normal mode of feeling and that of every other personality of religious genius that appeared in this Culture. The Faustian prime-sacrament of Contrition presupposes the strong and free will that can overcome itself. But it is precisely the *impossibility of an Ego as a free power* in the face of the divine that constitutes "Islam." Every attempt to meet the operations of God with a personal purpose or even a personal opinion is *masiga,*—that is, not an evil willing, but an evidence that the powers of darkness and evil have taken possession of a man and expelled the divine from him. The Magian waking-consciousness is merely the *theatre* of a battle between these two powers and not, so to say, a power in itself. Moreover, in this kind of world-happening there is no place for individual causes and effects, let alone any universally effective dynamic concatenation thereof, and consequently there is no *necessary* connexion between sin and punishment, no *claim* to reward, no old-Israelitish "righteousness."

From this basic feeling proceeds the Magian idea of Grace. This underlies all sacraments of this Culture (especially the Magian proto-sacrament of Baptism) and forms a contrast of the deepest intensity with the Faustian idea of Contrition. Contrition presupposes the will of an Ego, but Grace knows of no such thing. It was Augustine's high achievement to develop this essentially Islamic thought with an inexorable logic, and with a penetration so thorough that since Pelagius the Faustian Soul has tried by any and every route to circumvent this certainty— which for *it* constitutes an imminent danger of self-destruction —and in using Augustinian propositions to express its own proper consciousness of God has ever misunderstood and transvalued them. Actually, Augustine was the last great thinker of early-Arabian Scholasticism, anything but a Western intellect. For him grace is the substantial inflowing of something divine into the human Pneuma, itself also substantial. The Godhead radiates it; man receives it, but does not acquire it. From Augustine, as from Spinoza so many centuries later, the notion of force is absent, and for both the problem of freedom refers not to the Ego and its Will, but to the part of the universal Pneuma that is infused into a man and its relation to the rest of him. The conception that the idea of Grace excludes every individual will and every cause but the One, that it is sinful even to question why man suffers, finds an expression in one of the most powerful poems known to world-history, a poem that came into being in the midst of the Arabian pre-Culture and is in inward grandeur unparalleled by any product of that Culture itself—the Book of Job.[4] It is not Job but his friends who look for a sin as the cause of his troubles. They—like the bulk of mankind in this and every other Culture, present-day readers and critics of the work, therefore, included—lack the metaphysical depth to get near the ultimate meaning of suffering within the world-cavern.

THE CONSENSUS

The Magian contemplation is called by Spinoza "intellectual love of God," and his Sufist contemporaries in Asia "extinction in God" (*mahw*); it may be intensified to the Magian ecstasy that was vouchsafed to Plotinus several times, and to his pupil Porphyry once in old age. The other side, the rabbinical dialectic, appears in Spinoza as geometrical method and in the Arabian-Jewish "Late" philosophy in general as Kalaam. Both, however, rest upon the fact that in Magian there is no individual-ego, but a single Pneuma present simultaneously in each and all of the elect, which is likewise Truth. It cannot be too strongly emphasized that the resultant root-idea of the *ijma* is much more than a concept or notion, that it can be a lived experience of even overwhelming force and that all community of the Magian kind rests upon it. "The mystic Community of Islam extends from the here into the beyond; it reaches beyond the grave, in that it comprises the dead Moslems of earlier generations, nay, even the righteous of the times before Islam. The Moslem feels himself bound up in one unity with them all. They help him, and he, too, can in turn increase their beatitude by the application of his own merit." Augustine's famous *Civitas Dei* was neither a Classical Polis nor a Western Church, but a unity of believers, blessed and angels, exactly as were the communes of Mithras, of Islam, of Manichaeism and of Persia. As the community was based upon con-

---

[4] The period at which it was written corresponds to our Carolingian. Whether the latter really brought forth any poetry of like rank we do not know, but that it may possibly have done so is shown by creations like the Voluspa, Muspilli, the Heliand and the universe conceived by John Scotus Erigena.

sensus, it was in spiritual things infallible. "My people," said Mohammed, "can never agree in an error," and the same is premised in Augustine's State of God. With him there was not and could not be any question of an infallible Papal ego or of any other sort of authority to settle dogmatic truths; that would completely destroy the Magian concept of the Consensus. And the same applied in this Culture generally—not only to dogma but also to law and to the State. Within the Islamic community the State formed only a *smaller unit of the visible side,* a unit, therefore, of which the operations were governed by the major whole. In the Magian world, consequently, the separation of politics and religion is theoretically impossible and nonsensical, whereas in the Faustian Culture the battle of Church and State is inherent in the very conceptions—logical, necessary, unending. In the Magian, civil and ecclesiastical law are simply identical. Side by side with the Emperor of Constantinople stood the Patriarch, by the Shah was the Zarathustratema, by the Exilarch the Gaon, by the Caliph the Sheikh-ul-Islam, at once superiors and subjects. There is not in this the slightest affinity to the Gothic relation of Emperor and Pope; equally, all such ideas were alien to the Classical world. In the constitution of Diocletian this Magian embedding of the State in the community of the faithful was for the first time actualized, and by Constantine it was carried into full effect.

THE WORD AS SUBSTANCE

But besides the consensus there is another sort of revelation of Truth—namely, the "Word of God," in a perfectly definite and purely Magian sense of the phrase, which is equally remote from Classical and from Western thought, and has, in consequence, been the source of innumerable misunderstandings. The sacred book in which it has become visibly evident, in which it has been captured by the spell of a sacred script, is part of the stock of every Magian religion.[5] In this conception three Magian notions

---

[5] It is almost unnecessary to say that in all religions of the Germanic West the Bible stands in a quite other relationship to the faith—namely, in that of a *source* in the strictly historical sense, irrespective of whether it is taken as inspired and immune from textual criticism or not. The relation of Chinese thought to the canonical books is similar.

are interwoven—each of which, even by itself, presents extreme difficulties for us, while their simultaneous separateness and oneness is simply inaccessible to our religious thought, often though that thought has managed to persuade itself to the contrary. These ideas are: God, the Spirit of God, the Word of God. That which is written in the prologue of the John Gospel—"In the beginning was the Word, and the Word was with God, and the Word was God"—had long before come to perfectly natural expression as something self-evident in the Persian ideas of Spenta Mainyu,[6] and Vohu Mano,[7] and in corresponding Jewish and Chaldean conceptions. And it was the kernel for which the conflicts of the fourth and fifth centuries concerning the substance of Christ were fought. But, for Magian thought, truth is itself a substance, and lie (or error) second substance—again the same dualism that opposes light and darkness, life and death, good and evil. As substance, truth is identical now with God, now with the Spirit of God, now with the Word. Only in the light of this can we comprehend sayings like "I am the truth and the life" and "My word is the truth," sayings to be understood, as they were meant, with reference to substance. Only so, too, can we realize with what eyes the religious man of this Culture looked upon his sacred book: in it the invisible truth has entered into a visible kind of existence, or, in the words of John 1:14: "The Word became flesh and dwelt among us." *"Koran" means "reading."* Mohammed in a vision saw in the heaven treasured rolls of scripture that he (although he had never learned how to read) was able to decipher "in the name of the Lord." The first (and a very deliberate) example of a "Koran" is the book of Ezekiel, which the author received in a thought-out vision from God and "swallowed" (3:1–3). Here, expressed in the crudest imaginable form, is the basis on which later the idea and shape of all apocalyptic writing was founded. But by degrees this *substantial* form of reception came to be one of the requisites for any book to be canonical. It was in post-Exilic times that the idea arose of the Tables of the Law received by Moses on Sinai. From the Council of Jabna (about 90 B.C.) the whole word was regarded as inspired and delivered in the most literal sense. "Canon" is the

---

[6] The Holy Spirit, different from Ahuramazda and yet one with him, opposed to the Evil (Angra Mainyu).

[7] Identified by Mani with the Johannine Logos. Compare also Yasht 13, 31. Ahuramazda's shining soul is the Word.

technical expression for the totality of writings that arc accepted by a religion as delivered. It was as canons in this sense that the Hermetic collection and the corpus of Chaldean oracles came into being from 200—the latter a sacred book of the Neoplatonists which alone was admitted by Proclus, the "Father" of this Church, to stand with Plato's *Timaeus*.

Originally, the young Jesus-religion, like Jesus himself, recognized the Jewish canon. The first Gospels set up no sort of claim to be the Word made visible. *The John Gospel is the first Christian writing of which the evident purpose is that of a Koran.*

But such a Koran is by its very nature unconditionally right, and therefore unalterable and incapable of improvement. There arose, in consequence, the habit of secret interpretations meant to bring the text into harmony with the convictions of the time. A masterpiece of this kind is Justinian's Digests, but the same applies not only to every book of the Bible, but also (we need not doubt) to the Gathas of the Avesta and even to the then current manuscripts of Plato, Aristotle and other authorities of the Pagan theology. More important still is the assumption, traceable in every Magian religion, of a secret revelation, or a secret meaning of the Scriptures, preserved not by being written down, but in the memory of adepts and propagated orally. According to Jewish notions, Moses received at Sinai not only the written but *also a secret oral Torah,*[8] which it was forbidden to commit to writing. It has often been observed that Mark speaks of the Visitation and of the Resurrection only in hints, and that John only touches upon the doctrine of the Paraclete and omits the institution of the Lord's Supper entirely. The initiates understood what was meant, and the unbeliever ought not to know it. We ourselves, as it is upon the most important things that we are most emphatic and forthright, run the risk of misinterpreting Magian doctrines through taking the part that was expressed for the whole that existed, and the profane literal meaning of words for their real significance. Gothic Christianity had no secrets and hence it doubly mistrusted the Talmud, which it rightly regarded as being only the foreground of Jewish doctrine.

Pure Magian, too, is the Kabbalah, which out of numbers, letter-forms, points and strokes unfolds secret significances, and therefore cannot but be as old as the Word itself that was sent

[8] IV Ezra 14.

down as Substance. The secret dogma of the creation of the world out of the two and twenty letters of the Hebrew alphabet, and that of the throne-chariot of Ezekiel's Vision, are already traceable in Maccabaean times. Closely related to this is the allegorical exegesis of the sacred texts.

The only strictly *scientific* method that an unalterable Koran leaves open for progressive opinion is that of commentary. As by hypothesis the "word" of an authority cannot be improved upon, the only resource is reinterpretation. No one in Alexandria would ever have asserted that Plato was in "error"; instead, he was glossed upon. Following the procedure of the Gnostics, the Fathers compiled written commentaries upon the Bible, and similarly the Pehlevi commentary of the Zend appeared by the side of the Avesta, and the Midrash by the side of the Jewish canon. The Mishnah is one vast commentary upon the Torah. And when the oldest exegetes had become themselves authorities and their writings Korans, commentaries were written upon commentaries, as by Simplicius, the last Platonist, in the West, and by the jurists who compiled the Imperial Constitutions into the Digests at Byzantium.

This method, which fictitiously refers back every saying to an immediate inspired delivery, was brought to its keenest edge in the Talmudic and the Islamic theologies. A new Halakha or a Hadith is valid only when it can be referred through an unbroken chain of guarantors back to Moses or Mohammed.[9] Into the early-Christian literature this Halakha-form entered so self-evidently that no one remarked it for what it was. Apart altogether from the constant references to the Law and the Prophets, it appears in the superscription of the four Gospels (*"according to"* Mark), each of which had thus to present its warrant if authority was to be claimed for the words of the Lord that it presented.[1] And,

---

[9] In the West, Plato, Aristotle and above all Pythagoras were regarded as prophets in this sense. What could be referred back to them was valid. For this reason the succession of the heads of the schools became more and more important, and often more work was done in establishing—or inventing—them than was done upon the history of the doctrine itself.

[1] We today confuse *authorship* and *authority*. Arabian thought knew not the idea of "intellectual property." Such would have been absurd and sinful, for it is the *one* divine Pneuma that selects the individual as vessel and mouthpiece. Only to that extent is he the "author," and it does not matter even whether he or another actually writes down the material. "The Gospel *according to* Mark" means that Mark *vouches for* the truth of this evangel.

lastly, this is the metaphysical presupposition for the style and the deeper meaning of *citation,* which was employed alike by Fathers, Rabbis, "Greek" philosophers and "Roman" jurists—a fundamental notion, which differentiated the literary stock according to difference of *substance.*

THE GROUP OF THE MAGIAN RELIGIONS

With such researches to build upon, it will become possible in the future to write a history of the *Magian group of religions.* It forms an inseparable unit of spirit and evolution, and let no one imagine that any individual one of them can be really comprehended without reference to the rest. Their birth, unfolding and inward confirmation occupy the period 0–500. It corresponds exactly to the rise of the Western religion from the Cluniac movement to the Reformation.

In the wide realm of old-Babylonian fellahdom young peoples lived. There everything was making ready. The first premonitions of the future awoke about 700 B.C. in the prophetic religions of the Persians, Jews and Chaldeans. An image of creation of the same kind that later was to be the preface of the Torah showed itself in clear outlines, and with that an orientation, a direction, a goal of desire, was set. Something was descried in the far future, indefinitely and darkly still, but with a profound certainty that it would come. From that time on men lived with the vision of this, with the feeling of a mission.

The second wave swelled up steeply in the Apocalyptic currents after 300. Here it was the Magian waking-consciousness that arose and built itself a metaphysic of Last Things, based already upon the prime symbol of the coming Culture, the Cavern. Ideas of an awful End of the World, of the Last Judgment, of Resurrection, Paradise and Hell, and with them the grand thought of a process of salvation in which earth's destiny and man's were one, burst forth everywhere—we cannot say what land or people it was that created them—mantled in wondrous scenes and figures and names. The Messiah-figure presents itself, complete at one stroke. Satan's temptation of the Saviour [2] is told as a tale. But simultaneously there welled up a deep and

---

[2] Vendidad 19, 1; here it is Zarathustra who is tempted.

ever-increasing fear before this certainty of an implacable—and imminent—limit of all happening, before the moment in which there would be only Past. Magian Time, the "hour," directedness under the Cavern, imparted a new pulse to life and a new import to the word "Destiny."

The third upheaval came in the time of Caesar and brought to birth the great religions of Salvation. And with this the Culture rose to bright day, and what followed continuously throughout one or two centuries was an intensity of religious experience, both unsurpassable and at long last unbearable. Such a tension bordering upon the breaking point the Gothic, the Vedic and every other Culture-soul have known, once and once only, in their young morning.

Now arose in the Persian, the Mandaean, the Jewish, the Christian circles of belief, and in that of the Western Pseudomorphosis as well—just as in the Indian, the Classical and the Western ages of Chivalry—the Grand Myth. In this Arabian Culture religious and national heroism are no more distinctly separable than nation, church and state, or sacred and secular law. The powers of light and darkness, fabulous beings, angels and devils, Satan and the good spirits, wrestle together; all nature is a battle-ground from the beginning of the world to its annihilation. In the East the life of the Persian prophet inspired an epic poetry of grand outlines. At his birth the Zarathustra-laughter pealed through the heavens, and all nature echoed it. In the West the suffering of Jesus, ever broadening and developing, became *the veritable epic of the Christian nation,* and by its side there grew up a chain of legends of his childhood which in the end fructified a whole genre of poetry.

With the end of the second century the sounds of this exaltation die away. The flowering of epic poetry is past, and the mystical penetration and dogmatic analysis of the religious material begin. The doctrines of the new Churches are brought into theological systems. Heroism yields to Scholasticism, poetry to thought, the seer and seeker to the priest. The early Scholasticism, which ends about 200 (as the Western about 1200) comprises the whole Gnosis—in the very broadest sense, the great Contemplation—the author of the John Gospel, Valentinus, Bardesanes and Marcion, the Apologists and the early Fathers, up to Irenaeus and Tertullian, the last Tannaim up to Rabbi Jehuda, the completer of the Mishnah, the Neopythagoreans and Hermetics of Alexandria. All this corresponds with, in the West, the School of Chartres, Anselm, Joachim of Floris, Bernard of Clairvaux, Hugo de St. Victor. Full Scholasticism begins with Neoplatonism, with Clement and Origen, the first Amoraim and the creators of the newer Avesta under Ardeshir (226–41) and Sapor I, the Mazdaist high-priest Tanvasar above all. Simultaneously a higher religiousness begins to separate from the peasant's piety of the countryside, which still lingered in the apocalyptic disposition, and thenceforth maintained itself almost unaltered under various names right into the fellahdom of the Turkish age, while in the urban and more intellectual upper world the Persian, Jewish and Christian community was absorbed by that of Islam.

Slowly and steadily now the great Churches moved to fulfilment. To the third century belong the great mental structures of theology. A *modus vivendi* with historical actuality had been reached, the end of the world had receded into the distance and a new dogmatic grew up to explain the new world-picture.

A new religious founder appeared in 242, in the reign of Sapor I. This was Mani, who, rejecting "redeemerless" Judaism and Hellenism, knit together the whole mass of Magian religions in one of the most powerful theological creations of all times— for which in 276 the Mazdaist priesthood crucified him. Equipped by his father (who quite late in life abandoned his family to enter a Mandaean order) with all the knowledge of the period, he unified the basic ideas of the Chaldeans and Persians with those of Johannine, Eastern, Christianity. He conceived of the mystical figures of the Johannine Logos (for him identical with the Persian Vohu Mano), the Zarathustra of the Avesta legends and the Buddha of the late texts as divine Emanations, and himself he proclaimed to be the Paraclete of the John Gospel and the Saoshyant of the Persians. As we now know, thanks to the Turfan discoveries which included parts of Mani's works (till then completely lost), the Church-language of the Mazdaists, Manichaeans and Nestorians was—independently of the current languages—Pehlevi.

In the West *the two cult-Churches* developed (in Greek) a theology that was not only cognate with this but to a great extent identical with it. In the time of Mani began the theological fusion of the Aramaean-Chaldean sun-religion and the Aramaean-Persian Mithras cult into one system, whose first great "Father" was

Iamblichus (c. 300)—the contemporary of Athanasius, but also of Diocletian, the Emperor who in 295 made Mithras the God of a henotheistic State-religion. Spiritually, at any rate, its priests were in no wise distinguishable from those of Christianity. Proclus (he, too, a true "Father") received in dreams elucidations of a difficult text-passage; to him the *Timaeus* and the Chaldean oracles were canonical, and he would gladly have seen all other writings of the philosophers destroyed. His hymns, tokens of the lacerations of a true eremite, implore Helios and other helpers to protect him against evil spirits. Hierocles wrote a moral breviary for the believers of the Neopythagorean community, which it needs a keen eye to distinguish from Christian work. We possess Pagan gospels and hagiologies as well as Christian. Apollonius wrote the life of Pythagoras, Marinus that of Proclus, Damascius that of Isidore; and there is not the slightest difference between these works, which begin and end with prayers, and the Christian Acts of the Martyrs. Porphyry describes faith, love, hope and truth as the four divine elements.

Between these Churches of the East and the West we see, looking south from Edessa, the Talmudic Church (the "Synagogue") with Aramaic as its written language. Against these great and firm foundations Jewish-Christians (such as Ebionites and Elkazites), Mandaeans and likewise Chaldeans (unless we regard Manichaeism as a reconstruction of that religion) were unable to hold their own. Breaking down into numberless sects, they either faded out in the shadow of the great Churches or were structurally absorbed, as the last Marcionites and Montanists were absorbed into Manichaeism. By about 300, outside the Pagan, Christian, Persian, Jewish and Manichaean Churches no important Magian religions remained in being.

THE RELIGIONS OF MAGIAN CHRISTIANITY. THE END OF THEOLOGY

Christianity, which even in the second century was hardly more than an extended Order, and whose public influence was out of all proportion to the number of its adherents, grew suddenly vast about the year 250. This is the epochal moment in which the last city-cults of the Classical effaced themselves before, *not Christianity, but the new-born Pagan Church*. The records of the

Fratres Arvales in Rome break off in 241, and the last cult-inscriptions at Olympia are of 265. The Christian religion, on the other hand, was alone in spreading (*c.* 300) over the great Arabian field. And for that very reason it was inevitable that inner contradiction should now be set up in it. Due, not now to the spiritual dispositions of particular men, but to the spirit of the particular landscapes, these contradictions led to the break-up of Christianity into several religions—and forever.

The *controversy concerning the nature of Christ* was the issue on which this conflict came up for decision. The matter in dispute was just those problems of substance which in the same form and with the same tendency fill the thoughts of all other Magian theologies.

But the three Christian solutions predetermined by the three landscapes of East, West and South were all present from the first, implicit already in the main tendencies of Gnosticism, which we may indicate by the names of Bardesanes, Basilides and Valentinus. Their meeting-point was Edessa, where the streets rang with the battle-cries of the Nestorians against the victors of Ephesus and, anon, with the εἷς θεός shouts of the Monophysites, demanding that Bishop Ibas should be thrown to the wild beasts of the circus.

The great question was formulated by Athanasius, whose intellectual origins lay in the Pseudomorphosis and who had many affinities with his Pagan contemporary Iamblichus. Against Arius, who saw in Christ a demigod, merely *like* in substance to the Father, he maintained that Father and Son were of *the same* substance (θεότης), which in Christ had assumed a human σῶμα. "The Word became Flesh"—this formula of the West depends upon visible facts of the cult-Churches, and the understanding of the Word upon constant contemplation of the picturable.

With the recognition of the *homoousia* of Father and Son the real problem was for the first time posed—namely, the attitude of the Magian dualism to the historical phenomenon of the Son himself. In the world-cavern there was divine and human substance, in man a part in divine Pneuma and the individual soul somehow related to the "flesh." But what of Christ?

It was a decisive factor—one of the results of Actium—that the contest was fought out in the Greek tongue and in the territory of the Pseudomorphosis—that is, under the full influence of the "Caliph" of the Western Church. Constantine had even been the convener and president of the Council of Nicaea, where the doctrine of Athanasius carried the day. The breach between East and West, a consequence of the Council of Ephesus (431), separated two Christian *nations*, that of the "Persian Church" and that of the Greek Church, but this was no more than the manifestation of a difference, inherent from the first, between *modes of thought* proper to the two different landscapes. Nestorius and the whole East saw in Christ the Second Adam, the Divine Envoy of the last aeon. Mary had borne a *man*-child in whose human and created substance (*physis*) the godly, uncreated element *dwelt*. The West, on the contrary, saw in Mary the Mother of a *God:* the divine and the human substance formed in his body (*persona,* in the Classical idiom) a unity, named by Cyril ἕνωσις.[3] When the Council of Ephesus had recognized the mother of God, her who gave birth to God, the city of Diana's old renown burst into a truly Classical orgy of celebration.

But long ere this the Syrian Apollinaris had heralded the "Southern" idea of the matter—that in the living Christ there was not merely a substance, but a single substance. The divine had transmuted itself into, not mingled itself with, a human substance (no κρᾶσις, as Gregory Nazianzen maintained in opposition; significantly enough, the best way of expressing the Monophysite idea is through concepts of Spinoza—the *one* substance in another mode). The Monophysites called the Christ of the Council of Chalcedon (451, where the West once more prevailed) "the idol with the two faces." They not only fell away from the Church, they broke out in fierce risings in Palestine and Egypt; and when in Justinian's time the troops of Persia—that is, of Mazdaism— penetrated to the Nile, they were hailed by the Monophysites as liberators.

The fundamental meaning of this desperate conflict which raged for a century—not over scholarly concepts, but over the soul of a landscape that sought to be set free *in its people*—was the *reversal of the work of Paul.* If we can transport ourselves into the inmost soul of the two new-born nations, making no reservations and ignoring all minor points of dogmatics, then we

---

[3] The Nestorians protested against Mary *Theotokos* (she who bore God), opposing to her the concept of Christ the *Theophoros* (he who carried God in him). The deep difference between an image-loving and an image-hating religiousness is here clearly manifested.

see how the direction of Christianity towards the Greek West and its intellectual affinity with the Pagan Church culminated in the position that the Ruler of the West was the Head of Christianity in general. When the spirit of the Pseudomorphosis had, in the three determining councils of Nicaea, Ephesus and Chalcedon, put *its* seal upon dogma, once and for all, the real Arabian world rose up with the force of nature and set up a barrier against it. With the end of the Arabian springtime, Christianity fell apart for good into three religions, which can be symbolized by the names of Paul, Peter and John. These three religions are at the same time three nations, living in the old race-areas of Greeks, Jews and Persians, and the tongues that they used were the Church-languages borrowed from them—namely, Greek, Aramaic and Pehlevi.

The Eastern Church, since the Council of Nicaea, had organized itself with an episcopal constitution, at the head of which stood the Katholikos of Ctesiphon, and with councils, liturgy and law of its own. In 486 the Nestorian doctrine was accepted as binding, and the tie with Constantinople was thus broken. From that point on, Mazdaists, Manichaeans and Nestorians have a common destiny, of which the seed was sown in the Gnosis of Bardesanes. In the Monophysite Churches of the South, the spirit of the primitive Community emerged again and spread itself further; with its uncompromising monotheism and its hatred of images, its closest affinity was with Talmudic Judaism, and its old battle-cry of εἶς θεός had already marked it to be, with that Judaism, the starting-point of Islam (*"Allah il Allah"*). The Western Church continued to be bound up with the fate of the Roman Empire—that is, the cult-Church became the State. Gradually it absorbed into itself the adherents of the Pagan Church, and thenceforth its importance lay not so much in itself —for Islam almost annihilated it—but in the accident that it was *from it* that the young peoples of the Western Culture received the Christian system as the basis for a new creation,[4] receiving it, moreover, in the Latin guise of the extreme West—which for the Greek Church itself was unmeaning, since Rome was now a Greek city, and the Latin language was far more truly at home in Africa and Gaul.

The essential and elemental concept of the Magian nation, a

---

[4] And Russia, too, though hitherto Russia has kept it as a buried treasure.

being that consists in extension, had been from the beginning active in extending itself. All these Churches were, deliberately, forcefully and successfully, missionary Churches. But it was not until men had at last ceased to think of the end of the world as imminent, and dogma appropriate to prolonged existence in this World's Cavern had been built up, and the Magian religions had taken up their standpoint towards the problem of substance, that the extending of the Culture took up that swift, passionate tempo that distinguished it from all others and found in Islam its most impressive, its last, but by no means its only example.

But even before Christianity—and this is a fact of which the immense significance has never been observed, which has not even been correctly interpreted as *mission* effort—the Pagan Church had won for the Syncretic Cult the greater part of the population of North Africa, Spain, Gaul, Britain and the Rhine and Danube frontiers. Of the Druidism that Caesar had found in Gaul, little remained extant by the time of Constantine.

The Jews, as has been shown already, directed missionary effort on a large scale towards the East and the South. Through southern Arabia they drove into the heart of Africa, possibly even before the birth of Christ, while on the side of the East their presence in China is demonstrable, even in the second century. To the north the realm of the Khazars and its capital, Astrakhan, later went over to Judaism. From this area came the Mongols of Jewish religion who advanced into the heart of Germany and were defeated, along with the Hungarians, in the battle of the Lechfeld in 955.

From the Tigris, Mazdaists and Manichaeans penetrated the empires on either hand, Roman and Chinese, to their utmost frontiers. Persian, as the Mithras cult, invaded Britain; Manichaeism had by 400 become a danger to Greek Christianity, and there were Manichaean sects in Southern France as late as the Crusades; [5] but the two religions drove eastwards as well, along the Great Wall of China (where the great polyglot inscription of Kara Balgassun testifies to the introduction of the Manichaean faith in the Oigur realm) and even to Shantung. Persian fire-temples arose in the interior of China, and from 700 Persian expressions are found in Chinese astrological writings.

—————

[5] The Albigensian movement of the twelfth century.—*At.*

The three Christian Churches everywhere followed up the blazed trails. When the Western Church converted the Frankish King Clovis in 496, the missionaries of the Eastern Church had already reached Ceylon and the westernmost Chinese garrisons of the Great Wall, and those of the Southern were in the Empire of Axum. At the same time as, after Boniface (718), Germany became converted, the Nestorian missionaries were within an ace of winning China itself. They had entered Shantung in 638. It is in the highest degree significant that the Confucians, who cannot be called inexpert in religious matters, regarded the Nestorians, Mazdaists and Manichaeans as adherents of a single "Persian" religion, just as the population of the Western Roman provinces were unable to discriminate between Mithras and Christ.

Islam is to be regarded as the Puritanism of the whole group of early-Magian religions, emerging as a religion only formally new, and in the domain of the Southern Church and Talmudic Judaism. It is this deeper significance, and not merely the force of its warlike onslaught, that gives the key to its fabulous successes. The Katholikos of Seleucia, Jesujabh III, complains that tens of thousands of Christians went over to it as soon as it came on the scene, and in North Africa—the home of Augustine—the entire population fell away to Islam at once. Mohammed died in 632. In 641 the whole domain of the Monophysites and the Nestorians (and, therefore, of the Talmud and the Avesta) was in the possession of Islam. In 717 it stood before Constantinople, and the Greek Church was in peril of extinction. Already in 628 a relative of the prophet had brought presents to the Chinese Emperor T'ai Tsung and obtained leave to institute a mission. From 700 there were mosques in Shantung, and in 720 Damascus sent instructions to the Arabs long established in Southern France to conquer the realm of the Franks. Two centuries later, when in the West a new religious world was arising out of the remains of the old Western Church, Islam was in the Sudan and in Java.

For all this, Islam is significant only as a piece of *outward* religious history. The inner history of the Magian religion ends with Justinian's time, as truly as that of the Faustian ends with Charles V and the Council of Trent. Any book on religious history shows *"the"* Christian religion as having had *two ages of grand thought-movements*—0–500 in the East and 1000–1500 in the West. *But these are two springtimes of two Cultures*, and in

317

them are comprised also the non-Christian forms which belong to each religious development. The closing of the University of Athens by Justinian in 529 was not, as is always stated, the end of Classical philosophy—there had been no Classical philosophy for centuries. What he did, forty years before the birth of Mohammed, was to end the theology of the Pagan Church by closing this school and—as the historians forget to add—*to end the Christian theology also* by closing those of Antioch and Alexandria. Dogma was complete, finished—just as it was in the West with the Council of Trent (1564) and the Confession of Augsburg (1540), for with the city and intellectualism religious creative force comes to an end.

XVI

PROBLEMS OF
THE ARABIAN CULTURE:
PYTHAGORAS, MOHAMMED, CROMWELL

THE NATURE OF RELIGION; MORALITY AS SACRIFICE

RELIGION may be described as the Waking-Being of a living creature in the moments when it overcomes, masters, denies and even destroys Being. Worldly life and the pulse of its drive dwindles as the eyes gaze into an extended, tense and light-filled world, and *Time yields to Space.*

The higher religion requires tense alertness against the powers of blood and being that ever lurk in the depths ready to recapture their primeval rights over the *younger* side of life. "*Watch* and pray, that ye fall not into temptation." Nevertheless, "liberation" is a fundamental word in every religion and an eternal wish of every waking-being. In this general, almost prereligious, sense, it means the desire for freedom from the anxieties and anguishes of waking-consciousness; from the tensions of fear-born thought; from the consciousness of the Ego's loneliness in the universe, the rigid conditionedness of nature, the prospect of old age and death.

Sleep, too, liberates—"Death and his brother Sleep." And holy wine, intoxication, breaks the rigour of the spirit's tension, and dancing, the Dionysus art, and every other form of stupefaction and ecstasy. These are modes of slipping out of awareness by the aid of being, the cosmic, the "it," *the escape out of space into time.* But higher than all these stands the genuinely religious overcoming of fear *by means of the understanding itself.* The tension between microcosm and macrocosm becomes something that we can love, something in which we can wholly immerse ourselves.[1] We call this *faith,* and it is the beginning of all man's intellectual life. The viewing of the entire world as nature in relation to the individual consciousness as a single causally ordered concatenation is something perfectly unrealizable by our thought, inasmuch as our thinking proceeds always by single stages. It remains a belief. It is indeed Faith itself, for it is the basis of religious understanding of the world. The attitude of religious thought is to assess values and ranks within the causal succession, and it leads up to supreme beings or principles, as very first and "governing" causes; "dispensation" is the word used for the most comprehensive of all systems based upon valuation. Science, on the contrary, is a mode of understanding which fundamentally abhors distinctions of rank amongst causes; what it finds is not dispensation, but law.

The understanding of causes sets free. Belief in the linkages discovered compels the world-fear to retreat. God is man's refuge from the Destiny which he can feel and livingly experience, but not think on, or figure, or name, and which sinks into abeyance for so long—only for so long—as the "critical" (literally, the distinguishing) fear-born understanding can establish causes behind causes comprehensibly; that is, in order visible to the outer or the inner eye.

In the world-around something is established—that is, fixed, spellbound. Understanding man has the secret in the hands, whether this be, as of old, some potent charm or, as nowadays, a mathematical formula. Experience in this inorganic, killing, preserving sense, which is something quite different from life-experience and knowledge of men, takes place in two modes— *theory and technique,* or, in religious language, *myth and cult*— according as the believer's intention is to disclose or to compel the secrets of the world-around. The theorist is the critical seer, the technician is the priest, the discoverer is the prophet.

The means, however, in which the whole force of intellect concentrates itself is the *form* of the actual, which is abstracted from vision by speech, and of which not every waking-consciousness can discern the quintessence—the conceptual circumscription, the communicable law, name, number. Hence every

---

[1] "He who loves God with inmost soul, transforms himself into God" (Bernard of Clairvaux).

conjuration of the deity is based on the knowledge of its real name and the use of rites and sacraments, known and available only to the initiated, of which the form must be exact and the words correct. This applies not merely to primitive magic, but just as much to our physical (and particularly our medical) technique. The belief in a knowledge that needs no postulates is merely a mark of the immense naïveté of rationalist periods. A theory of natural science is nothing but a historically older dogma in another shape. And the only profit from it is that which life obtains, in the shape of a successful technique, to which theory has provided the key. It has already been said that the value of a working hypothesis resides not in its "correctness" but in its usableness. But discoveries of another sort, findings of insight, "Truths" in the optimistic sense, cannot be the outcome of purely scientific understanding, since this always presupposes an existing view upon which its critical, dissecting activity can operate; the natural science of the Baroque is one continuous dissection of the religious world-picture of the Gothic.

The aim of faith and science, fear and curiosity, is not to experience life, but to know the world-as-nature. Of world-as-history they are the express negation. *Only the Timeless is true.* Truths lie beyond history and life, and vice versa life is something beyond all causes, effects and truths. It follows that the distinction between faith and knowledge, or fear and curiosity, or revelation and criticism, is not, after all, an ultimate distinction. Knowledge is only a late form of belief. We can distinguish men, not according to what their modes of thinking are—religious or critical—nor according to the objects of their thought, but according to whether they are thinkers (no matter about what) *or doers.*

In the realm of doing the waking-consciousness takes charge only when it becomes *technique.* Religious knowledge, too, is power—man is not only ascertaining causations but handling them. He who knows the secret relationship between microcosm and macrocosm commands it also, whether the knowledge has come to him by revelation or by close attention.

From this starting-point we can understand (what the European-American world of today has well-nigh forgotten) the ultimate meaning of religious ethics, *Moral.* It is, wherever true and strong, a relation that has the full import of *ritual act and prac-*

tice; it is (to use Loyola's phrase) *"exercitium spirituale,"* performed before the deity,[2] who is to be softened and conjured thereby. "What shall I do to be saved?" This "What?" is the key to the understanding of all real moral. *There is only causal moral —that is, ethical technique—*on the background of a convinced metaphysic.

Moral is a conscious and planned causality of conduct, apart from all particulars of actual life and character, something eternal and universally valid, not only without time but hostile to time and for that very reason "true." Negation is expressed in its very phrases—religious moral contains prohibitions, not precepts. Taboo, even where it ostensibly affirms, is a list of disclaimers. Extreme tension of awareness is required lest we fall into sin. The world in general—meaning the world-as-history— is base. It fights instead of renouncing; it does not possess the idea of sacrifice. It prevails over truth by means of facts. And therefore the highest sacrifice that intellectual man can offer is to make a personal present of it to the powers of nature. *Every moral action is a piece of this sacrifice,* and an ethical life-course is an unbroken chain of such sacrifices. Above all, the offering of sympathy, com-passion, in which the inwardly strong gives up his superiority to the powerless. The compassionate man kills something within himself. But we must not confuse this sympathy in the grand religious sense with the vague sentimentality of the everyday man, who cannot command himself, still less with the *race-feeling of chivalry,* which is not a moral of reasons and rules at all, but an upstanding and self-evident *custom* bred of the unconscious pulsations of a keyed-up life. But Compassion likewise demands inward greatness of soul, and so it is those self-same springtimes that produce the most saintly servants of pity, Francis of Assisi, Bernard of Clairvaux, in whom renunciation was a pervading fragrance, to whom self-offering was bliss, whose *caritas* was ethereal, bloodless, timeless, historyless, in whom fear of the universe had dissolved itself into pure, flawless love, a summit of causal moral of which Late periods are simply no longer capable.

To constrain one's blood, one must have blood. Consequently it is only in knightly warrior-times that we find a monasticism of

---

[2] Anatole France's story *Le Jongleur de Notre-Dame* is something deeper than a beautiful fancy.—*At.*

the great style, and the highest symbol for the complete victory of Space over Time is the warrior become ascetic—not the born dreamer and weakling, who belongs by nature to the cloister, nor again the scholar, who works at a moral system in the study.

MORPHOLOGY OF RELIGIOUS HISTORY

If there were truths independent of the currents of being, there could be no history of truths. If there were one single eternally right religion, religious history would be an inconceivable idea. But, however highly developed the microcosmic side of an individual's life may be, it is nevertheless something stretched like a membrane over the developing life, perfused by the pulsing blood, ever betraying the hidden drive of cosmic directedness. Race dominates and forms all apprehension. It is the destiny of each moment of awareness to be a cast of Time's net over Space.

Not that "eternal truths" do not exist. Every man possesses them—plenty of them—to the extent that he exists and exercises the understanding faculty in a world of thoughts, in the connected ensemble of which they are, in and for the instant of thought, unalterable fixtures—ironbound as cause-effect combinations in hoops of premises and conclusions. Nothing in this disposition can become displaced, he believes. But in reality it is just *one* surge of life that is lifting his waking self and its world together. Its unity remains integral, but *as* a unit, a whole, *a fact,* it has a history. Absolute and relative are to one another as transverse and longitudinal sections of a succession of generations, the latter ignoring Space, and the former Time. The systematic thinker stays in the causal order of a moment; only the physiognomist who reviews the sequence of positions realizes the constant alteration of that which "is" true.

Alles Vergängliche ist nur ein Gleichnis holds good for the eternal truths also, as soon as we follow their course in the stream of history, and watch them move on as elements in the world-picture of the generations that live and die.

A morphology of religious history, therefore, is a task that the Faustian spirit alone could ever formulate, and one that it is only now, at this present stage of its development, fit to deal with. The problem is enunciated, and we must dare the effort of getting completely away from our own convictions and seeing before us everything indifferently as equally alien. And how hard it is! He who undertakes the task must possess the strength not merely to imagine himself in an illusory detachment from the truths of his world-understanding—illusory even to one for whom truths are just a set of concepts and methods—but actually to penetrate his own system physiognomically to its very last cells. And even then is it possible, in a single language, which structurally and spiritually carries the whole metaphysical content of its own Culture, to capture transmissible ideas of the truths of other-tongued men?

EGYPT AND THE ANCIENT WORLD

Primitive religions have something homeless about them, like the clouds and the wind. The mass-souls of the proto-peoples have accidentally and fugitively condensed into *one* being, and accidental, therefore, is and remains the "where"—which is an "anywhere"—of the linkages of waking-consciousness arising from the fear and defensiveness that spread over them. Whether they stay or move on, whether they alter or not, is immaterial so far as concerns their inward significance.

From life of this order the high Cultures are separated by deep soil ties. Here there is a mother-landscape behind all expression-forms, and just as the town, as temple and pyramid and cathedral, *must* fulfil their history *there* where their idea originated, so too the great religion of every springtime is bound by all the roots of its being to the land over which its world-image has risen. Sacral practices and dogmas may be carried far and wide, but their inner evolution stays spellbound in the place of their birth. It is simply an impossibility that the slightest trace of evolution of Classical city-cults should be found in Gaul, or a dogmatic advance of Faustian Christianity in America. Whatever disconnects itself from the land becomes rigid and hard.

Religion starts like a great shout. Gloomy apprehension is suddenly dispelled by a fervid wakening that blossoms plantwise from mother earth and at one glance takes in the depth of the light-world. In this moment—never earlier, and never (at least with the same deep intensity) later—it traverses the chosen spirits of the time like a grand light, which dissolves all fear in blissful love and lets the invisible appear, all suddenly, in a metaphysical radiance.

Every Culture actualizes here its prime symbol. Each has its own sort of love—we may call it heavenly or metaphysical as we choose—with which it contemplates, comprehends and takes into itself its godhead, and which remains to every other Culture inaccessible or unmeaning. Whether the world be something set under a domed light-cavern, as it was for Jesus and his companions, or just a vanishingly small bit of a star-filled infinity, as Giordano Bruno felt it; whether the Orphics take their bodily god into themselves, or the spirit of Plotinus, soaring in ecstasy, fuses in *henosis* with the spirit of God, or St. Bernard in his "mystic union" becomes one with the operation of infinite deity—the deep urge of the soul is governed always by the prime symbol of the particular Culture and of no other.

About 3000 begins the life-course of two great religions in Egypt and Babylon. In the Fifth Dynasty of Egypt (2450–2320), which followed that of the great pyramid-builders, the cult of the Horus-falcon, whose *ka* dwelt in the reigning monarch, faded. The old local cults and even the profound Thot religion of Hermopolis fell into the background. The sun-religion of Re appears. Out from his palace westward every king erects a Re-sanctuary by his tomb-temple, the latter a symbol of a life directional from birth to sarcophagus-chamber, the former a symbol of grand and eternal nature. Time and Space, being and waking-being, Destiny and sacred Causality, are set face to face in this mighty twin-creation as in no other architecture in the world. To both a covered way leads up; that to the Re is accompanied by reliefs figuring the power of the sun-god over the plant and animal worlds and the changings of seasons. No god-image, no temple, but only an altar of alabaster adorns the mighty terrace on which at daybreak, high above the land, the Pharaoh advances out of the darkness to greet the great god who is rising up in the East.[3] The beliefs of the peasant outside remain "eternal" and always the same. The Egyptian hind understood nothing of this Re. He heard the name, but while a grand chapter of religious history

---

[3] The Pharaoh is no longer an incarnation of godhead, and not yet, as the theology of the Middle Kingdom was to make him, the son of Re; notwithstanding all earthly greatness, he is small, a servant, as he stands before the god.

was passing over his head in the cities, he went on worshipping the old Thinite beast-gods, until with the Twenty-sixth Dynasty and its fellah-religion they regained supremacy.

But even in the towns one stratum hangs back, historically, relatively to another. Over the primitive religion of the country-side there is another popular religion, that of the small people in the underground of the towns and in the provinces. The higher a Culture rises—Middle Kingdom, Brahman period, Pre-Socratics, Pre-Confucians, Baroque—the narrower becomes the circle of those who possess the final truths of their time as reality and not as mere name and sound. How many of those who lived with Socrates, Augustine and Pascal understood them? In religion as otherwise the human pyramid rises with increasing sharpness, till at the end of the Culture it is complete—thereafter, bit by bit, to crumble.

In Egypt the "reformation" period at the end of the Old Kingdom saw solar monotheism firmly founded as the religion of priests and educated persons. All other gods and goddesses—whom the peasantry and the humble people continued to worship in their former meaning—are now only incarnations or servants of the one Re. Even the particular religion of Hermopolis, with its cosmology, was adapted to the grand system, and a theological negotiation brought even the Ptah of Memphis into harmony with dogma as an abstract prime-principle of creation. Exactly as in the time of Justinian and Charles V, the city-spirit asserted mastery over the soul of the land; the formative power of the springtime had come to an end; the dogma was essentially complete, and its subsequent treatment by rational processes abandoned more than it improved. Philosophy began. In respect of dogma, the Middle Kingdom was as unimportant as the Baroque.

From 1500 three new religious histories begin—first the Vedic in the Punjab, then the Early Chinese in the Hwang Ho and lastly the Classical on the north of the Aegean Sea. Distinctly as the Classical man's world-picture and his prime symbol of the unit body is presented to us, it is difficult even to guess the details of the great early-Classical religion. The new notion of godhead that was the special ideal of this Culture is the human-formed body in the light, the hero as mediator between man and god—so much, at any rate, the *Iliad* evidences. This body might be light-transfigured by Apollo or disjected to the winds by Dionysus, but in every case it was the basic form of Being.

A mighty upheaval there must have been at the beginning of this Culture, as at that of others—an upheaval extending from the Aegean Sea as far as Etruria—but the *Iliad* shows as few signs of it as the lays of the Nibelungs and of Roland show of the devotion and mysticism of Joachim of Floris, St. Francis and the Crusades, or of the inner fire of that *Dies Irae* of Thomas of Celano, which would probably have excited mirth at a thirteenth-century court of love. Great personalities there must have been to give a mystical-metaphysical form to the new world-outlook, but we know nothing of them and it is only the gay, bright, easy side of it that passed into the song of knightly halls. Was the "Trojan War" a feud, or was it also a Crusade? What is the meaning of Helen? Even the Fall of Jerusalem has been looked at from a worldly point of view as well as from a spiritual.

In the nobles' poetry of Homer, Dionysus and Demeter, as priests' gods, are unhonoured. But even in Hesiod, the herdsman of Ascra, the enthusiast-searcher inspired by his folk-beliefs, the ideas of the great early time are not to be found pure, any more than in Jakob Böhme the cobbler. That is the second difficulty. *The great early religions, too, were the possession of a class,* and neither accessible to or understandable by the generality.

But Aeschylus and Pindar, at any rate, were under the spell of a great priestly tradition, and before them there were the Pythagoreans, who made the Demeter-cult their centre (thereby indicating where the kernel of that mythology is to be sought), and earlier still were the Eleusinian Mysteries and the Orphic reformation of the seventh century; and, finally, there are the fragments of Pherecydes and Epimenides, who were not the first *but the last* dogmatists of a theology in reality ancient. The idea that impiety was a heritable sin, visited upon the children and the children's children, was known to Hesiod and Solon, as well as the doctrine (Apollinian also) of "Hybris." Plato, however, as an Orphic opponent of the Homeric conception of life, sets forth very ancient doctrines of hell and the judgment of the dead in his *Phaedo*. We know the tremendous formula of Orphism, the Nay of the mysteries that answered the Yea of the *agon*, which arose, certainly by 1100 at the latest, as a protest of Waking-Consciousness against Being—σῶμα σῆμα, that splendid Classical body a grave! Here man is no longer *feeling* himself as a thing of breeding, strength and movement; he *knows* himself and is terrified by what he knows. Here begins the Classical *askesis,*

327

which by strictest rites and expiations, even by voluntary suicide, seeks deliverance from this Euclidean body-being. From the self-immolation of Empedocles the line runs straight forward to the suicide of the Roman Stoic, and straight back to "Orpheus."

Out of these last surviving traces, however, an outline of the early-Classical religion emerges bright and distinct. Just as all Gothic devotion was centred upon Mary, Queen of Heaven and Virgin and Mother, so in that moment of the Classical world there arose a garland of myths, images and figures around Demeter, the bearing mother, around Gaia and Persephone, and also Dionysus the begetter, chthonian and phallic cults, festivals and mysteries of birth and death. All this, too, was characteristically Classical, conceived under the aspect of present corporeality. The Apollinian religion venerated body, the Orphic rejected it, that of Demeter celebrated the moments of fertilization and birth, in which body acquired being. There was a mysticism that reverently honoured the secret of life, in doctrine, symbol and mime, but side by side with it there was orgiasm too, for the squandering of the body is as deeply and closely akin to asceticism as sacred prostitution is to celibacy—both, all, are negations of time.

Putting the knightly poetry and folk-cults quite aside, then, we can even now determine something more of this (the) Classical religion. But in doing so there is a third pitfall to be avoided—the opposing of Greek religion to Roman religion. For in reality there was no such opposition. The Classical myth derives from a period when the Poleis with their festivals and sacral constitutions were not yet in existence, when there was not only no Rome but no Athens. With the religious duties and notions of the cities—which were eminently rational—it has no connexion at all. The myth, moreover, is in no way a creation of the Hellenic culture-field as a whole—it is not "Greek"—but originated (like the stories of Jesus' childhood and the Grail legend) in this and that group, quite local, under pressure of deep inward stirrings. For instance, the idea of Olympus arose in Thessaly and thence, as a common property of *all* educated persons, spread out to Cyprus and to Etruria, thus, of course, involving Rome. Etruscan painting presupposes it as a thing of common knowledge.

When this is taken into consideration, the Classical religion is seen to be a whole possessing an inner unity. The grand god-legends of the eleventh century, which have the dew of spring upon them, and in their tragic holiness remind us of Gethsemane, Balder's death and Francis, are the purest essence of *"theoria,"* contemplation, a world-picture before the inner eye, and born of the common inward awakening of a group of chosen souls from the world of chivalry. But the much later city-religions are wholly *technique,* formal worship, and as such represent only one side (and a different side) of piety.

The Chinese religion, of which the great "Gothic" period lies between 1300 and 1100 and covers the rise of the Chou dynasty, must be treated with extreme care. In the presence of the superficial profundity and pedantic enthusiasm of Chinese thinkers of the Confucius and Lao-tse type—who were all born in the *ancien régime* period of their state-world—it seems very hazardous to try to determine anything at all as to high mysticism and grand legends in the beginning. Nevertheless, such a mysticism and such legends must once have existed. But it is not from these over-rationalized philosophies of the great cities that we shall learn anything about them—as little as Homer can give us in the Classical parallel, though for another reason. What should we know about Gothic piety if all its works had undergone the censorship of Puritans and Rationalists like Locke, Rousseau and Wolff! And yet we treat the Confucian *close* of Chinese religion as its beginning—if, indeed, we do not go farther and describe the syncretism of Han times as "the" religion of China.

To the Chinese waking-consciousness heaven and earth were halves of the macrocosm, without opposition, each a mirror-image of the other. In this picture there was neither Magian dualism nor Faustian unity of active force. Becoming appears in the unconstrained reciprocal working of two principles, the *yang* and the *yin,* which were conceived rather as periodic than as polar. Accordingly, there are two souls in man, the *kwei,* which corresponded with the *yin,* the earthly, the dark, the cold, and disintegrated with the body; and the *sen,* which is higher, light and permanent. But, further, there are innumerable multitudes of souls of both kinds outside man. Troops of spirits fill the air and the water and the earth—all is peopled and moved by *kweis* and *sens.* The life of nature and that of man are in reality made out of the play of such units.

All this is concentrated in the basic word *tao.* The conflict between the *yang* and the *yin* in man is the *tao* of his life; the warp and woof of the spirit-swarms outside him are the *tao* of

Nature. The world possesses *tao* inasmuch as it possesses beat, rhythm and periodicity. It possesses *li*, tension, inasmuch as man knows it and abstracts from it fixed relationships for future use. Time, Destiny, Direction, Race, History—all this, contemplated with the great world-embracing vision of the early Chou times, lies in this one word. The path of the Pharaoh through the dark alley to his shrine is related to it, and so is the Faustian passion of the third dimension, but *tao* is nevertheless far removed from any idea of the technical conquest of Nature.

THE GOTHIC

When Alexander appeared on the Indus, the piety of these three Cultures—Chinese, Indian, Classical—had long been moulded into the historyless forms of a broad Taoism, Buddhism and Stoicism. But it was not long before the group of Magian religions arose in the region intermediate between the Classical and the Indian field, and it must have been at about the same time that the religious history of the Maya and Inca, now hopelessly lost to us, began. A thousand years later, when here also all was inwardly fulfilled and done with, there appeared on the unpromising soil of France, sudden and swiftly mounting, Germanic-Catholic Christianity.

The father-godhead men felt as Force itself, eternal, grand and ever-present activity, sacred causality, which could scarcely assume any form comprehensible by human eyes. But the whole longing of this "young" race, the whole desire of this strongly coursing blood, to bow itself in humility before the *meaning of the blood* found its expression in the figure of the Virgin and Mother Mary, whose crowning in the heavens was one of the earliest motives of Gothic art. She is a light-figure, in white, blue and gold, surrounded by the heavenly hosts. She leans over the new-born Child; she feels the sword in her heart; she stands at the foot of the cross; she holds the corpse of the dead Son. From the turn of the tenth century on, Petrus Damiani and Bernard of Clairvaux developed her cult; there arose the Ave Maria and the angelic greeting and later, among the Dominicans, the crown of roses. Countless legends gathered round her figure. She is the guardian of the Church's store of Grace, the Great Intercessor. Among the Franciscans arose the festival of the Visitation, amongst the English Benedictines (even before 1100) that of the Immaculate Conception, which elevated her completely above mortal humanity into the world of light.

But this world of purity, light and utter beauty of soul would have been unimaginable without the counter-idea, inseparable from it, an idea that constitutes one of the maxima of Gothic, one of its unfathomable creations—one that the present day forgets, and *deliberately* forgets. While she there sits enthroned, smiling in her beauty and tenderness, there lies in the background another world that throughout nature and throughout mankind weaves and breeds ill, pierces, destroys, seduces— namely, the realm of the Devil. It penetrates the whole of Creation, it lies ambushed everywhere. All around is an army of goblins, night-spirits, witches, werewolves, all in human shape. No man knows whether or not his neighbour has signed himself away to the Evil One. No one can say of an unfolding child that it is not already a devil's temptress. An appalling fear, such as is perhaps only paralleled in the early spring of Egypt, weighs upon man. Every moment he may stumble into the abyss. There were black magic, and devils' Masses and witches' Sabbaths, night feasts on mountaintops, magic draughts and charm-formulae. The Prince of Hell, with his relatives—mother and grandmother, for as his very existence denies and scorns the sacrament of marriage, he may not have wife or child—his fallen angels and his uncanny henchmen, is one of the most tremendous creations in all religious history. The Germanic Loki is hardly more than a preliminary hint of him. Their grotesque figures, with horns, claws and horses' hoofs, were already fully formed in the mystery plays of the eleventh century; everywhere the artist's fancy abounded in them, and, right up to Dürer and Grünewald, Gothic painting is unthinkable without them. The Devil is sly, malignant, malicious, but yet in the end the powers of light dupe him. He and his brood, bad-tempered, coarse, fiendishly inventive, are of a monstrous imaginativeness, incarnations of hellish laughter opposed to the illumined smile of the Queen of Heaven, but incarnations, too, of Faustian world-humour [4] opposed to the panic of the sinner's contrition.

~~~~~~

[4] Consider, for example, the fantastic paintings of Hieronymus Bosch. Breughel's similar humour, too, is unthinkable without the tradition of a rank-and-file of evil creatures.—*At.*

It is not possible to exaggerate either the grandeur of this forceful, insistent picture or the depth of sincerity with which it was accepted. The Mary-myths and the Devil-myth formed themselves side by side, neither possible without the other. Disbelief in either of them was deadly sin. There was a Mary-cult of prayer, and a Devil-cult of spells and exorcisms. Man walked continuously on the thin crust of the bottomless pit. Life in this world is a ceaseless and desperate contest with the Devil, into which every individual plunges as a member of the Church Militant, to do battle for himself and to win his knight's spurs. The Church Triumphant of angels and saints in their glory looks down from on high, and heavenly Grace is the warrior's shield in the battle. Mary is the protectress to whose bosom he can fly to be comforted, and the high lady who awards the prizes of valour. Both worlds have their legends, their art, their scholasticism and their mysticism—for the Devil, too, can work miracles. Characteristic of this alone among the religious springtimes is the symbolism of *colour*—to the Madonna belong white and blue, to the Devil black, sulphur-yellow and red. The saints and angels float in the aether, but the devils leap and crouch and the witches rustle through the night. It is the contrast, day and night, which gives Gothic art its indescribable appeal—this was no artistic fantasy. Every man knew the world to be peopled with angel and devil troops. The light-encircled angels of Fra Angelico and the early Rhenish masters, and the grimacing things on the portals of the great cathedrals, *really* filled the air. Men saw them, felt their presence everywhere. Today we no longer know what a myth is; for it is no mere aesthetically pleasing imagination, but a living actuality that shakes the innermost structure of being. These creatures were about one all the time. They were glimpsed without being seen. They were believed in with a faith that felt the very thought of proof as a desecration. What we call myth nowadays, our littérateur's and connoisseur's taste for Gothic colour, is nothing but Alexandrinism. In the old days men did not "enjoy" it—behind it stood Death.

For the Devil gained possession of human souls and seduced them into heresy, lechery and black arts. War was waged against him on earth, and waged with fire and sword upon those who had given themselves up to him. It is easy enough for us today to think ourselves out of such notions, but if we eliminate this appalling reality from Gothic, all that remains is mere romanticism. It was not only the love-glowing hymns to Mary but the cries of countless pyres as well that rose up to heaven. Hard by the Cathedral were the gallows and the wheel. Every man lived in those days in the consciousness of an immense danger, and it was hell, not the hangman, that he feared. Unnumbered thousands of witches genuinely imagined themselves to be so; they denounced themselves, prayed for absolution and in pure love of truth confessed their night rides and bargains with the Evil One. Inquisitors, in tears and compassion for the fallen wretches, doomed them to the rack in order to save their souls. That is the Gothic myth, out of which came the cathedral, the crusader, the deep and spiritual painting, the mysticism. In its shadow flowered that profound Gothic blissfulness of which to-day we cannot even form an idea.

In Carolingian times, all this was still strange and far. Charlemagne in the first Saxon Capitulary (787) put a ban on the ancient Germanic belief in werewolves and night-gangers (*strigae*), and as late as 1120 it was condemned as an error in the decree of Burkard of Worms. But twenty years later it was only in a dilute form that the anathema reappeared in the *Decretum Gratiani*. Caesarius of Heisterbach, already, was familiar with the whole devil-legend and in the *Legenda Aurea* it is just as actual and as effective as the Mary-legends. In 1233, when the Cathedrals of Mainz and Speyer were being vaulted, appeared the bull *Vox in Rama*, by which the belief in Devil and witch was made canonical. St. Francis's "Hymn to the Sun" had not long been written, and the Franciscans were kneeling in intimate prayer before Mary and spreading her cult afar, when the Dominicans armed themselves for battle with the Devil by setting up the Inquisition. Heavenly love found its focus in the Mary-image, and *eo ipso* earthly love became akin to the Devil. Woman is Sin—so the great ascetics felt, as their fellows of all ages had felt. The Devil rules only through woman. The witch is the propagator of deadly sin. It was Thomas Aquinas who evolved the repulsive theory of Incubus and Succuba. Devout mystics like Bonaventura, Albertus Magnus, Duns Scotus, developed a full metaphysic of the devilish.

The Renaissance had ever the strong faith of the Gothic at the back of its world-outlook. The Classical myth was entertainment-material, an allegorical play, through the thin veil of which men saw, no less definitely than before, the old Gothic actuality.

When Savonarola appeared on the scene the antique trappings vanished from the surface of Florentine life in an instant. It was all for the church that the Florentines laboured, and with conviction. Every one of them, painters, architects and humanists—however often the names of Cicero and Virgil, Venus and Apollo, were on their lips—looked upon the burning of witches as something entirely natural and wore amulets against the Devil. When Leonardo da Vinci, at the summit of the Renaissance, was working upon his *St. Anna,* the *Witches' Hammer* was being written in Rome (1487) in the finest Humanistic Latin.

It was the tremendous background of this myth that awakened in the Faustian soul a feeling of what it was. An Ego lost in Infinity, an Ego that was all force, but a force negligibly weak in an infinity of greater forces; [5] that was all will, but a will full of fear for its freedom. Never has the problem of free-will been meditated upon more deeply or more painfully. Other Cultures have simply not known it. But precisely because here Magian resignation was totally impossible—because that which thought was not an "it" or particle of an all-soul, but an individual, fighting Ego seeking to assert itself—every limitation upon freedom was felt as a chain that had to be dragged along through life, and life in turn was felt as a living death. And if so—why? For *what*?

The result of this introspection was that immense sense of guilt which runs throughout these centuries like one long, desperate lament. The cathedrals rose ever more supplicatingly to heaven, the Gothic vaulting became a joining of hands in prayer and little comfort of light shone through the high windows into the night of the long naves. The choking parallel-sequences of the church chants, the Latin hymns, tell of bruised knees and flagellations in the nocturnal cell. For Magian man the world-cavern had been close and the heaven impending, but for Gothic man heaven was infinitely far. No hand seemed to reach down from these spaces, and all about the lone Ego the mocking Devil's world lay in leaguer. And, therefore, the great longing of Mysticism was to lose created form (as Heinrich Seuse said), to be rid of self and all things (Meister Eckart), to abandon selfness

---

[5] The sense of such a relativity led to a mathematic (the calculus) which is literally based on the ignoring of second- and third-order magnitudes.—*At.*

(*Theologie deutsch*). And out of these longings there grew up an unending dogged subtilizing on notions which were ever more and more finely dissected to get at the "why," and finally a universal cry for Grace—not the Magian Grace coming down as substance, but the Faustian Grace that unbinds the Will.

To be able to will freely is, at the very bottom, the one gift that the Faustian soul asks of heaven. The seven sacraments of the Gothic, felt as one by Peter Lombard, elevated into dogma by the Lateran Council of 1215 and grounded in mystical foundations by Thomas Aquinas, mean this and only this. They accompany the unit soul from birth to death and protect it against the diabolical powers that seek to nest themselves in its will. For to sell oneself to the Devil means to deliver up *one's will to him.* The Church Militant on earth is the visible community of those who are enabled, by enjoyment of the sacraments, to will. This certainty of free being is held to be guaranteed in the altar-sacrament, which accordingly suffers a complete change of meaning. The miracle of the holy transformation which takes place daily under the hands of the priest—the consecrated Host in the high altar of the cathedral, wherein the believer sensed the presence of him who of old sacrificed himself to secure for his own the *freedom to will*—called forth a sigh of relief of such depth and sincerity as we moderns can hardly imagine. It was in thanksgiving, therefore, that the chief feast of the Catholic Church, Corpus Christi, was founded in 1264.

But more important still—and by far—was the essentially Faustian prime-sacrament of Contrition. The effect of the Magian baptism was to incorporate a man in the great *consensus*— the *one* great "it" of the divine spirit took up its abode in him as in the others, and thereafter resignation to all that should happen became his duty. But in the Faustian contrition the *idea of personality* was implicit. It is not true that the Renaissance discovered personality; what it did was to bring personality up to a brilliant surface, whereby it suddenly became visible to everyone. Its birth is in Gothic; it is the most intimate and peculiar property of Gothic; it is one and the same with Gothic soul. Contrition is something that each one accomplishes for himself alone. He alone can search his own conscience. He alone stands rueful in the presence of the Infinite. He alone can and must in confession understand and put into words his own past. And even the absolution that frees his Ego for new responsible action is personal to himself. Baptism is wholly impersonal—one receives it because one is *a* man, not because one is *this* man—but the idea of contrition presupposes that the value of every act depends uniquely upon the man who does it. This is what differentiates the Western drama from the Classical, the Chinese and the Indian. This is what directs our legislation more and more with reference to the doer rather than to the deed, and bases our primary ethical conceptions on individual doing and not typical behaviour. Faustian responsibility instead of Magian resignedness, the individual instead of the *consensus;* relief from, instead of submissiveness under, burdens—that is the difference between the most active and the most passive of all sacraments, and at the back of it again lies the difference between the world-cavern and infinity-dynamics. Baptism is something done upon one, Contrition something done by oneself within oneself. Every confession is an autobiography. This peculiar liberation of the will is to us so necessary that the refusal of absolution drives to despair, even to destruction. Only he who senses the bliss of such an inward acquittal can comprehend the old name of the *sacramentum resurgentium,* the sacrament of those who are risen again.[6]

When in this heaviest of decisions the soul is left to its own resources, something unresolved remains hanging over it like a perpetual cloud. It may be said, therefore, that perhaps no institution in any religion has brought so much happiness into the world as this. The whole inwardness and heavenly love of the Gothic rests upon the certainty of full absolution through the power invested in the priest. In the insecurity that ensued from the decline of this sacrament, both the Gothic joy of life and the Mary-world of Light faded out. Only the Devil's world, with its

---

[6] Hence it is that this sacrament has conferred a position of such immense power upon the Western priest. He receives the personal confession, and speaks personally, in the name of the Infinite, the absolution, without which life would be unbearable.

The notion of confession as a *duty,* which was finally established in 1215, first arose in England, whence came also the first confession-books (Penitentials). In England, too, originated the idea of the Immaculate Conception, and even the *idea* of the Papacy—at a time when Rome itself thought of it as a question of power and precedence. It is evidence of the independence of Faustian Christianity from Magian that its decisive ideas grew up in those remote parts of its field which lay beyond the Frankish Empire.

grim immediacy, remained. And then, in place of the blissfulness irrecoverably lost, came the Protestant, and especially Puritan, heroism, which could fight on, even hopeless, in a lost position. "Auricular confession," said Goethe once, "ought never to have been taken from mankind." Over the lands in which it had died out, a heavy earnestness spread itself. "Every man his own priest" is a conviction to which men could win through, but only as to that part of priesthood that involves duties, *not as to that which possesses powers*. No man confesses himself with the inward certainty of absolution. And as the need of the soul to be relieved of its past and to be redirected remained urgent as ever, all the higher forms of communication were transmuted, and in Protestant countries music and painting, letter-writing and memoirs, from being modes of description became modes of self-denunciation, penance and unbounded confession. Even in Catholic regions too—in Paris above all—art as psychology set in as doubt in the sacrament of Contrition and Absolution grew. Outlook on the world was lost in ceaseless mine-warfare within the self. In lieu of the Infinite, contemporaries and descendants were called in to be priests and judges. Personal art, in the sense that distinguishes Goethe from Dante, and Rembrandt from Michelangelo, was a substitute for the sacrament of confession. It was, also, the sign that this Culture was already in the condition of a Late period.

REFORMATION

In all Cultures, Reformation has the same meaning—the bringing back of the religion to the purity of its original idea as this manifested itself in the great centuries of the beginning. It was Destiny and not intellectual necessities of thought that led, in the Magian and Faustian worlds, to the budding off of new religions at this point. We know today that, under Charles V, Luther was within an ace of becoming the reformer of the whole undivided Church.

For Luther, like all reformers in all Cultures, was not the first, but *the last of a grand succession* which led from the great ascetics of the open country to the city-priest. Reformation is *Gothic*, the accomplishment and the testament thereof. Luther's chorale *"Ein' feste Burg"* does *not* belong to the spiritual lyrism of the Baroque. There rumbles in it still the splendid Latin of the *Dies Irae*. It is the Church Militant's last mighty Satan-song. Luther, like every reformer that had arisen since the year 1000, fought the Church not because it demanded too much, but because it demanded too little. So also with Marcion, Athanasius, the Monophysites and the Nestorians, who sought in the Councils of Ephesus and Chalcedon to purify the faith and lead it back to its origins. But so also the Orphics of the Classical seventh century were the last and not the first of a series that must have begun even before 1000 B.C. So with the establishment of the Re religion in Egypt at the close of the Old Kingdom, the Egyptian Gothic. It is an ending, not a new beginning, that these signify. Just so, again, a reform-fulfilment happened in the Vedic religion about the tenth century and was followed by the setting in of late Brahmanism. And in the ninth century a corresponding epochal point must have occurred in the religious history of China.

But the last reformers, the Luthers and Savonarolas, were *urban* monks, and this differentiates them profoundly from the Joachims and the Bernards. Their intellectual and urban askesis is the stepping-stone from the hermitages of quiet valleys to the scholar's study of the Baroque. The mystic experience of Luther which gave birth to his doctrine of justification is the experience, not of a St. Bernard in the presence of woods and hills and clouds and stars, but of a man who looks through narrow windows on the streets and house walls and gables.

The mighty act of Luther was a purely intellectual decision. Not for nothing has he been regarded as the last great Schoolman of the line of Occam. He completely liberated the Faustian personality—the intermediate person of the priest, which had formerly stood between it and the Infinite, was removed. And now it was wholly alone, self-oriented, its own priest and its own judge. But the common people could only feel, not understand, the element of liberation in it all. They welcomed, enthusiastically, indeed, the tearing up of visible duties, but they did not come to realize that these had been replaced by intellectual duties that were still stricter. Francis of Assisi had given much and taken little, but the urban Reformation took much and, as far as the majority of people were concerned, gave little.

The holy Causality of the Contrition-sacrament Luther replaced by the mystic experience of inward absolution "by faith alone." He came very near to Bernard of Clairvaux. Both of them understood absolution as a divine miracle: insofar as the man changes himself, it is God changing him. The one and the other preached: "Thou must believe that God has forgiven thee," but for Bernard belief was through the powers of the priest elevated to knowledge, whereas for Luther it sank to doubt and desperate insistence. Herein lies the ultimate meaning of the Western priest, who from 1215 was elevated above the rest of mankind by the sacrament of ordination and its *character indelebilis:* he was a hand with which even the poorest wretch could grasp God. This *visible* link with the Infinite, Protestantism destroyed. Strong souls could and did win it back for themselves, but for the weaker it was gradually lost. Bernard, although for him the inward miracle was successful of itself, would not deprive others of the gentler way, for the very illumination of his soul showed him the Mary-world of living nature, all-pervading, ever near and ever helpful. Luther, who knew himself only and not men, set postulated heroism in place of actual weakness. For him life was desperate battle against the Devil, and that battle he called upon everyone to fight. And everyone who fought it fought alone.

SCIENCE. PURITANISM

Intellectual creativeness of the Late period begins, not with, but after, the Reformation. Its most typical creation is free science. Even for Luther learning was still essentially the "handmaid of theology," and Calvin had the free-thinking doctor Servetus burnt.

Now, however, the critical powers of the city intellect have become so great that it is no longer content to affirm, but must test. The body of dogmas, accepted indeed by the head and not by the heart, was the first obvious target for dissecting activities. This distinguishes the springtime Scholasticism from the actuality-philosophy of the Baroque—as it distinguishes Neoplatonist from Islamic, Vedic from Brahmanic, Orphic from Pre-Socratic, thought.

Within Baroque philosophy, Western natural science stands by itself. No other Culture possesses anything like it, and assuredly it must have been from its beginnings, not a "handmaid of theology," but *the servant of the technical Will-to-Power,* oriented to that end both mathematically and experimentally—from its very foundations a practical *mechanics*. And as it is firstly technique and only secondly theory, it must be as old as Faustian man himself. Accordingly, we find technical works of an astounding energy of combination even by 1000. As early as the thirteenth century Robert Grosseteste [7] was treating space as a function of light. Petrus Peregrinus in 1289 wrote the best experimentally based treatise on magnetism that appeared before Gilbert (1600). Let us not deceive ourselves as to the fundamental motive-power of these explorations. Pure contemplative philosophy could have dispensed with experiment forever, but not so the Faustian symbol of the *machine*, which urged us to mechanical constructions even in the twelfth century and made "*perpetuum mobile*" the Prometheus-idea of the Western intellect. For us the first thing is ever the *working hypothesis*—the very kind of thought-product that is meaningless to other Cultures. It is an astounding fact (to which, however, we must accustom ourselves) that the idea of immediately exploiting in practice any knowledge of natural relations that may be acquired is alien to every sort of mankind except the Faustian (and those who, like Japanese, Jews and Russians, have today come under the intellectual spell of its Civilization). The very notion of the working hypothesis implicitly contains a dynamic lay-out of the universe. *Theoria*, contemplative vision of actuality, was for those subtly inquiring monks only secondary, and, being itself the outcome of the technical passion, it presently led them, quite imperceptibly, to the typically Faustian conception of God as the Grand Master of the machine, who could accomplish everything that they themselves in their impotence only dared to wish. Insensibly the world of God became, century by century, more and more like the *perpetuum mobile*. And, imperceptibly also, as the scanning of nature became sharper and sharper in the school of experiment and technique, and the Gothic myth became more and more shadowy, the concepts of monkish working hypotheses developed, from Galileo onwards, into the critically illuminated numina of modern science, fields of force, gravitation, the velocity of light and finally the "electricity" which in our electrodynamic world-picture has absorbed into itself the other forms of

[7] The famous Bishop of Lincoln (1175–1253), scholar and philosopher, scientist and statesman—the British Oresme.

energy and thereby attained to a sort of physical monotheism. They are the concepts that are set up behind the formulae, to endow them with a mythic visibility for the inner eye.

Every Late philosophy contains a critical protest against the uncritical intuitiveness of the Spring. But this criticism by the intellect that is sure of its own superiority affects also faith itself and evokes the one great creation in the field of religion that is the peculiarity of the Late period—every Late period—namely, Puritanism.

Milton's *Paradise Lost,* many surahs of the Koran, the little that we know of Pythagorean teachings—all come to the same thing. They are enthusiasms of a sober spirit, cold intensities, dry mysticism, pedantic ecstasy. And yet, even so, a wild piety flickers up once more in them. All the transcendent fervour that the City can produce after attaining to unconditional mastery over the soul of the Land is here concentrated, with a sort of terror lest it should prove unreal and evanescent, and is correspondingly impatient, pitiless and unforgiving. Puritanism—not in the West only, but in all Cultures—lacks the smile that had illumined the religion of the Spring—every Spring—the moments of profound joy in life, the humour of life. Nothing of the quiet blissfulness that in the Magian springtime flashes up so often in the stories of Jesus' childhood, or in Gregory Nazianzen, is to be found in the Koran, nothing in the palpable blitheness of St. Francis's songs in Milton. Deadly earnest broods over the Jansenist mind of Port Royal, over the meetings of the black-clothed Roundheads, by whom Shakespeare's "Merry England" —*Sybaris over again*—was annihilated in a few years. Now for the first time the battle against the Devil, whose bodily nearness they all felt, was fought with a dark and bitter fury. In the seventeenth century more than a million witches were burnt—alike in the Protestant North, the Catholic South and even the communities in America and India. Joyless and sour are the duty-doctrines of Islam (*fikh*), with its hard intellectuality, and the Westminster Cathechism of 1643, and the Jansenist ethics (Jansen's *Augustinus,* 1640) as well—for in the realm of Loyola, too, there was of inward necessity a Puritan movement. Religion is livingly experienced metaphysic, but the company of the "godly," as the Independents called themselves, and the Pythagoreans, and the disciples of Mohammed, all alike experienced it, not with the senses, but primarily as a concept. Pascal's wrestlings were about concepts and not, like Meister Eckart's, about shapes. Witches were burnt because they were proved, and not because they were seen in the air o' nights. The Madonnas of the early Gothic had appeared to their suppliants, but those of Bernini no man ever saw. Milton, Cromwell's great secretary of state, clothed concepts with shapes, and Bunyan brings a whole mythology of concepts into ethical-allegorical activity. From that it is but a step to Kant, in whose conceptual ethics the Devil assumes his final shape as the Radically Evil.

We have to knock down the fences by which uncoordinated studies have paddocked History before we can see that Pythagoras, Mohammed and Cromwell embody one and the same movement in three Cultures.

Pythagoras was not a philosopher. According to all statements of the Pre-Socratics, he was a saint, prophet and founder of a fanatically religious society that forced its truths upon the people around it by every political and military means. The destruction of Sybaris by Croton—an event which, we may be sure, has survived in historical memory only because it was the climax of a wild religious war—was an explosion of the same hate that saw in Charles I and his gay Cavaliers not merely doctrinal error but also a worldliness that must be destroyed root and branch. A myth purified and conceptually fortified, combined with rigorous ethical precepts, imbued the Pythagoreans with the conviction that they would attain salvation before all other men. It is the same certainty that the Koran gave to all believers who fought in the holy war against the infidel—the same which filled Cromwell's Ironsides when they scattered the "Philistines" and "Amalekites" at Marston Moor and Naseby.

Islam was no more a religion of the desert in particular than Zwingli's faith was a religion of the high mountains in particular. It is incident, and no more, that the Puritan movement for which the Magian world was ripe proceeded from a man of Mecca and not from a Monophysite or a Jew. At most Islam was a new religion only to the same extent as Lutheranism.[8] Actually,

---

[8] "Mahommedanism must be regarded as an eccentric heretical form of Eastern Christianity. This in fact was the ancient mode of regarding Mahommet. He was considered, not in the light of the founder of a new religion, but rather as one of the chief heresiarchs of the Church. Among them he is placed by Dante in the 'Inferno.' " Dean Stanley, *Eastern Church* (1861), Lecture VIII.—*At.*

it was the prolongation of the great early religions. Equally, its expansion was not (as is even now imagined) a "migration of peoples" proceeding from the Arabian Peninsula, but an onslaught of enthusiastic believers, which like an avalanche bore along with it Christians, Jews and Mazdaists and set them at once in its front rank as fanatical Moslems. It was Berbers from the homeland of St. Augustine who conquered Spain, and Persians from Iraq who drove on to the Oxus.

The great figures of Mohammed's entourage, such as Abu Bekr and Omar, are the near relatives of the Pyms and Hampdens of the English Revolution, and we should see this relationship to be nearer still if we knew more than we do about the Hanifs, the Arabian Puritans before and about the Prophet. All of them had won out of Predestination the guarantee that they were God's elect. The grand Old Testament exaltation in Parliament and the Independent armies—which left behind it, in many an English family, even to the nineteenth century, the belief that the English are the descendants of the ten Lost Tribes of Israel, a nation of saints predestined to govern the world—dominated also the emigration to America which began with the Pilgrim Fathers of 1620. It formed that which may be called the American religion of today, and bred and fostered the trait which gives the Englishman even now his particular political insouciance, an assurance that is essentially religious and has its roots in predestination. The Pythagoreans themselves, too (an unheard-of thing in the religious history of the Classical world), assumed political power for the furtherance of religious ends and sought to advance their Puritanism from Polis to Polis.

RATIONALISM

But in Puritanism there is hidden already the seed of Rationalism, and after a few enthusiastic generations have passed, this bursts forth everywhere and makes itself supreme. This is the step from Cromwell to Hume.

Rationalism signifies the belief in the data of critical understanding (that is, of the "reason") *alone*. In the springtime men could say *"Credo quia absurdum"* because they were certain that the comprehensible and the incomprehensible were *both* necessary constituents of the world—the nature which Giotto painted, in which the Mystics immersed themselves, and into which reason can penetrate, but only so far as the deity permits it to penetrate. But now a secret jealousy breeds the notion of the Irrational—that which, as incomprehensible, is *therefore* valueless. It may be scorned openly as superstition, or privily as metaphysic. Only critically established understanding possesses value. And secrets are merely evidences of ignorance. The new *secretless* religion is in its highest potentialities called wisdom (σοφία), its priests philosophers and its adherents "educated" people. According to Aristotle, the old religion is indispensable only to the uneducated, and his view is shared by Confucius and Gautama Buddha, Lessing and Voltaire. Systems were woven out of phenomenally guaranteed beginnings, but in the long run the result was merely to say "Force" instead of "God," and "Conservation of Energy" instead of "Eternity." Under all Classical rationalism is to be found Olympus, under all Western the dogma of the sacraments.

The great ideal of the educated of such periods is the Sage. The sage goes back to Nature—to Ferney or Ermenonville, to Attic gardens or Indian groves—which is the most intellectual way of being a megalopolitan. The sage is the man of the Golden Mean. His askesis consists in a judicious depreciation of the world in favour of meditation. The wisdom of the enlightenment never interferes with comfort. Moral with the great Myth to back it is always a sacrifice, a cult, even to extremes of asceticism, even to death; but Virtue with Wisdom at its back is a sort of secret enjoyment, a superfine intellectual egoism. And so the ethical teacher who is outside real religion becomes the Philistine. Buddha, Confucius, Rousseau, are arch-Philistines, for all the nobility of their ordered ideas, and the pedantry of the Socratic life-wisdom is insurmountable.

Along with this (shall we call it) scholasticism of sound reason, there must of inner necessity be a rationalistic mysticism of the educated. The Western Enlightenment is of English origin and Puritan parentage. The rationalism of the Continent comes wholly from Locke. In opposition to it there arose in Germany the Pietists (Herrnhut, 1700, Spener and Francke, and in Württemberg Oetinger) and in England the Methodists (Wesley "awakened" by Herrnhut, 1738). It was Luther and Calvin over again—the English at once organized themselves for a world-movement and the Germans lost themselves in mid-European conventicles. The Pietists of Islam are to be found in *Sufism,* which is not of "Persian" but of common Aramaean origin and in the eighth century spread all over the Arabian world. Pietists or Methodists, too, are the Indian lay preachers, who shortly before Buddha's time were teaching release from the cycle of life (*sansara*) through immersion in the identity of Atman and Brahman. But Pietists or Methodists, too, are Lao-tse and his disciples and—notwithstanding their rationalism—the Cynic mendicants and itinerant preachers and the Stoic tutors, domestic chaplains, and confessors of early Hellenism. And Pietism may ascend even to the peak of rationalist vision, of which Swedenborg is the great example, which created for Stoics and Sufists whole worlds of fancy, and by which Buddhism was prepared for its reconstruction as Mahayana. The expansion of Buddhism and that of Taoism in their original significations are closely analogous to the Methodist expansion in America, and it is no accident that they both reached their full maturity in those regions (lower Ganges and south of the Yangtze Kiang) which had cradled the respective Cultures.

THE SECOND RELIGIOUSNESS

Two centuries after Puritanism the mechanistic conception of the world stands at its zenith. It is the effective religion of the time. Even those who still thought themselves to be religious in the old sense, to be "believers in God," were only mistaking the world in which their waking-consciousness was mirroring itself. Culture is ever synonymous with religious creativeness. Every great Culture begins with a mighty theme that rises out of the pre-urban countryside, is carried through in the cities of art and intellect and closes with a finale of materialism in the world-cities. But even the last chords are strictly in the key of the whole. There are Chinese, Indian, Classical, Arabian, Western materialisms, and each is nothing but the original stock of myth-shapes, cleared of the elements of experience and contemplative vision and viewed mechanistically. The belief is belief in force and matter, even if the words used be "God" and "world," "Providence" and "man."

Unique and self-contained is the Faustian materialism, in the narrower sense of the word. In it the technical outlook upon the world reached fulfillment. The whole world a dynamic system, exact, mathematically disposed, capable down to its first causes of being experimentally probed and numerically fixed so that man can dominate it—this is what distinguishes our particular "return to Nature" from all others. That "Knowledge is Virtue" Confucius also believed, and Buddha, and Socrates, but "Knowledge is Power" is a phrase that possesses meaning only within the European-American Civilization. The Destiny element is mechanized as evolution, development, progress, and put into the centre of the system; the Will is an albumen-process; and all these doctrines of Monism, Darwinism, Positivism and what not are elevated into the fitness-moral which is the beacon of American businessmen, British politicians and German progress-Philistines alike—and turns out, in the last analysis, to be nothing but an intellectualist caricature of the old justification by faith.

Materialism would not be complete without the need of now and again easing the intellectual tension, by giving way to moods of myth, by performing rites of some sort or by enjoying the charms of the irrational, the unnatural, the repulsive and even, if need be, the merely silly. This tendency, which is visible enough, even to us, in the time of Mencius (372–289) and in those of the first Buddhist brotherhoods, is present also (and with the same significance) in Hellenism, of which indeed it is a leading characteristic. About 312 poetical scholars of the Callimachus type in Alexandria invented the Serapis-cult and provided it with an elaborate legend. The Isis-cult in Republican Rome was something very different both from the emperor-worship that succeeded it and from the deeply earnest Isis-religion of Egypt; it was a religious pastime of high society, which at times provoked public ridicule and at times led to public scandal and the closing of the cult-centres.[9] Correspondingly, we have in the European-American world of today the occultist and theosophist fraud, the American Christian Science, the untrue Buddhism of drawing-rooms, the religious arts-and-crafts business (brisker in Germany than even in England) that caters for groups and cults of Gothic or late-Classical or Taoist sentiment. Everywhere it is just a toying with myths that no one really be-

---

[9] Which was ordered no less than four times in the decade 58–49.

lieves, a tasting of cults that it is hoped might fill the inner void. Materialism is shallow and honest, mock-religion shallow and dishonest. But the fact that the latter is possible at all foreshadows a new and genuine spirit of seeking that declares itself, first quietly, but soon emphatically and openly, in the civilized waking-consciousness.

This next phase I call the *Second Religiousness*. It appears in all Civilizations as soon as they have fully formed themselves as such and are beginning to pass, slowly and imperceptibly, into the non-historical state in which time-periods cease to mean anything. (So far as the Western Civilization is concerned, therefore, we are still many generations short of that point.) The Second Religiousness is the necessary counterpart of Caesarism, which is the final *political* constitution of Late Civilization; it becomes visible, therefore, in the Augustan Age of the Classical and about the time of Shih Huang Ti in China. In both phenomena the creative young strength of the Early Culture is lacking. But both have their greatness nevertheless. That of the Second Religiousness consists in a deep piety that fills the waking-consciousness—the piety that impressed Herodotus in the (Late) Egyptians and impresses West Europeans in India and Islam—and that of Caesarism consists in its unchained might of colossal facts. But neither in the creations of this piety nor in the form of the Roman Imperium is there anything primary and spontaneous. Nothing is built up, no idea unfolds itself—it is only as if a mist cleared off the land and revealed the old forms, uncertainly at first, but presently with increasing distinctness. The material of the Second Religiousness is simply that of the first, genuine, young religiousness—only otherwise experienced and expressed. It starts with Rationalism's fading out in helplessness, then the forms of the springtime become visible, and finally the whole world of the primitive religion, which had receded before the grand forms of the early faith, returns to the foreground, powerful, in the guise of the popular syncretism that is to be found in every Culture at this phase.

Every "Age of Enlightenment" proceeds from an unlimited optimism of the reason—always associated with the type of the megalopolitan—to an equally unqualified scepticism. The sovereign waking-consciousness, cut off by walls and artificialities from living nature and the land about it and under it, cognizes nothing outside itself. It applies criticism to its imaginary world, which it has cleared of everyday sense-experience, and continues to do so till it has found the last and subtlest result, the form of the form—itself: namely, nothing. With this the possibilities of physics as a critical mode of world-understanding are exhausted, and the hunger for metaphysics presents itself afresh. But it is not the religious pastimes of educated and literature-soaked cliques, still less is it the intellect, that gives rise to the Second Religiousness. Its source is the naïve belief that arises, unremarked but spontaneous, among the masses that there is some sort of mystic constitution of actuality (as to which formal proofs are presently regarded as barren and tiresome word-jugglery), and an equally naïve heart-need reverently responding to the myth by means of a cult. The forms of neither can be foreseen, still less chosen—they appear of themselves, and as far as we are ourselves concerned, we are as yet far distant from them. But already the opinions of Comte and Spencer, the Materialism and the Monism and the Darwinism, which stirred the best minds of the nineteenth century to such passion, have become the world-view proper to country cousins.

JUDAISM

The religion of Jewry, too, is a fellah-religion since the time of Jehuda ben Halevi, who (like his Islamic teacher, al-Ghazali) regarded scientific philosophy with an unqualified scepticism, and in the *Kuzari* (1140) refused to it any role save that of handmaid of the orthodox theology. Neither in this period nor in any other is Judaism unique in religious history, though from the viewpoint that the Western Culture has taken up on its own ground, it may seem so. Nor is it peculiar to Jewry that, unperceived by those who bear it, its name is forever changing in meaning, for the same has happened, step by step, in the Persian story.

In the springtime (the first five centuries of the Christian era) this landless Consensus spread geographically from Spain to Shantung. This was the Jewish Age of Chivalry and its "Gothic" blossoming-time of religious creative-force. The later Apocalyptic, the Mishnah and also primitive Christianity (which was not cast off till after Trajan's and Hadrian's time) are creations of this nation. It is well known that in those days the Jews were peasants, artisans and dwellers in little towns, and "big business" was in the hands of Egyptians, Greeks and Romans—that is, members of the Classical world.

About 500 begins the Jewish Baroque, which Western observers are accustomed to regard, very onesidedly, as part of the picture of Spain's age of glory. The Jewish Consensus, like the Persian, Islamic and Byzantine, now advances to an urban and intellectual awareness, and thenceforward it is master of the forms of city-economics and city-science. Tarragona, Toledo and Granada are predominantly Jewish cities. Jews constitute an essential element in Moorish high society. Their finished forms, their *esprit,* their knightliness, amazed the Gothic nobility of the Crusades, which tried to imitate them; but the diplomacy also, and the war-management and the administration of the Moorish cities, would all have been unthinkable without the Jewish aristocracy, which was every whit as thoroughbred as the Islamic. As once in Arabia there had been a Jewish *Minnesang,* so now here there was a high literature of enlightened science.

But an entirely new situation was created when, from about the year 1000, the Western portion of the Consensus found itself suddenly in the field of the young Western Culture. The Jews, like the Parsees, the Byzantines and the Moslems, had become by then civilized and cosmopolitan, whereas the German-Roman world lived in the townless land, and the settlements that had just come (or were coming) into existence around monasteries and market-places were still many generations short of possessing souls of their own. While the Jews were already almost fellaheen, the Western peoples were still almost primitives. There was mutual hate and contempt, due not to race-distinction, but to *difference of phase.* Into all the hamlets and country towns the Jewish Consensus built its essentially megalopolitan—proletarian—ghettos. The *Judengasse* is a thousand years in advance of the Gothic town. Just so, in Jesus' day, the Roman towns stood in the midst of the villages on the Lake of Genesareth.

But these young nations were, besides, bound up with the soil and the idea of a fatherland, and the landless "Consensus," which was cemented, not by deliberate organization, but by a wholly unconscious, wholly metaphysical impulse—an expression of the Magian world-feeling in its simplest and directest form—appeared to them as something uncanny and incomprehensible. It was in this period that the legend of the Wandering Jew arose.

Jewry of the West European group had entirely lost the relation to the open land which had still existed in the Moorish period of Spain. There were no more peasants. The smallest ghetto was a fragment, however miserable, of megalopolis, and its inhabitants split into castes—the Rabbi is the Brahman or Mandarin of the ghetto—and a coolie-mass characterized by civilized, cold, superior intelligence and an undeviating eye to business. But this phenomenon, again, is not unique if our historical sense takes in the wider horizon, for *all* Magian nations have been in this condition since the Crusade period. The Parsee in India possesses exactly the same business-power as the Jews in the European-American world and the Armenians and Greeks in Southern Europe. The same phenomenon occurs in every other Civilization, when it pushes into a younger *milieu*—witness the Chinese in California (where they are the targets of a true anti-Semitism of western America), in Java and in Singapore; that of the Indian trader in East Africa; and that of *the Romans in the early-Arabian World*. In the last instance, indeed, the conditions were the exact reverse of those of today, for the "Jews" of those days were the Romans, and the Aramaean felt for them an apocalyptic hatred that is very closely akin to our West European anti-Semitism. The outbreak of 88, in which, at a sign from Mithridates, a hundred thousand Roman business-people were murdered by the exasperated population of Asia Minor, was a veritable *pogrom*.

Over and above these oppositions there was that of race, which passed from contempt into hate in proportion as the Western Culture itself caught up with the Civilization, and the "difference of age," expressed in the way of life and the increasing primacy of intelligence, became smaller. But all this has nothing to do with the silly catchwords "Aryan" and "Semite" that have been borrowed from philology. The "Aryan" Persians and Armenians are in our eyes entirely indistinguishable from the Jews, and even in Southern Europe and the Balkans there is almost no bodily difference between the Christian and Jewish inhabitants. The Jewish nation is, like every other nation of the Arabian Culture, the result of an immense *mission,* and up to well within the Crusades it was changed and changed again by accessions and secessions *en masse.* One part of Eastern Jewry conforms in bodily respects to the Christian inhabitants of the Caucasus, another to the South Russian Tatars, and a large portion of Western Jewry to the North African Moors. What has mattered in the West more than any other distinction is the difference *between the race-ideal of the Gothic springtime,* which has bred its human type, and that of the Sephardic Jew, which first formed itself in the ghettos of the West and was likewise the product of a particular spiritual breeding and training under exceedingly hard external conditions—to which, doubtless, we must add the effectual spell of the land and people about him, and his metaphysical defensive reaction to that spell. During the Gothic age this difference is deep and religious, and the object of hatred is the Consensus as religion; only with the beginning of the Western Civilization does it become materialist, and begin to attack Jewry on its intellectual and business sides, on which the West suddenly finds itself confronted by an even challenger.

But the deepest element of separation and bitterness has been one of which the full tragedy has been least understood. While Western man, from the days of the Saxon emperors to the present, has (in the most significant sense of the words) *lived* his history, and lived it with a consciousness of it that no other Culture can parallel, the Jewish Consensus ceased to have a history at all. Its problems were solved, its inner form was complete, conclusive and unalterable. For it, as for Islam, the Greek Church and the Parsees, centuries ceased to mean anything, and consequently no one belonging inwardly to the Consensus can even begin to comprehend the passion with which Faustians livingly experience the short crowded epochs in which their history and destiny take decisive turns—the beginning of the Crusades, the Reformation, the French Revolution, the German Wars of Liberation and each and every turning-point in the existence of the several peoples. All this, for the Jew, lies thirty generations back. A Jewish cavalry-general fought in the Thirty Years' War (he lies buried in the old Jewish cemetery at Prague) [1]—but what did the ideas of Luther or Loyola mean to him? What did the Byzantines—near relatives of the Jews—comprehend of the Crusades? Such things are among the tragic necessities of the

[1] Prague contains a veritable corpus of commentary upon these pages. —*At.*

higher history that consists in the life-courses of individual Cultures, and often have they repeated themselves. The European-American world has displayed a complete incomprehension of the fellah-revolutions of Turkey (1908) and China (1911); the inner life and thought of these peoples, and consequently even their notions of state and sovereignty (the Caliph in the one, the Son of Heaven in the other), being of an utterly different cast and, therefore, a sealed book, the course of events could neither be weighed up nor even reckoned upon in advance. The Jew of the Consensus follows the history of the present (which is nothing but that of the Faustian Civilization spread over continents and oceans) with the fundamental feelings of Magian mankind, even when he himself is firmly convinced of the Western character of his thought.

As every Magian Consensus is non-territorial and geographically unlimited, it involuntarily sees in all conflicts concerning the *Faustian* ideas of fatherland, mother tongue, ruling house, monarchy, constitution, a return from forms that are thoroughly alien (and therefore burdensome and meaningless) to him towards forms matching with his own nature. Hence the word "international," whether it be coupled with socialism, pacifism or capitalism, can excite him to enthusiasm, but what he hears in that word is *the essence of his landless and boundless Consensus*. Even when the force of the Consensus in him is broken and the life of his host-people exercises an outward attraction upon him to the point of an induced patriotism, yet the party that he supports is always that of which the aims are most nearly comparable with the Magian essence. Hence in Germany he is a democrat and in England (like the Parsee in India) an imperialist. It is exactly the same misunderstanding as when West Europeans regard Young Turks and Chinese reformers as kindred spirits—that is, as "constitutionalists." If there is inward relationship, a man affirms even where he destroys; if inward alienness, his effect is negative even where his desire is to be constructive. What Western Culture has destroyed, by reform-efforts of its own type where it has had power, hardly bears thinking of; and Jewry has been equally destructive where it has intervened. The sense of the inevitableness of this reciprocal misunderstanding leads to the appalling hatred that settles deep in the blood and, fastening upon visible marks like race, mode of life, profession, speech, leads both sides to waste, ruin and bloody excesses wherever these conditions occur.

Since the Napoleonic era the old-civilized Consensus has mingled unwelcome with the new-civilized Western "society" of the cities and has taken their economic and scientific methods into use with the cool superiority of age. A few generations later, the Japanese, also a very old intellect, did the same, and probably with still greater success. Yet another example is afforded by the Carthaginians, a rear-guard of the Babylonian Civilization, who, already highly developed when the Classical Culture was still in the Etrusco-Doric infancy, ended by surrendering to Late Hellenism—petrified in an end-state in all that concerned religion and art, but far superior to the Greeks and Romans as men of business, and hated accordingly.

Today this Magian nation, with its ghetto and its religion, itself is in danger of disappearing—not because the metaphysics of the two Cultures come closer to one another (for that is impossible), but because the intellectualized upper stratum of each side is ceasing to be metaphysical at all. It has lost every kind of inward cohesion, and what remains is simply a cohesion for practical questions. The lead that this nation has enjoyed from its long habituation to thinking in business terms becomes ever less and less (*vis-à-vis* the American, it has already almost gone), and with the loss of it will go the last potent means of keeping up a Consensus that has fallen regionally into parts. In the moment when the civilized methods of the European-American world-cities shall have arrived at full maturity, the destiny of Jewry—at least of the Jewry in our midst (that of Russia is another problem)—will be accomplished.

XVII

THE STATE:
THE PROBLEM OF THE ESTATES

MAN AND WOMAN

A FATHOMLESS secret of the cosmic flowings that we call Life is their separation into two sexes. Already in the earth-bound existence-streams of the plant world they are trying to part from one another, as the symbol of the flower tells us—into a something that *is* this existence and a something that keeps it going. Animals are free, little worlds in a big world—the cosmic —closed off as microcosms and set up against the macrocosm. And, more and more decisively as the animal kingdom unfolds its history, the dual direction of dual being, of the masculine and the feminine, manifests itself.

The feminine stands closer to the Cosmic. It is rooted deeper in the earth and it is immediately involved in the grand cyclic rhythms of Nature. The masculine is freer, more animal, more mobile—as to sensation and understanding as well as otherwise —more awake and more tense.

The male livingly experiences Destiny, and he *comprehends* Causality, the causal logic of the Become. The female, on the contrary, *is herself* Destiny and Time and the organic logic of the Becoming, and for that very reason the principle of Causality is forever alien to her. Whenever Man has tried to give Destiny any tangible form, he has felt it as of feminine form, and he has called it Moirai, Parcae, Norns. The supreme deity is never itself Destiny, but always either its representative or its master—just as man represents or controls woman. Primevally, too, woman is the seeress, and not because she knows the future, but because she *is* the future. The priest merely interprets the oracle; the woman is the oracle itself, and it is Time that speaks through her.

The man *makes* History, the woman *is* History. Here, strangely clear yet enigmatic still, we have a dual significance of all living happenings—on the one hand we sense cosmic flow as such, and on the other hand the chain and train of successive individuals brings us back to the microcosms themselves as the recipients, containers and preservers of the flow. It is this "second" history that is characteristically masculine—political, social, more conscious, freer and more agitated than the other. It reaches back deep into the animal world, and receives highest symbolic and world-historical expression in the life-courses of the great Cultures. Feminine, on the contrary, is the primary, the eternal, the maternal, the plant-like (for the plant ever has something female in it), *the cultureless history of the generation-sequence,* which never alters, but uniform and inconspicuous passes through the being of all animal and human species. In retrospect, it is synonymous with Life itself. This history, too, is not without its battles and its tragedies. Woman in childbed wins through to her victory. The Aztecs—the Romans of the Mexican Culture—honoured the woman in labour as a battling warrior, and if she died, she was interred with the same formulae as the fallen hero. Policy for Woman is eternally the conquest of the Man, through whom she can become mother of children, through whom she can become History and Destiny and Future. The target of her profound shyness, her tactical finesse, is ever the father of her son. The man, on the contrary, whose centre of gravity lies essentially in the other kind of History, wants that son as *his* son, as inheritor and carrier of his blood and historical tradition.

Here, in man and in woman, *the two kinds of History* are fighting for power. Woman is strong and wholly what she is, and she experiences the Man and the Sons only in relation to herself and her ordained role. In the masculine being, on the contrary, there is a certain contradiction; he is this man, and he is something else besides, which woman neither understands nor admits, which she feels as robbery and violence upon that which to her is holiest. This secret and fundamental war of the sexes has gone on ever since there were sexes, and will continue—silent, bitter, unforgiving, pitiless—while they continue. In it, too, there are policies, battles, alliances, treaties, treasons. Race-feelings of love and hate, which originate in depths of world-yearning and primary instincts of directedness, prevail between the sexes—and with a still more uncanny potency than in the other History that takes place between man and man. There are love-lyrics and war-lyrics, love-dances and weapon-dances, there are two kinds of tragedy—*Othello* and *Macbeth*. But nothing in the political world even begins to compare with the abysses of a Clytemnestra's or a Kriemhild's vengeance.

And so woman despises that other History—man's politics—which she never comprehends, and of which all that she sees is that it takes her sons from her.

Thus history has two meanings. It is cosmic or politic, it *is* being or it *preserves* being. There are two sorts of Destiny, two sorts of war, two sorts of tragedy—*public and private*. Nothing can eliminate this duality from the world. It is radical, founded in the essence of the animal that is both microcosm and participant in the cosmic. It appears at all significant conjunctures in the form of a conflict of duties, which exists only for the man, not for the woman, and in the course of a higher Culture it is never overcome, but only deepened. There are public life and private life, public law and private law, communal cults and domestic cults. As Estate, Being is "in form" for the one history; as race, breed, it is in flow as *itself* the other history. This is the old German distinction between the "sword side" and the "spindle side" of blood-relationships. The double significance of directional Time finds its highest expression in the ideas of *the State* and *the Family*.

RACE. BLOOD

On the other side, we see masses of individual beings streaming past, growing and passing, but *making* history. The purer, deeper, stronger, more taken-for-granted the common beat of these sequent generations is, the more blood, the more race they have. Out of the infinite they rise, every one with its soul,[1] bands that feel themselves in the common wave-beat of their being, as a whole—not mind-communities like orders, craft-guilds or schools of learning, which are linked by common truths, but blood-confederates in the melee of fighting life.

---

[1] Elsewhere Spengler uses the phrase "inspired mass-units."—*Tr.*

There are streams of being which are "in form" in the same sense in which the term is used in sports. A field of steeplechasers is "in form" when the legs swing surely over the fences, and the hoofs beat firmly and rhythmically on the flat. When wrestlers, fencers, ball-players, are "in form," the riskiest acts and moves come off easily and naturally. An art-period is in form when its tradition is second nature, as counterpoint was to Bach. An army is in form when it is like the army of Napoleon at Austerlitz and the army of Moltke at Sedan. Practically everything that has been achieved in world-history, in war and in that continuation of war by intellectual means that we call politics; in all successful diplomacy, tactics, strategy; in the competition of states or social classes or parties; has been the product of living unities that found themselves "in form."

The word for race- or breed-education is "training" (*Zucht, Züchtung*), as against the shaping (*Bildung*) which creates communities of waking-consciousness on a basis of uniform teachings or beliefs. Books, for example, are shaping agents, while the constant felt pulse and harmony of *milieu* into which one feels oneself, *lives* oneself—like a novice or a page of early Gothic times—are training influences. The "good form" and ceremonies of a given society are sense-presentations of the beat of a given species of Being, and to master them one must *have* the beat of them. Hence women, as more instinctive and nearer to cosmic rhythms, adapt themselves more readily than men to the forms of a new *milieu*. Women from the bottom strata move in elegant society with entire certainty after a few years—and sink again as quickly. But men alter slowly, because they are more awake and aware. The proletarian man never becomes wholly an aristocrat, the aristocrat never wholly a proletarian— only in the sons does the beat of the new *milieu* make its appearance.

The profounder the form, the stricter and more exclusive it is. To the outsider, therefore, it appears to be a slavery; the member, on the contrary, has a perfect and easy command of it. The Prince de Ligne was, no less than Mozart, master of the form and not its slave; and the same holds good of *every* born aristocrat, statesman and captain.

In all high Cultures, therefore, there is a *peasantry*, which is breed, stock, in the broad sense (and thus to a certain extent nature herself), and a *society* which is assertively and emphatically "in form." It is a set of classes or Estates, and no doubt artificial and transitory. But the history of these classes and estates is *world-history at highest potential*. It is only in relation to it that the peasant is seen as historyless.

This Culture is wholly unlike any other thing in the organic world. It is the one point at which man lifts himself above the powers of Nature and becomes himself a Creator. Even as to race, breed, he is Nature's creature—he *is* bred. But, as Estate, he breeds himself just as he breeds the varieties of animals and plants in which he is interested—and that process, too, is in the deepest and most final sense "Culture." Culture and estate are interchangeable expressions; they arise together and they vanish together. The breeding of select types of wines or fruit or flowers, the breeding of blood horses, *is* Culture, and the culture, in exactly the same sense, of the human elite arises as the expression of a Being that has brought itself into high "form."

True history is *not* "cultural" in the sense of anti-political, as the philosophers and doctrinaires of all commencing Civilizations assert. On the contrary, it is breed history, war history, diplomatic history, the history of being-streams in the form of man and woman, family, people, estate, state, reciprocally defensive and offensive in the wave-beat of grand facts. *Politics in the highest sense is life, and life is politics.* Every man is willy-nilly a member of this battle-drama, as subject or as object—there is no third alternative. The kingdom of the spirit is *not* of this world. True, but it presupposes it, as waking-being presupposes being. It is only possible as a consistent *saying* of "no" to the actuality that nevertheless exists and, indeed, must exist before it can be renounced. Race can dispense with language, but the very speaking of a language is an expression of antecedent race, as are religions and arts and styles of thought and everything else that happens in the history of the spirit—and that there *is* such a history is shown by the power that blood possesses over feeling and reason. For all these are active waking-consciousness "in form," expressive, in their evolution and symbolism and passion, of the blood (again the blood) that courses through these forms in the waking-being of generation after generation. A hero does not need to know anything at all of this second world—he is life through and through—but a saint can only by the severest asceticism beat down the life that is in him and gain solitary communion with his spirit—and his strength for this again comes from life itself. The hero despises death and the saint life, but in the contrast between the heroism of great ascetics and martyrs and the piety of most (which is of the kind described in Revelation 3: 16) we discover that greatness, even in religion, presupposes Race, that life must be strong indeed to be worthy of such wrestlers. The rest is mere philosophy.

For this reason nobility in the world-historical sense counts for much more than comfortable Late periods allow; it is not a sum of titles and privileges and ceremonies, but an inward possession, hard to acquire, hard to retain—worth, indeed, for those who understand, the sacrifice of a whole life. An old family betokens not simply a set of ancestors (we all have ancestors), but ancestors who lived through whole generations on the heights of history; who not merely had Destiny, but were Destiny; in whose blood the form of happening was bred up to its perfection by the experience of centuries. As history in the grand sense begins with the Culture, it was mere panache for a Colonna to trace back his ancestry into Late Roman times. But it was not meaningless for the grandee of Late Byzantium to derive himself from Constantine, nor is it so for an American of today to trace his ancestry to a *Mayflower* immigrant of 1620. In actual fact Classical nobility begins with the Trojan period and not the Mycenaean, and the Western with the Gothic and not the Franks and the Goths—in England with the Normans and not the Saxons. Only from these real starting-points is there History, and, therefore, only from then can there be an original aristocracy, as distinct from nobles and heroes. That which I earlier [2] called cosmic beat or pulse receives in this aristocracy its fulfilment. For all that in riper times we call diplomatic and social "tact" —which includes strategic and business flair, the collector's eye for precious things and the subtle insight of the judge of men—and generally all that which one has and does not learn; which arouses the impotent envy of the rest who cannot participate; which as "form" directs the course of events—is nothing but a particular case of the same cosmic and dreamlike sureness that is visibly expressed in the circlings of a flock of birds or the controlled movements of a thoroughbred horse.

~~~~~~~~

[2] Chapter XI.—*Tr.*

XVIII

STATE AND HISTORY

THE VESTING OF AUTHORITY

IN the historical world there are no ideals, but only facts—no truths, but only facts. There is no reason, no honesty, no equity, no final aim, but only facts, and anyone who does not realize this should write books on politics—let him not try to *make* politics. In the real world there are no states built according to ideals, but only states that have *grown,* and these are nothing but living peoples "in form." No doubt it is "the form impressed that living doth itself unfold," but the impress has been that of the blood and beat of a *being,* wholly instinctive and involuntary; and as to the unfolding, if it is guided by the master of politics, it takes the direction inherent in the blood; if by the idealist, that dictated by his own convictions—in other words, the way to nullity.

The destiny question, for States that exist in reality and not merely in intellectual schemes, is not that of their ideal task or structure, *but that of their inner authority,* which cannot in the long run be maintained by material means, but only by a belief—of friend *and* foe—in their effectiveness. The decisive problems lie, not in the working out of constitutions, but in the organization of a sound working government; not in the distribution of political rights according to "just" principles (which at bottom are simply the idea that a *class* forms of its own legitimate claims), but in the efficient pulse of the whole (efficient in the sense that the play of muscle and sinew is efficient when an extended racehorse nears the winning-post), in that rhythm which attracts even strong genius into syntony; not, lastly, in any world-alien moral, but in the steadiness, sureness and superiority of political leadership. The more self-evident all these things are, the less is said or argued about them; the more fully matured the State, the higher the standing, the historical capacity and therefore the Destiny of the Nation. State-majesty, sovereignty, is a life-symbol of the first order. It distinguishes *subjects and objects*. Strength of leadership, which comes to expression in the clear separation of these two factors, is the unmistakable sign of the life-force in a political unity—so much so that the shattering of existing authority (for example, by the supporters of an opposed constitutional ideal) almost always results not in this new party's making itself the subject of domestic policy, but in the whole nation's becoming the object of alien policy—and not seldom forever.

In every healthy State the letter of the written constitution is of small importance compared with the practice of the living constitution, the "form" (to use again the sporting term), which has developed of itself out of the experience of Time, the situation and, above all, the race-properties of the nation. The more powerfully the *natural* form of the body politic has built itself up, the more surely it works in unforeseen situations; indeed, in the end, it does not matter whether the actual leader is called King or Minister or party-leader, or even (as in the case of Cecil Rhodes) that he has no defined relation to the State. The nobility which managed Roman politics in the period of the three Punic Wars had, from the point of view of constitutional law, no existence whatever. The leader's responsibility is always to a minority that possesses the instincts of statesmanship and represents the rest of the nation in the struggle of history.

The fact, express and unequivocal, is that class-States—that is, States in which particular classes rule—are the *only* States. This must not be confused with the class-States to which the individual is merely *attached* in view of belonging to an estate, as in the case of the older Polis, the Norman States of England and Sicily, the France of the Constitution of 1791 and Soviet Russia today. The true class-State is an expression of the general historical experience that it is always a single social stratum which, constitutionally or otherwise, provides the political leading. It is always a definite minority that represents the world-historical tendency of a State; and, within that again, it is a more or less self-contained minority that in virtue of its aptitudes (and often enough against the spirit of the Constitution) actually holds the reins. In by far the greater number of cases this minority is one within the nobility—for example, the "gentry" which governed the Parliamentary style of England, the *nobiles* at the helm of Roman politics in Punic War times, the merchant-aristocracy of Venice, the Jesuit-trained nobles who conducted the diplomacy of the Papal Curia in the Baroque. Similarly, we find the political aptitude in self-contained groups within the religious Estate—not only in the Roman Catholic Church but also in Egypt and India and still more in Byzantium and Sassanid Persia. In the Third Estate—though this seldom produces it, not being itself a caste-unit—there are cases such as those of third-century Rome, where a stratum of the plebs contains men trained in commerce, and France since 1789, where an element of the bourgeoisie has been trained in law; in these cases, it is ensured by a closed circle of persons possessing homogeneous practical gifts, which constantly recruits itself and preserves in its midst the whole sum of unwritten political tradition and experience.

There is no best, or true, or right State that could possibly be actualized according to plan. Every State that emerges in history exists as it is but once and for a moment; the next moment it has, unperceived, become different, whatever the rigidity of its legal-constitutional crust. Therefore, words like "republic," "absolutism," "democracy," mean something different in every instance, and what turns them into catchwords is their use as definite concepts by philosophers and ideologues. A history of States is physiognomic and not systematic. Its business is not to show how "humanity" advances to the conquest of its eternal rights, to freedom and equality, to the evolving of a super-wise and super-just State, but to describe the political units that really exist in the fact-world, how they grow and flourish and fade and how they are really nothing but actual life "in form."

THE BOURGEOISIE

At the point when a Culture is beginning to turn itself into a Civilization, the non-Estate intervenes in affairs decisively—and for the first time—as an independent force. Under the Tyrannis and the Fronde,[1] the State has invoked its aid against the Estates proper, and it has for the first time learned to feel itself a power. Now it employs its strength *for itself,* and does so as a class

---

[1] Rebellion against the court during the minority of Louis XIV.—*Tr.*

standing for its freedom against the rest. It sees in the absolute State, in the Crown, in rooted institutions, the natural allies of the old Estates and the true and last representatives of symbolic tradition. This is the difference between the First and the Second Tyrannis, between Fronde and Bourgeois Revolution, between Cromwell and Robespierre.

The State, with its heavy demands on each individual in it, is felt by urban reason as a burden. So, in the same phase, the great forms of the Baroque arts begin to be felt as restrictive and become Classicist or Romanticist—that is, sickly or formless. German literature from 1770 is one long revolt of strong individual personalities against strict poetry. The idea of the whole nation being "in training" or "in form" for anything becomes intolerable, for the individual himself inwardly is no longer in condition. This holds good in morals, in arts and in modes of thought, but most of all in politics. Every bourgeois revolution has as its scene the great city, and as its hallmark the incomprehension of old symbols, which it replaces by tangible interests and the craving (or even the mere wish) of enthusiastic thinkers and world-improvers to see their conceptions actualized. Nothing now has value but that which can be justified by reason. But, deprived thus of the exaltation of a form that is essentially symbolical and works metaphysically, the national life loses the power of keeping its head up in the being-streams of history. Follow the desperate attempts of the French Government —the handful of capable and farsighted men under the mediocre Louis XVI—to keep their country in "condition" when, after the death of Vergennes in 1787, the whole gravity of the external situation had become manifest. With the death of this diplomatist France disappeared for years from the political combinations of Europe; at the same time the great reform that the Crown had carried through against all resistances—above all, the general administrative reform of that year, based on the freest self-management—remained completely ineffective, because in view of the pliancy of the State, the question of the moment for the Estates became, suddenly, the question of power. As a century before and a century afterwards, European war was drawing visibly nearer with an inexorable necessity, but no one now took any notice of the external situation. The nobility as an Estate had rarely, but the bourgeoisie as an Estate had never, thought in terms of foreign policy and world-history. Whether the State in its new form would be able to hold its own at all amongst the other States, no one asked. All that mattered was whether it secured men's "rights."

The bourgeoisie, the class of urban "freedom," strong as its class-feeling remained for generations (in West Europe even beyond 1848), was at no time wholly master of its actions. For, first of all, it became manifest in every critical situation that its unity was a *negative* unity, only really existent in moments of opposition to something, anything, else—"Tiers État" and "Opposition" are almost synonymous—and that when something constructive of its own had to be done, the interests of the various groups pulled all ways. To be free from something—that, all wanted. But the intellectual desired the State as an actualization of "justice" against the force of historical facts; or the "rights of man"; or freedom of criticism as against the dominant religion. And Money wanted a free path to business success. But there was another element, now and henceforth, that had not existed in the conflicts of the Fronde (the English Civil War included) or the First Tyrannis, but this time stood for a power—namely, that which is found in all Civilizations under different contemptuous labels—dregs, *canaille*, mob, *Pöbel*—but with the same tremendous connotation. In the great cities, which alone now spoke the decisive words—the countryside can at most accept or reject *faits accomplis,* as our eighteenth century proves—a mass of rootless fragments of population stands outside all social linkages. These do not feel themselves as attached either to an Estate or to a vocational class, nor even to the real working-class, although they are obliged to work. Elements drawn from all classes and conditions belong to it instinctively—uprooted peasantry, literates, ruined businessmen and above all (as the age of Catiline shows with terrifying clarity) derailed nobles. Their power is far in excess of their numbers, for they are always on the spot, always on hand at the big decisions, ready for anything, devoid of all respect for orderliness, even the orderliness of a revolutionary party. It is from them that events acquire the destructive force which distinguishes the French Revolution from the English, and the Second Tyrannis from the First. The bourgeoisie looks at these masses with real uneasiness, defensively, and seeks to separate itself from them—it was to a defensive act of this category, the thirteenth Vendémiaire, that Napoleon owed his rise. But in the pressure of facts the separating frontier cannot be drawn; wherever the bourgeoisie throws into the scale against the older orders its feeble weight of aggressiveness—feeble in relative numbers and feeble because its inner cohesion is risked at every moment—this mass has forced itself into their ranks, pushed to the front, imparted most of the drive that wins the victory and very often managed to secure the conquered position for itself—not seldom with the continued idealistic support of the educated who are intellectually captivated, or the material backing of the money powers, which seek to divert the danger from themselves onto the nobility and the clergy.

There is another aspect, too, under which this epoch has its importance—in it for the first time abstract truths seek to intervene in the world of facts. The capital cities have become so great, and urban man so superior and influential over the waking-consciousness of the whole Culture (*this influence is what we call Public Opinion*), that the powers of the blood and the tradition inherent in the blood are shaken in their hitherto unassailable position. For it must be remembered that the Baroque State and the absolute Polis in their final development of form are thoroughly living expressions of a *breed,* and that history, so far as it accomplishes itself in these forms, possesses the full pulse of that breed. Any theory of the State that may be fashioned here is one that is deduced from the facts, that bows to the greatness of the facts. The idea of the State had finally mastered the blood of the First Estate, and put it wholly and without reserve at the State's service. "Absolute" means that the great being-stream is *as a unit* in form, possesses *one* kind of pulse and instinct, whether the manifestations of that pulse be diplomatic or strategic flair, dignity of moral and manners, or fastidious taste in arts and thoughts.

It is now that the enemy of tradition—Rationalism—appears and spreads, that which has been described above as the *community of waking-consciousness in the educated,* whose religion is criticism and whose numina are not deities but concepts. Now begins the influence of books and general theories upon politics —in the China of Lao-tse as in the Athens of the Sophists and the Europe of Montesquieu—and the public opinion formed by them plants itself in the path of diplomacy as a political magnitude of quite a new sort. It would be absurd to suppose that Pisistratus or Richelieu or even Cromwell determined his actions under the influence of abstract systems, but after the victory of "Enlightenment" that is what actually happens.

Nevertheless the historical role of the great concepts of the "Civilization" is very different from the complexion that they presented in the minds of the ideologues who conceived them. The meaning of a truth always differs greatly from its tendency. In the world of facts, truths are simply *means*, effective insofar as they dominate spirits and therefore determine actions. Their historical position is determined not by whether they are deep, correct or even merely logical, but whether they *tell*. We see this in the word "catchword," "*Schlagwort.*" What certain symbols, livingly experienced, are for the springtime religions—the Holy Sepulchre for the Crusader, the Substance of Christ for the times of the Council of Nicaea—that two or three inspiriting word-sounds are for every Civilized revolution. It is only the catchwords that are facts—the residue of the philosophical or sociological system whence they come does not matter to history. But, *as* catchwords, they are for about two centuries powers of the first rank, stronger even than the pulse of the blood, which in the petrifying world of the outspread cities is beginning to be dulled.

But—the critical spirit is only one of the two tendencies which emerge out of the chaotic mass of the non-Estate. Along with abstract concepts abstract Money—money divorced from the prime values of the land—along with the study the counting-house, appear as political forces. If by "democracy" we mean the form which the Third Estate as such wishes to impart to public life as a whole, it must be concluded that democracy and plutocracy are the same thing under the two aspects of wish and actuality, theory and practice, knowing and doing. It is the tragic comedy of the world-improvers' and freedom-teachers' desperate fight against money that they are *ipso facto* assisting money to be effective. Respect for the big number—expressed in the principles of equality for all, natural rights and universal suffrage—is just as much a class-ideal of the unclassed as freedom of public opinion (and more particularly freedom of the press) is so. These are ideals, but in actuality the freedom of public opinion involves the preparation of public opinion, which costs money; and the freedom of the press brings with it the question of possession of the press, which again is a matter of money;

and with the franchise comes electioneering, in which he who pays the piper calls the tune. The representatives of the ideas look at one side only, while the representatives of money operate with the other. The concepts of Liberalism and Socialism are set in effective motion only by money. It was the Equites, the big-money party, which made Tiberius Gracchus' popular movement possible at all; and as soon as that part of the reforms that was advantageous to them had been successfully legalized, they withdrew and the movement collapsed. In England politicians of eminence laid it down as early as 1700 that "on 'Change one deals in votes as well as in stocks, and the price of a vote is as well known as the price of an acre of land." When the news of Waterloo reached Paris, the price of French Government stock rose—the Jacobins had destroyed the old obligations of the blood and so had emancipated money; now it stepped forward as lord of the land. There is no proletarian, not even a Communist, movement that has not operated in the interest of money, in the directions indicated by money and for the time permitted by money—and that without the idealist amongst its leaders having the slightest suspicion of the fact. Intellect rejects, money directs—so it runs in every last act of a Culture-drama, when the megalopolis has become master over the rest. And, in the limit, intellect has no cause of complaint. For, after all, it *has* won its victory—namely, in its own realm of truths, the realm of books and ideals that is not of this world. Its conceptions have become venerabilia of the beginning Civilization. But Money wins, through these very concepts, in *its* realm, which is *only* of this world.

In the Western world of States, it was in England that both sides of Third Estate politics, the ideal and the real, graduated. Here alone it was possible for the Third Estate to avoid the necessity of marching against an absolute State in order to destroy it and set up its own dominion on the ruins. For here it could grow up into the strong form of the First Estate, where it found a fully developed form of interest-politics, and from whose methods it could borrow for its own purposes a traditional tactic such as it could hardly wish to improve upon. Here was the home of Parliamentarism, genuine and quite inimitable, which had insular position instead of the State as its starting-point, and the habits of the First and not the Third Estate as its background.

Further, there was the circumstance that this form had grown up in the full bloom of Baroque and, therefore, had Music in it.[2]

But it was on British soil, too, that the rationalistic catchwords had, one and all, sprung up, and their relation to the principles of the Manchester School was intimate—Hume was the teacher of Adam Smith. "Liberty" self-evidently meant intellectual *and* trade freedom. An opposition between fact-politics and enthusiasm for abstract truths was as impossible in the England of George III as it was inevitable in the France of Louis XVI. Later, Edmund Burke could retort upon Mirabeau that "we demand our liberties, not as rights of man, but as rights of Englishmen." France received her revolutionary ideas without exception from England, as she had received the style of her absolute monarchy from Spain. To both she imparted a brilliant and irresistible shape that was taken as a model far and wide over the Continent, but of the practical employment of either she had no idea. The successful utilization of the bourgeois catchwords in politics presupposes the shrewd eye of a ruling class for the intellectual constitution of the stratum which intends to attain power but will not be capable of wielding it when attained. Hence in England it was successful. But it was in England too that money was most unhesitatingly used in politics— not the bribery of individual high personages which had been customary in the Spanish or Venetian style, but the "nursing" of the democratic forces themselves. In eighteenth-century England, first the Parliamentary elections and then the decisions of the elected Commons were systematically managed by money;[3] England, too, discovered the ideal of a Free Press, and discovered along with it that the press serves him who owns it. It does not spread "free" opinion—it generates it.

Both *together* constitute liberalism (in the broad sense); that is, freedom from the restrictions of the soil-bound life, be these

---

[2] Both the old parties possessed clear lines of tradition back to 1680.

[3] Pelham, the successor of Walpole, paid to members of the Commons, through his secretary, £500 to £800 at the end of each session according to the value of the services rendered by each recipient to the Government— i.e., the Whig party. The party agent Dodington described his parliamentary activities in these words: "I never attended a debate if I could help it, and I never missed a division that I could possibly take part in. I heard many arguments that convinced me, but never one that influenced my vote."

privileges, forms or feelings—freedom of the intellect for every kind of criticism, freedom of money for every kind of business. But both, too, unhesitatingly aim at the domination of a *class,* a domination which recognizes no overriding supremacy of the State. Mind and money, being both inorganic, want the State, not as a matured form of high symbolism to be venerated, but as an engine to serve a purpose. Only in England (it must be emphasized again and again) the Fronde had disarmed not only the State in open battle but also the Third Estate by its inward superiority, and so attained to the one kind of first-class form that democracy is capable of working up to, a form neither planned nor aped, but naturally matured, the expression of an old breed and an unbroken sure tact that can adapt itself to the use of every new means that the changes of Time put into its hands. Thus it came about that the English Parliament, while taking part in the Succession Wars of the Absolute States, handled them as economic wars with business aims. The mistrust felt for high form by the inwardly formless non-Estate is so deep that everywhere and always it is ready to rescue its freedom—*from* all form—by means of a dictatorship, which acknowledges no rules and is, therefore, hostile to all that has grown up, which, moreover, in virtue of its mechanizing tendency, is acceptable to the taste both of intellect and of money—consider, for example, the structure of the state-machine of France which Robespierre began and Napoleon completed. Dictatorship in the interests of a class-ideal appealed to Rousseau, Saint-Simon, Rodbertus and Lassalle as it had to the Classical ideologues of the fourth century—Xenophon in the Cyropaedia and Isocrates in the Nicocles.

The well-known saying of Robespierre that "the Government of the Revolution is the despotism of freedom against tyranny" expresses more than this. It reveals the deep fear that shakes every multitude which, in the presence of grave conjunctures, feels itself "not up to form." A regiment that is shaken in its discipline will readily concede to accidental leaders of the moment powers of an extent and a kind which the legitimate command could never acquire, and which *if* legitimate would be utterly intolerable. But this, on a larger scale, is the position of every commencing Civilization. Nothing reveals more tellingly the decline of political form than that upspringing of formless powers which we may conveniently designate, from its most conspicuous example, *Napoleonism.* How completely the being of

Richelieu or of Wallenstein was involved in the unshakable ante-
cedents of their period! And how instinct with form, under all
its outer uniform, was the English Revolution! The mere abolition of an order that had become obsolete was no novelty—
Cromwell and the heads of the First Tyrannis had done that. But,
that behind the ruins of the visible there is no longer the substance of an invisible form; that Robespierre and Napoleon find
nothing either around or in them to provide the *self-evident*
basis essential to any new creation; that for a government of
high tradition and experience they have no choice but to substitute an accidental regime, whose future no longer rests secure
on the qualities of a slowly and thoroughly trained minority,
but depends entirely on the chance of the adequate successor
turning up—such are the distinguishing marks of this turning
of the times, and hence comes the immense superiority that is
enjoyed for generations still by those states which manage to
retain a tradition longer than others.

TRADITION VERSUS THEORY

If it was an improbable piece of good luck in the destinies of the
Classical peoples that Rome was the only city-state to survive
the Revolution with an unimpaired constitution, it was, on the
contrary, almost a miracle that in our West—with its genealogical forms deep-rooted in the idea of duration—violent revolution broke out at all, even in one place—namely, Paris. It was
not the strength but the weakness of French Absolutism which
brought the English ideas, in combination with the power of
money, to the point of an explosion which gave living form to
the catchwords of the "Enlightenment," which bound together
virtue and terror, freedom and despotism, and which echoed still
even in the minor catastrophes of 1830 and 1848 and the more
recent Socialistic longing for catastrophe. In England itself,
there was certainly a small circle round Fox and Sheridan which
was enthusiastic for the ideas of the Revolution—all of which
were of English provenance—and men talked of universal suffrage and Parliamentary reform. But that was quite enough to
induce both parties, under the leadership of a Whig (the younger
Pitt), to take the sharpest measures to defeat any and every attempt to interfere in the slightest degree with the aristocratic

regime for the benefit of the bourgeoisie. The English nobility let loose the twenty-year war against France, and mobilized all the monarchs of Europe to bring about in the end, not the fall of Napoleon, but the fall of the Revolution—the Revolution that had had the naïve daring to introduce the opinions of private English thinkers into practical politics, and so to give a position to the Tiers État of which the consequences were all the better foreseen in the English lobbies for having been overlooked in the Paris salons.[4]

What was called "Opposition" in England was—the attitude of one aristocratic party while the other was running the Government. This Opposition was at once—and in complete ignorance of its social presuppositions—taken as a model for that which the educated in France and elsewhere aimed at creating, namely, a class-domination of the Tiers État under the eyes of a dynasty, no very clear idea being formed as to the latter's future. The English dispositions were, from Montesquieu onwards, lauded with enthusiastic misunderstanding—although these Continental countries, not being islands, lacked the first condition precedent for an "English" evolution.

The result of the turn, and the basic form of the Continental States at the beginning of the Civilization, is "Constitutional Monarchy," the extremest possibility of which appears as what we call nowadays a Republic. It is necessary to get clear, once and for all, of the mumblings of the doctrinaires who think in timeless and therefore unreal concepts and for whom "Republic" is a form-in-itself. The republican ideal of the nineteenth century has no more resemblance to the Classical *res publica,* or even to Venice or the original Swiss cantons, than the English constitution to a "constitution" in the Continental sense. That which *we* call republic is a *negation,* which of inward necessity postulates that the thing denied is an ever-present possibility. It is

---

[4] Afterwards—from 1832—the English nobility itself, through a series of prudent measures, drew the bourgeoisie into *co-operation* with it, but under its continued guidance and, above all, in the framework of tradition, within which consequently the young talent grew up. Democracy thus actualized itself here so that the Government remained strictly "in form"— the old aristocratic form—while the individual was free to practise politics according to his bent. This transition, in a peasantless society dominated by business interests, was the most remarkable achievement of inner politics in the nineteenth century.

non-monarchy in forms borrowed from the monarchy. The genealogical feeling is immensely strong in Western mankind; it strains its conscience so far as to pretend that Dynasty determines its political conduct even when Dynasty no longer exists at all. The historical is embodied therein, and unhistorically we cannot live. It makes a great difference whether, as in the case of the Classical world, the dynastic principle conveys absolutely nothing to the inner feelings of a man, or, as in the case of the West, it is real enough to need six generations of educated people to fight it down in themselves. Feeling is the secret enemy of all constitutions that are plans and not growths; they are in the last analysis nothing but defensive measures born of fear and mistrust. The urban conception of freedom—freedom *from* something—narrows itself to a merely anti-dynastic significance, and republican enthusiasm lives only on this feeling.

Such a negation inevitably involves a preponderance of theory. While Dynasty and its close congener Diplomacy conserve the old tradition and pulse, Constitutions contain an overweight of systems, bookishness and framed concepts—such as is entirely unthinkable in England, where nothing negative and defensive adheres to the form of government. It is not for nothing that the Faustian is *par excellence* the reading and writing Culture. The printed book is an emblem of temporal, the Press of spatial, infinity. In contrast with the immense power and tyranny of these symbols, even the Chinese Civilization seems almost empty of writing. In Constitutions, literature is put into the field against knowledge of men and things, language against race, abstract right against successful tradition—regardless of whether a nation involved in the tide of events is still capable of work and "maintaining its form." Mirabeau was quite alone and unsuccessful in combatting the Assembly, which "confused politics with fiction." Not only the three doctrinaire constitutions of the age—the French of 1791, the German of 1848 and 1919—but practically all such attempts shut their eyes to the great Destiny in the fact-world and imagine that that is the same as defeating it. It is symptomatic that no written constitution knows of money as a political force. It is pure theory that they contain, one and all.

It was only in England that race held its own against principle. Men had more than an inkling that real politics, politics aiming at historical success, is a matter of training and not of shaping. This was no aristocratic prejudice, but a cosmic fact that emerges much more distinctly in the experience of any English racehorse-trainer than in all the philosophical systems in the world. Shaping can refine training, but not replace it. And thus the higher society of England, Eton and Balliol, became training-grounds where politicians were formed with a consistent sureness the like of which is only to be found in the training of the Prussian officer-corps—trained, that is, as connoisseurs and masters of the underlying pulse of things (not excluding the hidden course of opinions and ideas). Thus prepared, they were able, in the great flood of bourgeois-revolutionary principles that swept over the years after 1832, to preserve and control the being-stream which they directed. They possessed "training," the suppleness and collectedness of the rider who, with a good horse under him, feels victory coming nearer and nearer. They allowed the great principles to move the mass because they knew well that it is money that is the "wherewithal" by which motion is imparted to these great principles, and they substituted, for the brutal methods of the eighteenth century, methods more refined and not less effective—one of the simpler of these being to threaten their opponents with the cost of a new election. The doctrinaire constitutions of the Continent saw only the one side of the fact democracy. Here, where there was no constitution, but men were in "condition," it was seen as a whole.

A vague feeling of all this was never quite lost on the Continent. For the absolute State of the Baroque there had been a perfectly clear form, but for "constitutional monarchy" there were only unsteady compromises, and Conservative and Liberal parties were distinguished—not, as in England after Canning, by the possession of different but well-tested modes of government, applied turn-and-about to the actual work of governing—but according to the direction in which they respectively desired to alter the constitution—namely, towards tradition or towards theory. Should the Parliament serve the Dynasty, or vice versa? —that was the bone of contention, and in disputing over it it was forgotten that *foreign* policy was the final aim. The "Spanish" and the misnamed "English" sides of a constitution would not and could not grow together, and thus it befell that during the nineteenth century the diplomatic service outwards and the Parliamentary activity inwards developed in two divergent directions. Each became in fundamental feeling alien to, and contemptuous of, the other. After Thermidor, France succumbed to the rule of the Bourse, mitigated from time to time by the setting up of a military dictature (1800, 1851, 1871, 1918). Bismarck's creation was in fundamentals of a dynastic nature, with a parliamentary component of decidedly subordinate importance, and in it the inner friction was so strong as to monopolize the available political energy, and finally, after 1916, to exhaust the organism itself. The Army had its own history, with a great tradition going back to Frederick William I, and so also had the administration. In them was the source of Socialism as one kind of true political "training," diametrically opposed to the English but, like it, a full expression of strong race-quality. The officer and the official were highly trained, but the necessity of breeding up a corresponding political type was not recognized. Higher policy was handled "administratively" and minor policy was hopeless squabbling. And so army and administration finally became aims in themselves, after Bismarck's disappearance had removed the one man who even without a supply of real politicians to back him (which tradition alone could have produced) was big enough to treat both as tools of policy. When the issue of the World War removed the upper layers, nothing remained but parties educated for opposition only, and these brought the activity of Government down to a level hitherto unknown in any Civilization.

Parliamentarism is not a summit as the absolute Polis and the Baroque State were summits, but a brief transition—namely, between the Late-Culture period with its mature forms and the age of great individuals in a formless world. It contains, like the houses and furniture of the first half of the nineteenth century, a residue of good Baroque. The parliamentary habit is English Rococo—but, no longer unselfconscious and in the blood, but retaining its sovereignty by a fiction. With the beginning of the twentieth century Parliamentarism (even English) is tending rapidly towards taking up itself the role that it once assigned to the kingship. It is becoming an impressive spectacle for the multitude of the Orthodox, while the centre of gravity of big policy, already *de jure* transferred from the Crown to the people's representatives, is passing *de facto* from the latter to unofficial groups and the will of unofficial personages. The World War almost completed this development. There is no way back to the old parliamentarism from the domination of Lloyd George and the Napoleonism of the French militarists. And for America, hitherto lying apart and self-contained, rather a region than a State, the parallelism of President and Congress which she derived from a theory of Montesquieu has, with her entry into world politics, become untenable, and must in times of real danger make way for formless powers such as those with which Mexico and South America have long been familiar.

THE PERIOD OF THE CONTENDING STATES

With this enters the age of gigantic conflicts, in which we find ourselves today. It is the *transition from Napoleonism to Caesarism,* a general phase of evolution, which occupies at least two centuries and can be shown to exist in all the Cultures. The Chinese call it Shan-Kwo, the "period of the Contending States."

For us this time of Contending States began with Napoleon and his violent-arbitrary government by order. He was the first in our world to make effective the notion of a military and at the same time popular world-domination—something altogether different from the Empire of Charles V and even the British Colonial Empire of his own day. If the nineteenth century was relatively poor in great wars—and revolutions—and overcame its worst crises diplomatically by means of congresses, this has been due precisely to the continuous and terrific war-preparedness which has made disputants, fearful at the eleventh hour of the consequences, postpone the definitive decision again and again, and led to the substitution of chess-moves for war. For this is the century of gigantic permanent armies and universal compulsory service. We ourselves are too near to it to see it under this terrifying aspect. In all world-history there is no parallel. Ever since Napoleon, hundreds of thousands, and latterly millions, of men have stood ready to march, and mighty fleets renewed every ten years have filled the harbours. It is a war without war, a war of overbidding in equipment and preparedness, a war of figures and tempo and technics, and the diplomatic dealings have been not of court with court, but of headquarters with headquarters. The longer the discharge was delayed, the more huge became the means and the more intolerable the tension. This is the Faustian, the dynamic, form of "the Contending States" during the first century of that period, but it ended with the explosion of the World War. For the demand of these four years has been altogether too much for the principle of universal service—child of the French Revolution, revolutionary through and through, as it is in this form—and all tactical methods evolved from it. The place of the permanent armies as we know them will gradually be taken by professional forces of volunteer war-keen soldiers; and from millions we shall revert to hundreds of thousands. But *ipso facto* this second century will be one of *actually* Contending States. *These* armies are not substitutes for war—they are *for* war, and they want war. Within two generations it will be their will that prevails over that of all the comfortables put together. In these wars of theirs for the heritage of the whole world, continents will be staked, India, China, South Africa, Russia, Islam, called out, new technics and tactics played and counterplayed. The great cosmopolitan foci of power will dispose at their pleasure of smaller states—their territory, their economy and their men alike—all that is now merely province, passive object, means to end, and its destinies are without importance to the great march of things. We ourselves, in a very few years, have learned to take little or no notice of events that before the War would have horrified the world; who today seriously thinks about the millions that perish in Russia?

Again and again between these catastrophes of blood and terror the cry rises up for reconciliation of the peoples and for peace on earth. It is but the background and the echo of the grand happening, but, as such, so necessary that we have to assume its existence even if, as in Hyksos Egypt, in Baghdad and Byzantium, no tradition tells of it. Esteem as we may the wish towards all this, we must have the courage to face facts as they are—that is the hallmark of men of race-quality and it is by the being of these men that *alone* history is. Life if it would be great, is hard; it lets choose *only* between victory and ruin, not between war and peace, and to the victory belong the sacrifices of victory. For that which shuffles querulously and jealously by the side of the events is only literature—written or thought or lived literature—mere truths that lose themselves in the moving crush of facts. History has never deigned to take notice of these propositions. In the Chinese world Hiang-Sui tried, as early as 535, to found a peace league. In the period of the Contending States, imperialism (*Lien-heng*) was opposed by the League of Nations idea (*Hoh-tsung*), particularly in the southern regions, but it was foredoomed like every half-measure that steps into the path of a whole, and it had vanished even before the victory of the North. But both tendencies alike rejected the political taste of the Taoists, who, in those fearful centuries, elected for intellectual self-disarmament, thereby reducing themselves to the level of mere material to be used up by others and for others in the grand decisions. Even Roman politics—deliberately improvident as the Classical spirit was in all other respects—at least made one attempt to bring the whole world into one system of equal co-ordinated forces which should do away with all necessity for further wars—that is, when at the fall of Hannibal Rome forwent the chance of incorporating the East. But reluctance was useless; the party of the younger Scipio went over to frank Imperialism in order to make an end of chaos, although its clear-sighted leader foresaw therein the doom of his city, which possessed (and in a high degree) the native Classical incapacity for organizing anything whatever. The way from Alexander to Caesar is unambiguous and unavoidable, and the strongest nation of any and every Culture, consciously or unconsciously, willing or unwilling, has had to tread it.

From the rigour of these facts there is no refuge. The Hague Conference of 1907 was the prelude of the World War; the Washington Conference of 1921 will have been that of other wars. The history of these times is no longer an intellectual match of wits in elegant forms for pluses and minuses, from which either side can withdraw when it pleases. The alternatives now are to stand fast or to go under—there is no middle course. The only moral that the logic of things permits to us now is that of the climber on the face of the crag—a moment's weakness and all is over. Today all "philosophy" is nothing but an inward abdication and resignation, or a craven hope of escaping realities by means of mysticisms. It was just the same in Roman times. Tacitus tells us how the famous Musonius Rufus tried, by exhortations on the blessings of peace and the evils of war, to influence the legions that in 70 stood before the gates of Rome, and barely escaped alive from their blows. The military commander Avidius Cassius called the Emperor Marcus Aurelius a "philosophical old woman."

In these conditions so much of old and great traditions as remains, so much of historical "fitness" and experience as has got into the blood of the twentieth-century nations, acquires an unequalled potency. For us *creative* piety, or (to use a more fundamental term) the pulse that has come down to us from first origins, adheres only to forms that are older than the Revolution and Napoleon,[5] forms which grew and were not made. Every remnant of them, however tiny, that has kept itself alive in the being of any self-contained minority whatever will before long rise to incalculable values and bring about historical effects which no one yet imagines to be possible. The traditions of an old monarchy, of an old aristocracy, of an old polite society, in so much as they are still healthy enough to keep clear of professional or professorial politics, insofar as they possess honour, abnegation, discipline, the genuine sense of a great mission (*race-quality*, that is, and training), sense of duty and sacrifice —can become a centre which holds together the being-stream of an entire people and enables it to outlast this time and make its landfall in the future. To be "in condition" is everything. It falls to us to live in the most trying times known to the history of a great Culture. The last race to keep its form, the last living tradition, the last leaders who have both at their back, will pass through and onward, victors.

CAESARISM

By the term "Caesarism" I mean that kind of government which, irrespective of any constitutional formulation that it may have, is in its inward self a return to thorough formlessness. It does not matter that Augustus in Rome, and Huang Ti in China, Amasis in Egypt and Alp Arslan in Baghdad disguised their position under antique forms. The spirit of these forms was dead,[6] and so all institutions, however carefully maintained, were thenceforth destitute of all meaning and weight. Real importance centred in the wholly personal power exercised by the Caesar, or by anybody else capable of exercising it in his place.

---

[5] Including the constitution of the United States of America. Only thus can we account for the reverence that the American cherishes for it, even where he clearly sees its insufficiency.

[6] Caesar recognized this clearly. "*Nihil esse rem publicam, appellationem modo sine corpore ac specie*" (Suetonius, *Caesar*, 77).

It is the *récidive* of a form-fulfilled world into primitivism, into the cosmic-historyless. Biological stretches of time once more take the place vacated by historical periods.

At the beginning, where the Civilization is developing to full bloom (today), there stands the miracle of the Cosmopolis, the great petrifact, a symbol of the formless—vast, splendid, spreading in insolence. It draws within itself the being-streams of the now impotent countryside, human masses that are wafted as dunes from one to another or flow like loose sand into the chinks of the stone. Here money and intellect celebrate their greatest and their last triumphs. It is the most artificial, the cleverest phenomenon manifested in the light-world of human eyes—uncanny, "too good to be true," standing already almost beyond the possibilities of cosmic formation.

Presently, however, the idea-less facts come forward again, naked and gigantic. The eternal-cosmic pulse has finally overcome the intellectual tensions of a few centuries. In the form of democracy, money has won. There has been a period in which politics were almost its preserve. But as soon as it has destroyed the old orders of the Culture, the chaos gives forth a new and overpowering factor that penetrates to the very elementals of Becoming—the Caesar-men. Before them the omnipotence of money collapses. *The Imperial Age, in every Culture alike, signifies the end of the politics of mind and money.* The powers of the blood, unbroken bodily forces, resume their ancient lordship. "Race" springs forth, pure and irresistible—the strongest win and the residue is their spoil. They seize the management of the world, and the realm of books and problems petrifies or vanishes from memory. There is no inward difference more between the lives of Septimius Severus and Gallienus and those of Alaric and Odoacer. Rameses, Trajan, Wu Ti, belong together in a uniform up-and-down of historyless time-stretches.

Once the Imperial Age has arrived, there are no more political problems. People manage with the situation as it is and the powers that be. In the period of the Contending States, torrents of blood had reddened the pavements of all world-cities, so that the great truths of Democracy might be turned into actualities, and for the winning of rights without which life seemed not worth the living. Now these rights are won, but the grandchildren cannot be moved, even by punishment, to make use of them. A hundred years more, and even the historians will no longer understand the old controversies. Already by Caesar's time reputable people had almost ceased to take part in the elections. It embittered the life of the great Tiberius that the most capable men of his time held aloof from politics, and Nero could not even by threats compel the Equites to come to Rome in order to exercise their rights. This is the end of the great politics.

The Julian-Claudian house destroyed Roman history, and the house of Shih Huang Ti (even from 206 B.C.) destroyed Chinese, and we darkly discern something of the same kind in the destinies of the Egyptian Queen Hatshepsut and her brothers (1501–1447). It is the last step to the definitive. With world-peace—*the peace of high policies*—the "sword side" of being retreats and the "spindle side" rules again; henceforth there are only *private* histories, private destinies, private ambitions, from top to bottom, from the miserable troubles of fellaheen to the dreary feuds of Caesars for the private possession of the world. The wars of the age of world-peace are private wars, more fearful than any State wars because they are formless.

For world-peace—which has often existed in fact—involves the private renunciation of war on the part of the immense majority, but along with this it involves an unavowed readiness to submit to being the booty of others who do *not* renounce it. It begins with the State-destroying wish for universal reconciliation, and it ends in nobody's moving a finger so long as misfortune only touches his neighbour. Already under Marcus Aurelius each city and each land-patch was thinking of itself, and the activities of the ruler were his private affair as other men's were theirs. The remoter peoples were as indifferent to him and his troops and his aims as they were to the projects of Germanic marauders. On this *spiritual* premiss a second Vikingism develops. The state of being "in form" passes from nations to bands and retinues of adventurers, self-styled Caesars, seceding generals, barbarian kings and what not—in whose eyes the population becomes in the end merely a part of the landscape. There is a deep relation between the heroes of the Mycenaean primitive age and the soldier-emperors of Rome, and between, say, Menes and Rameses II. In our Germanic world the spirits of Alaric and Theodoric will come again—there is a first hint of them in Cecil Rhodes—and the alien executioners of the Russian preface, from Genghis Khan to Trotski (with the episode of Petrine Tsarism between them), are, when all is said and done, very little different from most of the pretenders of the Latin-American republics, whose private struggles have long since put an end to the form-rich age of the Spanish Baroque.

With the formed state having finished its course, high history also lays itself down weary to sleep. Man becomes a plant again, adhering to the soil, dumb and enduring. The timeless village and the "eternal" peasant reappear, begetting children and burying seed in Mother Earth—a busy, easily contented swarm, over which the tempest of soldier-emperors passingly blows. In the midst of the land lie the old world-cities, empty receptacles of an extinguished soul, in which a historyless mankind slowly nests itself. Men live from hand to mouth, with petty thrifts and petty fortunes, and endure. Masses are trampled on in the conflicts of the conquerors who contend for the power and the spoil of this world, but the survivors fill up the gaps with a primitive fertility and suffer on. And while in high places there is eternal alternance of victory and defeat, those in the depths pray, pray with that mighty piety of the Second Religiousness that has overcome all doubts forever. There, in the souls, world-peace, the peace of God, the bliss of grey-haired monks and hermits, is become actual—and there alone. It has awakened that depth in the endurance of suffering which the historical man in the thousand years of his development has never known. Only with the end of grand History does holy, still Being reappear. It is a drama noble in its aimlessness, noble and aimless as the course of the stars, the rotation of the earth, and alternance of land and sea, of ice and virgin forest upon its face. We may marvel at it or we may lament it—but so it is.

XIX

PHILOSOPHY OF POLITICS

THE STATESMAN

TO be the centre of action and effective focus of a multitude, to make the inward form of one's own personality into that of whole peoples and periods, to be history's commanding officer, with the aim of bringing one's own people or family or purposes to the top of events—that is the scarcely conscious but irresistible impulse in every individual being possessing a historical vocation. There is only *personal* history, and consequently only *personal* politics. The struggle of, not principles but men, not ideals but race-qualities, for executive power is the alpha and omega. Even revolutions are no exception, for the "sovereignty of the people" only expresses the fact that the ruling power has assumed the title of people's leader instead of that of king. The method of governing is scarcely altered thereby, and the position of the governed not at all. And even world-peace, in every case where it has existed, has been nothing but the slavery of an entire humanity under the regimen imposed by a few strong natures determined to rule.

The conception of executive power implies that the life-unit—even in the case of the animals—is subdivided into subjects and objects of government. This is so self-evident that no mass-unit has ever for a moment, even in the severest crises (such as 1789), lost the sense of this inner structure of itself.

Politically gifted *peoples* do not exist. Those which are supposed to be so are simply peoples that are firmly in the hands of a ruling minority and in consequence feel themselves to be in good form. The English as a people are just as unthinking, narrow and unpractical in political matters as any other nation, but they possess—for all their liking for public debate—*a tradition of confidence*. The difference is simply that the Englishman is the object of a regimen of very old and successful habits, in which he acquiesces because experience has shown him their advantage. From an acquiescence that has the outward appearance of agreement, it is only one step to the conviction that this government depends upon his will, although paradoxically it is the government that, for technical reasons of its own, unceasingly hammers the notion into his head. The ruling class in England has developed its aims and methods quite independently of the "people," and it works with and within an unwritten constitution of which the refinements—which have arisen from practice and are wholly innocent of theory—are to the uninitiated as opaque as they are unintelligible. But the courage of a troop depends on its confidence in the leadership, and confidence means involuntary abstention from criticism. It is the officer who makes cowards into heroes, or heroes into cowards, and this holds good equally for armies, peoples, classes and parties. *Political talent in a people* is nothing but confidence in its leading. But that confidence has to be acquired; it will ripen only in its own good time, and success will stabilize it and make it into a tradition. What appears as a lack of the feeling of certainty in the ruled is really lack of leadership-talent in the ruling classes, which generates that sort of uninstinctive and meddlesome criticism which by its very existence shows that a people has got "out of condition."

The born statesman is above all a valuer—a valuer of men, situations and things. He has the "eye" which unhesitatingly and inflexibly embraces the round of possibilities. The judge of horses takes in an animal with one glance and knows what prospects it will have in a race. To do the correct thing without "knowing" it, to have the hands that imperceptibly tighten or ease the bit—his talent is the very opposite to that of the man of theory. The secret pulse of all being is one and the same in him and in the things of history. They sense one another, they exist for one another. The fact-man is immune from the risk of practising sentimental or program politics. He does not believe in the big words. Pilate's question is constantly on his lips— Truths? The born statesman stands beyond true and false. He does not confuse the logic of events with the logic of systems. He has convictions, certainly, that are dear to him, but he has them as a private person; no real politician ever felt himself tied to them when in action. "The doer is always conscienceless; no one has a conscience except the spectator," said Goethe, and it is equally true of Sulla and Robespierre as it is of Bismarck and

Pitt. The great Popes and the English party-leaders, so long as they had still to strive for the mastery of things, acted on the same principles as the conquerors and upstarts of all ages. Take the dealings of Innocent III, who very nearly succeeded in creating a world-dominion of the Church, and deduce therefrom the catechism of success; it will be found to be in the extremest contradiction with all religious moral. Yet without it there could have been no bearable existence for any Church, not to mention English Colonies, American fortunes, victorious revolutions or, for that matter, states or parties or peoples in general. It is *life*, not the individual, that is conscienceless.

The essential, therefore, is to understand the time *for* which one is born. He who does not sense and understand its most secret forces, who does not feel in himself something cognate that drives him forward on a path neither hedged nor defined by concepts, who trusts to the surface—public opinion, large phrases and ideals of the day—he is not of the stature for its events. He is in their power, not they in his. Look not back to the past for measuring-rods! Still less sideways for some system or other! There are times, like our own present and the Gracchan age, in which there are two most deadly kinds of idealism, the reactionary and the democratic. The one believes in the reversibility of history, the other in a teleology of history. But it makes no difference to the inevitable failure with which both burden a nation over whose destiny they have power, whether it is to a memory or to a concept that they sacrifice it. The genuine statesman is incarnate history, its directedness expressed as individual will and its organic logic as character.

But the true statesman must also be, in a large sense of the word, an educator—not the representative of a moral or a doctrine, but an exemplar in doing. It is a patent fact that a religion has never yet altered the style of an existence. It penetrated the waking-consciousness, the *intellectual* man, it threw new light on another world, it created an immense happiness by way of humanity, resignation and patience unto death, but over the forces of life it possessed no power. In the sphere of the living only the great personality—the "it," the race, the cosmic force bound up in that personality—has been creative (not shaping, but breeding and training) and has effectively modified the type of entire classes and peoples. It is not "the" truth or "the" good or "the" upright, but "the" Roman or "the" Puritan or "the" Prussian that is a fact. The sum of honour and duty, discipline, resolution, is a thing not learned from books, but *awakened* in the stream of being by a living exemplar; and that is why Frederick William I was one of those educators, great for all time, whose personal race-forming conduct does not vanish in the course of the generations. The genuine statesman is distinguished from the "mere politician"—the player who plays for the pleasure of the game, the *arriviste* on the heights of history, the seeker after wealth and rank—as also from the schoolmaster of an ideal, by the fact that he dares to demand sacrifices—*and* obtains them, because his feeling that he is necessary to the time and the nation is shared by thousands, transforms them to the core and renders them capable of deeds to which otherwise they could never have risen.[1]

Highest of all, however, is not action, but the *ability to command*. It is this that takes the individual up out of himself and makes him the centre of a world of action. There is one kind of commanding that makes obedience a proud, free and noble habit. That kind Napoleon, for example, did *not* possess. A residue of subaltern outlook in him prevented him from training men to be men and not bureau-personnel, and led him to govern through edicts instead of through personalities; as he did not understand this subtlest tact of command and, therefore, was obliged to do everything really decisive himself, he slowly collapsed from inability to reconcile the demands of his position with the limit of human capabilities. But one who, like Caesar or Frederick the Great, possesses this last and highest gift of complete humanity feels—on a battle-evening when operations are sweeping to the willed conclusion, and the victory is turning out to be conclusive of the campaign; or when the last signature is written that rounds off a historical epoch—a wondrous sense of power that the man of truth can never know. There are moments—and they indicate the maxima of cosmic flowings—when the individual feels himself to be identical with Destiny, the centre of the world, and his own personality seems to him almost as a

---

[1] The same, too, holds good of the Churches, which are different in kind from the Religion—namely, elements of the world of facts and, therefore, political and not religious in the type of their leadership. It was not the Christian evangel, but the Christian martyr, who conquered the world, and that which gave him his strength was not the doctrine, but the example, of the Man on the Cross.

covering in which the history of the future is about to clothe itself.

The first problem is to make oneself somebody: the second—less obvious, but harder and greater in its ultimate effects—*to create a tradition,* to bring on others so that one's work may be continued with one's own pulse and spirit, to release a current of like activity that does not need the original leader to maintain it in form. And here the statesman rises to something that in the Classical world would doubtless have been called divinity. He becomes the creator of a new life, the *spirit*-ancestor of a young race. He himself, as a unit, vanishes from the stream after a few years. But a minority called into being by him takes up his course and maintains it indefinitely. This cosmic something, this soul of a ruling stratum, an individual *can* generate and leave as a heritage, and throughout history it is this that has produced the durable effects. The great statesman is rare. Whether he comes, or wins through, too soon or too late, incident determines. Great individuals often destroy more than they have built up—by the gap that their death makes in the flow of happening. But *the creation of tradition means the elimination of the incident.* A tradition breeds a high average, with which the future can reckon—no Caesar, but a Senate, no Napoleon, but an incomparable officer-corps. A strong tradition attracts talents from all quarters, and out of small gifts produces great results. The schools of painting of Italy and Holland are proof of this, no less than the Prussian army and the diplomacy of the Roman Curia. It was the great flaw in Bismarck, as compared with Frederick William I, that he could achieve but could not form a tradition; that he did not parallel Moltke's officer-corps by a corresponding race of politicians who would identify themselves in feeling with his State and its new tasks, would constantly take up good men from below and so provide for the continuance of the Bismarckian action-pulse forever. If this creation of a tradition does not come off, then instead of a homogeneous ruling stratum we have a congeries of heads that are helpless when confronted by the unforeseen. If it does, we have a *Sovereign People* in the one sense of the phrase that is worthy of a people and possible in the world of fact—a highly trained, self-replenishing minority with sure and slowly ripened traditions, which attracts every talent into the charmed circle and uses it to the full, and *ipso facto* keeps itself in harmony with the remainder of the nation that it rules. Such a minority slowly develops into a true "breed," even when it had begun merely as a party, and the sureness of its decisions comes to be that of blood, not of reason. But this means that what happens in it happens "of itself" and does not need the Genius. *Great politics, so to put it, takes the place of the great politician.*

What then, *is* politics? It is the art of the possible—an old saying, and almost an all-inclusive saying. The gardener can obtain a plant from the seed, or he can improve its stock. He can bring to bloom, or let languish, the dispositions hidden in it, its growths and colour, its flower and fruit. On his eye for possibilities—and, therefore, necessities—depends its fulfilment, its strength, its whole Destiny. But the basic form and direction of its being, the stages and tempo and direction thereof, are *not* in his power. It must accomplish them or it decays, and the same is true of the immense plant that we call a "Culture" and the being-streams of human families that are bound up in its form-world. The great statesman is the gardener of a people. The worshippers of political ideals create out of nothing. Their intellectual freedom is astounding, but their castles of the mind, built of airy concepts like wisdom and righteousness, liberty and equality, are in the end all the same; they are built from the top story downwards. The master of fact, for his part, is content to direct imperceptibly that which he sees and accepts as plain reality. This does not seem very much, yet it is the very starting-point of freedom, in a grand sense of the word. The knack lies in the little things, the last careful touch of the helm, the fine sensing of the most delicate oscillations of collective and individual souls. The secret of all victory lies in the organization of the non-obvious. An adept in the game can, like Talleyrand, go to Vienna as ambassador of the vanquished party and make himself master of the victor. At the Lucca meeting, Caesar, whose position was well-nigh desperate, not only made Pompey's power serviceable to his own ends but undermined it at the same time, and without his opponent's becoming aware of the fact. But the domain of the possible has dangerous edges, and if the finished tact of the great Baroque diplomatists almost always managed to keep clear, it is the very privilege of the ideologues to be always stumbling over them. There have been turns in history in which the statecraftman has let himself drift with the current awhile, in order not to lose the leadership. Every situation has its elastic limit, and in the estimation of that limit not the smallest error is permissible.

Further, the necessary must be done *opportunely*—namely, while it is a present wherewith the governing power can buy confidence in itself, whereas if it has to be conceded as a sacrifice, it discloses a weakness and excites contempt. Political forms are living forms whose changes inexorably follow a definite direction, and to attempt to prevent this course or to divert it towards some ideal is to confess oneself "out of condition." In the period of mounting democracy we find again and again (as in France before 1789 and Germany before 1918) the arrival of a fatal moment when it is too late for the necessary reform to be given as a free gift; *then* that which should be refused with the sternest energy is given as a *sacrifice,* and so becomes the sign of dissolution. But those who fail to detect the first necessity in good time will all the more certainly fail to misunderstand the second situation. Even a journey to Canossa can be made too soon or too late—the timing may settle the future of whole peoples, whether they shall be Destiny for others, or themselves the objects of another's Destiny. But the declining democracy also repeats the same error of trying to hold what was the ideal of yesterday. This is the danger of our twentieth century. On the path towards Caesarism there is ever a Cato to be found.

The influence that a statesman—even one in an exceptionally strong position—possesses over the *methods* of politics is very small, and it is one of the characteristics of the high-grade statesman that he does not deceive himself on this matter. His task is to work in and with the historical form that he finds in existence; it is only the theorist who enthusiastically searches for more ideal forms. But to be politically "in form" means necessarily, amongst other things, an unconditional *command of the most modern means.* The danger of an aristocracy is that of being conservative in its means, the danger of a democracy is the confusion of formula and form. The means of the present are, and will be for many years, parliamentary—elections and the press. He may think what he pleases about them, he may respect them or despise them, but he *must command them.* Bach and Mozart *commanded* the musical means of their times. This is the hallmark of mastery in any and every field, and statecraft is no exception. The statesman knows that the extension of a franchise is quite unimportant in comparison with the technique

—Athenian or Roman, Jacobin or American or present-day German—of *operating* the votes. And as for the modern press, the sentimentalist may beam with contentment when it is constitutionally "free"—but the realist merely asks at whose disposal it is.

POLITICAL THEORY

Politico-social theory is only one of the bases of party politics, but it is a necessary one. The proud series that runs from Rousseau to Marx has its anti-type in the line of Classical Sophists up to Plato and Zeno. In the case of China the characteristics of the corresponding doctrines have still to be extracted from Confucian and Taoist literature; it suffices to name the Socialist Mo Ti. In the Byzantine and Arabian literature of the Abbassid period—in which radicalism, like everything else, is orthodox-religious in constitution—they hold a large place, and they were driving forces in all the crises of the ninth century. That they existed in Egypt and in India also is proved by the spirit of events in the Hyksos time and in Buddha's. Literary form is not essential to them—they are just as effectively disseminated by word of mouth, by sermon and propaganda in sects and associations, which indeed is the standard method at the close of the Puritan movements (Islam and Anglo-American Christianity amongst them).

Whether these doctrines are "true" or "false" is—we must reiterate and emphasize—a question without meaning for political history. The refutation of, say, Marxism belongs to the realm of academic dissertation and public debates, in which everyone is always right and his opponent always wrong. But whether they are *effective*—from when, and for how long, the belief that actuality can be ameliorated by a system of concepts is a real force that politics must reckon with—that does matter. We of today find ourselves in a period of boundless confidence in the omnipotence of reason. Great general ideas of freedom, justice, humanity, progress, are sacrosanct. The great theories are gospels. Their power to convince does not rest upon logical premises, for the mass of a party possesses neither the critical energy nor the detachment seriously to test them, but upon the sacramental hypostasis in their key-words. At the same time, the spell is limited to the populations of the great cities and the period of Rationalism as the "educated man's religion." On a peasantry it has no hold, and even on the city masses its effect lasts only for a certain time. But *for* that time it has all the irresistibleness of a new revelation. They are converted to it, hang fervently upon the words and the preachers thereof, go to martyrdom on barricades and battle-field and gallows; their gaze is set upon a political and social other-world, and dry sober criticism seems base, impious, worthy of death.

But for this very reason documents like the *Contrat Social* and the *Communist Manifesto* are engines of highest power in the hands of forceful men who have come to the top in party life and know how to form and to use the convictions of the dominated masses.

The power that these abstract ideals possess, however, scarcely extends in time beyond the two centuries that belong to party politics, and their end comes not from refutation, but from boredom—which has killed Rousseau long since and will shortly kill Marx. Men finally give up, not this or that theory, but the belief in theory of any kind and with it the sentimental optimism of an eighteenth century that imagined that unsatisfactory actualities could be improved by the application of concepts. When Plato, Aristotle and their contemporaries defined and blended the various kinds of Classical constitution so as to obtain a wise and beautiful resultant, all the world listened, and Plato himself tried to transform Syracuse in accordance with an ideological recipe— and sent the city downhill to its ruin. It appears to me equally certain that it was philosophical experimentation of this kind that put the Chinese southern states out of condition and delivered them up to the imperialism of Tsin The Jacobin fanatics of liberty and equality delivered France, from the Directory onward, into the hands of Army and Bourse, and every Socialist outbreak only blazes new paths for Capitalism. But by the time that Cicero wrote his *De re publica* for Pompey, and Sallust his two comminations for Caesar, nobody any longer paid attention. In the first century B.C. theories had become a threadbare school-exercise, and thenceforward power and power alone mattered.

For us, too—let there be no mistake about it—the age of theory is drawing to its end. The great systems of Liberalism and Socialism all arose between about 1750 and 1850. That of Marx is already half a century old, and it has had no successor. Inwardly it means, with its materialist view of history, that Nationalism has reached its extreme logical conclusion; it is therefore an end-term. Belief in program was the mark and the *glory* of our grandfathers—in our grandsons it will be a proof of provincialism. In its place is developing even now the seed of a new resigned piety, sprung from tortured conscience and spiritual hunger, whose task will be to found a new Hither-side (*Diesseits*) that looks for secrets instead of steel-bright concepts and in the end will find them in the deeps of the "Second Religiousness."

THE FATE OF DEMOCRACY

In the beginning of a democracy the field belongs to intellect alone. History has nothing nobler and purer to show than the night session of August 4, 1789, and the Tennis-Court Oath, or the assembly in the Frankfurt Paulskirche on May 18, 1848— when men, with power in their very hands, debated general truths so long that the forces of actuality were able to rally and thrust the dreamers aside. But, meantime, that other democratic quantity lost no time in making its appearance and reminding men of the fact that one can make use of constitutional rights only when one has money. That a franchise should work even approximately as the idealist supposes it to work presumes the absence of any organized leadership operating on the electors (in *its* interest) to the extent that its available money permits. As soon as such leadership does appear, the vote ceases to possess anything more than the significance of an opinion recorded by the multitude on the individual organizations, over whose structure it possesses in the end not the slightest positive influence.

In appearance, there are vast differences between the Western, parliamentary, democracy and the democracies of the Egyptian, Chinese and Arabian Civilizations, to which the idea of a universal popular franchise is wholly alien. But in reality, for us in this age of ours, the mass is "in form" as an *electorate* in exactly the same sense as it used to be "in form" as a collectivity of obedience—namely, as an *object for a subject*—as it was "in form" in Baghdad as the sects, and in Byzantium in its monks, and elsewhere again as a dominant army or a secret society or a "state within a state." Freedom is, as always, purely *negative*. It consists in the repudiation of tradition, dynasty, Caliphate; but the executive power passes, at once and undiminished, from these institutions to new forces—party leaders, dictators, presidents, prophets and their adherents—towards which the multitude continues to be unconditionally the passive object.

The fundamental rights of a Classical people (*demos, populus*) extended to the holding of the highest state and judicial offices. For the exercise of these the people was "in form" in its Forum, where the Euclidean point-mass was corporeally assembled, and there it was the object of an influencing process in the Classical style; namely, by bodily, near and sensuous means—by a rhetoric that worked upon every ear *and eye;* by devices many of which to us would be repellent and almost intolerable, such as rehearsed sob-effects and the rending of garments;[2] by shameless flattery of the audience, fantastic lies about opponents; by the employment of brilliant phrases and resounding cadenzas (of which there came to be a perfect repertory for this place and purpose); by games and presents; by threats and blows; but, above all, by money. We have its beginnings in the Athens of 400, and its appalling culmination in the Rome of Caesar and Cicero. As everywhere, the elections, from being nominations of class-representatives, have become the battle-ground of party candidates, an arena ready for the intervention of money, and, from Zama onwards, of ever bigger and bigger money. "The greater became the wealth which was capable of concentration in the hands of individuals, the more the fight for political power developed into a question of money." It is unnecessary to say more. And yet, in a deeper sense, it would be wrong to speak of corruption. It is not a matter of degeneracy, it is the democratic ethos itself that is foredoomed of necessity to take such forms when it reaches maturity. In the reforms of the Censor Appius Claudius (310), who was beyond doubt a true Hellenist and constitutional ideologue of the type of Madame Roland's circle, there was certainly no question but

---

[2] Even Caesar, at fifty years of age, was obliged to play this comedy at the Rubicon for his soldiers because they were used to it and expected it when anything was asked of them. It corresponds to the "chest-tones of deep conviction" of our political assemblies.

that of the franchise as such, and not at all of the arts of gerry-mandering—but the effect was simply to prepare the way for those arts. Not in the scheme as such, but from the first applications of it, race-quality emerged, and very rapidly it forced its way to complete dominance. After all, in a dictatorship of money it is hardly fair to describe the employment of money as a sign of decadence.

The career of office in Rome from the time when its course took form as a series of elections, required so large a capital that every politician was the debtor of his entire entourage. Dinners were offered to the electors of whole wards, or free seats for the gladiatorial shows, or even (as in the case of Milo) actual cash, delivered at home—out of respect, Cicero says, for traditional morals. Election-capital rose to American dimensions, sometimes hundreds of millions of sesterces; vast as was the stock of cash available in Rome, the elections of 54 locked up so much of it that the rate of interest rose from four to eight per cent. Caesar paid out so much as aedile that Crassus had to underwrite him for twenty million before his creditors would allow him to depart to his province, and in his candidature for the office of Pontifex Maximus he so overstrained his credit that failure would have ruined him, and his opponent Catulus could seriously offer to buy him off. But the conquest and exploitation of Gaul—this also an undertaking motived by finance—made him the richest man in the world. In truth, Pharsalus was won there in advance. For it was for *power* that Caesar amassed these milliards, like Cecil Rhodes, and not because he delighted in wealth like Verres or even like Crassus, who was first and foremost a financier and only secondarily a politician. Caesar grasped the fact that on the soil of a democracy constitutional rights signify nothing without money and everything with it.

THE PRESS

Now, whereas the Classical, and supremely the Forum of Rome, drew the mass of the people together as a visible body in order to compel it to make that use of its rights which was desired of it, the "contemporary" English-American politics have created *through the press* a force-field of world-wide intellectual and financial tensions in which every individual unconsciously takes up the place allotted to him, so that he must think, will and act as a ruling personality somewhere or other in the distance thinks fit. This is dynamics against statics, Faustian against Apollinian world-feeling, the passion of the third dimension against the pure sensible present. Man does not speak to man; the press and its associate, the electrical news-service, keep the waking-consciousness of whole peoples and continents under a deafening drum-fire of theses, catchwords, standpoints, scenes, feelings, day by day and year by year, so that every Ego becomes a mere function of a monstrous intellectual Something. Money does not pass, politically, from one hand to the other. It does not turn itself into cards and wine. It is turned into *force*, and its quantity determines the intensity of its working influence.

Gunpowder and printing belong together—both discovered at the culmination of the Gothic, both arising out of Germanic technical thought—as *the two* grand means of Faustian distance-tactics. The Reformation in the beginning of the Late period witnessed the first flysheets and the first field-guns, the French Revolution in the beginning of the Civilization witnessed the first tempest of pamphlets in the autumn of 1788 and the first mass-fire of artillery at Valmy. But with this the printed word, produced in vast quantity and distributed over enormous areas, became an uncanny weapon in the hands of him who knew how to use it. In France it was still in 1788 a matter of expressing private convictions, but England was already past that, and deliberately seeking to produce impressions on the reader. The war of articles, flysheets, spurious memoirs, that was waged from London on French soil against Napoleon is the first great example.

Today we live so cowed under the bombardment of this intellectual artillery that hardly anyone can attain to the inward detachment that is required for a clear view of the monstrous drama. The will-to-power operating under a pure democratic disguise has accomplished its task so well that the object's sense of freedom is actually flattered by the most thorough-going enslavement that has ever existed.

What is truth? For the multitude, that which it continually reads and hears. A forlorn little drop may settle somewhere and collect grounds on which to determine "the truth"—but what it obtains is just *its* truth. The other, the public truth of the moment, which alone matters for effects and successes in the fact-world, is today a product of the Press. What the Press wills, is true. Its commanders evoke, transform, interchange truths. Three weeks of press-work, and the "truth" is acknowledged by everybody.

With the political press is bound up the need of universal school-education, which in the Classical world was completely lacking. In this demand there is an element—quite unconscious —of desiring to shepherd the masses, as the object of party politics, into the newspaper's power-area. The idealist of the early democracy regarded popular education, without *arrière pensée,* as enlightenment pure and simple, and even today one finds here and there weak heads that become enthusiastic on the Freedom of the Press—but it is precisely this that smooths the path for the coming Caesars of the world-press. Those who have learnt to read succumb to their power, and the visionary self-determination of Late democracy becomes a thorough-going determination of the people by the powers whom the printed word obeys.

No tamer has his animals more under his power. Unleash the people as reader-mass and it will storm through the streets and hurl itself upon the target indicated, terrifying and breaking windows; a hint to the press-staff and it will become quiet and go home. The Press today is an army with carefully organized arms and branches, with journalists as officers, and readers as soldiers. But here, as in every army, the soldier obeys blindly, and war-aims and operation-plans change without his knowledge. The reader neither knows, nor is allowed to know, the purposes for which he is used, nor even the role that he is to play. A more appalling caricature of freedom of thought cannot be imagined. Formerly a man did not dare to think freely. Now he dares, but cannot; his will to think is only a willingness to think to order, and this is what he feels as *his* liberty.

The dictature of party leaders supports itself upon that of the Press. The competitors strive by means of money to detach readers—nay, peoples—*en masse* from the hostile allegiance and to bring them under their own mind-training. And all that they learn in this mind-training is what it is considered that they should know—a higher will puts together the picture of their world for them. There is no need now, as there was for Baroque princes, to impose military-service liability on the subject—one whips their souls with articles, telegrams and pictures until they *clamour* for weapons and force their leaders into a conflict to which they *willed* to be forced.

This is the end of Democracy. If in the world of truths it is *proof* that decides all, in that of facts it is *success*. Success means that one being triumphs over the others. Life has won through, and the dreams of the world-improvers have turned out to be but the tools of *master*-natures. In the Late Democracy, *race* bursts forth and either makes ideals its slaves or throws them scornfully into the pit. It was so, too, in Egyptian Thebes, in Rome, in China—but in no other Civilization has the will-to-power manifested itself in so inexorable a form as in this of ours. The thought, and consequently the action, of the mass are kept under iron pressure—for which reason, and for which reason only, men are permitted to be readers and voters—that is, in a dual slavery—while the parties become the obedient retinues of a few, and the shadow of coming Caesarism already touches them.

Through money, democracy becomes its own destroyer, after money has destroyed intellect. But, just *because* the illusion that actuality can allow itself to be improved by the ideas of any Zeno or Marx has fled away; because men have learned that in the realm of reality one power-will *can be overthrown only by another* (for that is the great human experience of Contending States periods); there wakes at last a deep yearning for all old and worthy tradition that still lingers alive. Men are tired to disgust of money-economy. They hope for salvation from somewhere or other, for some true ideal of honour and chivalry, of inward nobility, of unselfishness and duty. And now dawns the time when the form-filled powers of the blood, which the rationalism of the Megalopolis has suppressed, reawaken in the depths. Everything in the order of dynastic tradition and old nobility that has saved itself up for the future, everything that there is of high money-disdaining ethic, everything that is intrinsically sound enough to be, in Frederick the Great's words, the *servant*—the hard-working, self-sacrificing, caring *servant* —of the State—all this becomes suddenly the focus of immense life-forces. Caesarism *grows* on the soil of Democracy, but its roots thread deeply into the underground of blood tradition. The Classical Caesar derived his power from the Tribunate, and his dignity and therewith his permanency from his being the Princeps. Here too the soul of old Gothic wakens anew. The spirit of the knightly orders overpowers plunderous Vikingism. The mighty ones of the future may possess the earth as their private property—for the great political form of the Culture is irremediably in ruin—but it matters not, for, formless and limitless as their power may be, it has a task. And this task is the unwearying care for this world as it is, which is the very opposite of the interestedness of the money-power age, and demands high honour and conscientiousness. But for this very reason there now sets in the final battle between Democracy and Caesarism, between the leading forces of dictatorial money-economics and the *purely political* will-to-order of the Caesars.

XX

THE FORM-WORLD OF
ECONOMIC LIFE:
MONEY

ECONOMIC LIFE

THE standpoint from which to comprehend the economic history of great Cultures is not to be looked for on economic ground. That which we call national economy today is built up on premisses that are openly and specifically English. Credit-money, in the special form imparted to it by the relations of world-trade and export-industry in a peasantless England, serves as the foundation whereupon to define words like capital, value, price, property—and the definitions are then transferred without more ado to other Culture-stages and life-cycles. The creators of this economic *picture* were David Hume and Adam Smith. Everything that has since been written about them or against them always presupposes the critical structure and methods of their systems. This is as true of Carey and List as it is of Fourier and Lassalle. As for Smith's greatest adversary, Marx, it matters little how loudly one protests against English capitalism when one is thoroughly imbued with its images; the protest is itself a recognition, and its only aim is, through a new kind of accounting, to confer upon objects the advantage of being subjects.

From Adam Smith to Marx economic thought is nothing but self-analysis of the economic thinking of a single Culture on a particular development-level. Rationalistic through and through, it starts from Material and its conditions, needs and motives, instead of from the *Soul*—of generations, Estates and peoples— and its creative power. It takes economic life to be something that can be accounted for without remainder by visible causes and effects, something of which the structure is quite mechanical and completely self-contained and even, finally, something that stands in some sort of causal relation to religion and politics —these again being considered as individual self-contained domains. As this outlook is the systematic and not the historical, the timeless and universal validity of its concepts and rules is an article of faith, and its ambition is to establish the one and only correct scientific method of economic management. And accordingly, wherever its truths have come into contact with the facts, it has experienced a complete fiasco—as was the case with the prophecies of bourgeois theorists concerning the World War,[1] and with those of proletarian theorists on the induction of the Soviet economy.

Up to now, therefore, there has been no national economy, in the sense of a morphology of the economic *side* of life and more particularly of that side in the life of the high Cultures, with their individual styles according to stage, tempo and duration. Economics has no system, but a physiognomy. To fathom the secret of its inner form, its *soul*, demands the physiognomic flair. But this faculty of "judgment" can be awakened, and the way to awaken it is through the sympathetic outlook on history which gives a shrewd idea of the race-instincts, which are at work in the economic as in other constituents of active existence, symbolically shaping the external position—the economic "stuff," the need—in harmony with their own inner character. *All economic life is the expression of a soul-life.*

The attempt which follows is meant only as a fleeting survey of the possibilities here available.

ECONOMICS AND POLITICS

Economics and politics are sides of the *one* livingly flowing current of being, and not of the waking-consciousness, the intellect. Being "in form" has two sides—political and economic. They overlie, they support, they oppose each other, but the political is unconditionally the first. Life's will is to preserve itself and to prevail, or, rather, to make itself stronger in order that it may prevail. But in the economic state of fitness the being-streams

---

[1] It was the opinion of the expert, almost everywhere, that the economic consequences of general mobilization would compel the breaking up of hostilities within a few weeks.

are in order as *self*-regarding, whereas in a political they must be *other*-regarding. Whole peoples have lost the tense force of their race through the gnawing wretchedness of their living. Here men die *of* something and not *for* something. Politics sacrifices men for an idea, they fall for an idea; but economy merely wastes them away. In war life is elevated by death, often to that point of irresistible force whose mere existence guarantees victory, but in the economic life hunger awakens the ugly, vulgar and wholly unmetaphysical sort of fearfulness for one's life under which the higher form-world of a Culture miserably collapses and the naked struggle for existence of the human beasts begins.

For this very reason the significance of economic history is something quite different from that of political. Economics is only a foundation, for Being that is in any way meaningful. What really signifies is not *that* an individual or a people is "in condition," well nourished and fruitful, but *for what* he or it is so; and the higher man climbs historically, the more conspicuously his political and religious will to inward symbolism and force of expression towers above everything in the way of form and depth that the economic life as such possesses. It is only with the coming of the "Civilization," when the whole form-world begins to ebb, that mere life-preserving begins to outline itself, nakedly and insistently—this is the time when the banal assertion that "hunger and love" are the driving forces of life ceases to be ashamed of itself; when life comes to mean, not a waxing in strength for the task, but a matter of "happiness of the greatest number," of comfort and ease, of *"panem et circenses"*; and when, in the place of grand politics, we have economic politics as an end in itself.

Since economics belongs to the race side of life, it possesses, like politics, a customary ethic and not a moral—yet again the distinction of nobility and priesthood, facts and truths. A vocation-class, like an Estate, possesses a *matter-of-course* feeling for (not good and evil, but) good and bad. Not to have this feeling is to be void of honour. For those engaged *in* the economic life, too, honour stands as central criterion, with its tact and fine flair for what is "the right thing"—something quite separate from the sin-idea underlying the religious contemplation *of* the world. There exist, not only a very definite vocational honour amongst merchants, craftsmen and peasants, but equally definite gradations downward for the shopkeeper, the exporter, the banker, the contractor and even, as we all know, for thieves and beggars, insofar as two or three of them feel themselves as fellow-practitioners. No one has stated or written out these customary-ethics, but they exist, and, like class-ethics everywhere and always, they are binding only within the circle of membership. Along with the noble virtues of loyalty and courage, chivalry and comradeship, which are found in every vocational society, there appear clean-cut notions of the ethical value of industry, of success, of work, and an astonishing sense of distinction and apartness. This sort of thing a man *has*—and without knowing much about it, for custom is evidenced to consciousness only when it is infringed—while, on the contrary, the prohibitions of religion which are timeless, universally valid, but never realizable ideals, must be learned before a man can know or attempt to follow them.

Religious-ascetic fundamentals such as "selfless," "sinless," are without meaning in the economic life. For the true saint business in itself is sinful, and not merely taking of interest, or pleasure in riches, or the envy of the poor. The saying concerning the "lilies of the field" is for deeply religious (and philosophical) natures unreservedly true. The whole weight of their being lies outside economics and politics and general facts of "this world." We see it in Jesus' times and St. Bernard's and in the Russian soul of today; we see it too in the way of life of a Diogenes and a Kant. For its sake men choose voluntary poverty and itinerancy and hide themselves in cells and studies. Economic activity is *never* found in a religion or a philosophy, always only in the political organism of a *church* or the social organism of a theorizing fellowship; it is ever a compromise with "this world" and an index of the presence of a will-to-power.

All higher economic life develops itself on and over a peasantry. Peasantry, *per se*, does not presuppose any basis but itself. It is, so to say, race-in-itself, plant-like and historyless, producing and using wholly for itself, with an outlook on the world that sweepingly regards every other economic existence as incidental and contemptible. To this *producing* kind of economy there is presently opposed an *acquisitive* kind, which makes use of the former as an object—as a source of nourishment, tribute or plunder. Politics and trade are in their beginnings quite inseparable, both being masterful, personal, warlike, both with a hunger for power and booty. Primitive war is always also booty-war, and primitive trade intimately related to plunder and piracy. The Icelandic sagas often narrate how the Vikings would agree with a town population for a market-peace of a fortnight, after which weapons were drawn and booty-making started.

Politics and trade in developed form—the art of achieving material successes over an opponent by means of intellectual superiority—are both a replacement of war by other means. Every kind of diplomacy is of a business nature, every business of a diplomatic, and both are based upon penetrative judgment of men and physiognomic tact.

But the genuine prince and statesman wants to rule, and the genuine merchant wants only to be wealthy, and here the acquisitive economy divides to pursue aim and means separately. One may aim at booty for the sake of power, or at power for the sake of booty.

He who is out for purely economic advantages—as the Carthaginians were in Roman times and, in a far greater degree still, the Americans in ours—is correspondingly incapable of purely political *thinking*. In the decisions of high politics he is ever deceived and made a tool of, as the case of Wilson shows—especially when the absence of statesmanlike instinct leaves a chair vacant for moral sentiments. This is why the great economic groupings of the present day (for example, employers' and employees' unions) pile one political failure on another, unless indeed they find a real political politician as leader, and he—makes use of them. Economic and political thinking, in spite of a high degree of consonance of form, are in direction (and therefore in all tactical details) basically different. Great business successes awaken an unbridled sense of *public* power—in the very word "capital" one catches an unmistakable undertone of this. But it is only in a few individuals that the colour and direction of their willing and their criteria of situations of things undergo change. Only when a man has really ceased to feel his enterprise as "his own business," and its aim as the simple amassing of property, does it become possible for the captain of industry to become the statesman, the Cecil Rhodes.

All this, however, is the very manifestation of the hidden course of a high Culture. In the beginning appear the primary orders, nobility and priesthood, with their symbolism of Time and Space. Political life, like religious experience, has its fixed place, its ordained adepts and its allotted aims for facts and truths alike, in a well-ordered society, and down below, the economic life moves unconscious along a sure path. Then the stream of being becomes entangled in the stone structures of the town, and intellect and money thenceforward take over its historical guidance. The heroic and the saintly with their youthful symbolic force become rarer, and withdraw into narrower and narrower circles. Cool bourgeois clarity takes their place. In the frictions of the city the stream of being loses its strict rich form. Elementary economic factors come to the surface and interplay with the remains of form-imbued politics, just as sovereign science at the same time adds religion to its stock of objects. Over a life of economics political self-satisfaction spreads a critical-edifying world-sentiment. But out of it all emerge, in place of the decayed Estates, the individual life-courses, big with true political or religious force, that are to become destiny for the whole.

THINKING IN TERMS OF GOODS AND IN TERMS OF MONEY

With the coming of its Spring there begins in every Culture an economic life of settled form. The life of the population is entirely that of the peasant in the countryside.

That which separates out from a life in which everyone is alike producer and consumer is *goods,* and traffic in goods is the mark of all early intercourse. We say that a man is endowed with this world's "goods," the word *"possession"* takes us back right into the plant-like origin of property, into which this particular being—no other—has grown, from the roots up. Exchange in these periods is a process whereby goods pass from one circle of life into another. They are valued with reference to life, according to a sliding-scale of *felt* relation to the moment. There is neither a conception of value nor a kind or amount of goods that constitutes a general measure—for gold and coin are goods too, whose rarity and indestructibility causes them to be highly prized.

Into the rhythm and course of this barter the dealer comes only as an intervener. In the market the acquisitive and the creative economics encounter one another, but even at places where fleets and caravans unload, trade appears only as the *organ* of countryside traffic.[2]

With the soul of the town a quite other kind of life awakens. The decisive point is this—the true urban man is *not* a producer in the prime terrene sense. He has not the inward linkage with soil or with the goods that pass through his hands.

With this, goods become wares, exchange turnover, *and in place of thinking in goods we have thinking in money.*

With this, a purely extensional something, a form of limit-defining, is abstracted from the visible objects of economics just as mathematical thought abstracts something from the mechanistically conceived environment. Abstract money corresponds exactly to abstract number. Both are entirely inorganic. The economic picture is reduced exclusively to quantities, whereas the important point about "goods" had been their quality.

It is an error of all modern money-theories that they start from the value-token or even the material of the payment-medium instead of from the form of economic thought.[3] In reality, money, like number and law, is a *category of thought*. Money-value is a numerical value measured by a unit of reckoning. This exact "value-in-itself," like number-in-itself, the man of the town, the man without roots, is the first to imagine. Only in the economy-picture of the real townsman are there objective values and kinds of values which have an existence apart from his private needs, as thought-elements of a generalized validity, although in actuality every individual has his proper system of values and

---

[2] And, consequently, on a very small scale. As foreign trade was in those days highly adventurous and appealed to the imagination, it was as a rule immensely exaggerated. The "great" merchants of Venice and the Hansa about 1300 were hardly the equals of the more distinguished craftsmen. The turnover of even the Medici or the Fugger about 1400 was equivalent to that of a shop-business in a small town today. The largest merchant vessels, in which usually several traders held part shares, were much smaller than modern German river-barges, and made only *one* considerable voyage each year. The celebrated wool-export of England, a main element of Hanseatic trade, amounted about 1270 to hardly as much as the contents of two modern goods-trains.

[3] Marks and dollars are no more "money" than metres and grammes are "forces." *Pieces* of money are real values. It is only our ignorance of Classical physics that has saved us from confusing gravitation with a pound-weight—in our mathematics, with its Classical basis, we still mix number with magnitude, and our imitation of Classical coinage has brought about the same confusion between money and pieces of money.

his proper stock of the most varied kinds of value, and feels the ruling prices of the market as "cheap" or "dear" with reference to these.[4]

Whereas the earlier mankind *compares* goods, and does so not by means of the reason only, the later *reckons* the values of wares, and does so by rigid unqualitative measures. Whether and how this measure of value finds symbolic expression in a value-sign—as the written, spoken or represented number-sign is, in a sense, number—depends on the economic style of the particular Culture, each of which produces a different sort of money. The common condition for the appearance of this is the existence of an urban population that thinks economically in terms of it, and it is its particular character that settles whether the value-token shall serve also as payment-medium; thus the Classical coin and *probably* the Babylonian silver did so serve, whereas the Egyptian *deben* (raw copper weighed out in pounds) was a measure of exchange, but neither token nor payment-medium. The Western and the "contemporary" Chinese banknote,[5] again, is a medium, but not a measure.

The outcome of this way of thinking is that the old *property,* bound up with life and the soil, gives way to the *fortune,* which is essentially mobile and qualitatively undefined: it does not *consist in* goods, but it is *laid out in* them. Considered by itself, it is a purely numerical quantum of money-value.

As the seat of this thinking, the city becomes the money-market, the centre of values, and a stream of money-values begins to infuse, intellectualize and command the stream of goods. *And with this the trader, from being an organ of economic life, becomes its master.* Thinking in money is always, in one way or another, trade or business thinking. It presupposes the productive economy of the land, and, therefore, is always primarily

~~~~~~

[4] Similarly all value-theories, however objective they are meant to be, are developed—and inevitably so—out of a subjective principle. That of Marx, for example, defines value in the way that promotes the interest of the manual worker, the effort of the discoverer or the organizer seeming to him, therefore, valueless. But it would be wrong to describe this as "erroneous." All these theories are "right" for their supporters and "wrong" for their opponents, and it is not reasons but *life* that settles whether one is a supporter or an opponent.

[5] The Western introduced (on a very modest scale) by the Bank of England from the end of the eighteenth century, the Chinese dating from the period of the Contending States.

acquisitive, for there is no third course. The very words "acquisition," "gain," "speculation," point to a profit tricked off from the goods *en route* to the consumer—an *intellectual plunder*—and for that reason are inapplicable to the early peasantry. With money-traffic there appears between producer and consumer, as though between two separate worlds, the third party, the *middleman,* whose thought is dominated *a priori* by the business side of life. He forces the producer to offer, and the consumer to inquire of him. He elevates mediation to a monopoly and thereafter to economic primacy, and forces the other two to be "in form" in *his* interest, to prepare the wares according to *his* reckonings and to cheapen them under the pressure of *his* offers.

He who commands this mode of thinking is the master of money. In all the Cultures evolution takes this road. Lysias informs us in his oration against the corn-merchants that the speculators at the Piraeus frequently spread reports of the wreck of a grain-fleet or of the outbreak of war, in order to produce a panic. In Hellenistic-Roman times it was a widespread practice to arrange for land to go out of cultivation, or for imports to be held in bond, in order to force up prices. In the Egyptian New Empire wheat-corners in the American style were made possible by a bill-discounting that is fully comparable with the banking operations of the West. Cleomenes, Alexander the Great's administrator for Egypt, was able by book transactions to get the whole corn-supply into his own hands, thereby producing a famine far and wide in Greece and raking in immense gains for himself. To think economically on any terms but these is simply to become a mere pawn in the money-operations of the great city. All highly developed economy is urban economy. World-economy itself, the characteristic economy of all Civilizations, ought properly to be called world-city-economy. The destinies even of this world-economy are now decided in a few places, the "money-markets" of the world. Finally, money is the form of intellectual energy in which the ruler-will, the political and social, technical and mental, creative power, the craving for a full-sized life, are concentrated. Shaw is entirely right when he says: "The universal regard for money is the one hopeful fact in our civilization . . . the two things [money and life] are inseparable: money is the counter that enables life to be distributed socially: it *is* life. . . ." What is here described as Civilization, then, is the stage of a Culture at which tradition and personality have lost their immediate effectiveness, and every idea, to be actualized, has to be put into terms of money.

CLASSICAL AND WESTERN MONEY-THOUGHT

[*Every culture has its own way of thinking in money and its own money-symbol according to its principle of valuation. The Apollinian idea of money as magnitude and the Faustian conception of money as function are in direct opposition to one another. Economically, as in other ways, Classical man saw the world surrounding him as a sum of bodies; money is also a body. Value as magnitude had long existed (the talent). About 650 appeared the coin. The coin as money is a purely Classical phenomenon and only possible according to Euclidean ideas but then creatively dominant over economic life. Notions like Income, Property, Debt, Capital, here mean a sum of valuable objects in hand. Property was always mobile cash. It resulted that in the period of unlimited plutocracy, after Hannibal, the naturally limited quantity of valuable metals became quite inadequate to cover needs. The slave, who was a thing not a person, came to have a negotiable value. Wars were waged for the sake of booty in slaves. Private enterprises hunted slaves along the Mediterranean coast.*

The discovery of double-entry book-keeping in 1496 "coincided" with the discovery of Classical coinage (650). Double-entry book-keeping is a pure analysis of the "value-space," referred to a co-ordinate system which starts with the "Firm." A field of money tensions lies in space and assigns to every object a positive or negative effect-value, which is represented by a book entry. The symbol of the functional money, thus imagined, and which can be compared only with the Classical coin, is not the actual book entry, nor yet the share-voucher, cheque, or note, but the act by which the function is performed in writing and the role of the security is simply to be historical evidence of this act. Our economy-world is ordered by force and mass as the Classical is related to stuff and magnitude.

The West has followed the Classical habit of striking coins in the same way that, in Gothic times, it adopted Roman law

*with its equating of things to bodily magnitudes, and the
Euclidean mathematic, which rested upon the conception
of number as magnitude. So it befell that the evolution of
these three intellectual form-worlds took the shape of a
progressive emancipation from the notion of magnitude.*]

MONEY AND WORK

It is entirely consonant with the illusion that money and pieces
of money are the same, to measure the value of a thing against
the magnitude of a quantity of work. The purely executive work
(which alone Marx takes into account) is in reality nothing but
the function of an inventive, ordering and organizing work; it
is from this that the other derives its meaning, relative value,
and even possibility of being done at all. The whole world-
economy since the discovery of the steam-engine has been the
creation of a quite small number of superior heads, without
whose high-grade work everything else would never have come
into being. But this achievement is of creative thinking, not a
quantum, and its value is not to be weighed against a certain
number of coins. Rather it *is* itself money—Faustian money,
namely, which is not minted, but mentally devised as an instrument by Faustian life—and it is the quality of that life which
elevates the thought to the significance of a fact. *Thinking in
money generates money*—that is the secret of the world-
economy. When an organizing magnate writes down a million
on paper, that million exists, for the personality as an economic
centre vouches for a corresponding heightening of the economic
energy of his field. This, and nothing else, is the meaning of the
word "Credit" for us. As every stream of Being consists of a
minority of leaders and huge majority of led, so *every sort of
economy consists in leader work and executive work.*

And, similarly, thinking in money has subjects and objects:
those who by force of their personality generate and guide
money, and those who are maintained by money. Money of the
Faustian brand is the *force* distilled from economy-dynamics of
the Faustian brand, and it appertains to the destiny of the individual (on the economic side of his life-destiny) whether he is
inwardly constituted to represent a part of this force, or whether,
on the contrary, he is nothing in relation to it but mass.

XXI

THE FORM-WORLD OF
ECONOMIC LIFE:
THE MACHINE

TECHNIQUE is as old as free-moving life itself. The original relation between a waking-microcosm and its macrocosm—"Nature"—consists in a mental sensation which rises from mere sense-*impressions* to sense-*judgment,* so that already it works critically (that is, separatingly) or, what comes to the same thing, *causal-analytically.*

The decisive turn in the history of the higher life occurs when the ascertaining of nature's laws is followed by their practical application. With this, technique becomes more or less sovereign and the instinctive prime-experience changes into a definitely "conscious" prime-*knowing.* Thought has emancipated itself from sensation. It is the *language of words* that brings about this epochal change.

With that, the system of identification-marks develops into a theory, a *picture* which is arrived at from the technique of the day and not vice versa—whether this be a day of high-level Civilized technics or a day of simplest beginnings—by way of *abstraction,* as a piece of waking-consciousness uncommitted to activity. One "knows" what one wants, but much must have happened for one to have that knowledge, and we must make no mistake as to its character. By numerical experience man is enabled to switch the secret on and off, but he has not discovered it. But through this technique the waking-consciousness does, all the same, intervene masterfully in the fact-world. Life *makes use* of thought as an "open sesame," and at the peak of many a Civilization, in its great cities, there arrives finally the moment when technical critique becomes tired of being life's servant and makes itself tyrant. Western Culture is even now experiencing an orgy of this unbridled thought, and on a tragic scale. The stock of discoveries grew and grew. Often they were made and forgotten and made again, were imitated, shunned, improved. But in the end they constituted for whole continents a store of *self-evident* resources.

On this foundation arose the technique of the higher Cultures, expressive in quality and colour and passion of the whole soul of these major entities. It need hardly be said that Classical man, who felt himself and his environment alike Euclidean, set himself *a priori* in hostile opposition to the very idea of technique. If by "Classical" technique we mean something that (along with the rest that we comprehend in the adjective) rose with determined effort above the universal dead perfection of the Mycenaean age, then there was no Classical technique. Its triremes were glorified row-boats, its catapults and onagers mere substitutes for arms and fists—not to be named in the same breath with the war-engines of Assyria and China—and as for Hero and his like, it was flukes and not discoveries that they achieved. They lacked the inner weight, the fatedness of their moment, the deep necessity.

Very different is the Faustian technics, which with all its passion of the third dimension, and from earliest Gothic days, thrusts itself upon Nature, with the firm resolve to *be its master*. Here, and only here, is the connexion of insight and utilization a matter of course. Theory is working hypothesis [1] from the outset. The Classical investigator "contemplated" like Aristotle's deity, the Arabian sought as alchemist for magical means (such as the Philosophers' Stone) whereby to possess himself of Nature's treasures *without effort,* but the Western strives to *direct* the world according to his will.

The Faustian inventor and discoverer is a unique type. The primitive force of his will, the brilliance of his visions, the steely energy of his practical ponderings, must appear queer and incomprehensible to anyone at the standpoint of another Culture, but for us they are in the blood. Our whole Culture has a discoverer's soul. To *dis*-cover that which is not seen, to draw it

[1] The Chinese Culture, too, made almost all these European discoveries on its own account—including compass, telescope, printing, gunpowder, paper, porcelain—but the Chinese did not wrest, but *wheedled,* things out of Nature. No doubt he felt the advantages of his knowledge and turned it to account, but he did not hurl himself upon it to exploit it.

into the light-world of the inner eye so as to master it—that was its stubborn passion from the first days on. All its great inventions slowly ripened in the deeps, to emerge at last with the necessity of a Destiny. All of them were very nearly approached by the high-hearted, happy research of the early Gothic monks. Here, if anywhere, the religious origins of all technical thought are manifested. These meditative discoverers in their cells, who with prayers and fastings *wrung* God's secret out of him, felt that they were *serving* God thereby. But for all of them, too, there was the truly Faustian danger of the Devil's having a hand in the game, the risk that he was leading them in spirit to that mountain on which he promises all the power of the earth. Again and again they succumbed to this ambition; they forced this secret out of God in order themselves to be God. They listened for the laws of the cosmic pulse in order to overpower it. And so they created the *idea of the machine* as a small cosmos obeying the will of man alone.

Then followed, however, simultaneously with Rationalism, the discovery of the steam-engine, which upset everything and transformed economic life from the foundations up. Till then Nature had rendered services, but now she was tied to the yoke as *a slave*, and her work was as though in contempt measured by a standard of horse-power. As the horse-powers run to millions and milliards, the numbers of the population increase and increase, on a scale that no other Culture ever thought possible. This growth is a *product of the Machine*, which insists on being used and directed, and to that end centuples the powers of each individual. For the sake of the machine, human life becomes precious. *Work* becomes the great word of ethical thinking; in the eighteenth century it loses its derogatory implication in all languages. The machine works and forces man to co-operate.

And what now develops, in the space of hardly a century, is a drama of such greatness that the men of a future Culture, with other soul and other passions, will hardly be able to resist the conviction that "in those days" Nature herself was tottering. The technique will leave traces of its heyday behind it when all else is lost and forgotten. For this Faustian passion has altered the Face of the Earth.

This is the outward- and upward-straining life-feeling—true descendant, therefore, of the Gothic—as expressed in Goethe's Faust monologue when the steam-engine was yet young. The intoxicated soul wills to fly above Space and Time. An ineffable longing tempts him to indefinable horizons.

Never save here has a microcosm felt itself superior to its macrocosm, but here the little life-units have by the sheer force of their intellect mastered inert matter. It is a triumph, so far as we can see, unparalleled. Only this our Culture has achieved it, and perhaps only for a few centuries.

But for that very reason Faustian man has become *the slave of his creation*. The machine has forcibly increased his numbers and changed his habits in a direction from which there is no return. The peasant, the hand-worker, even the merchant, appear suddenly as inessential in comparison with the *three great figures that the Machine has bred and trained up in the cause of its development: the entrepreneur, the engineer and the factory-worker*. Out of a quite small branch of manual work there has grown up (*in this one Culture alone*) a mighty tree that casts it shadow over all the other vocations—namely, *the economy of the machine-industry*.[2] It forces the entrepreneur not less than the workman to obedience. *Both* become slaves, and not masters, of the machine, which now for the first time develops its devilish and occult power. Not merely the importance but the very existence of industry depends upon the existence of the hundred thousand talented, rigorously schooled brains that command the technique and develop it onward and onward. The quiet engineer it is who is the machine's master and destiny. His thought is as possibility what the machine is as actuality. There have been fears, thoroughly materialistic fears, of the exhaustion of the coal-fields. But so long as there are worthy technical path-finders, dangers of this sort have no existence. When, and only when, the crop of recruits for this army fails—this army whose thought-work forms one inward unit with

---

[2] So long as it dominates the earth, every non-European tries and will try to fathom the secret of this terrible weapon. Nevertheless, inwardly he abhors it, be he Indian or Japanese, Russian or Arab. It is something fundamental in the essence of the Magian soul that leads the Jew, as entrepreneur and engineer, to stand aside from the creation proper of machines and devote himself to the business side of their production. But so also the Russian looks with fear and hatred at this tyranny of wheels, cables and rails, and if he adapts himself for today and tomorrow to the inevitable, yet there will come a time when he will *blot out the whole thing from his memory and his environment,* and create about himself a wholly new world, in which nothing of this Devil's technique is left.

the work of the machine—the industry must flicker out in spite of all that managerial energy and the workers can do. Suppose that, in future generations, the most gifted minds were to find their soul's health more important than all the powers of this world; suppose that, under the influence of the metaphysic and mysticism that is taking the place of rationalism today, the very elite of intellect that is now concerned with the machine comes to be overpowered by a growing sense of its *Satanism* (it is the step from Roger Bacon to Bernard of Clairvaux)—then nothing can hinder the end of this grand drama that has been a play of intellects, with hands as mere auxiliaries.

But titanic, too, is the onslaught of money upon this intellectual force. Industry, too, is earth-bound like the yeoman. It has its station, and its materials stream up out of the earth. Only high finance is *wholly* free, wholly intangible. Since 1789 the banks, and with them the bourses, have developed themselves on the credit-needs of an industry growing ever more enormous, as a power on their own account, and they will (as money wills in every Civilization) to be the only power. The ancient wrestle between the productive and the acquisitive economies intensifies now into a silent gigantomachy of intellects, fought out in the lists of the world-cities. This battle is the despairing struggle of technical thought to maintain its liberty against money-thought.[3]

The dictature of money marches on, tending to its material peak, in the Faustian Civilization as in every other. And now something happens that is intelligible only to one who has penetrated to the essence of money. If it were anything tangible, then its existence would be forever—but, as it is a form of thought, *it fades out as soon as it has thought its economic world to finality,* and has no more material upon which to feed. It thrust into the life of the yeoman's countryside and set the earth moving; its thought transformed every sort of handicraft; today it presses victoriously upon industry to make the productive work of entrepreneur and engineer and labourer alike its spoil. The machine with its human retinue, the real queen of this century, is in danger of succumbing to a stronger power. Money, also, is

---

[3] Compared with this mighty contest between the two handfuls of steel-hard men of race and of immense intellect—which the simple citizen neither observes nor comprehends—the battle of mere interests between the employing class and the workers' Socialism sinks into insignificance when regarded from the distant world-historical viewpoint.

beginning to lose its authority, and the last conflict is at hand in which Civilization receives its conclusive form—the conflict *between* money and blood.

The coming of Caesarism breaks the dictature of money and its political weapon, democracy. After a long triumph of world-city economy and its interests over political creative force, the political side of life manifests itself after all as the stronger of the two. The sword is victorious over money, the master-will subdues again the plunderer-will. If we call these money-powers "Capitalism," [4] then we may designate as Socialism the will to call into life a mighty politico-economic order that transcends all class interests, a system of *lofty* thoughtfulness and duty-sense that keeps the whole in fine condition for the decisive battle of its history, and this battle is also the battle of money and law. The *private* powers of the economy want free paths for their acquisition of great resources. No legislation must stand in their way. They want to make the laws themselves, in their interests, and to that end they make use of the tool they have made for themselves, democracy, the subsidized party. Law needs, in order to resist this onslaught, a high tradition that finds its satisfaction not in the heaping up of riches, but in the tasks of true rulership, above and beyond all money-advantage. *A power can be overthrown only by another power,* not by a principle, and only one power that can confront money is left. Money is overthrown and abolished by blood. *Life* is alpha and omega, the cosmic stream in microcosmic form. It is *the* fact of facts within the world-as-history. Before the irresistible rhythm of the generation-sequence, everything built up by the waking-consciousness in its intellectual world vanishes at the last. Ever in History it is life and life only—race-quality, the triumph of the will-to-power—and not the victory of truths, discoveries or money that signifies. And so the drama of a high Culture—that wondrous world of deities, arts, thoughts, battles, cities—closes with the return of the pristine facts of the blood eternal that is one and the same as the ever-circling cosmic flow. The bright imaginative Waking-Being submerges itself into the silent service of Being, as the Chinese and Roman empires tell us. Time triumphs over Space, and it is

---

[4] In this sense the interest-politics of the workers' movements also belong to it, in that their object is not to overcome the money-values, but to possess them.

Time whose inexorable movement embeds the ephemeral incident of Culture, on this planet, in the incident of Man—a form wherein the incident of life flows on for a time, while behind it all the streaming horizons of geological and stellar histories pile up in the light-world of our eyes.

For us, however, whom a Destiny has placed in this Culture and at this moment of its development—the moment when money is celebrating its last victories, and the Caesarism that is to succeed approaches with quiet, firm step—our direction, willed and obligatory at once, is set for us within narrow limits, and on any other terms life is not worth the living. We have not the freedom to reach to this or to that, but the freedom to do the necessary or to do nothing. And a task that historic necessity has set *will* be accomplished with the individual or against him.

Ducunt Fata volentem, nolentem trahunt.

INDEX

Abaca, Evaristo F. Dall', sonatas, 150

Abbassids, court life, 275

Abel, Niels H., mathematic problems, 64

Absolutism. *See* Politics

Abu Bekr, Puritanism, 343

Act, and portrait, 136, 139, 142

Actium, battle, importance, 270

Activity, as Western trait, 167; as quality of Socialism, 186–7

Actuality, as test of philosophy, 32; significance of, 87–8; and abstract thought, 260–1

Addison, Joseph, type, 134

Aeschylus, and deity, 164; tragic form and method, 167, 168; and religion, 327

Aggregates, theory, 223–4

Agriculture, effect on man, 245; farmhouse as symbol, 245

Ahmes, arithmetic, 44

Ahuramazda, as deity, 282*n.;* and Spenta Mainyu and Vohu Mano, 306*n.*

Alaric, historyless, 379

Albani, Francesco, colour, 128

Albigensians, Manichaeans, 316*n.*

Alcamenes, contemporary mathematic, 58; period, 151

Al-Chazali, and Science, 348

Alchemy, as symbol, 130; as Arabian physics, 191; and substance, 191

Alembert, Jean B. le R. d', mathematic, 58; mechanics and deism, 209

Alexander the Great, analogies, 4; romantic, 29. *See also* Macedonians

Alexander I of Russia, and Napoleon, 82

Alexandria, as a cultural left-over, 59; as irreligious, 185; as world-city, 247

Algebra, defined, significance of letter notation, 53; Western liberation, 65. *See also* Mathematics

"Alien" and "proper," 41

Al-Khwarizmi, mathematic, 53

Alphabet. *See* Writing

Alsidzshi, mathematic, 53

Amenhotep (Amenophis) IV, city, 250*n.*

American, as race, Indian influence, 254; as people, creation of events, 264–5; and predestination, 343; fate of government, 375; basis of reverence for constitution, 378*n.;* economics and politics, 402

Amos, as Arabian prophet, 281

Analogies, superficial and real historical, 4, 21, 29, 30

Analysis, and Classical mathematic, 51; in Western mathematic, 54, 55; inadequacy as term, 61; and double-entry book-keeping, 407. *See also* Mathematics

Anamnesis, and comprehension of depth, 93

Anaxagoras, on atoms, 193; and mechanical necessity, 198

Anaximander, and chaos, 47

Animal, essential character, microcosm in macrocosm, 227; cosmic beat and tension, 227; sense, 227; sight as supreme sense, 227; being and waking-being, 227; sense and understanding, 228; and language, 257–8; involuntary technique, 409

Anselm, St., Arabian contemporaries, 311

Antioch, as un-Classical, 249*n.*

Anti-Semitism, rationale, 349–53

Antonello da Messina, Dutch influence, 123–4

Aphrodite, as goddess, 140; in Classical art, 140

Apocalyptic, predecessors of Mohammed, 280; related Arabian, 280–2, 284; Arabian development, 283; Jewish law and the prophets, 284; end of Jewish, 285; and Arabian awakening, 286; Jesus' teaching, 289; and Resurrection, 290; Paul's attitude, 291; basis of writing, 306. *See also* Religion

Apollinaris, Monophysite, 314

i

Memling, Hans, in Italy, 123

Mencius, practical philosophy, 34

Menzel, Adolf F. E., impressionism, 153

Messiah, as common Arabian idea, 281–2; of Mandaeanism, 286–7; attitude of Jesus, 287; effect of Resurrection, 290

Metaphysics, Western, and pairs of concepts, 163. *See also* Ethics; Philosophy; Religion

Mexican (Mayan) Culture, and historical scheme, 13–14; development, 239; violent death, 239; Civilization and Aztecs, 239; reconstruction of history, 239–40; depopulation, 351

Michelangelo, and passing of sculpture, 116; as dissatisfied thinker, 144; unsuccessful quest of the Classical, 144–6, 148; and marble, 145; architecture as final expression, 145; liberation of architecture, beginning of Baroque, 164

Microcosm, animal as, in macrocosm, 226–7, 229; waking-being, 227; and history and nature, 230; and megalopolitanism, 245; language as essential element, 258; and sex, 354; and Western technique, 412. *See also* Animal; Cosmic; Waking-being

Middleman, as economic master, 405–6; as agent of Western technique, 410. *See also* Economics; Money

Millennianism, as Western phenomenon, 187, 219–20

Milton, John, and concepts, 242

Ming Chu, period, 236

Ming Ti, as ruler, 236

Minkowski, Hermann, and relativity, 215

Mino da Fiesole, and portrait, 143

Mirabeau, Comte de, and imperialism, 81

Mishnah, development, 283–4; as commentary, 308; origin, 348

Missionarism, Arabian, 316; Islam, 342–3; Jewish, 316

Mithraism, form-language of Mithraea, 117; cult in Rome, 205, 205*n.*; in Syncretism, 278, 312

Mithridates, cultural basis of wars, 350

Mo Ti, practical philosophy, 34; and politics, 389

Modern History, as irrational term, 12–14

Mohammed, predecessors as prophets, 280; Paul's analogy, 291; as Logos, 301; and consensus, 304–5; revelation, 306. *See also* Islam

Moltke, Count Helmuth von, leadership, 386

Monasticism, and Western morale, 165*n.*; mendicant orders, 179; in Paganism, 280; Western rural and urban, 338; sage, 344

Money, as power of Civilization, 26–7, 406; rise as political force, and Rationalism, 365–6; in English politics, 367; and class dictatorship, 369; Caesarism and overthrow, 378–9, 396, 414, 415; and democracy, 391; in Roman politics, 392–3; in Western politics, and press, 394–5; and end of democracy, 395; early status of coin as goods, 403–4; beginning of concept as category, 404–5; value-token and payment-medium, 405; trader as master, 405, 406; struggle against, 406; Classical magnitude concept, 407; irrelation with Classical land value, 407; Classical slaves as, 407; Western function-concept, book-keeping, 407; Western Culture and metallic, 407; and work, quantity, 407–8; struggle with technique, 412–13; and Socialism, 413*n. See also* Economics

Monophysites, and starting point of Islam, 113, 315; as alchemistic problem, 191; and Mary-cult, 293; origin, 314; missionarism, 317; and reform, 338

Monotheism, relation to Arabian Culture, 278*n.*

Monteverde, Claudio, music, 118, 120, 131, 150

Morale, Western moral imperative, 176, 177; Western purposeful motion, ethic of deed, 177, 178; Western Christian, 177, 179; plurality, cultural basis, no conversions, 177–9; morphology, 178; compassion, cultural types of manly virtue, 178–80; real and presumed, phrases and meanings, 179; instinctive and problematic, 182; end phenomena, cultural basis, 183–5; qualities and aim of Socialism, 185–7; and cultural atomic theories, 193. *See also* Ethics; Spirit; Truth

Mörike, Eduard, poetry, 155

Morphology, concept of historical, 5–6, 21, 29–30; historical, and symbolism, 35; historical, ignored, 37; histori-

INDEX

Will, free will and destiny, 79; as Western concept, 160–4; and reason, 160; and Western concept of God, 163; and character, 165; and Western morale, 176–80; Arabian attitude, submission, 300–3; Arabian Grace, 303–4; Western free will and sacraments, 335

Witchcraft, Western cult, 333–4; persecution, 341

Wolfram von Eschenbach, forest-longing, 99; tragic method, 171; and popularity, 173

Woman. *See* Sex

Word, relation to number, 43; and conscious technique, 409. *See also* Language; Names

Work, Protestant works, 165*n.;* and Socialism, 186; Western concept, quantity and quality, 210, 408

World, and soul and life, 41–2

World-city. *See* Megalopolitanism

World conceptions, historical and natural, overlapping, 71–2, 84–5; symbolic, 87–8. *See also* History; Macrocosm; Nature

World-end, as symbol of Western soul, 187, 220

World-fear, creative expression, 59–60

World-longing, development, and world-fear, 58–60

World War, and Spengler's theories, xv; as type of historical change,

36–8; effect on universal military service, 376

Writing, grammatical decomposition, 261–2; cultural relation, 262; technique of signs and thoughts, 262; and linguistic history, 263; relation to race, as taboo, ornament, 263; Arabian religions and scripts, 295*n.* *See also* Language

Xenophon, and class dictatorship, 369

Yahweh, dualism, 203; cult, 278

Yoga doctrine, 183

Zarathustra, Jewish contemporaries, 281. *See also* Mazdaism; Zend Avesta

Zechariah, Persian influence, 283

Zend Avesta, commentary, 308; new, Mazdaism, 311

Zeno the Stoic, ethic, 178, 183; character of Nihilism, 184

Zero, Classical mathematic and, 49–50; and theory of the limit, 64–5

Zoroaster, Nietzsche's "Zarathustra," 177, 187; unimposed mystic benefits, 177*n.* *See also* Zarathustra; Zend Avesta

Zwinger, of Dresden, in style history 75, 152

MODERN LIBRARY GIANTS

A series of sturdily bound and handsomely printed, full-sized library editions of books formerly available only in expensive sets. These volumes contain from 600 to 1,400 pages each.

THE MODERN LIBRARY GIANTS REPRESENT A
SELECTION OF THE WORLD'S GREATEST BOOKS